Readings in
LATIN
AMERICAN
HISTORY

VOLUME I: TO 1810

LEWIS HANKE

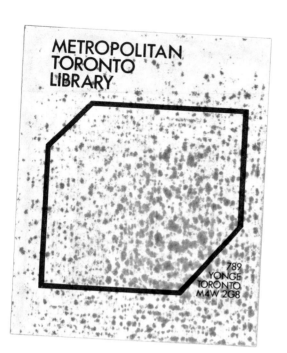

Readings in Latin American History
Volume I: To 1810

Readings in
Latin American History

Volume I: To 1810

Selected Articles from the
Hispanic American Historical Review

EDITED BY

LEWIS HANKE

THOMAS Y. CROWELL COMPANY
Established 1834 New York

380
H39

Dedicated
to
the authors, editors, proofreaders, and
secretaries whose labors prepare
The Hispanic American Historical Review
and to
the enlightened institution
that makes its publication possible
Duke University Press

PREFACE

This two-volume anthology consists of selected articles from the *Hispanic American Historical Review* which, by their lively scholarship and range of subject matter, are intended to attract the interest of students, primarily undergraduates, taking general courses on Latin America with the Columbus-to-Castro sweep.

Every anthologist, including this one, learns to accept the inevitable fact that, to keep his collection of reasonable size he must omit many valuable pieces which he would like to include. In order to convey something of the quality, flavor, and variety of the *HAHR*, I have chosen for each volume articles which, throughout the nearly fifty years of the *Review*, have made permanent contributions on significant topics, sometimes embodying new approaches to the study of Latin American history, and in general representing a balance between the work of veteran historians and younger scholars in the field. The text of each article appears in its entirety, minus the footnotes but with a brief introductory note to identify the author and to suggest the relation of his article to the relevant literature on the topic he treats.

The *HAHR* itself has not been used intensively by undergraduates, partly because librarians naturally cherish professional journals and attempt to protect them from damage or loss. Thus there is need for an easily accessible anthology which will bring students face to face with some of the valuable material the *Review* has published. At the end of most of the selections a list is given of other relevant articles, at times with descriptive notes that have been taken, with the permission of Duke University Press, from the two guides to the *Review*. In this way readers of this anthology will have access to a considerable part of the total contents of the *Review*. In addition, at the end of each volume a list appears of a number of important bibliographical articles published in recent numbers of the *Review*, which will be especially useful to students preparing term papers or special reports.

Many persons and institutions have built and sustained the *Review*, fulfilling President Woodrow Wilson's hope, expressed in his letter printed in the first issue, that the new *Review* would lead "to very important results both for scholarship and for the increase of cordial feeling throughout the Americas." One institution, Duke University, deserves special mention, because it assumed in 1926 the responsibility for publication of the *Review* by the Duke University Press. This generous support has enabled the *HAHR* to survive financially. Its quality, however, depends and will continue to depend upon its editors and its contributors. One may with reason hope that some of these will surely be found in the future among readers of this anthology.

The introductory notes for the individual articles were prepared in Santiago, Chile, where I was able to use the excellent collection of the *Review* in the Sociedad Chilena de Historia y Geografía, thanks to the kindness of my long-time colleague Dr. Ricardo Donoso, whose valuable aid is hereby gratefully acknowledged.

LEWIS HANKE

New York City
February, 1966

CONTENTS

CHAPTER ONE

BACKGROUND

1. The Peninsular Background of Latin American Cattle Ranching
   CHARLES JULIAN BISHKO   1
2. The Incidence and Significance of Disease among the Aztecs
   and Related Tribes   SHERBURNE F. COOK   16

CHAPTER TWO

GENERAL

3. William Hickling Prescott: The Man and the Historian
   R. A. HUMPHREYS   29
4. Two Articles on the Same Topic: Bernal Díaz del Castillo and
   Popularism in Spanish Historiography and Bernal Díaz del Castillo's Criticisms of the *History of the Conquest of Mexico*, by
   Francisco López de Gómara   RAMÓN IGLESIA   42
5. The Puerto Bello Fairs   ALLYN C. LOOSLEY   65
6. Spanish Seamen in the New World During the Colonial Period
   PAUL S. TAYLOR   79
7. The Archives of the Indies at Seville   IRENE A. WRIGHT   97

CHAPTER THREE

VICEROYALTY OF NEW SPAIN

8. Civil Congregations of the Indians in New Spain, 1598–1606
   HOWARD F. CLINE   101
9. Grain Legislation in Colonial Mexico, 1575–1585
   RAYMOND L. LEE   115
10. Conquerors and Amazons in Mexico   IRVING A. LEONARD   125
11. The Birth of the Mestizo in New Spain   C. E. MARSHALL   139
12. Social Structure and Social Change in New Spain
    L. N. MC ALISTER   154
13. Music in the Cathedral of Mexico in the Sixteenth Century
    LOTA M. SPELL   171

CHAPTER FOUR

SPANISH SOUTH AMERICA

14. Intendants and Cabildos in the Viceroyalty of La Plata,
    1782–1810   JOHN LYNCH   189
15. Colonial Tucumán   MADALINE W. NICHOLS   208
16. The Encomienda in Paraguay   ELMAN R. SERVICE   222
17. Indian Warfare on the Pampa During the Colonial Period
    ALFRED J. TAPSON   239
18. Antonio de Ulloa   ARTHUR P. WHITAKER   257

CHAPTER FIVE

COLONIAL BRAZIL

19. Padre António Vieira, S.J., and the Institution of the Brazil
    Company in 1649   C. R. BOXER   278
20. The Guerra dos Emboabas, Civil War in Minas Gerais,
    1708–1709   MANOEL S. CARDOZO   295
21. The Rise of the Brazilian Aristocracy   ALAN K. MANCHESTER   308
22. Feudal and Capitalistic Elements in the Portuguese Settlement
    of Brazil   ALEXANDER MARCHANT   318

A List of Recent Articles on Historiography   331

A List of Editors of the *Hispanic American Historical Review* 333

Readings in Latin American History
Volume I: To 1810

CHAPTER ONE

BACKGROUND

1. The Peninsular Background of Latin American Cattle Ranching

CHARLES JULIAN BISHKO

Professor Bishko of the University of Virginia here brings his deep knowledge of Iberian medieval history to bear upon the rich and absorbing story of cattle ranching in Latin America. The article contains many important suggestions on "certain hitherto unnoticed factors explaining the cattleman's early rise to major prominence in the overseas colonies."

The history of Spanish and Portuguese cattle ranching and its expansion to the Western hemisphere has never been seriously investigated on either side of the Atlantic. Descriptions of medieval Iberian pastoralism, whether in the older, narrowly juridical works of Redonet, Camacho, and Moreno Calderón or the superior modern treatments of Klein and Ribeiro, deal almost exclusively with sheep raising, the "clásica ganadería española." Latin Americanists, on the other hand, have long recognized that in the Luso-Hispanic colonization and development of the Americas it is not sheep raising but cattle raising that plays by far the major role. Yet they have failed to explore the reasons for this striking reversal; and, in spite of much loose generalization on the subject by Latin-American and Anglo-American writers, we still know astonishingly little about the peninsular background from which sprang the greatest cattle empire in world history, one still flourishing from the Argentine pampa to the plains of Wyoming.

The fact is that, since the sixteenth century, historians of the Indies have tended to limit their discussion of colonial cattle ranching to only three of its many aspects: (1) the identification of the supposed first importers of the Iberian cow, such as Colón for Española, Villalobos and Cortés for New Spain, Fernán Gutiérrez for Peru, the brothers Goes for Brazil, and in the River Plate country, Gaete with his famous "siete vacas y un toro"; (2) the territorial lines of bovine diffusion; and (3) the mounting statistics of herds and hides. But the recent studies of Miranda,

Chevalier and Morrisey on the colonial cattle frontier as a cutting edge
of Hispanic settlement in Mexico, and the many unsolved problems connected with the cattle country's participation in the Wars of Independence
and in subsequent political and economic evolution, underline our urgent
need of comprehensive institutional histories of *ganadería vacuna* for all
parts of Latin America. Such histories, however, require as an indispensable preliminary an account of the organization and conditions of operation of the ranch cattle industry in Spain and Portugal before 1500,
and this, even in brief or inadequate form, has simply not been obtainable.

The sources of information for this peninsular background of the cattle kingdoms of the Americas are widely scattered and often difficult of
access. Of first importance are the royal and municipal law codes of
medieval and early modern Iberia, and the numerous royal, ecclesiastical,
and private charters. Many of the latter still lie unpublished in peninsular
archives, such as those of the Mesta, the Duque de Osuna, the Castilian
and Portuguese military orders, and the Extremaduran, Andalusian and
Alentejan towns: archives which have never been searched for the cattle
materials they undoubtedly contain. Valuable also for the light they throw
upon antecedent Iberian institutions are the colonial American histories,
relaciones, leyes, cédulas, actas de cabildo, etc. Even current ranching
practices in Spain, Portugal and Ibero-America merit attention for their
preservation of ancient usages that never attained the level of written
notice. Until all these several sources have been thoroughly exploited, a
definitive history of Iberian cattle ranching in the Middle Ages cannot
be written. But enough material is available in published form to justify
this initial, tentative and of necessity sparsely annotated survey. Its purpose
is to outline broadly the peninsular ranching institutions that lie back of
those of the Americas, and to suggest certain hitherto unnoticed factors
explaining the cattleman's early rise to major prominence in the overseas
colonies.

I

The first essential is to recognize that, like so many other features
of Iberian civilization, cattle ranching in the Middle Ages was virtually
peculiar to the Peninsula, a *cosa de España*. Cattle were, of course, raised
almost everywhere in medieval Europe, for their dairy products—milk,
cheese, butter; as draft animals—the indispensable ox; and for their meat,
tallow, and hides. But such cattle were either a strictly subordinate element in manorial crop agriculture, in which peasants might own at best a
few cows and a yoke or two of oxen; or they were bred, e.g., in certain
parts of Normandy, Wales and Ireland, on small dairy or feeder farms.
In the medieval Peninsula, cattle raising of these two types was widely
distributed, but most strongly established in what might be called the
Iberian Humid Crescent—the rainy, fertile crop and grasslands that

stretch from Beira in central Portugal up through Galicia, swing east across the Cantabrian and Pyrenean valleys, with certain southern salients like the Leonese Tierra de Campos, the *comarca* of Burgos and the Rioja Alta, and finally turn south into Catalonia. Throughout this region nobles, peasants, churches and monasteries raised considerable stock on the basis of small herds (*greyes*) averaging twenty to thirty head. These humid-zone cattle belonged to still surviving northern Iberian *razas:* Gallegas, Minhotas, Barrosãs, Arouquesas and Mirandesas in Galicia, Minho, Trás-os-Montes and Beira Alta; Asturianas in the Cantabrians; and various sub-breeds of Pirenaicas between the Basque Provinces and the Mediterranean. In color they ran predominantly to solid or mixed shades of white, cream, dun, yellow and the lighter and medium reds and browns; and they were in general docile, easily handled and admirably suited to dairy, beef, and draft needs.

But the raising of cattle on dairy or stock farms, or as a subsidiary to dirt-farming, is not ranching, which implies the ranging of cattle in considerable numbers over extensive grazing grounds for the primary purpose of large-scale production of beef and hides. With the possible exception of the Hungarian Plain and western portions of the British Isles, for both of which areas we badly need careful pastoral studies, medieval Iberia appears to have been the only part, as it was unquestionably the most important part, of medieval Europe to advance to this third level of cattle raising. While the precise circumstances must remain obscure, the available charters and *fueros* enable us to determine that a genuine ranch cattle industry evolved in the Peninsula in the late eleventh and twelfth centuries, under Alfonso VI and Alfonso VII of León-Castile. Its birthplace was not the Humid Crescent, but that portion of the subhumid or arid interior tableland of the Meseta Central lying between the middle course of the Duero River and the massive sierras of Gata, Gredos, and Guadarrama; or, more specifically, the *tierras* of Zamora and Salamanca in León, and those of Segovia and Avila in southern Old Castile.

From this original area of its nativity cattle ranching, on an ever increasing scale, expanded southward in the van of *reconquista* colonization. By the later twelfth century it had moved, along with the sheep industry of León, Castile and Portugal, into the broad pasturelands of New Castile, Extremadura and Alentejo, the latter region apparently being the cradle of the Portuguese ranching system which was later extended into Algarve, the Atlantic Islands and the Brazilian *sertão*. On this southern half of the *meseta*, chiefly to the west of a line running through central New Castile, Castilian and Portuguese military orders, nobles and townsmen grazed thousands of cattle, although in both numbers and economic importance these were less significant than the great sheep flocks of the Mesta and other owners. But this situation was reversed after 1250, with Ferdinand III's reconquest of Andalusia, when royal *repartimientos* assigned to cattlemen rather than to sheep raisers the bulk of the *campos, campiñas* and *marismas* of the Guadalquivir valley. As a result, the Andalusian plain became in the latter Middle Ages the one region of the Peninsula, and perhaps of all Europe, where pastoral life, and indeed agricultural life in general, was dominated by a thriving, highly organized cattle-ranching economy. The fact that many of the early colonists of the Canaries and the Indies came from this Andalusian cattle kingdom, which was at its height in the fifteenth and early sixteenth centuries, or from the not too dissimilar cattle *ambiente* of Extremadura, provides one significant clue to the promotion of cattle over sheep ranching in the American colonies.

Just why medieval Castile and Portuguese Alentejo became the site of this widespread ranch cattle industry is a complex question. The only factor usually mentioned, the taking over or imitation of an already established Moorish cattle-ranching system, is clearly of secondary consequence. Some Moorish influence there undoubtedly was, especially in Andalusia, but the Berber was not much of a cattleman in North Africa, nor did he abandon in the Peninsula his typically Mediterranean preference for mutton over beef. Comparatively little in the techniques, vocabulary, dress or equipment of the Castilian and Portuguese cowboy can be traced to Moorish sources; and it is significant that the predominance of the old Iberian breeds of cattle was not adversely affected by African strains, as happened after the Moorish importation of the merino sheep and the Barb horse.

The really decisive factors determining the development of medieval Iberian cattle ranching appear to have been four in number, all of them native to the Peninsula:

(1) the presence, as in almost every phase of medieval Luso-Hispanic life, of numerous active, enterprising and ambitious individuals, many of whom were already familiar with Humid Crescent pastoralism and swiftly realized the broader opportunities presented by the conquest of the *meseta* grazing grounds. Whether nobles, churchmen or town-dwelling *ganaderos*, such men were the first true prototypes of the cattle ranchers of the Indies.

(2) the transformation imposed upon Castilian and Portuguese agriculture by the frontier advance from northern, rainy, good-soiled "European" conditions onto the interior subhumid plains of the *meseta* (Köppen BS; Thornthwaite DB′d, DB′s), with their scarcity of water, poor soils and predominantly *mattoral*-type bush vegetation (the *monte bajo* of the stockman)—an environmental change that affected medieval Iberian life as radically as, in W. P. Webb's view, occupation of the Great Plains did American. Extremes of aridity and deficiencies of browse restricted cattle ranching chiefly to the western half of the *meseta;* Aragon was always strong sheep country, and in eastern New Castile, i.e., La Mancha, cattlemen were relatively few.

(3) the Reconquista, which for centuries created frontier areas on the *meseta* where Christians and Moors often raided or fought; where the population huddled in large, widely spaced towns separated by *despo-*

blados; where rural labor was scarce and crop-farming hazardous; and where cattle and sheep, being mobile and little demanding, had obvious advantages. Royal colonization policies, with their predilection for large seigneurial and municipal grants, further accentuated pastoral trends.

(4) the special breed of cattle that developed on the *meseta* and the Andalusian Plain, cattle unique in medieval Europe. Moorish strains, as already observed, never became prominent; some North-African stock was brought in, but these were, as the reference to them in Cabeza de Vaca shows, the brown Atlas shorthorns still found in Morocco, and not to be confused with the native breeds of the Peninsula.

The cattle of Castilian and Portuguese ranching were—as nearly as a very amateur zoötechnician can determine—the result of various degrees of crossing between lighter-colored European types of all-purpose cow found in the Humid Crescent, and the wild, or semi-wild, black, dark red, and dark brown descendants of that uniquely Iberian strain, *Bos taurus ibericus,* the ancestor of the modern fighting bull. Mingling upon the *meseta* as the *reconquista* frontier drove southward, these two *razas* produced a very hardy hybrid stock, varying astonishingly in color and color combinations from creams, yellows and duns to deep browns, reds and blacks—a stock characterized by markedly feral instincts and often complete wildness. Such cattle were valuable chiefly for their tough hides and stringy beef. Medieval Castilians, however, were proud of them. The *Siete Partidas* notes with satisfaction that animals born in the hot frontier country were larger and stronger than those of the humid region; one fifteenth century writer, Fernando de la Torre, calls Castile the "tierra de bravos toros"; another claims for her "los mas grandes y mejores toros del mundo." These cattle, unsuited for dairy or draft purposes, compelled the *criaderos, charros* and *serranos* of Castile and Portugal to abandon their cosy little cowpastures for the open range, to take to the horse for herding, to perfect systematic methods of long-distance grazing, periodical round-ups, branding, overland drives, and so forth—in short, to invent cattle ranching. These too are the cows whose long, stern faces, low-swinging heads, formidable horns, narrow sides and long legs appear on the opening pages of the family photograph albums of nearly every *criollo* breed of the Americas from the longhorns of the pampas to the longhorns of Texas.

These range cattle of the *meseta* and Andalusian Plain gave rise to a characteristic Iberian and, later, Ibero-American phenomenon, the *ganado bravo* or unbranded wild cattle existing in some numbers on the fringes of the ranching industry as a result of loose herding methods and the frontier conditions of the cattle country. The co-existence of herded, branded cows and wild, ownerless ones was a regular feature of peninsular *ganadería vacuna* long before there appeared across the ocean the very much larger wild herds of Española, New Spain, Brazil, the River Plate, and other regions; just as the medieval hunts of *ganado bravo* by mounted hunters, using dogs and armed with lances and pikes, anticipated the great *monterías* and *vaquerías* of Cuba, Española and the pampas.

From this same cattle background arose the *fiesta brava*, the bullfight, a prominent element in Iberian and Ibero-American social history that has too long been left to amateur historians. Much imaginative nonsense has been written about the alleged Roman or Moorish origins of the bullfight; but if one relies solely on historical evidence it seems highly probable that *toreo* first developed in the cattle *ambiente* of the *meseta* in the twelfth and thirteenth centuries. To this day the *suerte de picar* and the *suerte de banderillear* display old traditional techniques of handling and hunting range cattle, and the still archaic organization of bull raising and the *corrida* illumines certain otherwise obscure aspects of medieval ranching. For the intimate relationship existing in the Iberian mind between cowpunching, *ganado bravo*, and the bullfight, no better example can be cited than the familiar descriptions of the discovery of the buffalo in Cabeza de Vaca, Oñate, Villagrá, Castañeda, and others, passages whose strong ranching, cowhunting, and bullfighting flavor has never been fully appreciated. When, on the Great Plains of North America, as absolutely nowhere else in the Western hemisphere, Castilians encountered animals resembling cows, they naturally looked upon them as the *ganado bravo* declared by the *Siete Partidas* to be in the public domain. Despite certain visible evidence to the contrary, it followed that these animals must be ferocious, longhorned, risky to approach and, like difficult *toros de lidia*, given to attacking from the side and exceedingly dangerous to horses. Doubtless someone dismounted to try a *verónica* with his cape. In any case, the Plains Indians were obviously *vaqueros* who were already engaged in *vaquerías* which, if under Castilian management, would furnish hides for a lucrative trade.

II

In the sixteenth century not only the cow but the organization, methods and customs of the peninsular ranching system reached the Indies, there to become the enduring foundation of Latin-American ranching to the present day, the trunk from which have stemmed the various regional traditions that distinguish Mexican cattle techniques from Argentine, or Brazilian from Venezuelan. What was the nature of these parent institutions?

The ecological and frontier conditions of the *reconquista*, together with the steady demand for beef and hides, produced in portions of medieval Castile and Alentejo a fairly numerous class of cattle ranchers, although only in Andalusia did these outnumber the ubiquitous sheepmen. Of these peninsular cowmen a small but powerful seigneurial group were large operators, with herds (*cabañas, hatos*) running up to a thousand or more head. Such, for example was the rancher-noble Don Juan Alfonso de Benavides, who *ca.* 1306 ranged up to around 800 cows; or the famous

Castilian nunneries of Santo Domingo de Caleruega, Santo Domingo de Madrid and Santa Clara de Guadalajara, with 1000, 1500, and 1000 head, respectively. The military orders of Castile and Portugal also belonged to this group, with their extensive ranges held as *encomiendas* in New Castile, Andalusia, Alentejo and Algarve. In 1302, the Castilian branch at Uclés of the Order of Santiago had at least a thousand head, while the Orders of Santiago de León and of Calatrava found it necessary to appoint special administrative officials for their great herds, the *comendadores de las vacas*, who were subject to supervision by *visitadores*. The figures just cited of 800, 1000, and 1500 represent the known maximum herd sizes for the Peninsula before 1500 and lie back of the amusing passages in Oviedo's *Historia general y natural de las Indias* (III, 11; XII, 9), where that writer astonishes his readers with herds in the Caribbean area running to five, ten, twenty thousand or more cows.

Most peninsular cattlemen, however, had much smaller holdings than the wealthier magnates and ecclesiastical corporations. Even among nobles and monasteries were many, like the Premonstratensian house of Nuestra Señora de la Vid, which in 1292 owned 4000 sheep and only 200 cows, for whom cattle ranching was a relatively minor interest. But the great majority of medieval *ganaderos* in the cattle business were *vecinos* of the towns, whose herds rarely exceeded a few hundred head and often ran very much lower. In thirteenth and fourteenth century New Castile, for example, the royal *privilegios* establish three categories of municipal cowmen: those with under 40 head; those owning 40 to 100; and those with above 100. Yet it is essential to recognize that these *dueños de ganado*, for all their small herds, were not mere stockfarmers of Humid Crescent type; their cattle grazed not on small farms but great municipal ranges and were often driven long distances for seasonal pasturage; and small *vacadas* were frequently combined on an *aparcería* basis into larger herds, the *aparceros* thus becoming partners in an enterprise of some size. Furthermore, in the fourteenth and fifteenth centuries, notably in Extremadura and Andalusia, the *vecinos* owning over 100 cows increased markedly in number and in the size of their herds. The *fueros* of Cáceres and Usagre set a minimum of 400 cows for pasturage drives northward, thus compelling *vecinos* to form *aparcerías* of this scale; and ca. 1491 Málaga found it impossible to enforce a 150 head limit for grazing on its ranges. The *cabildo* of Seville in 1493 defined an *hato de vacas* as consisting of as many as 500 cattle, and even allowed for larger herds in the hands of its citizens, some of whom evidently ran stock on their own *dehesas, montes, prados* and *pastos* as well as on the municipal ranges.

Recognition of the dividing line between municipal and seigneurial cattle ranching in medieval Iberia is basic to its proper understanding. The distinction finds reflection not merely in disparity of size between town ranching outfits and those of the nobles, monasteries and military orders at the top of the industry, but in differences of organization, land use and pasturage and marketing rights. Seigneurial ranching operated far more freely than municipal, which partly explains why the *cabildos* of the Indies had so much difficulty imposing livestock controls upon the new colonial landed classes. While abundant data on *vaqueros'* wages and the prices of hides, leather and meat can be found in the *cuadernos* of the medieval Castilian and Portuguese Cortes, neither these nor the royal law codes contain any considerable body of restrictive legislation aimed at close control of seigneurial cattle ranching. It is not necessary to review here the history of medieval Iberian grazing rights, stock taxes and royal transhumancy laws, so definitively treated for Castile by Klein, although we still lack a comparable study for Portugal; such regulations of course affected seigneurial ranchers. It is however significant to note that the great Castilian cattlemen never organized, either voluntarily or under royal compulsion, a counterpart to the sheepmen's Real Consejo de la Mesta, even though in Extremadura and Andalusia their struggle over pasturage with that powerful national gild must have suggested the advantages of union and royal support. Very likely the Mesta itself opposed any inclination of the Castilian kings from Alfonso X on to charter a parallel society of cattle raisers; and perhaps the inclusion of some cattle owners in the Mesta, as attested by its documents and by the bull prominently displayed alongside the merino sheep on its coat-of-arms, reflects an unsuccessful attempt to win over seigneurial cattlemen into a kind of national stockmen's association.

Municipal ranchers, on the other hand, were rigorously supervised by the local town government, the *concejo* or *concelho*, which controlled their grazing grounds. The later medieval *fueros* and ordinances of Castilian and Alentejan towns regulate almost every aspect of cattle ranching: grazing rights; compensations for crop damage; wages of cowboys; branding; penalties for rustling, brand-changing, or killing another man's stock; marketing and sale of cattle in the town's markets, butchershops and *ferias*; slaughtering practices; and many other related subjects. Some towns, although clearly not all, possessed a stockmen's gild or *mesta*, which operated as a kind of municipal bureau of pastoral affairs, and must be carefully distinguished from the national Mesta Real of the transhumant sheepmen. Jurisdiction of the local *mesta* was confined to the town's *términos;* all *vecinos* grazing cattle, sheep, horses, goats, pigs, and other animals on the municipal ranges were required to join, while strenuous efforts were made to impose membership upon non-*vecinos* holding pasturelands adjacent to those of the town. While subordinate to the supreme authority of the *concejo*, such local *mestas*, which held meetings two or three times a year under their elected *alcaldes de la mesta*, were powerful bodies, administering all the livestock provisions of the local law code. In the cattle country, these *mestas* at times subdivided along the lines of *ganado mayor* and *menor;* this meant that the local cowmen had their own organization, a kind of sub-*mesta*, under their own duly elected *alcalde* or *alcaldes de la mesta*, who fined or otherwise punished violators of cattle laws and settled disputes among the ranchers. A major function of municipal *mestas* was to regulate and protect the use of brands and earmarks, and to facilitate recovery of lost cattle. Cattlemen were commonly required to work their herds in the spring and fall for all stray stock (*mesteños, mostrencos*) and turn these over to the *mesta* officials. The latter, after recording the brands and other distinguishing features of the strays, and having the *pregón* or crier proclaim these details at intervals in the plaza mayor, held the animals for a fixed period of months in a corral pending identification by the owners. The best and most colorful picture we have of such a local *mesta* connected with a genuine cowtown is contained in the 1527 *Ordenanças* of Seville, which describe in detail the old semi-annual meetings of the ranchers outside the Hospital de los Criadores in the Calle de Arrayán. Here in the open air, amid the dust of *dueños de ganado* and *mayorales* galloping in from the *campo*, while *mesteños* turned into the nearby corral bawled their protests, the *alcalde de la mesta* heard *pleitos*, administered justice, settled quarrels, and supervised his *escribano* in the registration of brands in the official *libro de la mesta*. These Seville *alcaldes de la mesta*, like those of sixteenth-century Mexico City, also traveled on circuit to district *mestas* in more remote parts of the municipal territory.

In other towns of the cattle country, however, no trace of a municipal *mesta* can be found in the *fueros* or *ordenanzas;* here the *concejo* or *concelho* itself administered pastoral affairs, and its own alcaldes and their *escribano* performed the functions elsewhere assigned to the *mesta* officials. This appears to have been the precedent generally followed in the Americas, where, from the sixteenth century on, *cabildos* like those of Lima, Caracas, Habana, and many others exercised direct control over the ranch cattle industry, as their *actas capitulares* testify. In Mexico City, however, an important exception occurs; here, in 1537, under order of Charles V and Viceroy Mendoza, the *cabildo* organized a *mesta* for handling livestock problems, which deserves further study. Recent writers have regarded its establishment as marking the introduction into New Spain of the Real Concejo de la Mesta, but its creation by, and subjection to, the *cabildo*, its municipal membership, and the general character of its organization and aims, indicate that it was closer to a municipal *mesta* of Andalusian type adapted to New World conditions than a colonial counterpart of the national Mesta of the Castilian transhumant sheep industry.

As for the cowboys themselves, only the briefest mention of questions requiring further examination can be made. Their life, and that of the cowgirls as well, finds its most vivid memorial in the fourteenth century picaresque poem of Juan Ruiz, archpriest of Hita; students have yet to recognize how thoroughly this masterpiece of medieval Castilian literature reflects the life of the range cattle country between Segovia and Toledo. In the municipal sources, these medieval ancestors of the *vaqueros, vaqueiros, gauchos, huasos* and *llaneros* of the Indies always appear as freemen, who hire themselves out for a year's time, usually from one *día de San Juan* to the next, and receive an annual wage (*soldada*) paid in cash, a percentage of calves, or a combination of these. Whether, as seems inherently likely, unfree cowboys could also be found, performing compulsory herding services for seigneurial *dueños de ganado* like some *indios de encomienda* in the New World, is unknown. *Vaqueros* were held liable to deduction of pay for stock lost; in cases of rustling, sworn statements supported by other men of trust were required; and when an animal died, it was necessary to produce the hide and affirm under oath that the death was due to natural causes or the attacks of wolves or bears. When express permission was granted, the peninsular cowboy might graze a few cows, marked with his own brand, alongside those of his employer. The herds were not left to roam at will, but kept under standing guard to avoid both stock losses and the heavy penalties imposed for trespass against the *cinco cosas vedadas:* orchards, grain fields, vineyards, ox pastures and mown meadows. As with sheep, dogs were used to assist the vaqueros in guarding and on round-ups. Herds of any size were tended by a foreman (*mayoral, rabadán, mayordomo*) and from three to four *vaqueros* on up. Large outfits often had both a *mayoral* and *rabadán*, and perhaps a dozen or more hands. In Andalusia such crews normally included a *conocedor*, who memorized each cow's appearance as an aid in detecting strays or identifying the owner's own lost stock. Such a post could, of course, exist only where, as seen, cattle varied infinitely in color, and where also Spanish and Portuguese provided that remarkably rich, syncopated terminology of color and marking terms for cows and horses such as no other European language possesses. The *conocedor* clearly filled an important need in the period prior to official registration of brands, but the advent of the municipal *libro de marcas y señales* in the late fifteenth century soon ended his usefulness; although he can be found still flourishing in the 1527 *Ordenanças* of Seville, he does not appear to have crossed the ocean.

The dress and equipment of Latin-American cowmen owe much to peninsular models. Students of costume could doubtless trace back to the twelfth century regional dress of the *charros* and *serranos* of Salamanca and southern Old Castile, the cradle of the ranch cattle industry, the cowboy costume that appears with many local variations in the Indies: the low-crowned, broad-brimmed hat, the bolero jacket, the sash and tight-fitting trousers, the spurred boots. Since, for herding on the open range, mounted *vaqueros* were indispensable, the rise of Iberian cattle ranching could hardly have occurred if the Peninsula had not been in the Middle Ages the one European region where saddle horses were at once relatively abundant and cheap enough to escape being an aristocratic monopoly. Numerous references to horses and horse-breeding in the cattle documents indicate that the horse herd, the later *remuda* or *caballada*, was a normal feature of peninsular cowboy life, although much work remains to be done on the regional origins of the cowhorse, the evolution of the saddle, bridle, stirrups and spurs, and the relative importance of the northern *silla de brida* and the Moorish *silla de ginete* riding styles, both of which appear among Latin-American cattlemen.

For working stock the Castilian and Alentejan *vaquero* carried the long pike-like *garrocha*, which still survives in peninsular ranching and bullfighting use, and can be found also among Venezuelan *llaneros*, Brazilian *sertanejos* and other American cowboys. Carrying of arms was strictly regulated by the *concejos* in an effort to check brawls, *vaqueros* being ordinarily forbidden to possess any other weapons than the *garrocha* and the *puñal pastoril*, perhaps a distant forerunner of the Bowie knife. That the *reata* or *lazo* was known in the Peninsula has been denied, but while it is impossible to decide, from the few known medieval references to ropes (*sogas*) used on cattle, whether or not these were noosed, the apparently early diffusion of the rawhide *reata*, with its remarkably complex techniques and vocabulary, throughout the New-World cattle industry points to an Iberian origin. In any case peninsular cowboys also handled *reses vacunos* with the *garrocha*, with the aid of trained, belled steers (*cabestros*) and by their dexterity in throwing animals to the ground with a twist of the tail or horns, all of which alternatives to roping are still used in Ibero-America.

For grazing purposes, cattle were ranged either as *estantes* in local pastures that often varied seasonally from lowland to nearby sierra; or as *transhumantes* that might be driven as much as 400 miles over the official trails or *cañadas* linking the summer pastures (*agostaderos*) of León and Castile with the winter *invernaderos* of the south. The proportion of migrant to nonmigrant herds is difficult to determine; cows were less transhumant than sheep, but even so large numbers were trailed each year *á los extremos*, over the some routes as the Mesta flocks. Royal charters granting towns and military orders along the *cañadas* the right to collect *montazgo* from the transhumants reckon this toll for units as high as 1000 and even 2000 cows. At certain seasons the collective trail herds of the towns, and others belonging to nobles, monasteries and military orders, must have marched along the *cañadas* in a great series, accompanied by their heavily armed cavalry escorts (the *rafalas*), and by *dueños* and *vaqueros* who doubtless entertained their charges by day with the profaner aspects of diverse Leonese and Castillian dialects, soothed them at night with renditions of secular and ecclesiastical songs—cf. the *vaquero* songs in the Arcipreste—and defended them from the perils of drought, storm, stampede and attack by Moorish or other foe. Yet, in many parts of the *meseta*, *reses estantes* predominated. In Andalusia long distance transhumancy seems to have consisted more of northern herds moving in from the *meseta* than of Guadalquivir valley ranchers trailing stock north of the Sierra Morena. The Ordenanças of Seville, which apply to all the many towns of its *tierra* as well as to the capital itself, make no mention of the migrations so carefully regulated in *fueros* such as those of Cáceres and Usagre.

The traditional Latin-American cycle of ranching life, with the rounding-up and branding of calves in the spring *herredero* and the cutting-out of beef for slaughter in the autumn, comes straight from peninsular practice. Miranda claims the *rodeo*, or round-up, as an "institución castizamente americana," but this is far from certain. Municipal laws forced ranchers to work their herds at least once, and commonly twice, a year in order to brand calves, remove strays and cut out stock for market; although this involved, strictly speaking, only each *criadero's* rounding up his own cows, it is difficult to believe that some from of coöperative *rodeo* had not emerged before 1500. But this question must remain open until we have had further research upon the whole history of the *rodeo*, its role in the pastoral organization of the Indies, and the connection between its *alcaldes* or *jueces del campo* (the round-up bosses or captains of Texas) and the municipal *alcaldes de la mesta*.

Branding is unquestionably a very ancient peninsular livestock practice, dating from at least the Roman period. The oldest medieval brand yet discovered is a heart-shaped one depicted on the flanks of a bull and a horse in two tenth-century manuscripts of the Leonese abbey of San Miguel de Escalada. No study has yet been attempted of peninsular cattle brands (*hierros, marcas*) or of the supplementary system of earcrops (*señales*), although it is obvious that they are the immediate prototypes of the intricate symbols and monograms common to Latin-American and Anglo-American ranching. Branding was originally optional in the Peninsula, being used by the stockmen for their own protection, but from at least the thirteenth century the *fueros* require it of all municipal ranchers. The brand book, destined to become universal in the Americas, is a comparatively late device; down to the fifteenth century the *concejos* kept simply a temporary record of the brands of strays turned into the town corral. Only in the latter part of that century do we find evidence that at least in Andalusia some towns were compelling the cattlemen of their *tierra* to register brands and earmarks with the town or *mesta escribano*, by whom they were inscribed in a genuine brand register, the *libro de marcas y señales* or *libro de la mesta*. The relative novelty of the *libro de marcas* may help explain why in New Spain, New Castile and elsewhere *cabildos* and royal officials encountered so much difficulty in getting *ganaderos* to register brands or even to brand at all. Whether any peninsular brand book of the Middle Ages still exists in some unsearched archive is unknown, but probable enough; at present the oldest known such register for the entire Luso-Hispanic and Ibero-American world seems to be the remarkable *Relación de los hierros de bacas y obejas y bestias*, which the cabildo of Mexico City opened in 1530, seven years before it established the New Spanish *mesta*.

A final question of prime importance for colonial agrarian institutions is that of the peninsular or American origin of the cattle ranch, variously styled in the Indies *sitio de ganado mayor, hacienda de ganado, fazenda, finca, hato, sitio de estancia, estancia* and the like. From the fact that throughout the Middle Ages royal pasturage rights in *realengo* land were conceded by the Castilian and Portuguese crowns to towns, nobles and ecclesiastical corporations, and by them granted or rented to their *vecinos*, vassals or others, it has been contended that ranching based upon private ownership of large estates was a New World invention. The subject is too involved for more than brief mention here, but it should be noted that this view rests solely upon documents dealing with transhumancy and municipal ranching, fields in which rights would naturally loom larger than land titles. Yet evidence that seigneurial ranchers frequently possessed extensive domains that were in effect true *estancias* is readily discoverable. The *pergaminos* of Madrid mention privately owned grazing grounds in New Castile, while those of Cáceres reveal that in late medieval Extremadura private pasturelands were threatening to absorb, by purchase or usurpation, the communal ranges of towns and villages. The military orders held great *dehesas* in Extremadura, New Castile and Andalusia, some of which they grazed directly, while others were allotted to their stock-raising vassals. The Seville Ordenanças cite *campiñas, cortijos, casas fuertes, donadíos* and other large *heredades*, located in the *marismas* and *islas* of the Guadalquivir, from which the municipal herds were barred and which were evidently being operated as seigneurial ranches. Even among municipal ranchers there were those who in addition to grazing cattle on town lands had their own *dehesas, dehesas dehesadas, prados, sotos* and *pastos*, some of which were certainly larger than mere cowpastures. It is noteworthy that ca. 1500, probably in response to seigneurial influence, some Castilian and Andalusian towns, instead of allowing, as previously, unrestricted movement of herds within their *términos*, were siting (*asentar*) *reses estantes* on assigned portions of their *tierra;* this trend toward municipal allocation of grazing sites may have given rise in the Indies to the term *estancia* (commonly classified as an Americanism) and to the grants of *sitio de ganado, sitio de estancia,* etc., for which a municipal origin may be conjectured.

Even in our present state of knowledge regarding the development of *latifundismo* in late medieval Spain and Portugal, it seems possible to reach two principal conclusions about the estancia. The first is that by the fourteenth and fifteenth centuries the ranch (i.e., the seigneurial estate devoted to large-scale stockraising) and the landed *ganadero* were both well established in the peninsular cattle kingdom, probably to a much greater extent than in the more heavily transhumant sheep industry upon which alone previous judgments have been based. The second conclusion is that not only was peninsular ranching thus characterized *ca.* 1500 by a dual system of pasturage rights and large landed estates, but that the system was in a state of flux, with the domanial element in the ascendent. It is this dualism, in process of transition from rights to tenures, that finds reflection in sixteenth-century colonial documents. In New Spain, New Castile, and the Brazilian *capitanias*, as in Iberia, grazing rights in royal and municipal land coëxisted with *sitios de ganado, tierras de señorío* and *fazendas*. The seigneurial estancia triumphed early under New-World conditions of conquest and settlement, but, like so many other elements in the Ibero-American cattle tradition, it was almost certainly an importation from the Peninsula.

III

That the ranch cattle industry of Castile and Alentejo expanded between 1200 and 1500 in both territorial extent and volume of production, in response to increasing demand for beef and hides, is a safe inference, but nearly all aspects of this process have been neglected by historians. Marketing centered about the towns, especially the great cattle fairs (*ferias de ganado, feiras de gado*) that were held annually by old cowtowns like Segovia, Avila, Plasencia, Béjar, Cáceres, Córdoba, Seville, Evora, Beja and others. At these, local slaughterers competed with professional itinerant cattle buyers, who traveled from one town to another and drove their purchases north to markets or feeding grounds outside the cattle country. Galicia, already in the Middle Ages what she remains to this day—Spain's chief milch cow center—was also, it would seem, an important beef feeder region for *meseta* cattle, like present-day western Buenos Aires and eastern La Pampa provinces, southern Brazil or the northern Great Plains of the United States. Hamilton's statistics suggest that prices on beef, hides, tallow, and other cattle products rose markedly in the fourteenth and fifteenth centuries, in line with the price structure as a whole. To a degree unusual in the cereal-consuming Middle Ages, meat, whether fresh, salted, or dried (*carne seca*), was a staple foodstuff for Spaniards and inland Portuguese, a fact which explains another curious Iberian and Ibero-American phenomenon, the Bula de la Cruzada, with its virtual repeal of the dietary meat restrictions of medieval Catholic Europe.

As for hides, their mounting output can be linked to the significant late medieval shift of the peninsular tanning and leather trades from goat and sheep skins, which the Moors had preferred for their Córdoban and Moroccan leathers, to the tougher, if less workable, cowhide. From the limited data thus far assembled on this subject, it looks as if cowhides were not only in heavy demand at home but were also the basis of an important export trade to Italy, France, the Low Countries, and perhaps other areas. Furthermore, this does not imply a surplus, for in late medieval Andalusia hides were being imported from North Africa, England, Ireland and, within the Peninsula itself, from dairy-farming Galicia and other districts. Presumably this means that peninsular hide production ca. 1500 was insufficient to satisfy home and export demands; if so, this enables us to grasp the immediate economic circumstances under which colonial Latin-American cattle raising and early large-scale export of cowhides from the colonies first developed.

The demands of the home market, mercantilist preference for colonial rather than foreign sources of raw material, the colonists' own need for a commodity yielding quick overseas revenues, and the natural disinclination of the Crown and the Real Concejo de la Mesta to foster a competitive wool industry in the Indies, must all have combined to swing the New-World decision to the cow instead of the sheep. To be sure, sheep raising was by no means neglected; in New Spain, for example, Viceroy Mendoza encouraged it strongly, and in Peru, as Cieza de León's frequent references indicate, large numbers of imported Iberian sheep along with the native llamas dominated the livestock picture. Yet this colonial wool seems to have been almost wholly intended for local use and not for export to the Peninsula, where the Mesta successfully protected its markets against colonial competition. What effect the rise of a far more productive American cattle industry had upon the eventual decline of peninsular cattle ranching, and to what extent this decline contributed to insuring the complete triumph of the Spanish sheepmen in the Hapsburg period, are interesting questions to which no answer is now possible.

Such, in broad and tentative outline, is the peninsular background of Latin-American cattle ranching. To students of colonial and modern Latin America it should not seem altogether unfamiliar. Changes there certainly were in the organization of the industry when it crossed the ocean; but the coëxistence of seigneurial and municipal ranching; their common conflict with the agriculturist, whether *encomendero* or Indian; the regulatory activities of government, both royal and municipal, in connection with pasturage, branding, marketing and the like; the commerce in hides; the traditional cycle of the cowman's year; above all, the *ganaderos* and *vaqueros* themselves, galloping along in the dust of their wild or half-wild herds—these are the stuff of colonial and post-colonial ranching no less than of that of the Peninsula. In the New World a vaster cattle kingdom was founded, but, as every reader of *Os Sertões* and *Doña Bárbara* discovers, it continued to preserve tenaciously its traditional institutions, many of which still flourish. It was with a cattle country in mind, and in words that apply to many other stockraising regions of the Western Hemisphere, that Sarmiento declared in *Facundo* (chap. ii): "En la República Argentina se ven a un tiempo dos civilizaciones distintas en un mismo suelo. . . . El siglo xix y el siglo xii viven juntos; el uno dentro de las ciudades, el otro en las campañas." No more perfectly expressed estimate could be made of the enduring influence of medieval Iberian cattle ranching upon the history of the Americas.

Other Articles of Interest

Cunningham, Charles H. "The Institutional Background of Spanish American History." I (1918), 24–39.
Modern research has shown that Spain's colonial system was admirably suited to the problems of the New World. By the thirteenth century four political factors—royal power, the nobility, the municipalities, and the Church— had developed into a definite pattern. By the sixteenth century the colonial administration was already designed, incorporating these four factors with necessary modifications. Spain's political institutions were, however, far more successful than her commercial organization; and the failure of Spain in America was due to her inability to readjust her commercial system and to compete with other nations.

Verlinden, Charles. "Italian Influence in Iberian Colonization." XXXII (1953), 199–211.
Italy was the only true colonizing nation in the Middle Ages. Spanish and Portuguese economic colonization depended upon Italian, notably Genoese, precedent and experience in the Levant and on the shores of the Black Sea. Italian influence in the Iberian peninsula increased continually from the mid-thirteenth century and was strong in the early sixteenth century, when a number of Italians moved from there to America.

---

2. The Incidence and Significance of Disease among the Aztecs and Related Tribes

SHERBURNE F. COOK

The medical history of Latin America remains largely unwritten, despite such studies as the present article. Professor Cook, a scientist at the University of California who has done important research over the years on Latin American history, demonstrates in this article his close knowledge of medical data in sources on Aztec history as well as his flair for interpreting the facts in a meaningful and challenging way.

For many years students of epidemiology and sociology have recognized the importance of diseases introduced from Europe into the New World,

From Volume XXVI (1946), pages 320–335.

for the profound dislocations in population and in economic life caused by smallpox, measles, and similar maladies can scarcely be overestimated. On the other hand little attempt has been made, save in a casual way by some anthropologists, to assess the importance of endemic disease to the native population prior to the advent of the white man. Yet a study of this factor should logically precede consideration of introduced pathology if the entire course of the health-disease relationship in any region is to be fully understood.

A great deal of attention has been devoted to the decline of population in Mexico subsequent to the conquest by Cortés, a decline which was caused primarily by malnutrition and violent epidemics, and which has left its mark on the country to this day. Nevertheless, very little consideration has been given to the status of public health among the Aztec and related tribes which had held the territory for centuries prior to 1520. It is true that even from the sixteenth century down to modern times several comprehensive discussions have appeared dealing with medicine and therapeutics in the pre-colonial era. Nevertheless, these works have treated in only a secondary fashion the significance of the various diseases in their relation to the welfare of the civilization at large.

The question requiring a definitive answer is specifically this: What was the intensity of incidence of the various diseases known to be present in the late pre-conquest era? There are five possible lines of approach to the solution of this problem.

1. Consideration of the prevalence of certain infections among both Spanish and Indians after the conquest.
2. Indirect evidence from the materia medica of the natives.
3. Direct statements by observers in the sixteenth century.
4. Archaeological evidence developed by physical anthropologists.
5. Statements and accounts of epidemics by historians and chroniclers.

1. In the sixteenth century several very severe scourges afflicted the natives of central Mexico. Of these the most notable were smallpox, measles, and *matlazahuatl*. The first two were unquestionably introduced and were unknown in the land prior to 1519. Concerning the third there is considerable controversy, particularly with respect to its identification. Many authorities have stated it to be *typhus exanthematicus*. It first appeared in virulent form in 1576 and attacked the native population with terrific force. On the contrary, no white man was ever known to suffer from it, despite extreme exposure in many cases. From this circumstance it has been argued that the disease was introduced from Europe. But *typhus exanthematicus* certainly attacks Europeans; and hence the opposite view has been advanced that it was an endemic disease that for some obscure reason suddenly acquired virulence insofar as the natives were concerned. Regardless of the merits of this controversy, it is clear that between 1519, when the

Spanish first landed, and 1576, the disease was unknown. The remaining point is whether it had likewise been unknown prior to 1519. The two principal modern writers on Aztec medicine are of the opinion that *matlazahuatl* was known before the conquest. Flores says that it was typhus and that it was represented pictographically in the codices. Ocaranza is, however, more skeptical, saying "its existence before the conquest is founded on one codex where an Indian appears who is suffering from epistaxis, and in a passage of Hernández where . . . he mentions some fever which might be typhus exanthematicus: . . . *exantematis, et punctis quae ex sanguine sicitatas febres comitare solent.*" With regard to the statement of Hernández it must be remembered that this author wrote at the end of the sixteenth century. He was familiar with the diseases of his time in Mexico, but he nowhere makes reference to or displays any interest in those of the natives prior to the Spanish occupancy. There is no reason, therefore, to assume that the sentence quoted by Ocaranza referred to any but Hernández' own time. The pictograph cited by both Flores and Ocaranza is allocated by neither to its documentary source. It may well exist, but I have been unable to find any other reference to it. One other modern opinion may be mentioned. In the *Anales de Quauhtitlán* as translated by Lehmann the statement appears with reference to the Valley of Mexico at approximately 1320: ". . . Denn hier gedeiht 'die Krankheit' Blutdurchfall, Bluthusten, Schüttelfrost, Auszehrung." In a parenthesis, Lehmann gives as equivalent for "die Krankheit" *Flecktyphus*, or *typhus exanthematicus.* The Nahuatl in the original text uses *yn cocolliztli*, which Lehmann properly renders into German as "die Krankheit." The difficulty lies in the meaning of the word *cocolliztli*, which can clearly be shown to imply illness, sickness, or epidemic. Consequently Lehmann has proceeded only upon assumption in stating that the disease was typhus, and hence *matlazahuatl*. There is no internal proof whatsoever that such was the case. The evidence is consequently exceedingly tenuous that the disease which caused the great epidemic of 1576 had been recognized at all prior to the date. Even if known there is no record whatever that the *matlazahuatl* had constituted a serious menace to the health of the inhabitants.

Two other diseases of colonial importance deserve mention in the present category: malaria and syphilis. With respect to the latter, wholly apart from the perennial argument concerning origin, there is general agreement that whether or not it was present it caused no great damage. The occasional reference by native writers to "buboes" implies merely that lesions of this character were recognized, but proves nothing as to their pathogenicity. Malaria proved quite destructive to the coastal Indians in the early colonial period, and still constitutes a serious problem in public health, but how severe were its effects prior to 1520 is unknown. That the mosquito has always been present is highly probable, but the opinion is widely held that the organism—or at least *an* organism—was brought by the Spanish from the Mediterranean basin. It is extremely difficult to reconcile two facts with the pre-existence of a virulent form of malaria along the coast: (1) there was a very high native population density in these regions, and (2) of the original 1,300-odd conquistadores not a single one contracted the disease. On the other hand, this type of fever was known in general to the Nahua peoples. Thus Flores says: "The Mexicans were perfectly well acquainted with intermittent fevers and came to distinguish them, according to the type of onset, as quotidian, tertian, quartan, etc." Ocaranza agrees in effect: "It is very probable that they understood malaria as a transmissible disease, distinct from the rest; but nevertheless we know the name of only the tertian fever, *viptlatica*."

If the natives derived their worst plagues from the white man it would be reasonable to suppose that the latter would suffer most severely from diseases to which the Indians had long been accustomed and to which during the course of many centuries they had become relatively immune. Apart from the presumptive evidence contained in the herbals of Hernández and others, we possess two very clear expositions of the pathology of the white settlers. One of these is by Agustín Farfán, written in 1579. He lists the principal afflictions of the Spanish residents, as follows:

1. *Weakness and indigestion of the stomach.* "It is very sad to see in this land the weakness and indigestion of the stomach of almost everyone. . . ."
2. Typhoid.
3. Tuberculosis (extreme pain in chest, fever, bloody sputum).
4. Dysentery.
5. Diphtheria.
6. Appendicitis—or enteritis.

The other source of data is Juan de Cárdenas, who devotes a chapter to the subject. He says regarding gastric ills: "But certainly . . . in the Indies . . . there is scarcely a man who does not go around complaining of his stomach, no matter whether he be old or young, man or woman, born in the Indies or come from Spain. . . ." He remarks that nearly every woman of Spanish descent is afflicted with menstrual difficulties whereas the Indians escape these entirely. In another place he states: ". . . the Spanish scarcely arrive, in their twenties, when they begin to complain of rheumatism, headache and stomachache . . . and rarely has an Indian been seen to complain of rheumatism, liver trouble, urinary difficulty, or other ills which are so ordinary and continuous among the Spanish. . . ."

From the evidence presented up to the present point the deduction is possible that smallpox, measles, *matlazahuatl*, malaria, and syphilis were either absent completely or present in very mild form among the aboriginal tribes. Various gastro-intestinal disturbances and respiratory infections had been endemic but over a period of hundreds of years the natives had built up a high resistance to them.

2. A great many specific maladies and ailments were known to the

central Mexican tribes, some possibly important, others presumably insignificant. The most complete compilation of these is that given by Flores, who apparently exhausted the original sources. His list contains well over one hundred items, all of which are recognized pathological states. Many of them pertain to organic and nervous ailments, menstruation and parturition, wounds, and skin lesions of various sorts. Those infectious and possibly fatal diseases which could react seriously upon public health and population are fewer in number and are as follows:

pneumonia	gastro-enteritis	yellow fever
tuberculosis	dysentery	intermittent fever
pleurisy		

A mere list, however, although it be very extensive, gives no indication of the severity of any malady beyond the mere fact of its existence. A somewhat more quantitative insight may be obtained from an examination of the therapeutics of the time. The materia medica of Europe, and hence of the Spanish, throughout the Middle Ages had been largely herbalistic, a state of affairs which persisted throughout the sixteenth century. Similarly, the treatment of diseases in aboriginal Mexico depended almost exclusively upon the use of plant preparations. On both continents over a series of generations a large number of plants had been found to possess medicinal value. Now in a general way and in spite of various disturbing factors any civilization relying upon an herbalistic rationale of medicine inevitably tends to find a preponderance of medicines for those ailments which are both most common and most lethal. If, therefore, the Mexican native materia medica differed from that of contemporary Europe with respect to the number of remedies available for specific types of disease, there would be a probability that the incidence of such types differed in parallel fashion between the two regions. In order to apply this hypothesis, three lists of plants have been compared with respect to the number of plants stated to be of curative value for various classes and for certain specific diseases. The first is that of Parkinson, chosen as an exhaustive and a representative work applying strictly to Europe. The second is that of Hernández who, in the latter half of the sixteenth century compiled information concerning many hundred Mexican plants of medicinal value. Hernández, nevertheless, thought in terms of the current European medical philosophy and was interested in the treatment of Europeans and their descendants. His work hence reflects the condition of the white men exposed to the New World environment. Thirdly we have the discussion and list of Sahagún who, although European himself, wrote with reference to the aboriginal Mexican scene. His informants, whom he lists by name and describes as "*médicos*," were all Indians who spoke from the purely native point of view.

In both Parkinson and Hernández there is an index or table of "virtues" in which all pathological states mentioned are listed alphabetically and under each one the plants noted which are supposed to be efficacious in the particular instance. For Sahagún it was necessary to construct such a table. The Parkinson list is the most extensive, with 8,177 items. Hernández has 2,254 and Sahagún 202. In all cases, moreover, it is necessary to delete one broad category of materials, those which were designed to induce some particular response or excite some specific function. Here would be included drugs designated only as purgatives, astringents, soporifics, diuretics, tonics, etc., without stating explicitly for what diseases they were to be employed. Deducting these there remain for Parkinson 7,373, for Hernández 1,797, and for Sahagún 162. It is impossible to get an exact cross-check on the diseases themselves, owing to language differences (Latin, Spanish, English) and to variations in medical terminology. Certain broad but reasonably distinct categories can be set up, however, which convey all essential information. These are listed in the table below, together with the per cent of the remedies shown in the three herbals as applying to each (after the deduction mentioned above):

Neglecting minor categories two important trends are apparent: the reduction in non-infectious organic ailments in Mexico, and the corre-

TYPE OF AILMENT	PARKINSON	HERNÁNDEZ	SAHAGÚN
1. Specifics for internal and animal poisons	5.8	2.6	0.0
2. Animal parasites, internal and external	1.8	1.2	1.2
3. Wounds, burns, fractures, bruises ..	7.6	3.3	5.6
4. Female reproductive system: parturition, menstruation, lactation, uterine	9.1	7.1	3.7
5. Organic ailments and symptoms, primarily non-infectious	38.4	36.9	18.5
6. Minor non-infectious ailments	3.4	3.4	4.3
7. Tumors and cysts	1.7	3.6	0
8. Skin diseases: bacterial, mycotic, zootic	13.3	9.5	19.8
9. Infectious diseases: inflammatory, febrile, venereal	18.1	32.0	40.2
10. Unidentifiable diseases	0.6	0.4	6.8

sponding increase in infectious diseases. Even allowing for perhaps dubious statistical validity, it is evident, as one might expect, that the inflammatory and febrile infections assumed a relatively more important position in semi-tropical Mexico than in temperate Europe. This trend, moreover, is still pronounced when we compare Hernández and Sahagún, indicating that the native population was, or had been, very definitely subject to the effect of such diseases.

The field may be still further narrowed down if certain more specific categories are selected. For three of these in particular the data are quite clear cut:

TYPE OF AILMENT	PARKINSON	HERNÁNDEZ	SAHAGÚN
Respiratory infections: nose, throat, lungs	5.7	8.5	9.3
Diarrhea and dysentery	2.6	9.0	13.0
Fevers of all types	3.4	7.7	13.0

It is clear that, relative to the entire pathology of the region, Mexico in general and the aboriginal tribes in particular, suffered extensively from infections of the respiratory and gastro-intestinal tracts.

3. The evidence hitherto adduced can give us some picture of what diseases were present among the pre-conquest Mexicans as well as an approximate idea of their *relative* incidence. We still have to enquire concerning their *absolute* intensity: conceding their presence, what was their influence upon the condition of the whole population?

Among modern writers the prevailing opinion seems to be that the native tribes were in quite good shape insofar as their physical well-being is concerned. This view is illustrated by Bancroft, who states that "The Nahuas were a healthy race . . . ," and by Flores. The latter, referring to tuberculosis, says that ". . . this important pathological state which probably was rare among them . . . was nevertheless perfectly well known to them." And, regarding pneumonia: "It is not possible to affirm in a final manner whether the pneumonias were known to them . . . but it is impossible to suppose that such an important pathological state would have passed unnoticed by them." The implication is that neither of these diseases was of any particular consequence.

Very few of the sixteenth-century chroniclers make any positive assertions respecting epidemiology among the Aztecs and their neighbors. There is, however, an interesting passage by Cárdenas in connection with a discussion of the savage northern tribes known collectively as Chichimecas. These people, he says, are very healthy in their natural habitat, but when captured they rapidly sicken and die: ". . . the stronger and fiercer and healthier they are in their own land, the worse food they eat, . . . the fewer clothes they wear, the more miserably wasted and sick they become on falling into our hands . . . and scarcely do they become afflicted with a bit of a pain or a slight dysentery than they immediately die. . . ." More positive are the assertions of Pomar, one of the native Nahua writers: "It is stated . . . that in the time of their heathendom they lived very healthy without ever knowing what a pestilence was . . . and it is not found that their fathers or ancestors left any word of ever having had plagues and mortality, as they have had since their conversion."

Of the opposite opinion was Herrera, writing in approximately 1600
A.D. He says: No se guardavan de malos contagiosos y enfermedades y
bestialmente se dexaban morir." Also, referring to the Popoloca of Tepeaca
province, he says: "The principal illnesses which ran through these people
were an abundance of *colera, flema,* and other *malos humores,* caused by
bad food and lack of protection in their clothing." It is probable, on the
other hand that Herrera, who never saw Mexico, did not clearly distinguish
the pre-conquest natives from their descendants, who certainly were in a
miserable condition subsequent to 1520.

Although the weight of published opinion, for what it is worth, holds
that the pre-colonial inhabitants were relatively free from severe epidemics
we must go to such primary sources as are available for more concrete
evidence.

4. One type of data which might prove of value is the findings of the
archaeologists and the physical anthropologists who have disinterred hundreds of skeletons. The results to date which have been published are
surprisingly meager, although several highly competent persons have pursued this line of investigation. Two specific items have come to my attention. The first is the observation of Rubín de la Borbolla on dental caries
in skulls found at Tzintzuntzán in Michoacan. Rubín states: "Las caries
dentarias son en exceso abundantes al grado de llamar la atención por el
número en comparación con las piezas completas." He ascribes this condition to faulty diet. The second is an isolated case of "exostasis osea" in one
skeleton which "might indicate osseous tuberculosis or syphilis" found by
Caso and Rubín at Mitla in Oaxaca.

George C. Vaillant tabulated several score burials with respect to age.
His final conclusion was that "Disease has left no trace but over a quarter
of the dead were children and few individuals reached old age." Some
years previously, he had published a table showing the age of 138 skeletons
disinterred at three different sites. Of these, thirty-three are listed as children, twenty-four as "young," fifty-eight as "middle age," and twenty-
three as "old." Aside from the obvious smallness of the sample, it is doubtful
whether this type of age distribution shows any evidence of unduly high
infant mortality or whether the relative scarcity of very old persons is
not wholly to be expected in a primitive population. Vaillant furthermore
contradicts his implication of abnormal mortality by his introductory statement that "Disease has left no trace."

A reasonable conclusion to be drawn from the relative lack of archaeological data is that there were few if any really critical epidemics or any
unusual incidence of internal organic pathology among the peoples whose
osseous remains have been discovered.

5. There still remains to examine the written record of the central
Mexican tribes before the conquest and their immediate descendants thereafter. This source of information should be of crucial significance because
wars, famines, natural disasters, and decimating pestilences are the four

categories of material events which invariably leave their mark upon the social consciousness and which therefore find expression in oral and written tradition.

The earliest reference to anything approaching an epidemic which I have been able to find is a pictograph from the *Codex Boturini*, Plate, or *Lámina* 8. According to Orozco y Berra this plate represents the period of approximately 780 A.D. during the early migrations of the Aztecs, before their settlement in the Valley of Mexico. "The naked figure with closed eyes and exhausted appearance near the day sign 6 *acatl* signifies that a plague swept over the land during this period." The general interpretation of illness may be accepted but the use of the word "plague" in the modern medical sense may be questioned, as also the assertion that it "swept over the land." The *Codex* was composed probably in the middle of the fifteenth century and could represent only the haziest tradition of what happened seven or eight hundred years previously. Moreover the Nahua tribes in the eighth century were small groups of wandering nomads. A much more conservative statement of the probable meaning of the picture would be that at a remote period the Aztecs had been afflicted with some kind of sickness sufficiently severe to leave a trace in the memory of subsequent annalists.

The next mention of disease is derived from the *Codex Aubin*. During the late thirteenth century while the Aztecs were still migrating and reached Pantitlán, ". . . allí les sobrevino una epidemia de rajarseles todas las carnes (grietas)." Literally this means "splitting or cracking of all the flesh," evidently referring to some type of severe skin infection. The exact nature cannot be determined, nor is there any evidence of high mortality. Had the latter occurred the *Codex* would very probably have so indicated.

At or near the year 1330, after the Aztecs had settled finally in their home on Lake Tezcoco the valley seems to have been subject to some kind of debilitating illness. This localized in at least two points: at the northern end of the valley and at the southern end at Coyoacán. It was to this period that the *Anales de Quautitlán* ascribed the list of diseases to which reference has already been made. Apparently there was a widespread incidence of dysentery and respiratory diseases at least among the Tepanecs. At the same time occurred the fabulous epidemic at Coyoacán. According to later accounts—and it is noteworthy that only the later accounts carry the story in full detail—the Aztecs on the lake cooked large amounts of fish. The smell of this cookery, carried by the wind a few miles to the shore at Coyoacán, caused a violent reaction. Tezózomoc says that the Aztecs had previously tried to starve out the people at Coyocacán by withholding the supply of fish, hence the profound effect of the odor: "Little by little the old men and women, the boys and girls began to feel ill and suffer from swelling of the eyelids. The small boys and girls began to die, after them the old men and women. And the young men and women began to show bloody diarrhea, with no remedy whatever to cure them. . . ." Durán says

". . . and such was the smoke that entered the streets of Coyoacán that it made the women miscarry from desire to eat what the Mexicans were cooking and made the children cry for it; it gave diarrhea to the old people from desire to eat; it made the faces of the women and feet of the children swell, from which many suffered and died. . . ." Torquemada adds that "many died" and that the symptoms included "enfermedad de garganta" and "pujamento de sangre."

Summing the symptoms and accepting the statements that there was a high mortality, it is clear that in 1320 to 1330 there was unusually severe illness in central Mexico. On the other hand there is evidence that the fundamental cause was nutritional. From the multiplicity of symptoms it may be inferred that several distinct diseases were rampant: certainly dysenteries and acute respiratory infections. The fanciful account of the fish smell has all the appearance of an attempt upon the part of later historians to interpret an otherwise mysterious malady. On the other hand it is quite possible that there was a food shortage. If so the intensity of disease onset is quite logically explained by assuming a reduced resistance on the part of the general population to the normal endemic disease pattern. Furthermore the eye inflammation, the diarrhea, and the tendency toward edema could very easily have resulted from an acute avitaminosis accompanying a critical shortage of food, particularly of certain types of food. If this concept of the situation may be accepted, then what was observed was not an epidemic in the sense of the decimation of an otherwise healthy population by an invading organism, but merely the sequelae of semi-starvation.

This close association in Mexico of famine and epidemic is seen even more clearly in the famous mortality of 1454–1457 which, it will be noted, was the first severe experience of the sort suffered by the Nahua peoples subsequent to 1330, or in a period of 120 years. The natural disasters occurring at this time have been fully described in histories of pre-colonial Mexico and need not be discussed at length here. They began apparently with an unprecedented freeze and snowfall in the winter of 1453–1454 which caught the inhabitants totally unprepared. This was followed by utter drouth throughout 1454, 1455, and 1456, such that food production was completely prevented and the food reserves utterly exhausted. In the resulting famine thousands perished from acute starvation. The pertinent question in connection with the present discussion concerns the possibility of an epidemic which caused mortality apart from starvation.

The local sources and in general the earlier speak only of famine. In the *Atlas* of Durán, *Lámina* 17, there is shown "the terrible famine that raged over the land for a period of three years. . . ." The *Codex Telleriano-Remensis* states simply that "there was so much snow that the people died" and "there was such a famine that the people died." Two illustrations are given in Plate 7, one showing or representing snow, the other hunger. The *Codex Aubin* describes the famine and then says "The people scattered through the mountains to secure the flesh of animals or birds . . . nor did they have hunting nets; they wandered among the valleys, the birds of prey ate them, for there was no one to bury them." In *Historia de los mexicanos por sus pinturas* there is merely the statement: "In the year one hundred and thirty-two there was an intense frost and a famine." The *Anales de Chimalpahin* says that "there were many deaths. The people died of thirst. . . ." The *Codex Ramírez* gives a circumstantial account of the famine. Regarding mortality there is only the statement that ". . . the people began to grow thin and weak from the hunger which they suffered and many died, and others fled. . . ." The *Anales de Quautitlán* states there was a "fearful famine, in which many people perished."

Disease comes to be mentioned in conjunction with the famine only by the chroniclers of the sixteenth century. The most important references of this type are as follows. Diego Durán says that "the people began to weaken and grow thin with the hunger they suffered; some began to fall ill eating things contrary to health. . . ." Ixtlilxóchitl in the *Historia chichimeca* is rather detailed in his account. In the great cold winter of 1454 "there was a pestilential catarrh from which many people died especially the older persons, and in the three following years all the crops and fruits of the earth were lost such that the greater part of the people perished . . . and soon the sickness increased and so many people died that it seemed as if not a single person would survive. . . ." Tezózomoc mentions no disease until he comes to the end of his description where he uses the terms "hambre, pestilencia y mortandad." He then proceeds: ". . . the old Mexicans called this famine and mortality *Nezetochhuiloc*, others applied the name *Netotonacahuiloc*, the pest of the coasts of Cuextlan." These terms are illuminating in themselves. The first is derived from *Ne* (from), *ce* (one) *toch* (rabbit) and *huiloc* (illness), that is: from the illness of (the year) 1 rabbit. The other is derived from *Ne* (from) *totonaca* (the Totonacs) and *huiloc* (illness), or from the illness of the Totonacs. The first expression therefore refers to some illness or debilitating condition which occurred at a certain date. The other ascribes this condition to the Totonacs, a tribe living on the Gulf Coast in the present state of Veracruz. Neither defines or qualifies the illness in the pathological sense. One other citation may be mentioned. There is a statement in the "Anales mexicanos: Mexico-Azcapotzalco" that ". . . there was much hunger and for that reason it was said that they suffered such *fuego* (skin eruption, rash)." Since later writers merely repeated the ideas set forth immediately above, nothing further would be gained by citing them in detail.

Tezózomoc's account indicates that there was severe illness among the starved and dying Mexicans. But such illness is an inevitable accompaniment of any acute famine. There is no evidence of any epidemic beyond that directly caused by starvation, or one which affected persons in a nutritionally good condition, or one which carried beyond the borders of the stricken region. In fact many famine sufferers migrated to or were sold into slavery among the surrounding tribes, particularly the Totonacs, but there is no record of any spread of illness to these groups. Such would inevitably have happened if the Mexicans had been afflicted with a serious contagion. Durán's statement is no more specific than that of Tezózomoc. He merely accounts for the general debility by referring it to the very inferior food eaten by the desperate sufferers. Ixtlilxóchitl's claim of an epidemic of respiratory disease may well carry weight, although he is the first writer to mention it. He, however, distinctly ascribes the condition to the cold weather. It is entirely reasonable to assume that the extreme exposure suffered by the inhabitants wearing few clothes and living in unheated houses would result in a much increased incidence of the normally occurring respiratory infections such as pneumonia, bronchitis, laryngitis, colds, and the like. The *fuego*, or skin eruptions, rashes or lesions referred to in the fourth citation are more difficult to place but could easily have arisen as a result of acute dietary deficiencies plus generally lowered resistance to ordinary skin infections.

If we sum up the testimony concerning the misfortunes of 1454-1457 we find two points clearly emerging: (1) None of several primary documentary sources mention any disease at all (unless pure hunger is a disease). (2) The maladies mentioned in four other sources, somewhat later in origin, can all be regarded as secondary to exposure and famine, either in the form of acute avitaminosis or in the form of normally occurring infectious diseases operating on subjects badly weakened by starvation. There is no presumption whatever of a true epidemic.

In the years 1504-1506, there was another famine in which on a smaller scale the events of fifty years previously were repeated. All authorities agree upon the facts, insofar as the crop failures and consequent hunger are concerned. There is no reference in any of the annals, codices, or chronicles to death by any agency but simple starvation, no direct or oblique claim of an epidemic, or even abnormal illness. Yet this famine occurred only fifteen years before the Spaniards arrived and was well within the memory of such persons as Tezózomoc, Ixtlilxóchitl, and the informants of Sahagún. Had a pestilence of noticeable magnitude afflicted the country some record of it would unquestionably have been preserved.

Certain final conclusions are now possible. From the accounts of both whites and Indians after the conquest, as well as from the materia medica of both races, it is clear that the pathology expected in a semitropical region was present in central Mexico, probably for centuries before 1520. The natives were subject to these diseases but over a long period of occupancy had probably developed a high level of immunity and resistance. This is demonstrated in part by the susceptibility shown by the incoming white men. The archaeological and historical record indicates a race which was remarkably free from devastating epidemics and from generalized chronic endemic ailments. There are few cases of serious or widespread illness in historic times and within at least two hundred years of the conquest; all of these can be classified as secondary to physical exposure and starvation.

The biological and demographic implications of this surprisingly high level of public health were profound, for one of the most important factors commonly limiting population increase was absent or substantially inoperative. As a consequence the aboriginal population increased notably prior to 1520 until it pressed close upon the food supply. Furthermore, the terrible epidemics following the conquest were all the more fearful, particularly in their psychological effect, since the social group which suffered them was intellectually and emotionally unprepared to meet them.

GENERAL

3. William Hickling Prescott: The Man and the Historian

R. A. HUMPHREYS

The February, 1949, issue of the *HAHR* was prepared as a memorial volume to mark the hundredth anniversary of the death of Prescott, who first turned the attention of readers in the English-speaking world to the dramatic story of the Spanish conquest of Mexico and of Peru. The lead article of that issue appears below. Professor Humphreys is dean of Latin Americanists in Britain today and director of the newly established Institute of Latin American Studies in London.

"There is only one way to look at life," wrote Henry Adams to the young Henry Cabot Lodge in 1872, "and that is the practical way . . . Sentiment is very attractive and I like it as well as most people, but nothing in the way of action is worth much which is not practically sound. The question is whether the historico-literary line is practically worth following, not whether it will amuse or improve you. Can you make it *pay?* either in money, reputation, or any other solid value. Now if you will think for a moment," Adams continued, "of the most respectable and respected products of our town of Boston, I think you will see at once that this profession does pay. No one has done better and won more in any business or pursuit, than has been acquired by men like Prescott, Motley, Frank Parkman, Bancroft, and so on in historical writing; none of them men of extraordinary gifts, or who would have been likely to do very much in the world if they had chosen differently. What they did can be done by others."

That is a revealing letter. It says something of Henry Adams and something of Boston, and, incidentally, it passes a judgment on William Hickling Prescott, with which Prescott—a man of singular modesty as well as of singular charm—would have been the first to agree. Whether he would also have agreed with the very worldly advice which Adams gave to Lodge on the reasons why a talented young man should choose to follow "the historico-literary line" is another question.

The Boston mind, of course, in Prescott's day, as in Adams's, was not

From Volume XXXIX (1959), pages 1-19.

indifferent to "money, reputation, or any other solid value." And Prescott, though he had been born not at Boston but at Salem, in 1796, was very much a Boston man. A New England gentleman, moreover, however well-to-do, was not expected to pass a life of idleness and pleasure. And Prescott was very much a New Englander and a gentleman. His grandfather was old Colonel William Prescott of Bunker Hill fame. His father was Judge Prescott, who had amassed a comfortable fortune at the Massachusetts Bar. He himself had not only been born of the right stock; he had been sent to one of the best schools—that of Dr. Gardiner, the Rector of Trinity Church; he had gone to the right university—indeed, for a Bostonian, the only university—Harvard; he held the right opinions—federalist, in the language of the day, or, in more modern terms, conservative; and he belonged to the right church—Unitarian. And in the normal course of events the young man should have become, like his father, a successful lawyer and a respected man of affairs. Nothing in his bright and happy boyhood and early youth foreshadowed any different future, except, perhaps, a love of reading and of telling stories. And both at school and college he seems to have aimed at acquiring no more than that ordinary stock of learning which would enable him to do himself and his family credit.

But an accident which happened in his second, or junior, year at Harvard changed his whole life. Leaving the dining hall one day, he was struck in the left eye by a crust of bread and was instantly and permanently blinded. Nevertheless, he was able to complete his college course, graduated with moderate distinction—the family marked the occasion by giving a dinner for five hundred in a tent—and began to read law in his father's office. Then in January, 1815, acute rheumatism attacked his right eye and other parts of his body also, and for weeks he lay in darkness. Recovering, he sailed for the Azores to stay with his maternal grandfather, Thomas Hickling, who was the American consul in the island of St. Michael's. The visit gave him his one glimpse of the kind of tropical scenery he was later so vividly to describe. But on November 1st darkness again fell, and for three months he was shut up in a single room, walking backwards and forwards, throwing out his elbows to feel the walls, and—for he was already beginning to cultivate those powers of memory which were later to be his—singing, reciting, and composing a Latin ode for one of his friends.

The light returning and his rheumatism lifting, he visited England, where the specialists told him that there was no hope of a permanent cure and that he must abandon all thought of his profession—a sentence which he received with the utmost calm. "Do not think that I feel any despondency," he wrote to his parents. "My spirits are full as high as my pulse; fifteen degrees above the proper temperament." He now bought his famous noctograph or writing case—a frame with brass wires stretched across it and holding a piece of carbon paper tightly clamped to a piece of ordinary paper. Guided by the wires and using an ivory stylus, he could write without having to try to read what he had written, and without the lines running into one another, though the resulting hieroglyphics were the despair of his friends and of his future secretaries. The autumn saw him in Paris and the winter in Italy, crossing without note, as Ticknor observes, the battlefields of Gonsalvo de Córdoba, but with a Horace and a Livy in his travelling carriage and a shrewd eye for the contemporary scene. On his way back to England in the following spring, however, he was again prostrated, and at mid-summer, 1817, he was glad to leave Europe and England for Boston and home.

Home, yes, to a devoted family. But to what else? Prescott had now turned twenty-one. Tall, handsome, and extremely entertaining, he was everywhere a favorite. His light-heartedness was infectious, his smile irresistible. But what was he to do? "I can't say that I like to be called blind . . . ," he wrote, many years later. "I have it is true but one eye, but that has done me some service, and with fair usage will I trust do me some more." But his journal records the careful examination he made of his habits and way of life in order to determine how best to preserve his halting sight and to keep at bay the dreaded rheumatic attacks, and it records also how often all precaution was in vain. Fortunately, there was no need for him to earn his living, for it was increasingly obvious that all ordinary careers were closed to him. But in Prescott the ancestral and New England virtues were too strong, he had too much force of character, too fine a sense of moral obligation, too ardent and gallant a nature, to allow his physical disabilities to serve as an excuse for idleness. For a while he was content to watch and weigh himself. Then, in 1820, the year also of his most happy marriage, he made up his mind. His life should be given to literature.

It was a courageous choice. For Prescott knew that only by the most rigorous self-discipline could he preserve his health and his sight. And he knew also that he must depend much upon the sight of others. But literature was his natural bent. There were friends to encourage and help him— George Ticknor, for example, the new Professor of the French and Spanish languages at Harvard, who had only recently returned from Göttingen and Europe with incredible stories of German scholarship and a library of Spanish books the like of which Boston had not seen before. And, fortunately, he could afford to employ a secretary. He began to do so regularly in 1824. Meanwhile, he had laid down for himself a course of study. It is best given in his own words. "I am now twenty-six years of age, nearly," he wrote in 1822. "By the time I am thirty, God willing, I propose, with what stock I have already on hand, to be a very well-read English scholar; to be acquainted with the classical and useful authors, prose and poetry, in Latin, French, and Italian, and especially in history . . . The two following years, 31-32, I may hope to learn German, and to have read the classical German writers; and the translations, if my eye continues weak, of the Greek. And this is enough for general discipline."

Enough, indeed. But the program was carried out, except that German proved too difficult a language to master for a man who could only use his one eye with great caution and for short periods at a time. Reluctantly, Prescott substituted Spanish for German. Ticknor's Harvard lectures on Spanish literature, read over to Prescott in the evenings, seem to have been the origin of this momentous change. But it was made without enthusiasm. "I am battling with the Spaniards this winter," he wrote in 1824, "but I have not the heart for it that I had for the Italians." And in view of what was to come, his further comment was indeed ironic. "I doubt whether there are many valuable things that the key of knowledge will unlock in that language!"

All of this was preliminary. Prescott was fast becoming a man of letters. Working hard—"*never* put up with a smaller average than 7 hours intellectual occupation per diem" was one of his resolutions—he was writing as well as reading and noting. "State with confidence what I know to be true," he observes in October, 1824; "Never introduce what is irrelevant or superfluous or unconnected for the sake of crowding in more facts," he remarks in July, 1828—both admirable maxims. And, beginning in 1821, each year till 1833 he contributed what he called his "annual peppercorn" to the *North American Review*—the "old North," which was the American equivalent of the *Edinburgh* and of the *Quarterly*.

But he had yet to discover his all-absorbing field of study. History had always attracted him—history, that is, as a branch of literature, history in the grand manner of Robertson or Gibbon. An American history, a Roman history, a history of Italian literature, he considered them all. But, more and more, he began to feel the lure of Spain. Unexpected riches opened before him in the language which he had at first been tempted to underrate. And as he reflected on the course of Spanish history between the Arab invasion of the peninsula and the consolidation of the monarchy under Charles V, suddenly his mind took fire. Here was the age of Ferdinand and Isabella; here the age which contained "the germs of the modern system of European politics." It was full of brilliant episodes and striking events—the conquest of Granada, the exploits of the Great Captain, Gonsalvo de Córdoba, in Italy, "the discovery of a new world, my own country," the establishment of the Inquisition. "Untried ground," he noted early in January, 1826, "and in my opinion a rich one." But could he rise to the subject? Was he not more at home in literary history, particularly Italian literary history? He hesitated painfully. Then, on January 19th, he entered in his journal: "I subscribe to the History of the Reign of Ferdinand and Isabella." He was twenty-nine, and he had found his theme.

Then years of almost unremitting toil followed. At first, while he read widely in the literature of English and European history in order to lay a firm foundation for his work, doubts continued to assail him, as well they might, for at this time he was deprived almost entirely of the use of his eye. But, soon, books and manuscripts arrived from Spain. The subject began to unfold in his imagination. And by the summer of 1828 all hesitation had vanished. Six hours a day his secretary would read to him in a darkened room while Prescott made notes on his noctograph, and then, sitting alone, he would "digest" what he had heard. Presently, in October, 1829, he began to compose, "ripening" a chapter in his mind during his early morning rides or on his walks, and striving never to write until he should know exactly what he wanted to say. Later, at the height of his powers, he could retain in his memory as much as sixty or seventy pages of future print without putting a single word on paper, and he could amend and correct what lay in his mind just as if he had the manuscript in front of him. Yet, all the while, Prescott had to force himself to work. He hated early rising, but always rose early, and his servant had instructions to take away the bedclothes if he did not get up so soon as he was called. He hated having to begin a new chapter. And he was always making bets with his secretary that he would get through a certain amount of writing by a given time and imposing penalties on himself if he failed.

At last, in June, 1836, the *History of the Reign of Ferdinand and Isabella* was finished. Few people in Boston, or anywhere else, knew that young Mr. Prescott had been writing a book. Indeed, says Ticknor, "most of his friends thought that he led rather an idle, unprofitable life, but attributed it to his infirmity, and pardoned or overlooked it as a misfortune, rather than as anything discreditable." And Prescott himself, having finished the book, was in two minds whether to publish it. He need never have doubted. "Their Catholic Majesties," as he called it, appeared on Christmas Day, 1837, to captivate all Boston and to win for the author the respect and admiration of the scholarly world not only in America but in England and Europe.

The book was not a masterpiece of historical interpretation. It was not a penetrating analysis of a great historical period. And it did not provide that "thorough view of the literary and social, as well as the political condition of Spain" which Prescott seemed to think that it provided. Literature indeed he discussed, and at length. He was accustomed to writing on literature in the pages of the *North American Review*. But Prescott never ranked his critical and literary essays highly, and there is no reason to dissent from his judgment. His comment, when a collected edition came out, was characteristic. "My portrait," he wrote, "is to be prefixed thereto —which they consider, I suppose, putting a good face on the matter." As for social, constitutional, and economic history, it cannot be denied that Prescott's interest in these matters in *Ferdinand and Isabella* was of a very limited kind. It was the politics, the personalities, the conflicts of wills and of arms, that fascinated Prescott. History, as he saw it, was a story, full, as he says, of "picturesque delineations of incident" and "dramatic exhibitions of character." And this is what *The Reign of Ferdinand and Isabella* was— a narrative history, splendidly conceived and solidly based. "Much new material has been discovered," wrote one of the greatest of Prescott's successors in the field of Spanish history, Roger Merriman in 1918, ". . . and the fashions of historical writing have greatly changed; but Prescott's work still remains the standard authority on the reign of the Catholic Kings." And testifying to the "profound learning" and "unfailing honesty" of Prescott's writing, Merriman added: "Such errors as he made were due to lack of material, and to a really noble inability to comprehend a policy of treachery or deceit."

Ferdinand and Isabella was the story of the rise of Spain from "chaos," as Prescott puts it, "not to the first class only, but to the first place, in the scale of European powers." In it he had traced the unification of the country and the consolidation of its monarchy, and he had traced also the progress of maritime discovery and the foundation of the first great European empire overseas. And as he closed his survey of what he believed to be "the most glorious epoch" in Spanish history, the future was already calling. "Scarcely was Ferdinand's reign brought to a close," he wrote, "before Magellan completed, (1520), what that monarch had projected, the circumnavigation of the southern continent; the victorious banners of Cortes had already (1518) penetrated into the golden realms of Montezuma; and Pizarro, a very few years later, (1524), following up the lead of Balboa, embarked on the enterprise which ended in the downfall of the splendid dynasty of the Incas."

Here was the theme of Prescott's next and greatest books—*The Conquest of Mexico* and *The Conquest of Peru*. And it was exactly suited to his talents. His comments are revealing. "An epic in prose," he notes in his journal. "As full of incident as any tale of chivalry," he tells his publisher. "More like a romance than a history," he says a little later, and, again, it is, he writes, "as brilliant a subject, with adventures as daring and wonderful as ever occupied the pen of a historian."

Yet for some time after he had "knocked their Catholic highnesses on the head"—his own phrase—Prescott hesitated. He even thought of writing a life of Molière. But his heart, as he well knew, was elsewhere. What deterred him was the problem of sources. "Your manuscripts," he wrote, "is the only staple for the historic web—at least the only one to make the stuff which will stand the wear and tear of old Father Time." Could he get them?

His doubts were soon dispelled. Obadiah Rich, a bibliophile and bibliographer, who, after serving as an American consul in Spain and in the Balearic Islands, became a bookseller in London, had collected materials for *Ferdinand and Isabella*. *Ferdinand and Isabella* brought the friendship of the great Arabic scholar, Pascual de Gayangos, who later catalogued the Spanish manuscripts in the British Museum. It brought the friendship of the Spanish Minister to the United States, Ángel Calderón de la Barca, who was shortly to be transferred to Mexico. It brought election to the Royal Academy of History in Madrid. All doors were opened. The Academy placed its great resources at Prescott's disposal and allowed him to employ copyists, and here he could consult the immense collection of documentary materials which the celebrated Cosmographer of the Indies,

Juan Bautista Muñoz, had brought together in preparation for that history of the new world which Charles III had commissioned him to write, and of which one volume only appeared. The aging President of the Academy, Martín Fernández de Navarrete, who had long been engaged in compiling and editing, with loving care, the records of Spanish maritime discovery in America, made available his own fine collection of manuscripts. The representative of the family of Cortés opened his private archives. Everywhere Prescott found willing helpers. In the end he came to possess an unrivalled corpus of materials—8,000 folio pages of manuscript from Spain alone, enriched with further gleanings from public and private archives in Mexico, France, England, Italy and Sicily.

Prescott records that he began his "scattered reading" on *The Conquest of Mexico* in May, 1838, and began "to read in earnest" in April, 1839. Meanwhile he was dismayed to learn that "the most popular of American authors," Washington Irving, was engaged on the same subject. Twice already Irving had crossed Prescott's path. In 1828, two years after Prescott had begun his work on *Ferdinand and Isabella*, Irving had published his *Life and Voyages of Christopher Columbus*. This was the author of Rip Van Winkle in a new role. Southey, reading the book for John Murray, had remarked that it displayed "neither much power of mind nor much knowledge" but that it presented "a most remarkable portion of history in a popular form" and was "therefore likely to succeed." It was in fact chiefly based, with very inadequate acknowledgements, on Navarrete's collection of voyages. But the story was romantically told in Irving's characteristic style; only with the years were its pretensions to independent scholarship exposed; and succeed it did. It was followed in 1829 by *The Conquest of Granada*, fiction rather than history, indeed, but, once again, Prescott's ground, and Prescott, though he paid a handsome tribute to Irving in the preface to *Ferdinand and Isabella*, had been "sorely troubled." But in 1838 the boot was on the other leg. For Irving, once he knew of Prescott's plans, impulsively, but also wisely as well as generously, withdrew from the field, taking, as he said, to "planting cabbages most desperately."

Thenceforth all was plain, or relatively plain, sailing. The introductory section to *The Conquest of Mexico*, which dealt with what Prescott called "the moonshine period of the old Aztecs," was hard labour and cost him two years. But by the middle of 1841 he was "in full march" with Cortés across the mountains. And by August, 1843, the book was finished. *The Conquest of Peru*, which came next, was even more rapidly completed. The first words were written in August, 1844, and the last in November, 1846. But despite this heavenly speed, Prescott enjoyed the work less. The first chapter, in which he began his discussion of the civilization of the Incas, was, he complained, "a perfectly painful task, as painful as ever I performed at school." For the rest, the history of the conquest of Peru lacked, he felt, that dramatic inevitability which the conquest of Mexico possessed. It had less of a unity. And besides, while Cortés had all the character of a hero,

Prescott could only express the wish that Pizarro had been "more of a gentleman and less of a bandit."

But, like its predecessor, the book was a magnificent achievement. Both in the Peruvian and in the Mexican story, Robertson, in the eigtheenth century, had covered the same ground; and for Robertson Prescott had a great respect. But the plan of Robertson's famous *History of America* allowed, as Prescott said, "only an outline of the Mexican campaigns" and a "masterly sketch" of the conquest of Peru. Prescott provided the detailed narrative. And it is the measure of his success that after more than a hundred years there is still no narrative history of the Spanish conquest of America to equal his.

Like Robertson, of course, Prescott was greatly hampered in his discussion of the native civilizations of America by the novelty of the subject. His literary sources, it is true, were far more extensive than those available to Robertson. He could read Sahagún, for example, as Robertson could not. He reaped the benefit, moreover, of Humboldt's researches, for Humboldt had spent nearly five years in Spanish America, exploring, collecting, and describing, and every subject, from archaeology to mineralogy, had been grist to Humboldt's mill. And he could draw both on the magnificent collection of the *Antiquities of Mexico*, which Lord Kingsborough had published, hoping to prove that the American Indians were really Jews, and on the great folios of the *Antiquités Mexicains*, printed at Paris in 1834, which contained, as indeed did Kingsborough's volumes, reports of the archaeological expeditions which Captain Guillaume Dupaix, a discharged French officer, had led to various sites in Mexico.

But the archaeological evidence at Prescott's disposal was all too scanty. In the "shadowy field" which he was now exploring, he could derive little help from contemporary studies in anthropology and ethnology. These sciences were in their infancy. And though, since Robertson's day, much more information had become available to illustrate the character of the native Indian societies which the Spaniards had found in the Valley of Mexico, the most remarkable of all pre-conquest civilizations—that of the Maya—was still unknown. Two or three Mayan sites had been cursorily examined, and, even as Prescott wrote, John Lloyd Stephens and Frederick Catherwood were uncovering in the jungles of Central America and on the limestone plains of Yucatán the lost cities of the Maya world. But it was long before these discoveries were followed up. Prescott saw quite clearly —and the conclusions of Stephens confirmed his own—that the ruins of such cities at Mitla, Palenque and Uxmal argued, as he said, "a higher civilisation than anything yet found on the American continent." Like Stephens, he strongly distrusted the great antiquity commonly ascribed to them. And he was inclined to think that they were Toltec in origin. But beyond this he could not go. Of the inscriptions at Palenque he remarked that "the language of the race" who devised them, and "the race itself," were unknown. And he doubted whether their "mysterious import" would ever be revealed.

Yet whatever the limitations set by the then boundaries of knowledge, Prescott's account of pre-conquest Mexico and pre-conquest Peru, read in the light of what had gone before, was a remarkable achievement; and, seen in the light of what has come after, it appears more impressive still. A later generation, it is true, found Prescott's colors exaggerated and his sources suspect. Prescott, for example, follows Cortés and Bernal Díaz del Castillo in describing the "barbaric splendour" of Montezuma's household, the state in which the "emperor" dined, the retinue which attended him, the dishes which he ate, the Cholula earthenware on which they were served, the golden goblets from which he drank, and Prescott's description was still further elaborated by H. H. Bancroft in 1875. But to the pioneer ethnologists of the school of Lewis H. Morgan, the so-called "social evolutionists," this picture was absurd. Morgan had lived and worked among the Iroquois. He knew an Indian when he saw one, and none that he had met remotely resembled Montezuma. The explanation was plain. The picture of ancient Mexico as drawn by the first Europeans was delusive and fictitious. The halls of Montezuma were nothing more than a "joint-tenement house of the aboriginal American model, owned by a large number of related families and occupied by them as joint-proprietors." The dinner which Montezuma ate was simply "the usual single daily meal of a communal household, prepared in a common cook-house from common stores, and divided, Indian fashion, from the kettle." All that the Spaniards found in Mexico, wrote Morgan, was a "simple confederacy of three Indian tribes, the counterpart of which was found in all parts of America." And while Montezuma, under Morgan's hand, was reduced to the stature of some early Pontiac or primitive Tecumseh, Prescott himself was dismissed as a romantic who had allowed his critical judgment to be warped by the picturesque tales of the conquistadores and others.

These are ancient controversies. The terms of discussion have long since changed and the world of American archaeology has been revolutionized. But Prescott's scholarship has been vindicated and his reputation rehabilitated. Prescott, of course, had been fully alive to the "proneness to exaggerate, which was natural," he says, to the early conquistadores. He was always careful to test and weigh the credibility of his Spanish sources. But it never occurred to him to reject their testimony out of hand. Like the Spaniards, no doubt, he was constrained to describe the political organization of semi-civilized indigenous societies in terms of European institutions, though he was well aware of the dangers which such analogies entailed; and to illustrate the development of these societies he made use of classical, oriental and Egyptian parallels which carried greater conviction in the eighteen-forties than they do in the nineteen-fifties. But Prescott's description of the pre-Columbian civilizations of the New World was the most penetrating appraisal that had yet been made. And though much has been discovered since his day, though there were fields into which he could not enter, it approached far closer to the truth than his later nineteenth-century detractors were disposed to allow.

But all of this, of course, was merely preliminary to Prescott's main purpose—to tell the story of the conquest itself; and, however much these introductory surveys may need to be revised and amplified, from the moment when the Europeans first set foot on American soil Prescott was on firm ground. And he built to last. Such is his mastery of his materials that even his descriptions of landscape and seascape leave the impression that Prescott had seen it all himself. And so he had, in his vivid imagination and through the eyes of others. "I want to dip my pencil in your colours," he writes to Fanny Calderón de la Barca, the charming Scottish wife of the first Spanish Minister to Mexico—"the colours of truth, gently touched with fancy, at least feeling." And as her enchanting *Life in Mexico* shows, no one who had Fanny for a correspondent could ask for more.

Prescott's style, it is true, was a little magniloquent. His grass is "verdant" rather than green. His "monarchs" are "sagacious" and his "soldiery" "licentious." He was even capable of referring to "the feathered tribes" when he meant birds. He himself was aware of this weakness. "Finished text of chap. 1. Book 3rd," he notes in 1841. "Full of the picturesque—read very like Miss Porter—rather boarding-schoolish finery." And "boarding-schoolish finery" some of it is. Prescott prefers "gales" to "winds" and "groves" to "woods" and when insects appear he cannot refrain from painting them with "enamelled wings, glistening "like diamonds in the bright sun of the tropics." But there is good, plain, homespun stuff too—the Prescott of the letters and journals, and, whatever his love of the conventional ornament and the rhetorical word, sooner or later every reader succumbs to the spell he weaves. For Prescott was an artist. The easy flow of his narrative, its admirable clarity, never reveal the enormous pains which he had taken to master the difficulties of construction and to ensure, both in *The Conquest of Mexico* and in *The Conquest of Peru*, that his book should be a whole in which every part was exactly right.

They never conceal, either, the absolute integrity both of the man and of his writing. For though Prescott trod enchanted ground, no one was less capable of sacrificing truth to effect. His passion for accuracy was unquenchable. And while he sought to establish his narrative, as he says, "on as broad a basis as possible of contemporary evidence," he sought also to see the sixteenth century through sixteenth-century eyes. He burkes no awkward facts. "Never shrink from the truth . . . ," he notes in his private journals. "I spoke fearlessly in 'F[erdinand] and I[sabella].' Do so now." But the historian, he thought, gained nothing "by throwing about hard names . . . like Southey and others of that plain spoken school." And the Spanish conquistadores, those "antique heroes whose great deeds were so nearly allied to great crimes," were to be judged not by the standards of the nineteenth century but by those of their own times. So, he remarks, after describing the massacre at Cholula, "It is far from my intention to vindicate the cruel deeds of the old Conquerors. Let them lie heavy on their heads. They were an iron race, who periled life and fortune in the cause; and as they made little account of danger and suffering for themselves, they had little sympathy to spare for their unfortunate enemies. But, to judge them fairly, we must not do it by the lights of our own age. We must carry ourselves back to theirs."

And Prescott, in his fine imagination, had lived with the Spaniards. He knew their sixteenth-century world in all its violence and vitality. Side by side with the "capricious cruelty of the conqueror" and the "cupidity of the colonist," he saw also the courage which "no danger could appal," the lure of the unknown which charmed the Spanish mind, the sense of high adventure. And more than this, even amid the "coarse and covetous spirit" which marked, he says, "the adventurers of Peru," he recognized something else. "One might have supposed," he writes of Pizarro and his men as they prepared to seize the Inca, "one might have supposed them a company of martyrs, about to lay down their lives in defence of their faith, instead of a licentious band of adventurers, meditating one of the most atrocious acts of perfidy on the record of history! Yet, whatever were the vices of the Castilian cavalier, hypocrisy was not among the number. He felt that he was battling for the Cross, and under this conviction, exalted as it was at such a moment as this into the predominant impulse, he was blind to the baser motives which mingled with the enterprise." For the Spaniard, Prescott says again, "was ever a Crusader. He was, in the sixteenth century, what *Coeur de Lion* and his brave knights were in the twelfth, with this difference; the cavalier of that day fought for the Cross and for glory, while gold and the Cross were the watchwords of the Spaniards."

The New World was conquered in the name of the Cross of Christ as well as in a search for gold. This dual motive is the paradox, or rather it is one of the paradoxes, the seemingly contradictory impulses, in the mind of the sixteenth-century Spaniard. Prescott recognized it fully, as he recognized also the contrast between the humane intentions of the Crown and the "practical license," as he says, of the colonists. His view of history was not profound. As Theodore Parker observed, in a famous comment, he was fond of referring events to Providence "which other men would be content to ascribing to human agency." But, like Lady Bertram of Mansfield Park, if Prescott did not think deeply, he always thought justly. His writings, as Stirling Maxwell remarked in 1859, reflect that "calm good sense" which "directed every action of his life." *The Conquest of Mexico* and *The Conquest of Peru* do not present the total picture of the action of Spain in America in the first half of the sixteenth century. They need to be supplemented by studies of a different kind, in administration, in economic life, in political thought. But they must always remain two of the great adventure stories of history, and stories which, at every point, are solidly tied to established fact.

"Of late years," wrote Prescott in April, 1846, "I have had a fair use of my eyes. But I fear I am not to count on this for the future. The sight has grown much dimmer, and I have at times pain which warns me not to press the matter further. So I complete 'Peru' as I began 'Ferdinand and Isabella.' But I shall not abandon the historian's career. For how can I?" He had, indeed, long been collecting materials for what was to be his last important book—the *History of the Reign of Philip the Second*. He had been thinking about it as early as 1833. The idea constantly recurred to him, and in December, 1841, his journal records: "I have had the satisfaction to learn from that accomplished scholar, Gayangos, that he will undertake the collection of manuscripts for me relating to Philip the Second's history, so far as it can be effected in Paris and London."

From that moment the work went merrily forward. In 1842 Gayangos wrote that he had four copyists at work in the British Museum and another one in Holland House. From the British Museum he proceeded to the Public Record Office—a disgrace to the country, he writes. "Not only it requires great favour to obtain admission; but when admitted the papers are only trusted into your hands after a succession of ridiculous formalities." The papers themselves were in a lamentable state of confusion. No one could be employed as a copyist, copying being a perquisite of the clerks, who charged eight pence per folio of 72 words. And the office was only open from 11 to 2. The great collection of Sir Thomas Phillipps was also laid under requisition—a collection so large that the papers flowed into Sir Thomas's bedroom and even under his bed. And then Gayangos was off to Brussels, the Hague and Paris, and finally to Madrid and Simancas.

If the Public Record Office, or State Papers Office, as it was then called, was a disgrace, it is difficult to know what term to apply to Simancas. Gayangos was one of the first scholars ever to be admitted within its precincts. Visitors, he found, were forbidden to copy, to take extracts or notes, or even to make a summary of the documents they were allowed to examine. The confusion of the papers was appalling, and though in Simancas one could work four hours a day instead of three, as in London, the archives were closed every saint's day, of which, in Spain, there was a profusion.

Gayangos, however, triumphed over all difficulties. Other friends assisted Prescott in Florence, Vienna and Berlin. And by 1847, when Prescott was ready to start, he had as noble a collection of manuscripts on his shelves as the heart could desire. But he had already had to resolve "to relinquish *all* use of the eye" for the future in his studies, and to be content, as he records, if he "could preserve it for the more vulgar purposes of life." The mere sight of his collection filled him "with apprehension bordering on despair." He doubted much whether he would be able to produce anything more than a series of memoirs, and hardly had he begun to write, in July 1849, when his strength began to fail.

Urged by his friends, Prescott decided to try a change of scene, and this was the reason for his visit to England in 1850, "the most brilliant visit ever made . . . ," as Ticknor says, "by an American citizen not clothed with the prestige of official station." He met everyone and was invited everywhere. He stayed at Alnwick with the Duke of Northumberland, at Inverary with the Duke of Argyll, at Naworth and Castle Howard with the Earl of Carlisle, and at Trentham with the Duchess of Sutherland. He was presented at Court. Oxford made him a Doctor of Civil Law. Lockhart, Hallam, Macaulay, Lyell, Ford, Milman, all welcomed him. "Pray," said Disraeli, "are you related to the great American author—the author of the Spanish Histories?" "I squeezed his arm," says Prescott, "telling him that I could not answer for the greatness, but I was the man himself."

The visit was short. But it did much to revive Prescott's spirits. And he had made a brief excursion to Brussels, Antwerp and Holland—Motley's country, for Motley, with Prescott's blessing, was hard at work on *The Rise of the Dutch Republic*. Still, he had to describe the revolt of the Netherlands himself, and so soon as he had returned to America he was back at work, enlarging his plans and resolving that he would treat the reign of Philip II *in extenso* and not in the more desultory manner that he had at first envisaged. And by April, 1852, the first volume was finished. The second was ready by August, 1854, and Prescott then turned aside to prepare a new conclusion to Robertson's famous *History of the Reign of the Emperor Charles V* in the light of documents unknown to Robertson and dealing with Charles's life after his abdication. Soon, however, he was "Philippizing" (his own word) again. "Rebellion of the Moriscoes," he records, in June, 1857, "making in all 289 pages—more than half a volume! As bad as Macaulay—without his merits to redeem it." And, a few days later, "Finished Battle of Lepanto. I hope it will smell of the ocean."

It does. The set pieces of *Philip II* show no decline in Prescott's dramatic powers. But the book was never to be completed. In February, 1858, Prescott suffered a slight stroke. He carried on and managed to produce a conclusion to this third volume. He even started to work on the fourth, though he was not able to begin to write. "As to not working, as you kindly recommend," he wrote to Gayangos in September, 1858, "—to use Scott's words on a similar recommendation to him, 'Molly, when she puts the kettle on, might as well say, Don't boil, kettle.' But then I manage matters with more prudence, and make it a rule, one indeed that I have generally followed, never to sacrifice pleasure to business. But in truth long habit makes me find business—that is literary labor—the greatest pleasure." On January 28th, 1859, however, Prescott suffered a second stroke and in a few hours was dead.

It is related of the great Spanish scholar, Navarrete, to whom Prescott owed much, that "on the evening that he died, finding himself alone in his bedroom after having received extreme unction, he managed to get up without being heard by anyone and tottered into his study. He was found there by his daughters and when they asked him what he was doing he replied that he was bidding farewell to his books." So, also, Prescott had expressed the wish that he might lie for a time in the library which he had built for himself. And, there, he, too, bade farewell to the books and manuscripts which had been the friends of his life.

Other Articles of Interest

Gardiner, C. Harvey. "Prescott's Most Indispensable Aide: Pascual de Gayangos." XXXIX (1959), 81–115.

Lohman Villena, Guillermo. "Notes on Prescott's Interpretation of the Conquest of Peru." XXXIX (1959), 46–80.

Levin, David. "History as Romantic Art: Structure, Characterization, and Style in *The Conquest of Mexico.*" XXXIX (1959), 20–45.

Patterson, Jerry E. "A Checklist of Prescott Manuscripts." XXXIX (1959), 116–128.

---

4. Two Articles on the Same Topic: Bernal Díaz del Castillo and Popularism in Spanish Historiography and Bernal Díaz del Castillo's Criticisms of the *History of the Conquest of Mexico*, by Francisco López de Gómara

RAMÓN IGLESIA

Professor Iglesia achieved in these two articles the remarkable feat of examining his own ideas on history at two crucial periods in his life: first, when he was a calm researcher in Madrid before the outbreak of the Spanish Civil War and was preparing a critical edition of *The True History of the Conquest of New Spain* by the foot soldier of Cortés, the renowned Bernal Díaz del Castillo; second, after he had himself fought for

Republican Spain as a "foot soldier" and was making a new life for himself in the New World. His direct experience of military problems and of war profoundly affected his conceptions of history. One of his friends wrote of him later: "In those heart-breaking years [of the Civil War] he learned something of history in the raw and a great deal about the virtues of military leadership, and by 1939 he found himself in complete disagreement with the Ramón Iglesia of 1936 with respect to Bernal Díaz' evaluation of Cortés." * At the time of Iglesia's death he was on the faculty of the University of Wisconsin.

* * *

In a piece of historical writing, arrangement is argument; statements of fact, every one of which is true, can be arranged in many ways, and as some arrangement is always necessary, no history can be truly "impartial." (Shotwell, *The History of History*, p. 198.)

Today there is little to envy in the situation of those of us who have been brought up on historical studies within the confident, cheerful atmosphere of the positivist creed. In this atmosphere we were being put to sleep while we devoted ourselves to the placid gleaning of documents, the contribution of "facts," and our scruples were dispelled with the assertion that interpretation and synthesis would come later, would be a task for subsequent generations who could build upon the solid foundation which we were going to hand to them.

What a serene life our teachers led in spite of their painstaking research! No philosophical preoccupations, no visions of history as a whole, no shadow of disputable or contradictory ideas to trouble them. Look for facts, bring in new documents, refine your philological techniques, increase your materials, and the truth will then issue of its own accord like ripe fruit.

And today? Do we, by chance, have anything left of these confident illusions? Have we really learned so many things from the heaps of material which our predecessors have so diligently accumulated? Or, on the contrary, do we find ourselves overwhelmed, thoroughly weary, in danger of suffering the fate of Anatole France's scholar who was buried beneath the torrent of his own notes?

It is a serious matter to have to accept this last situation as the one we actually face. After the confident attitude, the passive and essentially comfortable attitude of the positivists, who, after all, did no more than repeat—consciously or unconsciously—"after me, the deluge," we find that the deluge has already begun and that its waters threaten to swallow us.

At first sight this situation could not be more discouraging. Positivism took the human element out of history and, what is more serious, took

---

* Lesley Byrd Simpson, "Ramòn Iglesia y Parga, 1905-1948," *HAHR*, XXVIII (1948), 163.
From Volume XX (1940), pages 517-550.

the human element out of the historian. It required that the latter be as detached as a recording machine, that he remain apart from every conflict and every idea of his times, and that he become empty of all spiritual content. Only in this way could the historian analyze and criticize the productions of other periods and cultures different from his own, acquiring the elusive possession of historic knowledge.

Has this end been attained? When the historian became empty of spiritual content, his work remained empty too. Instead of achieving a higher standard, what he has done has been to lower his standard, and one sees the result in the fact that people do not generally read history today. The historian has gradually been converted into a narrow individual who exchanges notes with colleagues, as he might exchange stamps or solve chess moves by postal card. In the best of cases the man of the street thinks of the historian as a poor creature who is incapable of facing life and who takes refuge in study of the past because there he finds no opposition, no struggle, with which he does not feel fit to cope. The man of the street is today, as he always has been, eager for history, and he pounces upon the production of those who, because they have taken an active part in the whirlwind of contemporary events, give to the account of their own and others' lives a vitality, a breath of passion, something which is never found in the works of professional historians.

In my opinion it cannot be denied that if any type of historiography has kept alive in our times, it has been biography, which has been cultivated—with more or less impurity—by persons who do not represent the field of historical studies, strictly speaking, but who have been careful to avoid that coldness, that gravity, and that deathly quality which have infested the productions of "scientific" history.

Can this not serve as an indication of the road we are to follow? Does not the success of some recently published biographies make it clear that the public perceives and appreciates in these works the existence of elements which have always been essential to history, the polished style of the account and the task of intelligent selection which emphasizes certain aspects while it disregards all confusing and irrelevant points? But there is more to be said. Of all the types of historical literature, biography is the only one which has managed to keep in contact with human life, contrary to the mechanizing process in which the "scientific" historians have gloried. This has saved it from catastrophe, because history is, as Huizinga says, the subject which maintains closest contact with life, and it is immediately killed if one wishes to disregard this intimate relationship.

One may think, then, that everything is not lost—that there is a road to salvation for the historian, and that the direction of this road is opposite that of the road over which he has recently been travelling. The historian will have to become human; he will have to admit the humble truth that he too is a being with limitations, a complex of ideas and passions and instincts—a man, in short, with all the grandeur and the servitude this implies. Only thus, by accepting beforehand all his limitations with respect to time, space, culture, and way of life—that is to say, with respect to his total environment—can he focus his attention upon the past, enrich his vision with first-hand experience, and let himself in turn be enriched by the selfsame past.

These considerations, among others which preoccupy and disturb many history scholars, have claimed my attention in a very special way because of conflicting impressions which have been made upon me by some studies I had been pursuing, and the vicissitudes of my own life. I know it sounds like heresy for the historian to talk about himself, but I cannot avoid it—nor do I wish to. Before the beginning of the war in Spain, I was working on the preparation of a critical edition of the *Verdadera Historia de la Conquista de la Nueva España*, by Bernal Díaz del Castillo. Since I needed to submit a paper for the Twenty-sixth Congress of Americanists which was held in Seville in October, 1935, I had to summarize in a somewhat risky fashion—as one always must—my viewpoints on some aspects of Spanish historiography and, in particular, on Bernal Díaz's book. This summary constitutes the first of the following articles. In it I accept as true Bernal's version of the Mexican conquest. The men who surround Cortés, and not the conqueror himself, are the ones who bear the entire burden, who have initiative and responsibility in the most difficult moments. Cortés is just one of the group.

If the war had not taken place in Spain, the prologue to my edition of Bernal—of which the article cited is only a preliminary study—might have been conceived and drawn up in analogous terms. But the war broke out, I took part in it, and in this manner I acquired a direct, vivid experience in connection with military problems, an experience which all the history books in the world would not have given me. And I saw at close range what there is to war—that touchstone of every human value, since in it the presence of death, which is ordinarily more faint and hidden, is ever existent: the rôle of the leaders who know how to command, and that of the soldiers who know how to obey and to die; the profound need of hierarchy and discipline in an army; all things that we had been forgetting, perhaps scorning, in our civilized, liberal, and individualistic society. This made me completely revise my ideas about a series of historical problems, and about Bernal's book also. After the war ended, I read it again, I studied Gómara's text with greater attention than before, I compared the two, and I arrived at the conclusions stated in the second of the articles published here. In these conclusions, although I do not altogether accept Gómara's partiality toward Cortés, I admit that Cortés played a much more outstanding rôle in the conquest than the one assigned him by Bernal.

Would my judgment have changed thus, if the tremendous experience of the Spanish war had not occurred during my lifetime? Probably not. The change has led me to believe that the joint publication of the two articles might be interesting, as it may give food for thought to the confident believers in the simple accumulation of data as the only possible generator of better understanding. In my case there has been no simple accumulation of data, but a "change in viewpoint," which is not the result of readings and reflections, but the consequence of a vivid experience. The same person—if I can say I am now the same person that I was before the war—working on the same subject, using the same method, can arrive at different and even contrary conclusions, if a change in his life takes place. Is not this a topic worthy of the attention of scientific historians? I believe so. For this reason I have thought that the simultaneous publication of my two articles may constitute a contribution not lacking in interest with regard to meditation on subjects which preoccupy many cultivators of history today. Is it possible, as we have recently been told, that the historian lays personality entirely aside when he begins work? If this is not possible, to what extent can, and should, his personality and that of his period and environment influence his vision of the past? What complex of ideas and sentiments does the historian use, consciously or subconsciously, to analyze facts, to select them, and to interpret them, now that selection, interpretation, and synthesis are becoming prime necessities? Will this subjective element spoil the unity and cohesion of historic learning attained after the output of great effort? These urgent questions are bound to keep positivist historians awake, to interrupt their siesta of an endless publication of documents. While it is true that these problems complicate the historian's mission dreadfully, it is also true that, if they are not stated in an honest, uncompromising manner, his efforts run the risk of proving fruitless.

Bernal Díaz del Castillo and Popularism in Spanish Historiography

Of all the sciences, History is the one closest to life. In this indestructible relationship are inherent History's weakness and strength. This makes History's standards variable, its certainty doubtful; but at the same time it gives History its universality, its importance, its seriousness.

These words of Huizinga have, without doubt, universal significance, but I consider them more applicable to Spain than to any other country. In Spain history is so intimately connected with life that our most valuable historical productions are those which have been written in the very wake of events, those which have sprung from a direct vision, from living the incidents related.

Frequently when the Spanish scholar prepares a history of the high scientific type based on documents and books, he fails to reach his goal. In this respect it will be sufficient for us to remember what happened with the official chronicle of the Indies. On the other hand, any witness of, or participant in, outstanding events generally has in our ranks a talent, a plastic force in description, a liveliness and exactitude in detail, which I do not believe have been attained in the historical writings of other countries. On our soil historical works have abounded. The purpose of the medieval chronicle was to relate facts about kings, according to what we are told in the chronicle of Alfonso XI, a model of this type of literature in Fueter's opinion. In fact, from the time of Alfonso X on, each Spanish monarch has one or several chronicles dedicated to the account of events during his reign. The authors of these works are not always known.

In the fifteenth century, when royal power declines under the weak monarchs of the Trastamara dynasty, not only the deeds of the king, but also those of the noblemen, furnish the chronicles with material. So, beside the chronicle of Enrique III will appear the magnificent one of Don Pero Niño, Count of Buelna, a model knight; beside the chronicle of Juan II, that of his favorite, Don Alvaro de Luna; beside the chronicles of Enrique IV, that of his favorite, the lord high constable Miguel Lucas de Iranzo, that of Don Alfonso de Monroy, treasurer of Alcántara, and others. Kings and noblemen parade in the wonderful gallery of pictures found in Pérez de Guzmán's *Generaciones y Semblanzas*.

In the fifteenth century there also appears in Spain the book of travels, represented by the delightful *Andanças* of Pero Tafur, a knight of a noble Andalusian family, who, taking advantage of the truces with the Moors of Granada, makes a trip to the Holy Land and travels through various countries. Pero Tafur, whose work lent itself to the narration of every kind of marvel, will tell us: "I had good information about the city of Damasco, but, since I did not see it, I leave that for one who has seen it."

At the height of the Renaissance during the reign of Ferdinand and Isabella, when history tries to raise its standards by imitating models of ancient times—which procedure merely fills the account with confused dissertations, as occurs in Hernando del Pulgar's chronicle—there appears a magnificent representative of the direct narrative, of the popular type, in Andrés Bernáldez, a priest of Los Palacios. The latter will not be above telling us that he writes his book at the request of a grandmother of his:

At the age of twelve I, the author of these memoirs, was reading in the register of a deceased grandfather, who was public clerk in the town of Fuentes, in the region of León, where I was born. I then came across some chapters concerning heroic things which had happened in his time. Upon hearing these things read, my widowed grandmother, his wife, who was already quite old, said to me: "Son, why don't you write that way about things of the present? For you must not be lazy about writing the good things which may happen during your lifetime, so that people who come afterwards may read those things and, marvelling as they read, may give thanks to God."

Nor will he fail to mention that Queen Isabella tore out her hair when she learned of the rebellious attitude which the Archbishop of Toledo, Don Alonso Carillo, had taken:

And the archbishop, with bad judgment, sent a message to the queen in order that she might definitely know that, if she went there, as soon as she entered Alcalá through one gate, he would go flying through the other. And as the queen learned this during mass, after the mass she was so angry that she flung her hands to her hair.

The dawn of a new Spain will begin to reveal itself in the simple notes of a childish song:

After the beginning of the wars in Castile between King Enrique and the noblemen of his kingdom, and before the marriage of Ferdinand to Queen Isabella, in Castile there was sung to a good tune a song which young people, who are generally fond of music, used to sing: "Flowers of Aragon are within Castile." And the children would take little banners, and mounted on sticks like knights on horseback, they would sing: "Banner of Aragon, banner of Aragon!" And I used to sing it, and I sang it more than five times. Now then we can well say here, in accordance with later experience: "Domine, ex ore infantium et lactantium perfecisti laudem. . . ."

Without dropping this familiar tone Bernáldez writes unexcelled pages on the capture of Granada, the expulsion of the Jews, and the discovery of America. Only too well known is his biographical sketch of Christopher Columbus.

While havoc is wrought in Spain by the erudite tendency in historiography, which gives us involved accounts of the life of the Great Captain, Latin texts concerning the life of Cisneros, and a multitude of outlines and collections of material for the life of Carlos V, the uncultured Spaniard, with his high-spirited eagerness to contemplate spectacles never before seen and to accomplish extraordinary feats, turns up and runs loose in America. From now on, neither kings nor noblemen, but any leader or soldier in any expedition of conquest, carries out the heroic deeds. Consequently there is a change in the social level of topics and authors of chronicles. Fernández de Oviedo asserts that it is a matter of a typically Spanish feature:

A rare thing and a precious gift of nature, and one not seen in any other nation so bounteously and generously bestowed as on the Spanish people; because in Italy, France, and the other kingdoms of the world, only the knights are specially or naturally trained for war and dedicated to it, or inclined or disposed toward it; and of the other classes, those who are devoted to mechanical trades and to agriculture, and the populace, few are the ones who engage in arms or like to wage war abroad. But in our Spanish nation it seems utterly common that all men were born to be dedicated principally and specially to arms and their practice, and arms and war are so fitting to them that everything else is accessory, and they willingly abandon all occupations for the militia. And for this reason, although few in number, the Spanish conquerors have always done in these places what many from other nations could not have done nor brought about.

It is a foreigner—Friederici—who tells us that in no country is there so great a number of soldier-chroniclers as in Spain. Characteristic of these is their scorn for bookish erudition, even though they try to exhibit their own ingenuously and repeatedly. A genuine representative of this attitude is Gonzalo Fernández de Oviedo, who at every step says that elegance of style and erudition are of no use unless one has lived what he wishes to relate. His attacks are directed against Peter Martyr, a palatine chronicler who wrote his *Decadas de Orbe Novo* without stirring from Spain. "All the more because past writers, not as experimenters like our Spaniards, searching for the world, but as spectators, standing still, spoke to his liking." "I have not taken the material of these books from two thousand thousands of books I have read, as Plinius writes in the passage alluded to . . . , but I accumulated everything that I write here from two thousand millions of hardships and privations and dangers in the twenty-two years and over that I have been seeing and experiencing these things personally."

Sentences like these are continually arising in Oviedo's pages. And if Oviedo was at heart frightened at the thought that he was deficient in culture, still more frightened must have been Bernal Díaz del Castillo, one of the fighters who won greatest distinction in the conquest of Mexico. He himself tells us he stopped writing his chronicle when that of Gómara, Cortés' chaplain, reached his hands. Nevertheless, he resumed the work after he became convinced of the falsehoods which the commander's panegyrical clergyman was reciting. Bernal Díaz adopts before Gómara the same attitude that Oviedo does before Peter Martyr. And although his book offers wonderful, unique qualities, posterity has not done its merits justice, but rather has accepted the adverse judgment of Antonio Solís, the seventeenth-century chronicler who, thanks to his marvellous prose, has given the classic version of the account of the Mexican conquest by the Spaniards. With regard to Bernal's book, Solís says:

Today it is considered true history, as the very negligence of its style and its lack of adornment serve to make it resemble the truth and to verify for some persons the author's sincerity; but although it is to his advantage that he witnessed what he wrote, one perceives from his own book that he did not look at things dispassionately so that his pen might be well controlled: he proves to be as satisfied with his ingenuity as he is dissatisfied with his luck; between the lines envy and ambition are very obvious; and many times the display of these feelings ends in complaints against Hernán Cortés, the principal hero of this history, as he tries to fathom Cortés' intentions and to amend his counsels; and often he presents as infallible not what his captain ordained and directed, but what was being murmured by the soldiers, among whose ranks the common element is as great as elsewhere, since everywhere there is equal danger that those who were born to obey be allowed to express their opinions.

The historians who criticize Bernal's chronicle usually limit themselves to dwelling on what Solís has said, and they all speak of our chronicler's unpolished style, his arrogance, and even his animosity toward Cortés. All this is inaccurate. Bernal's style can hardly be excelled in descriptive force or narrative ease. He has a feeling for preciseness in details, which is strengthened by a surprising memory. If Alonso de Grado, a captain of whom Cortés used to complain, is put in stocks for two days, Bernal will give us the news, adding: "I remember that the wood of those stocks had a scent of onions or garlic." Extremely anxious to attain the maximum veracity, he does not consider the most minute details unworthy of his account. He never forgets to count the steps of the temples. "And then we went down the steps, and as they numbered one hundred and fourteen, and as some of our soldiers were suffering from tumours and abscesses, their legs were tired by the descent." Neither do the piles of skulls escape his attention. "I remember that in the plaza where some of their oratories stood, there were piles of human skulls so regularly arranged that one could count them, and I estimated them at more than a hundred thousand. . . . And in another part of the plaza there were so many piles of dead men's thigh bones that one could not count them."

However, no matter how expressive and savory these minute details may be, they are not sufficient to make a great artist of Bernal. His pen maintains its exactitude and vigor when extensive accounts are being treated, and he describes the incidents of a battle the same as he does the tumult of the big Mexican market or Moctezuma's mode of life.

Let us consider one scene taken at random:

They then asked us by signs to go with them to their town, and we took council together as to what we should do, and decided to go with them, keeping well on the alert and in good formation. They led us to some large houses very well built of masonry, which were the Temples of their Idols, and on the walls were figured the bodies of many great serpents and snakes and other pictures of evil-looking Idols. These walls surrounded a sort of Altar covered with clotted blood. On the other side of the Idols were symbols like crosses, and all were coloured. At all this we stood wondering, as they were things never seen or heard of before. It seemed as though certain Indians had just offered sacrifices to their Idols so as to ensure victory over us. However, many Indian women moved about us, laughing, and with every appearance of good will, but the Indians gathered in such numbers that we began to fear that there might be some trap set for us at Catoche. While this was happening, many other Indians approached us, wearing very ragged mantles and carrying dry reeds, which they deposited upon the plain, and behind them came two squadrons of Indian archers in cotton armour, carrying lances and shields, slings and stones, and each captain drew up his squadron at a short distance from where we stood. At that moment, there sallied from another house, which was an oratory of their Idols, ten Indians clad in long white cotton cloaks, reaching to their feet, and with their long hair reeking with blood, and so matted together, that it could never be parted or even combed out again, unless it were cut. These were the priests of the Idols, who in New Spain are commonly called "papas" and such I shall call them hereafter. These priests brought us incense of a sort of resin which they call "copal," and with pottery braziers full of live coals, they began to fumigate us, and by signs they made us understand that we should quit their land before the firewood which they had piled up there should burn out, otherwise they would attack us and kill us. After ordering fire to be put to the reeds, the priests withdrew without further speech. Then the warriors who were drawn up in battle array began to whistle and sound their trumpets and drums.

After reading passages like this, one does not understand the unfavorable opinion of a historian of Prescott's category: "The literary merits of the work are of a very humble order; as might be expected from the condition of the writer." And it is Prescott too who speaks to us of Bernal's vulgar vanity which bursts forth with truly comic ostentation on every page of his book. The great American historian must have had a strange idea of human nature if, according to him, feats like the conquest of Mexico may not engender pride in the persons who accomplish them. The conquerors are fully aware of the historical perspective of their acts, and sentences like these are frequent in Bernal:

As to what you say, sirs, that the most renowned Roman captains have never done such great deeds as we have—you tell the truth. And from now onwards, God helping us, they will say in the histories that record these events far more than they may have said about those that happened before.

What men have there been in the world who, numbering four hundred soldiers (we did not even reach that number), would have dared to enter into such a strong city as Mexico, which is larger than Venice, and is distant from our own Castile more than fifteen hundred leagues, and take prisoner so great a Prince, and punish his Captains before his eyes!

If what is being discussed is our chronicler's personal participation in the great enterprise, one ought to read the last chapters of his book, particularly the wonderful "Record of the Battles and Encounters in Which I Was Present." The man who had such deeds to his credit might well say, without being accused of vulgar vanity: "And among the brave conquistadores, my comrades (and there were very valiant ones among them) they included me as being the oldest of them all. I once more assert, and I repeat it so many times, that I am the oldest of them, and have served as a very good soldier of His Majesty."

Bernal's attitude toward Cortés, and the relationship which existed between the soldiers and their captain, set before us an extremely delicate problem: nothing less than that of the relationship between a genial individual and the mass of people. Solís solved this question all at once, in the words already mentioned, with his aristocratic thesis. And yet the expeditions of conquest may well cause us to think that the truth was otherwise, that the ones who took part in them played a rôle very different from that of a common soldier in our day, that it was necessary to rely upon such men for the most serious decisions. This lessens the exclusive, conspicuous grandeur of the leader, and converts the mass of people into the principal agent of the epic. It is the populace itself who carries out the epic, it is the mass itself which is gifted with extraordinary, unique qualities. Bernal's pages are kept alive constantly by this breath of the group, whose driving force is directed toward a common goal:

> It is here that the historian Gómara says that when Cortés ordered the ships to be scuttled that he did not dare to let the soldiers know that he wished to go to Mexico in search of the great Montezuma. It was not as he states, for what sort of Spaniards should we be not to wish to go ahead, but to linger in places where there was neither profit nor fighting?
>
> Being in that town without any plans beyond finishing the fort, for we were still at work on it, most of us soldiers suggested to Cortés to let the fort stand as it was, for a memorial (it was just ready to be roofed), for we had already been over three months in the country and it seemed to us better to go and see what this great Montezuma might be like and to earn an honest living and make our fortune.

According to Bernal, Cortés used to assemble his captains and distinguished soldiers in council whenever any important resolution was to be taken: "Our Captain determined to take counsel of certain captains and soldiers whom he knew to be well disposed towards him (who besides being very valiant, were wise counsellors), because he never did anything without first asking our advice about it." This should not surprise us if we remember that, when the expedition was organized, the very soldiers could exert influence in the designation of the leader: "Most of us soldiers who were there said that we should prefer to go again under Juan de Grijalva, for he was a good captain, and there was no fault to be found either with his person or his capacity for command." Vargas Machuca confirms for us this state of affairs in his *Milicia y descripción de las Indias*: "The soldier must recognize this obligation to be submissive to his leader's mandates, a thing which the soldier of the Indies observes very badly, with the arrogance that he knows as much as his leader, and, as he is a practical person, he needs no one to direct him, and, confident in this, soldiers commit a thousand errors worthy of punishment."

As for animosity toward Cortés, Bernal never had any. "Never in the world was a captain obeyed with more respect and punctuality," he tells us. And he informs us that he will limit himself to calling Cortés by his name, without other titles, because Cortés' name alone surpasses all praise:

> Although he was such a valiant, energetic and daring captain, I will not, from now on, call him by any of these epithets of valiant, or energetic, nor will I speak of him as Marqués del Valle, but simply as Hernando Cortés. For the name Cortés alone was held in as high respect throughout the Indies as well as in Spain, as was the name of Alexander in Macedonia, and those of Julius Caesar and Pompey and Scipio among the Romans, and Hannibal among the Carthaginians, or in our own Castille the name of Gonzalo Hernández, the Great Captain. And the valiant Cortés himself was better pleased not to be called by lofty titles but simply by his name.

What happens is that Bernal draws a living silhouette of Cortés; he gives us a man of flesh and blood, not a character from an academic tragedy.

In his pages Cortés, without losing his heroic quality, takes purgatives, and laughs, and jokes with the Indians. He does not use a solemn language, but one that is unaffected and popular. "Cortés replied that he could not rest, that 'a lame goat must not nap,' that he would go in person with the soldiers he had brought with him." "Cortés answered half angrily that 'It was better to die in a good cause, as the Psalms said, than to live dishonoured!' " Nor will Bernal fail to tell us how, in the distribution of the booty, Cortés and his captains were the ones who took the lion's share for themselves, especially in the case of the captive Indian women, when they left the old ugly ones for the poor soldiers. Doubtless the serious Solís was thinking of information of this type when he wrote: ". . . nor wasting time on insignificant details, which either soil the paper with what is indecent or fill it with the most unworthy material, as they accord more attention to the quantity than to the quality of the history."

I do not believe anyone will share that opinion today. History's greatness lies precisely in the fact that its characters are men and not gods. And Solís, who, figuratively speaking, heightened Cortés on Buskins, could not help but know that the shoe used by the leader and his soldiers in the conquest was the fiber sandal.

Where the importance of the chronicler's book has been most noticeable is in America, particularly in Mexico and Guatemala. The Mexican historian, Carlos Pereyra, has written pages warm with admiration for Bernal's work. Nevertheless, it is a Mexican, Genaro García, the editor of Bernal's chronicle, who makes a new charge against our author. He says that the latter lowers the Indians and elevates the Spaniards more than is fitting, "by way of contrast, or perhaps to weaken the interest which the Indians might arouse in the readers." That this is untrue is proved to us by careful reading of Bernal's pages. Our chronicler greatly admires the military virtues of the Mexicans. He speaks with enormous respect and affection of Moctezuma and his lordly qualities. He loves those who are under his command and is glad to hear that they are to be good Christians.

The conduct of the conquerors was more humane than that of any colonial army of our times. This is well proved by Gonzalo de Sandoval's expedition of chastisement to a village under Texcoco's rule:

Much blood of the Spaniards who had been killed was found on the walls of the Temple in that pueblo, for they had sprinkled their Idols with it, and he also found two faces which had been flayed, and the skin tanned like skin for gloves, the beards were left on, and they had been placed as offerings upon one of the altars. There were also found four tanned skins of horses very well prepared, with the hair on and the horse shoes, and they were hung up before the Idols in the great Cue. There were also found many garments of the Spaniards who had been killed hung up as offerings to these same Idols, and on the pillar of a house where they had been imprisoned, there was found written with charcoal: "Here was imprisoned the unfortunate Juan Yuste and many others whom I brought in my company." This Juan Yuste was a gentleman, and one of the horsemen whom they killed here, and was one of the persons of quality whom Narváez had brought with him. Sandoval and all his soldiers were moved to pity by all this and it grieved them greatly, but, how could the matter now be remembered except by being merciful to the people of the pueblo, however they had fled and would not wait, and had taken their women and children with them. A few women who were captured wept for their husbands and fathers, and when Sandoval saw this, he liberated four chieftains whom he had captured and all the women and sent them to summon the inhabitants of the pueblo, who came and begged for pardon.

I have spoken before of a democratizing tendency in the chronicles, a tendency which has more to do with their subject matter than with the manner in which they are written. There is a greater popular element, a more direct style in the first royal chronicles than in those of the nobles during the fifteenth century in Spain. The cultured trend, which had mixed harmoniously with the popular one in Pero López de Ayala—to a lesser degree in Alonso de Palencia—breaks openly with the popular movement at the beginning of the Renaissance period during the reign of Ferdinand and Isabella. The Renaissance opposition between the commoner and the scholar becomes irreducible in historiography. And while the ambitious commoner opens the way for himself after his fashion, producing the splendid flora of the chronicles of the Indies, which culminates in Bernal's work, the peninsular scholars lose their way in their collections of material and the polishing of their prose. Only direct contact with events will bring to life accounts like those of Hurtado de Mendoza and Mármol Carvajal about the war with the Moriscos of Granada. The concern for form, so marked in these two authors, will lead in Spain's seventeenth century to such an extreme that not history is produced, but treatises on the manner of writing history, in which the qualities and talents befitting the historian are discussed—Cabrera de Córdoba, Fr. Jerónimo de San José. The baroque movement will twist facts in its search for moral interpretations and maxims. Scholars of Nicolás Antonio's category will open the way to eighteenth-century research. But popular historiography will no longer raise its head. It remains buried in America, with the soldiers who wrote it.

Bernal Díaz del Castillo's Criticisms of the
History of the Conquest of Mexico,
by Francisco López de Gómara

Prescott has said that the two pillars upon which rests the history of the Mexican conquest by the Spaniards are the chronicles of Gómara and Bernal Díaz del Castillo. Now then, these two pillars, on the contrary, with their immutable symmetry, appear to me like sensitive thermometrical columns which vary continually as specific changes are produced in the atmosphere.

At the present time we are witnessing the ascendancy of Bernal Díaz, who seems to have definitely surpassed Gómara, without leaving the latter any possibility of regaining the ground lost. I, myself, in the Twenty-sixth Congress of Americanists, held in Seville in 1935, went to the defense of Bernal, whose chronicle I was then busy editing. I echoed the usual criticisms against Gómara, and I called him Cortés' panegyrist, servile adulator, and I do not know what else.

What was really the matter with me then was that I had not read Gómara with sufficient care. I do not wish to suggest that all those who today maintain the attitude maintained by me in 1935 are in the same situation. Not at all. But the truth is that, after reading Gómara more carefully and comparing his book with that of Bernal Díaz, I have reached conclusions which differ considerably from my former ones, to such an extent that the present article turns out to be a defense of Gómara, or, at least, an attempt to restore the equilibrium which is so greatly inclined in Bernal Díaz's favor today.

As it is well known, this conqueror was already an old man when he undertook the relation of the conquest. He had some chapters written when Gómara's book reached his hands. The first impression that its reading produced was one of discouragement; he thought that his account could never compete with that of the clergyman, and he was about to give it up; but he continued reading, and found—according to what he tells us— that Gómara's book was so full of falsehoods that he felt encouraged to resume his own, with the intention of refuting these falsehoods. "I wish to return to my story pen in hand as a good pilot carries his lead in hand at sea, looking out for the shoals ahead, when he knows that they will be met with, so will I do in speaking of the errors of the historians, but I shall not mention them all, for if one had to follow them item by item, the trouble of discarding the rubbish would be greater than that of gathering in the harvest."

Today, in broad outline, this opinion of Bernal Díaz is considered correct. His history of the conquest is the true one, as he called it. This seems to imply that Gómara's is not. And I should like to call the reader's attention briefly to this matter.

Before continuing I must make a remark. I do not believe in historical impartiality in the sense that liberal positivist historiography has given this term: that of the existence of an exclusive, unique truth which it is always possible to attain. When I was an undergraduate studying chemistry —and I make this reservation because I am not very well informed about the present status of the question—there was a certain number of simple bodies beyond which one could not arrive in the decomposition of a material which was supposed to be unique. In an analogous manner one might explain what I understand by historical truth. Facts have been produced, without doubt, in a specific way, in a unique way; but in the verification of these facts, as in their analysis, we can go no further than the viewpoint of the persons who have witnessed and lived them, and told about them. The viewpoint of the immediate narrator is the simple body against which we come in our investigation. When there are several participants or witnesses narrating events, we can collect their viewpoints in related groups; but, if there is disparity among them, in the selection we make will enter a new factor which will be, whether or not we so wish, our own viewpoint, as conditioned and as limited by a complex series of factors as are the viewpoints we submit to examination. I do not believe, as has normally been accepted, that a greater distance automatically provides a better vision of historic events.

A typical case of this kind is the one which arises with the history of the conquest of America by the Spaniards. According to who the writers are, according to their races and beliefs, opinions clash fearlessly and pens prolong the struggles they narrate. In the Congress of Americanists previously mentioned, there was a session in which the congressmen almost came to blows over the discussion of Padre Las Casas' personality and work. "What a lamentable spectacle!" some said. "What an inevitable spectacle!" I thought. If life is always struggle and conflict, the narration of this struggle, history, must be passionate, partial. We can be satisfied if passion is confined to noble limits and the narration of events is not deliberately falsified; but what we can never avoid is the variance of the point at issue according to the attitude of the one who is studying and analyzing it.

I fear my digression has been too long but I believe it necessary so that one may see clearly what I have been leading up to. By admitting the relativity, the contingency of historic knowledge, we acquire a greater liberty of movement, a greater validity for our conclusions, since we recognize their limitations "a priori."

Let us come concretely to the problem presented by the historiography of the Mexican conquest, to a valuation of its two basic texts. Today, in the name of a would-be historical impartiality, Bernal's book is preferred to Gómara's. Why? Is Bernal really more sincere, more detached in relating events? I think that what I shall here present will show that he is not. Are literary reasons, reasons of style, those that motivate the preference? Neither is this the case. Because, even if it is true that Bernal's book has unique qualities of spontaneity and freshness, Gómara's book is one of the most beautiful products of the Castilian language. But, then, to what is the preference due? How can one explain the frequent reprints of Bernal, while Gómara, who enjoyed unprecedented success immediately after the publication of his work, is today an author whom one can hardly find and whom few people have read—except specialists, of course—in Spain as well as in Mexico?

The preference is due to what I said before about viewpoint. Through

Bernal's pages, despite his constant protests of loyalty and admiration, there runs an almost open dissatisfaction with Cortés, a resentful desire to belittle his merits; on the other hand, in the pages of Gómara's book the conqueror is glorified. And so Bernal's viewpoint happens to coincide with that of a period which has striven to put all things on the same level, which has regarded genial individuals with suspicion, especially in the field of political and military action. Let it be understood that I am not an anti-democrat. What I am doing is pointing out certain tendencies of democratic thought which in the sphere of historical investigation have led to completely demagogical attitudes. I have not the slightest doubt that the conquest of America was an enterprise of the popular type, that the mass played an outstanding rôle in it; but what this mass does by itself when it does not find superior men to clarify its ideals and direct its energies, we see in the conquest of the West Indies, in the civil wars of Peru, and in a whole series of episodes not necessary to recollect here.

Cortés, with all his defects—he would not be human if he did not have them—was a superior man. And this is what Bernal did not want to admit: the exceptional character of Cortés' personality. For Bernal, Cortés was a good captain and no more—a good captain, something which abounded among the Spaniards at that time. For Gómara, Cortés was a genius. And today historians look sympathetically upon Bernal's testimony, for the same reason that makes them unearth any servant's statement that may prove unfavorable to the conqueror in the investigation of his conduct. All this happens, of course, in the name of historical impartiality.

Things would perhaps be made clear if we admitted that Bernal Díaz is as partial as Gómara, and that their viewpoints are opposite, which is particularly obvious when they pass judgment on Cortés' work. Gómara, chaplain of the Marqués del Valle, who is closely connected with him during his stay in Spain, writes his life and receives money for doing so. On the other hand, Bernal, a soldier whose name would have remained unknown if he himself had not done something to prevent it, has a grudge against Cortés because the latter always handles with great ease the first person singular, forgetting his companions' merits, which were not few. Bernal accuses him without mincing words: "This I assert that when in the beginning Cortés wrote to His Majesty, instead of ink, pearls and gold flowed from his pen, and all in his own praise and not about us valiant soldiers." "As we understood, he gave no account in his letter of Francisco Hernández de Córdova nor of Grijalva, but attributed the discovery, and the honour and glory of it all, to himself alone, and he said that now at this time it would be better to write thus, and not to report it to His Majesty. There were not wanting those who said to him that to our King and Lord nothing that had happened should be left untold."

If Cortés adulterates the truth, according to Bernal, he does so for selfish purposes, to obtain favors from the Emperor, without remembering the others at all. When he was in Spain, "he did not seek to ask a single thing for us that might have benefited us, only for himself alone." This was a very harsh accusation on the part of Bernal, who was not exactly a model of disinterestedness. He complains constantly of his poverty and neediness, in complete disagreement with the documentary data referring to the last period of his life, when he carries his complaints to the extreme. "And I say it with sorrow in my heart, for I find myself poor and very old, with a marriageable daughter and my sons young men already grown up with beards, and others to be educated, and I am not able to go to Castile to His Majesty to put before him things which are necessary for his Royal Service, and also that he should grant me favours, for they owe me many debts." If we compare these statements with the results shown by the documents mentioned, we shall see that one must treat what Bernal says with the greatest caution. He had the same unlimited greed as his companions, which he does not conceal, since he gives the search for riches as one of the motives of the conquest. "They died that cruel death in the service of God and His Majesty, and to give light to those who were in the darkness, and also to acquire riches, which all of us men usually came to seek."

Bernal has the mentality of a resentful person. He always reproaches Cortés for having kept the lion's share in the spoils of the conquest. Nor can he bear not having his own name occupy an important place in the relation of the enterprise. As his rôle must have been a secondary one, he has to raise the level of the group and lower that of Cortés in order to put himself on the highest plane. Besides the desire for riches was not Bernal's only incentive; he was also driven by the desire for glory, so typical among men of this Renaissance period. At the end of his book there is a short dialogue with "the good and illustrious Fame," where he makes no secret of his grudge. Fame "loudly clamors, saying, that it would be just and reasonable that we should have good incomes and more advantages than other persons have who have not done service in these conquests nor in other parts for His Majesty. So it (Fame) inquires: 'Where are our palaces and mansions, and what coats of arms are there on them distinguishing us from the others?' And, 'Are our heroic deeds and arms carved on them and placed as a memorial in the manner that gentlemen have them in Spain?'" Fame also asks where the conquerors' tombs are, and Bernal replies that "they are the bellies of the Indians who ate their legs and thighs, arms and flesh, and feet and heads, and the rest found sepulchre in, and their entrails were thrown to, the tigers and serpents and falcons which at that time they kept for show in strong houses, and those were their tombs and there are their blazons." Greed, the desire for glory, and resentment go hand in hand in the conclusion of the dialogue. "To this (question) which I have put to the most Virtuous Fame, she answers and says that she will very willingly do it, and adds that she is astonished that we do not possess the best assignments of Indians in the land, for we have conquered it, and His Majesty orders them to be given in the same way as to the

Marquis Cortés (it is not understood that it would be to the same extent but in moderation)."

If Cortés leaves his companions without due reward, Gómara's account takes from them the very last hope of obtaining it, since he overlooks their deeds. Hence, Bernal implicates both in his reproaches. Often he repeats that, if Gómara wrote in the fashion he did, praising Cortés alone and failing to state the deeds of the other captains and soldiers, he did so because "his palms were greased," because they paid him for it. Gómara's information is false; but the falsifier is Cortés. "And what he writes is mere nonsense. As I understand it the fault is not his, but that of the man who gave him the information."

According to Bernal, Cortés sins as much by adulterating the truth as Gómara does by undertaking the relation of something he has not seen. Typical features of every war are the scorn of the combatants for the persons in the rear guard, and their indignation because people talk about military events without having taken part in them. Bernal, who felt all the pride of a soldier, rebukes Gómara continually on this account. The "Let us drop this subject then, which Gómara says he knows about because 'they told him so,' " the "he was not well informed," contrast strongly with the precision of his own recollections: "Now that I am writing about it, it all comes before my eyes as though it had happened but yesterday." A licentiate "who was very eloquent and had a very good opinion of himself," to whom Bernal showed his manuscript, reproached him for speaking too much about himself. Bernal answers that the only one who can speak about war is the person who has been in it; "but for one who is not present in a war, and does not see it or understand it, how is he able to do it? Are the clouds to utter praise or the birds that flew over us when we were fighting our battles? Only the Captains and soldiers who were present (could do so)."

This is directed against Gómara, who, to make Bernal's despair the greater, possessed a style which added much to the attractiveness of his narration. Bernal pretends to attach no importance to this, but in his heart he feels otherwise. "Whoever sees Gómara's history will believe it to be true, as it is expressed with such eloquence, although it is quite the reverse of what really took place." "And let him (the reader) ignore eloquence and ornate language which is evidently pleasanter than my coarse (manner)." That this modesty on Bernal's part was false, and that literary elegance did not mean so little to him as he pretended, is seen in the conversation with the licentiates, to which reference has been made, for these men made the remark about his manuscript that "it followed the customary speech of Old Castile, and that in these times it is accounted the more agreeable because there are no elaborate arguments nor gilded elegance such as some writers are wont (to display), but all is in plain simple language, and that all really good narration is comprised in this true statement."

Gómara has not been in the conquest; Gómara, who possesses literary talent, is, to top misfortunes, a clergyman. Now then, Bernal shares the ideas of Cortés and a certain number of conquerors with regard to the action of clergymen in the Indies. As great as the respect and veneration he feels for the friars is his animosity toward the priests. One need not search far in his book to find sentence like these:

I call this story to mind here to show my curious readers, and even the priests who nowadays have charge of administering the holy sacraments and teaching the doctrine to the natives of the country, that because the poor soldier stole two fowls in a friendly town, it nearly cost him his life, so that they can see how one ought to act towards the Indians, and not seize their property.

And they (the Indians) paid the same attentions to the priests, but after they had seen and known some of these and the covetousness of the rest, and that they committed irregularities in the pueblos, they took no (further) notice of them and did not want them as Curas in their pueblos, but Franciscans and Dominicans. It does not mend matters that the poor Indians say to a prelate that they do not hear him or . . . , but what more there is to be said about this subject had better remain in the inkpot.

With this amount of phobias against Gómara, one cannot expect the lead of which Bernal spoke to function with precision. In fact the majority of his comments have the nature of simple outbursts. "From beginning to end they did not tell correctly what took place in New Spain"; it is all "nonsense that has been written about the affairs of New Spain"; "in all they write, they speak with prejudice, so why should I go on dipping my pen to mention each item separately, it is merely wasting ink and paper, moreover I should say it badly . . ."; "and if all his writings in other Spanish chronicles are like this, I condemn them as a matter of lies and fables, however good his style may be."

All this interests us as the key to a state of mind which we cannot ignore if we are to put a true value on the criticisms, strictly speaking, which Bernal makes of Gómara. My article has not the character of an exhaustive comparison, which would be very desirable to make, but which would be out of place here. It merely calls attention to this matter.

What are, in concrete terms, the objections which Bernal makes to Gómara in the relation of events? Frequently, after a careful comparison of the two texts, one discovers there is no justification for the remark with which Bernal customarily concludes his chapters: "This is what happened, and not the account given to Gómara," "here the chronicler Gómara says many things about which they did not inform him correctly," etc. See both authors' accounts of Cortés' preparations for the enterprise, or of the meeting with Jerónimo de Aguilar, or of the interview with Moctezuma's emissaries in San Juan de Ulúa. I candidly confess that I find no essential differences to justify the remarks and observations made by Bernal Díaz. Doubtless, since he had a great feeling for detail and a surprisingly trustworthy memory, he could appreciate small differences which escape our notice. But his comment is always exaggerated. And two episodes I wish to emphasize prove to us that it is impossible to speak of a great exactitude in the management of the lead. Bernal, in his desire to contradict Gómara, not only disagrees with him openly upon the conclusions of fundamentally identical episodes, but makes Gómara say things which appear nowhere in the latter's work. That is what happens when the Spaniards' stay in Cempoala is mentioned. "The historian, Gómara, says that Cortés remained many days in Cempoala and planned a league and rebellion against Montezuma, but he was not correctly informed, because, as I have said, we left Cempoala on the following morning, and where the rebellion was planned and what was the reason for it, I will relate further on." Now then, if we consult Gómara's account, we shall see that he says nothing whatsoever about the formation of a league against Moctezuma in Cempoala. What he says is that the Indian chief of Cempoala, "the fat Indian chief," complained to Cortés about the terrible slavery to which they were subject—the same as Bernal says—and that the rebellion and league against the Aztec monarch were planned later in Quiahuiztlán—as Bernal also says.

The same thing occurs in the account of the occupation of Cingapacinga. Bernal states: "This affair of Cingapacinga was the first expedition made by Cortés in New Spain, and it was very successful, and we did not, as the historian Gómara says, kill and capture and destroy thousands of men in this affair at Cingapacinga." Let us see what Gómara says, and we shall find that he does not speak of the combat at all, for the simple reason that there was none, since the natives offered no resistance and Moctezuma's force deserted the place. "And Cortés asked," Gómara relates, "that no harm be done the residents, and that the soldiers who were protecting the place be left free, but without arms or banners. It was a new thing for the Indians." The story of the slaughter of thousands of Indians is a device which Bernal invents in his frantic desire to discredit Gómara.

So far Bernal's criticisms are unjustified. They have another aspect which merits closer examination—the one referring to what Gómara says about Cortés' action. In this respect, without doubt, Gómara gave free rein to his pen. His book might better have been entitled "Vida de Hernán Cortés" than "Conquista de México." In it there is an exclusive concentration on the Estremenian hero, a constant attribution of every kind of feat to him, which may justify Bernal's indignant exclamation: "Cortés never did or said anything (important) without first asking well considered advice, and acting in concert with us. Although the historian Gómara says Cortés did this and that, and came here and went there, and says many other things without reason, even if Cortés were made of iron, as Gómara in his history says he was, he could not be everywhere at once."

Let us admit that Bernal was right in this, as he was right in the appreciation of matters of detail: that it was not Cortés who entered the Alvarado River, that it was not Cortés but Alvarado who for the first time penetrated the interior of the country, shortly after the landing of the Spaniards, etc. All this is very well, but what we cannot accept is Bernal's continual plural, with the "we agreed," "we ordered," "we did," which reduces Cortés to a mere tool in the hands of his captains. "It seems that God gave us soldiers grace and good counsel to advise Cortés how to do all things in the right way." "And let me relate how one and all we put heart into Cortés, and told him that he must get well again and reckon upon us." Despite the onesidedness of Gómara's vision in overlooking Cortés' companions, I believe it less distant from the truth than Bernal's vision when he gives us a Cortés subject to the opinions of a clique.

I am sorry I have not more precise information about the organization of the military hierarchy in those times. Of course there did not exist then what we call staffs today, with their specific mission of preparing the decisions of the leaders. But then, as today, and as always, the decision, with or without previous consultation, was an attribute of the leader and not of the subordinate. Bernal contradicts himself on this point since, in sketching for us Cortés character, he insists that the latter was very obstinate.

He was very obstinate, especially about warlike matters, however much advice and persuasion we might offer to him about imprudent attacks and expeditions which he ordered us to undertake—(such as) when we marched round the great pueblos of the Lake, or on the rocky hills which they now call the "Peñoles del Marqués," when we told him that we could not climb up to the fortifications and rocky heights, but that we would keep them beleaguered, because of the many boulders which came bounding down hurled at us from the top of the fortress, for it was impossible to protect ourselves from the shock and impetus with which they came, and it was risking all our lives, for valour and counsel and prudence were of no avail; yet still he contended against all of us, and we had to begin to ascend again and were in extreme danger, and eight soldiers were killed, and all the rest of us injured in the head and wounded, without accomplishing anything worth mentioning until we changed to other plans.

All this is said against Cortés, but it contradicts the statement that the conqueror was carried here and there by the opinions of his captains. Reality must have been exactly the opposite. What happens is that Cortés was so clever and explained his plans to the men in such a manner that the latter came to believe the plans had been their own ideas. The reflection of Orozco y Berra upon speaking about the capture of Moctezuma is correct: "The general had his plans made, but, as usual, he pretended to agree with the opinion of others, so that he might not be alone in responsibility, in case there were any."

This is the truth, and Bernal's attempts to disfigure it are vain. At the time of the destruction of the ships, Bernal himself admits that the idea came from Cortés. "As far as I can make out, this matter of destroying the ships which we suggested to Cortés during our conversation, had already been decided on by him, but he wished it to appear as though it came from us, so that if any one should ask him to pay for the ships, he could say that he had acted on our advice and we would all be concerned in their payment." Then he becomes very indignant because Gómara declares that the conqueror kept his plans in the greatest secrecy possible, and he insinuates that the soldiers knew about it. "It is here that the historian Gómara says that when Cortés ordered the ships to be scuttled that he did not dare to let the soldiers know that he wished to go to Mexico in search of the great Moctezuma. It was not as he states for what sort of Spaniards should we be not to wish to go ahead, but to linger in places where there was neither profit nor fighting?"

This estimate of the Spaniards' courage and greed is all right; but it is a pity that Bernal contradicts himself once more, since, in mentioning the statements of some soldiers who are anxious for Cortés to renounce the enterprise, he makes them say: "And that now the ships which we sunk would have been useful to us, and we might have left at least two of them in case of necessity arising, but without consulting them about this, or about anything else, by advice of those who did not know how to provide for changes of fortune, he (Cortés) had ordered them all to be sunk."

Really this famous impartiality and truthfulness of Bernal's muddle things terribly. If the soldiers had known that the ships were going to be destroyed, why did they complain afterwards that they had not been informed about it? Lying requires a good memory, friend Bernal. You would have done better to limit yourself to saying that Cortés occasionally consulted some of his captains, but without forever insinuating that they and the soldiers are the ones who decide everything, as if Cortés did not exist. Questions of war are not settled by committees and votes as Bernal wishes to indicate in his account of the meeting held in Cholula, when the Spaniards believe themselves in danger of an attack by the natives:

That night Cortés took counsel of us as to what should be done, for he had very able men with him whose advice was worth having, but as in such cases frequently happens, some said that it would be advisable to change our course and go to Huexotzingo, others that we must manage to preserve the peace by every possible means and that it would be better to return to Tlaxcala, others of us gave our opinion that if we allowed such treachery to pass unpunished, wherever we went we should be treated to worse (treachery), and that being there in town, with ample provisions, we ought to make an attack, for the Indians would feel the effect of it more in their own homes than they would in the open, and that we should at once warn the Tlaxcalans so that they might join in it. All thought well of this last advice.

Cortés does not open his mouth. Of course, Bernal lets it be known that it is Cortés who decides in critical moments, as at the junction of the two roads which lead to Mexico City: "Then Cortés said that he wished to go by the blocked up road." Yet this is the exception. Bernal's Cortés is as colorless as his companions are in Gómara's history, but, if there is omission in Gómara's work, there is deformation in Bernal's. As a last example consider the account of Moctezuma's capture. There Bernal tells us who compose Cortés' clique, that clique which is the advisory and executive organ without which the conqueror takes no step. Naturally Bernal forms part of the group. "Four of our captains took Cortés aside in the church, with a dozen soldiers in whom he trusted and confided, and I was one of them." They, and not Cortés, are the ones who conceive the idea of taking Moctezuma prisoner, who determine even the slightest details concerning the manner in which the daring capture is to be carried out. Cortés—such an irresolute man, of course—doesn't see well how it is going to be possible to seize Moctezuma in the midst of his warriors. "Our Captains replied, (that is Juan Velásquez de León and Diego de Ordás, Gonzalo de Sandoval and Pedro de Alvarado,) that with smooth speeches he should be got out of his halls and brought to our quarters, and should be told that he must remain a prisoner, and if he made a disturbance or cried out, that he would pay for it with his life; that if Cortés did not want to do this at once, he should give them permission to do it, as they were ready for the work."

I do not believe there is a better comment on Bernal's unscrupulousness (which, as we see, is no less marked than Gómara's) than that paragraph from the second letter of Cortés' report in which he refers to the first loss. "And I still remember that, with regard to the question of this lord, I volunteered much more than was in my power, for I guaranteed Your Majesty that I should have taken him prisoner, or killed him, or made him subject to Your Majesty's royal crown." In other words, the idea of capturing the sovereign was conceived by Cortés the very moment he learned of this person's existence.

Regarding Bernal's statements, it will be enough to grant the existence of a group of captains—the part about the soldiers seems less likely—with whom Cortés took counsel before making any important decisions; but without this group being the axis of the conquest, Cortés' inspiration and fortifier, as Bernal tells us. At any rate the criticisms pointed out do not justify the burial of Gómara's book in discredit and oblivion. Bear in mind that Bernal does not refute Gómara's work as a whole, but only in the outburst mentioned. He lets pass without contradiction the essential facts of the conquest: the war of Tlaxcala, the massacre of Cholula, the entrance into Mexico City, the struggle with Narváez, the flight from the capital, the siege and taking of the same, the trips to the Hibueras. And do not tell me it is because Bernal announces his resolution not to mention Gómara again shortly after relating the first entry into Mexico City. "As I am already tired of noting the things in which this historian goes outside of what really happened, I will stop speaking of it." This is beyond the power of Bernal, who renews his attack on Gómara whenever he finds, or believes he finds, occasion for it. So he does, for example, in his comment on Alvarado's leap: "I assert that at the time not a single soldier stopped to see if he leaped much or little, for we could hardly save our own lives."

Before I conclude, I should like to make a remark which I offer for the attention of some patient student. Let the comparison of the texts of

Bernal and Gómara be given greater emphasis and perhaps it may be found that the latter lent the former a valuable service, helping him to shape his work, to divide the chapters, etc. It is a mere suggestion which I cannot altogether justify now but I believe that Gómara not only stimulated Bernal but served him as a guide in his account. This alone would be a merit for Gómara, an author who deserves our attention for many reasons. Let Bernal be edited and studied as much as you like—no one can say that more sincerely than I, since I devoted almost four years to an edition of his chronicle which the war in Spain prevented my finishing—but do not let resentment be the motive for the enthusiastic cult of Bernal and the forgetting of Gómara. For the work of the latter, like that of Cortés, may be discussed as much as you wish, but may never be ignored.

Other Articles of Interest

Simpson, Lesley B. "Bernal Díaz del Castillo died in 1584." XV (1935), 99–100.

Wagner, Henry R. "Three Studies on the Same Subject." XXV (1945), 155–211.
Part I, entitled "Bernal Díaz del Castillo," contains a discussion of Díaz's contemporaries, Gómara, Illescas, and Giovio; biographical details concerning Díaz; and an appraisal of his book and of editions of it up to 1939, with an analysis of the text. Part II is concerned with Díaz's family, and Part III with notes on writings by and about him.

---

5. The Puerto Bello Fairs

ALLYN C. LOOSLEY

Between, roughly, 1575 and 1750 the Puerto Bello fairs in Panama played an essential and colorful role in the commerce of colonial Spanish America. Silver, cacao, sugar, tobacco, and other products were transshipped at the Isthmus after their arrival from Peru, and a wide variety of goods brought from Spain were sold there for the use of the colonists. Briefly, once a year, Puerto Bello was the scene of feverish activity, and death by disease or violence lay in wait for many of those who went to the fair to do business. Professor Loosley, who wrote this article while a member of St. Mary's College in California, tells the interesting story of the rise and decline of this extraordinary institution.

From Volume XIII (1933), pages 314–35.

The commerce of the Isthmus of Panama during the colonial period may roughly be divided into two parts, although there was considerable overlapping between the two divisions. First and most important was the transshipment trade which was carried on by the isthmus by virtue of its position as the port of entry for Peru and the other Spanish South American areas; second was the local trade which grew up for the support of the Spanish forces on the isthmus.

It is the first of these which claims our attention in this study. With the restrictions which were placed by the Spanish government upon the entry of goods into the Indies—that is, the limiting of the entry to a few specially designated ports—the isthmus became the distributing center for the whole of the Central and South American areas. Through the greater part of the colonial period there were no open ports on the eastern or western coasts of Spanish South America. All goods shipped to the South American areas were required to go by way of the Isthmus of Panama. This applied not only to those commodities destined for Peru, but also to those shipped to Potosí, Chile, Tucuman, and the Río de la Plata area—even as far as Buenos Aires. Rather than extend the number of ports of entry in the Indies, the commodities for these areas were carried across the Atlantic to Puerto Bello on the periodic fleets. From Puerto Bello they were transported across the isthmus by mule or river boat to Panama, where they were transhipped to Callao. There they were again loaded on mules and packed over the long routes to Potosí, Chile, Tucuman, and the Río de la Plata area. It is not to be implied, however, that all the commodities which reached these areas actually took this route. Officially, the route described was to be followed. But the distances involved in this long journey, the time required, and the addition it made to the prices of the commodities, made the inhabitants of those areas willing and even eager to purchase smuggled goods, which usually could be introduced clandestinely at lower prices than the Spanish goods. The colonial officials frequently disregarded the contraband trade or even connived at it, with the result that there early grew up a vast and profitable smuggling trade on the eastern coast of South America, with Buenos Aires as its "capital."

The return current of the Spanish South American trade originated largely in the precious metals from Peru and Potosí, which were packed to Callao, and there loaded on ships bound for Panama. Arrived there, they were transported across the isthmus by mule, and at Nombre de Dios and later at Puerto Bello were placed aboard the galleons for the voyage to Spain. The precious metals, while the most important single item in this return current, were not the only commodities of importance. In addition, such staple commodities as cacao, quinine, sugar, tobacco, and vicuña wool figured prominently in the trade.

The exchanges in the Spanish-Peruvian trade first took place at the port of Nombre de Dios. In the beginning, ships from Spain had gone to the isthmus singly as the occasion demanded, although, even before the inauguration of the fleet system, it had become the practice to organize occasional fleets in order to thwart the activities of corsairs and pirates. Before the middle of the sixteenth century, the number of ships arriving at Nombre de Dios from Spain was not large. According to the historian Girolamo Benzoni, who visited Nombre de Dios in 1541, but fourteen or fifteen vessels annually arrived there about that time. The largest of these appears to have been of about three hundred sixty tons. The cargos brought from Spain at that time consisted of miscellaneous wares, but principally of wine, flour, biscuit, oil, cloth, silk, and household articles. Even at this early date, Benzoni observed the glutting of the isthmian market, which at a later time became chronic. According to him, there were instances where quantities of such items as oil, figs, and raisins were left on the hands of the Spanish merchants. They, not being able to obtain any price for them, were frequently obliged to give them to the shipmasters in payment of the freight. While not intending, in his own words, to "deteriorate from the glory and ambition of the Spanish nation", Benzoni commented that at the time "undoubtedly, ten Venetian merchants would suffice to buy up all the merchandise that once a year is brought here, as well as the town itself." The volume of commodities passing to the isthmus at this time was not substantial for, although the city of Lima had been founded and the flow of gold from Peru had begun, the population of the Peruvian and isthmian areas had not attained any large proportions.

But as the South American area was further opened up, the increased population and the continued exploitation of the Peruvian and Potosí mines contributed to the expansion of the Spanish American trade. In 1552, the fleet system was installed. With the establishment of the fleets, the exchanges in the Spanish-Peruvian trade were concentrated in the short time that the fleets remained in Nombre de Dios. There, sometime after 1575, the famous annual fair was established to facilitate the exchanges in the trade. At Nombre de Dios the fairs had but a short life for, in 1597, the city was removed to Puerto Bello, and that city became the seat of the annual exchanges.

Function of the Fairs

Of the various fairs held in the Indies, that at Puerto Bello was the most important, not only from the point of view of its particular function, but also in point of the volume and the value of the commodities handled. The Vera Cruz and Cartagena fairs, while exceedingly important in the distribution of commodities to their respective hinterlands and the concentration of the Spain-bound commodities for the return voyage, were somewhat local by comparison with that at Puerto Bello. The full significance of the isthmian fairs, and the importance to which they attained, can only be appreciated by an understanding of the particular function which they performed. They were not merely an aggregation of merchants from the surrounding area, who used the fair as a distributing center for a part of the Tierra Firme region. Their chief function was that of an entrepôt for the whole of the Spanish-South American trade. The essential feature was the exchange of the commodities of Spain for the precious metals and other products of Peru and the other South American areas. Thus, the fairs became the focal point around which the whole of Spain's trade with its South American dominions revolved. The existence of the fairs in this form was the result of an agreement between the Spanish and the Peruvian merchants, sanctioned by the crown, regarding the method by which the trade of Spain with Peru was to be transacted. Paramount in this connection was the fact that Spanish merchants could trade on their own account only as far as Puerto Bello, and conversely, that the Peruvian merchants could trade on their own account only as far as the isthmus.

With this restriction of their movement, the merchants of Spain and Peru, or their representatives, met annually at Puerto Bello to effect their exchanges. Essentially they were organized as two companies or merchant guilds, the Seville merchants being the members of the one, and the Peruvian merchants constituting the membership of the other. The body of rules and regulations which grew up had as its purpose the securing of a monopoly of the Spanish-Peruvian trade to these two organizations, as well as equality of opportunity for the merchants who took part in that commerce. At the fairs, the Spanish merchants were represented by the *almirante* of the galleons, and the Peruvian merchants by the president of Panama.

Duration of the Fairs

After the organization of the fleet system, but before the Atlantic terminus had been transferred to Puerto Bello, the exchanges in the Spanish-Peruvian trade were conducted at Nombre de Dios, where the annual fairs began after 1575. The exchange period at first was of uncertain duration, lasting as long as was necesary to complete the transactions. The transfer of the Caribbean terminus to Puerto Bello was ordered in 1584, but did not become a fact until thirteen years later, in 1597. At first, the fairs at Puerto Bello were limited to no particular time. As late as 1637, when the English friar Thomas Gage visited the isthmus, the fair period was fixed at a fortnight, but this duration was dictated more by the sanitary situation than by the volume of trade passing through the fair. The growing population in the Tierra Firme and Peruvian areas, and the consequent increase in the volume of commodities flowing in both directions through the fairs, made the two week period inadequate for the transaction of the exchanges. The duration of the fairs was therefore extended by degrees. In 1685, when William Dampier passed through the isthmus, the fair lasted for thirty days, while in 1735, when the two Spanish naval captains Juan and Ulloa undertook a survey of Spanish South America, they found that the duration was forty days.

The limit set was intended to provide as long a time as was possible for the transactions, consistent with the unhealthful nature of the Puerto Bello region. While Puerto Bello was considered a more healthful site than Nombre de Dios had been, it left much to be desired. Because of the ring of mountains which surrounded the town, the heat was continually excessive. From January to May, the breezes reaching the city were somewhat cooler than those during the remainder of the year, but were heavily laden with moisture. From May to January, they became warmer and drier, but more healthful. Precipitation was heavy and continuous throughout the year. The climate was enervating. Casualties from fevers were high, especially during the time of the fleets, when it was common for from three to four hundred of the sailors and soldiers to succumb to disease. At the beginning of the seventeenth century, the French traveler Samuel Champlain called Puerto Bello "the most evil and pitiful residence in the world," and called attention to the great number of sailors, soldiers, and merchants who died while the fleets remained there. Nearly half a century later the situation had not improved, for in 1637 Thomas Gage thus characterized the city:

... when the Fleet is there, it is an open grave, ready to swallow in part of that numerous people, which at that time resort unto it, as was seen the year that I was there, when about five hundred of the Souldiers, Merchants, and Mariners ... lost their lives, finding it to be to them not *Porto Bello*, but *Porto malo*.

It was not always possible to adhere to the time limit which was set for the fairs. As was the case with fleet sailings, the duration of the fairs depended somewhat on the success in completing the transactions, the loading and the unloading in the allotted time. On some occasions the *almirante* of the galleons would delay several days or a week before sailing, in order to accommodate merchants who were behind schedule. Officially, however, the fairs were expected to close promptly at the designated time, and Spanish merchants not completing their transactions were in danger of being left behind, for the ships were expected to weigh anchor precisely on the last day of the fair period. The round trip from the time the galleons left Spain until they again anchored at San Lucar usually occupied from eight to twelve months. In the later period, however, when foreign merchandise was finding its way to the fairs in great volume, the Spanish merchants experienced greater difficulty in disposing of their wares, and the fleets often were delayed beyond that time.

The Fair

Upon their arrival at Cartagena, the galleons disposed of that portion of their cargo which was consigned to that city. They then laid up at Cartagena until such time as they received advice that the Peru fleet had arrived at the city of Panama. This policy was dictated not only by the desire to make the stay in the unhealthful Puerto Bello region as short as possible, but also because of the poor state of the Puerto Bello defenses, which made the city an easy prey for the pirates who infested the area. The word of the arrival of the Peruvian fleet having been received at Cartagena, the galleons then proceeded to Puerto Bello.

Meanwhile, with the receipt of the word that the galleons had left Cartagena, the city of Panama became the scene of feverish activity. Seamen and Negro slaves were occupied in unloading the treasure and other commodities from Peru. The *recuas*, or droves of mules, made their way across the isthmus to Puerto Bello laden with the precious metals. *Barcos*, or river boats, made the journey down the Río Chagre loaded with the more bulky materials. At the same time, there began an exodus from Panama. Royal officials, merchants, factors, and artisans took up the journey to Puerto Bello to perform their functions or to ply their trades at the fair. At Puerto Bello the townspeople were busy vacating their houses, or certain portions of them, in preparation for the arrival of the fleet. When it is realized that in addition to the officials, merchants, and artisans, sometimes between 4,000 and 5,000 soldiers and sailors arrived with the galleons, some idea may be gained of the strain which was placed on the housing facilities of such a small place as Puerto Bello. Many of the householders moved into one or two rooms of their houses, renting the balance to merchants and seamen. Some moved out entirely to take up a temporary residence in the poorer quarters and slave district of the town, called Guinea. Here many temporary cottages were erected, while in the large open area to the west of the town temporary barracks were erected, principally to accommodate the crews and soldiers from the ships.

Entering the harbor and anchoring, the ships were boarded by the royal officials who had come from Panama for the event. They inspected the *registros* and the cargos, to see that the merchandise was properly registered, and that no unauthorized articles were aboard. The manifests and cargos having been inspected and found correct, the order for unloading was given. Supervised by the general of the fleet, the royal officials, and the *alcalde* mayor of Puerto Bello, the seamen and slaves then proceded to unload the cargos. A tent of the ship's sails was constructed in the plaza of the city to receive the cargo of the particular ship. As the commodities were unloaded, they were drawn on sledges to the proper tent, where the owners of the goods or their representatives watched for the markings which distinguished their respective shipments. The money given to the seamen for their work in unloading was then divided proportionately among them. Meanwhile meetings of the officials and the representatives of the Spanish and the Peruvian merchants were taking place. At these, prices were established for the various classes of merchandise. These, together with a statement of the merchandise carried in the fleet, were then publicly announced, and each merchant was expected to adhere to them.

These preliminaries accomplished, the principal business of the fair began, and Puerto Bello became a scene of animation perhaps not duplicated in the Indies. Where before the arrival of the fleet there had been practically an empty town, there was now a multitude of people, all engaged in some activity connected with the Spanish-Peruvian trade. Merchants hired shops and houses in which to display and sell their wares. Houses were crowded, and the streets, squares, houses, and shops were filled with bales and boxes of commodities of all kinds, and chests of gold and silver. Even the seamen from the ships took part in the trade which occupied the attention of everyone during the fair. They kept stalls for the sale of sweetmeats and others edibles which they had brought from Spain.

As the deals were accomplished, the goods purchased by the Peruvian and Panama merchants were loaded on mules, or on the small river boats. The pack trains, once loaded, moved out of Puerto Bello on the Panama road, while the *barcos* coasted west to the Río Chagre, entered the mouth, and commenced the ascent of the river. And, while the transactions were being effected, the *recuas* continued to enter Puerto Bello, laden with chests of gold and silver. The precious metals apparently could be left about without fear that they would be stolen. Thomas Gage, who witnessed the fair in 1637, thus describes the unloading of the metals:

> . . . but what I most wondered at was to see the *Requa's* of mules which came thither from *Panama* laden with Wedges of Silver; in one day I told 200 Mules, laden with nothing else, which were unladen in the publick Market place, so that the heaps of Silver Wedges lay like heaps of Stones in the Street, without any fear of being lost.

The time allotted for the fair having elapsed, and the precious metals and other commodities having all been loaded, the galleons weighed anchor and started on the return voyage to Spain. The transfer of the commodities to Panama by mule or river boat, if not already accomplished, was completed. Temporary buildings and barracks, erected to take care of the influx during the fair, were taken down, and the officials, merchants, factors, and artisans returned to Panama. Thus the famous Puerto Bello fair ended, and Puerto Bello entered upon a comparatively inactive period, which extended until the time of preparation for the next fair.

Commodities

The Spanish commodities placed on sale at the Puerto Bello fairs consisted of a wide variety of goods for the use of the Spanish forces on the isthmus, in Peru, and the other Spanish South American areas. For the most part they were finished goods, in contrast to the commodities which flowed back to Spain. Chief among them were the fabrics, which constituted probably the largest single item in the trade. These included linens, both white and blue, striped linens for mattresses, damask, canvas, and sail cloth. Other commodities which figured in the fair trade were: clothing for Negroes, tanned leather, leather goods, sesame oil, almond oil, cinnamon, cloves, caper, black pepper, cumin seed, anise, figs, prunes, marjoram, raisins, licorice sticks, hazelnuts, walnuts, chestnuts, gall nuts, almonds, vinegar, beer, cider, wines, spiritous liquors, lavender, rosemary, incense, hard soap, gum for ink, drugs and compounds, crude and refined wax, sulphur, white lead, copperas, linseed oil, minium, vermillion, verdigris, saffron, tar, pitch, gypsum, rope, cordage of all sizes, emery, whetstones, steel, lead, iron in bars and in plates, iron work and grating, sheets of tin plate, shovels, hoes, nails, wire, hammers, axes, musket balls, gunpowder, ramrods, weapons, paper, colored papers, glassware, writing desks, clocks, tables and other furniture, books of both Spanish and foreign impression, bricks, tile, and gravestones.

Officially the shipments by Spanish merchants to the Indies were to consist, not of bulk shipments of one or some few commodities, but in shipments of a very diversified nature. In spite of this, however, it was common for bulk shipments of a few commodities to be made, and for the American merchants to acquire these *en bloc*, at times even before their unloading, and at reduced prices because of the quantity purchase.

By far the major item for value in the Peru-Spain exchange were the precious metals. Certain staple commodities such as cacao, quinine, sugar, tobacco, and vicuña wool also figured prominently in the trade. Other items, mostly raw materials, which returned to Spain via the isthmus were: copper, tin, lead, shells, tortoise shells, hides, vicuña hides, tanned leather, tanned goatskins, tanning materials, jaguar skins, horsehair, seeded and unseeded cotton, wool, alpaca wool, guanaco wool, earthenware vessels, indigo, *carmin* (cochineal), *annatto* (a yellowish-red dye made from the annatta tree), *copal* (a transparent resin used for varnish), mangle gum, *caraña* (an American gum), *cedadilla* (Indian caustic barley, the seeds of which were used as an insecticide and for snuff), canime oil, *oruca* (a refuse of grapes, cottonseed, olives), Peruvian beans, chocolate paste, ginger, coffee, cocoa butter, cassia (a coarse variety of cinnamon), *canchalagua* (a Peruvian medicinal herb), *calagula* (a Peruvian herb), *contrahierba* (a South American medicinal antidote), anacardic, balsam, rhubarb, and extract of cascarilla (used as a tonic and stomachic).

An analysis of the value of the commodities which passed through the Puerto Bello fairs when they were at their height would constitute a study in itself. Bernardo Ulloa estimates, however, that each of the twelve fleets which left Spain for the isthmus between August 4, 1628, and June 3, 1645, carried Spanish commodities ranging in value from eight to twelve million pesos, and that they returned to Spain with gold, silver, vicuña wool, and other commodities to the value of between twenty and forty million pesos. This was at a time, it will be remembered, when the fair lasted but a fortnight.

The Transactions

In contrast with the fair at Vera Cruz, the transactions at the Puerto Bello fairs were largely conducted on a cash basis. The volume of precious metals flowing through the fair made this possible, but credit was not unknown, and became increasingly important in the later history of the fairs. Most of the transactions at the fairs were handled by brokers or by the factors of the Spanish and the Peruvian merchants. For the most part the transactions seem to have taken place on a basis of extremely good faith. There were instances of fraud, sometimes on a large scale, but on the whole a fine *esprit de corps* seems to have been built up among the Spanish merchants and their representatives and the Peruvian merchants and factors. The fairs ultimately reached the point where the exchange of Spanish commodities for the precious metals and the other products of Peru was largely carried on by invoice, the chests of gold and silver as well as the bales and packages of Spanish goods not being opened for inspection by the purchasing merchants. According to Bernardo Ulloa, this good faith at the fairs even survived the incident of 1654, in which it was discovered that most of the silver arriving at the fair that year was considerably alloyed. In this case, the ultimate blame was fastened upon the tesorero of the Casa de Moneda at Lima, who paid with his life for his part in the affair. The Peruvian merchants ignored the whole fraud, and the entire loss was borne by the Spanish merchants.

In some cases, errors in packing resulted in the inclusion of sacks or bars of gold in the shipments of silver. In others the shipments contained more metals than was called for in the invoice. According to the practice which grew up, the first person noticing the error was to notify the parties concerned, and restore the surplus metal. If the fleet sailed before restitution could be made, the error was to be rectified in the following voyage.

But the transaction of trade by the use of factors was not without its objectionable features. Early in 1538, the Seville merchants called the attention of the crown to the fact that many of the factors were gambling with money that they had collected for the account of their masters. The crown took cognizance of the situation, and directed the Casa de Contratación to order that no playing cards or dice be thenceforth taken to the Indies. In November of the same year a *cédula* was dispatched to the audiencia of Panama calling attention to the losses which were being sustained by the Spanish merchants who had entrusted their funds to the gambling factors. It was ordered that no factor might play at cards, dice, or any other game involving the use of money. Penalties were provided, not only for the erring factors, but also for those who joined them in the gambling. The latter, if apprehended, were to spend thirty days in jail, while the money confiscated was to be restored to its rightful owners. Any surplus was to be divided equally between the informer, the magistrate who sentenced the offender, and the royal treasury. In spite of all these edicts, the gambling continued, as also did the complaints of the Seville merchants. The factors were not, moreover, the only ones who transgressed the general rules against gambling. During the fairs, there was also much gambling and gaming among the officials, soldiers, sailors, and the inhabitants of Puerto Bello, who sometimes sustained large losses. This gambling apparently was sanctioned by the officials, but as a result of the reports which reached Spain, the president of Panama was ordered not to permit any gaming among the passengers and soldiers in the houses of any of the inhabitants of Puerto Bello. As far as enforcement was concerned, this edict suffered the same fate as the edicts against gambling by factors.

In addition to their penchant for gambling, there was another objectionable feature in the employment of factors at the fairs. At times, there was considerable difficulty in securing prompt remittances from factors of the moneys which they had collected for the account of their principals. This tardiness usually resulted from their gambling affairs or from the employment of the moneys in their own speculations. The crown early ordered them to send the proceeds of their collections back to Spain on the first ship leaving the isthmus after the moneys had been received, but there is no indication that this decree was any better enforced than the general run of Spanish colonial legislation.

Prices and Profits

The period of the fair saw a marked rise in the price level of goods and services. Lodging and quarters for merchants, being at a premium, commanded exceedingly high prices, depending of course on the size and location of the shop or lodging. Even at a time when the fair lasted but two weeks, an ordinary shop sometimes rented for as much as a thousand crowns. In the later period, when the fair lasted forty days, stalls were rented for a thousand crowns, and large houses for as much as four thousand to six thousand crowns. Lodging was proportionately dear, a poor lodging costing as much as 110 crowns for the period of the fair. Foodstuffs likewise underwent a rise in price. Gage complained that while he was at the fair in 1637, a fowl, which could be obtained elsewhere for one *real*, there cost twelve, and beef, which he frequently had purchased elsewhere at thirteen pounds for one *real*, at the fair cost two *reales* per pound.

Prices of the commodities entering into the Spanish-Peruvian trade were fixed at the opening of each fair. Before the commodities were unloaded and placed on sale, the representatives of the Spanish and Peruvian merchants, together with the royal officials, met on board the *capitana*, or admiral's flagship. Here, with the *almirante* of the galleons as patron of the Spanish merchants and the president of Panama as sponsor of the Peruvian merchants, the prices of the various classes of merchandise were fixed. These, together with a statement of the commodities which the fleet carried, were then publicly announced, and everyone was expected to conform to the schedule of prices without alteration. No transactions were to take place before the price schedule had been announced, notwithstanding any obligations, bargains, and agreements which might previously have been made by the merchants.

It is somewhat difficult to determine the exact basis upon which the prices at the fairs were fixed. The cost of the goods to the Spanish merchant was the first of the series of influences which finally determined the price schedule. With this and the supply of, and the demand for, the particular commodity as the basis of calculation, it appears that the customary procedure was to multiply the price which the merchant had paid for the goods in Spain. Double the price seems to have been the usual figure. This, after allowing for the cost of transportation, deterioration, customs duties, and other expenses involved, apparently was designed to leave about fifty per cent profit to the merchant. In the case of certain commodities, the announced price was set at from 150 to 300 per cent or more of the cost price to the merchants, depending on the supply which was present at the time, and the possibility that there might be a shortage of the commodity on the next fleet.

During the period before the establishment of the fleet system, when the departure of the ships from Spain was relatively free of regulation, prices were influenced considerably by the expectancy of ships in the near future. With the regularization of the fleets, this factor became less important, although there was always speculation as to the probable supply of a commodity that might arrive with the next fleet. When the interloping trade had become substantial, the influx of foreign commodities was sufficient to glut the market and to depress prices considerably. In some cases the fleets arrived at Puerto Bello only to find that foreign ships had preceded them. Considerable quantities of merchandise were thus thrown on the market, to the great detriment of the Spanish merchant, who sometimes found himself unable to dispose of his wares at any price.

There is some indication that the prices at the fairs may also have been fixed with reference to the volume of the precious metals which flowed through the particular fair. Bernardo Ulloa says:

> . . . all it [the silver], the gold, and the [other] products had to be allotted in proportion to the clothing and other materials which came from Spain, without there being any excess of silver, nor [of] clothing. . . .

The cost of the commodities to the merchant in Spain, the expectancy of a greater or lesser supply with the next fleet, and the amount of the precious metals flowing through the fair, then, were some of the factors which influenced prices at the fairs. Aside from these considerations, there was no rule or standard for prices in the trade between the Spanish and the Peruvian merchants. Prices were fixed freely with reference to these factors, without legislative interference. By a law of April 8, 1538, confirmed in 1633, it was decreed that:

> . . . we shall not consent that the merchants of these kingdoms, who carry wine, breadstuffs, or other sustenance, or merchandise to the Indies and adjacent islands, shall place on them a standard price . . . we permit them to sell them for as much or as little as they can. . . .

But in the ordinary retail trade, the consumer was protected by a clause in the same law which provided that, in the case of merchants who bought commodities for the retail trade, prices might be fixed by the local authorities.

On the basis of the cost of the commodities to the merchant in Spain, the average profit at the fairs seems to have been about 100 per cent, although profits of 150 to 300 and even 500 per cent were not uncommon. By virtue of the risks involved in the Spanish-Peruvian trade, it would seem that the average profit was not excessive. The element of risks was great, for it was extremely difficult for the merchants to judge the market. Before the inauguration of the fleet system it was difficult to determine when ships would arrive, and what commodities they would carry. Even during the time when the galleons were employed, it frequently was not possible for the merchant to ascertain what amounts and varieties of commodities were being carried by the other merchants. The result was that merchants often arrived at the fair only to discover the supply of a particular commodity out of all proportion to the demand, with the consequence that prices declined or the merchant was unable to dispose of his wares. As the interloping trade became more brisk, it became correspondingly more difficult for the Spanish merchant to estimate the state of the market.

The question of profits at the fairs also turned somewhat on the quality of the goods carried to the isthmus by the Spanish merchants. Some of the traders were of such small means that they were unable to traffic in commodities of really excellent quality. The distinctly inferior goods which they handled were frequently resold at the fairs at prices far out of proportion to their original cost, the profits of these merchants sometimes ranging as high as 500 per cent. But it was early discovered by the colonists that the foreign commodities carried by the interlopers were frequently of higher quality than those carried by the Spanish merchants. The competition with smuggled goods, then, was not only a question of price, but also of quality.

Decline of the Fairs

In spite of the attempts of the Spanish crown to restrict the trade with the Indies to Spaniards or naturalized foreigners, there was from the outset a vast and profitable smuggling trade. This took two forms: the running of the customs by the Spanish merchants themselves, and the direct introduction of goods by foreigners. While the running of the customs resulted in the loss of considerable revenue to the crown, it made little difference in the status of the Puerto Bello fairs, for the trade was still in the hands of the Spanish. It was the interloping trade which struck at the roots of Spain's commerce with its Indies, and which indicated the general breakdown of the Spanish commercial organization.

While there were no parts of Spanish America free from it, the interloping trade flourished particularly in the region of Buenos Aires and at Panama. That the extraordinarily facile way in which the goods were introduced and the quantities in which they were thrown on the American market was the result of the attitude of the colonial officials and merchants, hardly needs to be mentioned. The interloping trade began and continued because it was profitable not only to the foreign merchant, but to the colonial merchants and officials as well. At best the colonists were but meagerly supplied through the medium of the Spanish fleets. The list of commodities which already has been cited as passing to South America through the Puerto Bello fairs seems to be an imposing one. But it should be noted, without seeming to minimize the importance of the Spanish-American trade, that the volume of commodities was small relative to the population of the American areas. Restriction of the Spanish commerce to a few selected ports, and the concentration of the authorized trade in so few channels has a tendency to make the trade appear more substantial than it really was. In the middle of the seventeenth century, for instance, the capacity of the Tierra Firme fleets seems to have been about 3,000 tons, although this was far from invariable. The ships rarely exceeded two to three hundred tons burden, and the fleets for the most part sailed only every two or three years. Commodities destined for western South America were packed across the isthmus with the help of but five to six hundred mules and half a hundred small river boats. The load of a mule was limited to a little more than two hundred pounds, while the largest of the river boats did not carry in excess of thirty or thirty-five tons. The volume of commodities which could be handled with such transport media, it is obvious, was relatively small.

The activities of pirates, and the numerous wars in which Spain was involved, were a further aid to the interloping trade. These interferences drove the Spanish commerce to cover while the place of the Spanish commodities was taken by the foreign products, which were eagerly sought by the colonists. And there was another side to the story. This was that the foreign goods frequently were of better quality and of lower price than those which arrived on the periodic Spanish fleets. This appeal to the pocketbook was one which it was hard to resist, and so from the outset Portuguese, Dutch, French, and English interlopers plied their trade in relative security.

The Puerto Bello fairs, being the focal point for the trade of Spain with South America, became the target for the interlopers and the piratical groups which operated in the Caribbean areas. At an early time, Jamaica and other of the West Indian islands had become complete entrepôts for the smuggling trade, and from them merchandise was poured onto the market in quantity. Not the least of these interferences to the established order of things were the various slave *asientos* made with foreign powers. These were masks behind which the contraband trade flourished. The contracts usually allowed the *asentistas* to convey to Puerto Bello, as well as the other ports indicated for the trade, provisions for the use of their slaves and factors. This privilege was grossly abused. The mere presence at Puerto Bello of the commercial agents of a foreign power was objectionable, for they often were better informed as to the state of the American market than were the Spanish merchants themselves. While contraband trade took place under all of the slave *asientos*, it was the contract with the English that proved most disastrous to the Spanish commerce on the isthmus. This was not the fault of the slave *asiento* itself, but of the provision of the Treaty of Utrecht of 1713 which allowed the South Sea Company to send annually to the Puerto Bello fair for purposes of trade one ship of five hundred tons. On its face the provision for the *navío de permiso* might seem to have been relatively harmless, but it actually proved the means by which the English secured a firm foothold in Spanish commerce. It was specified in the treaty that this ship was not to exceed five hundred tons burden, but by a clever artifice, the ship was made to carry many times its normal burden. Relieved of the necessity of carrying large amounts of supplies by a stop at Jamaica, the ship would proceed to Puerto Bello, accompanied by five or six tenders. There the merchandise on board the *navío de permiso* would be unloaded, and its place taken by more merchandise which was transferred from the tenders. In this way, the single ship was made to carry as much as perhaps five or six of the Spanish galleons.

Where contraband merchandise was concerned, Panama in the latter seventeenth and early eighteenth centuries was like the fabulous milk pitcher which was continually full no matter how much was poured out of it. The extent of the illegal traffic on the isthmus may be gauged by the fact that between 1730, when a Spanish fleet arrived at Puerto Bello, and 1736, there was still in Puerto Bello and Panama European merchandise which went under the guise of "fleet" merchandise. This undoubtedly may be set down as a result of the untiring efforts of the South Sea Company. Although the merchandise was continually being carried on to Peru, it never seemed to be exhausted. With this situation existing continuously, the decline of the Tierra Firme fleets, and likewise the Puerto Bello fairs, becomes no mystery.

As they have been here described, the periodic Puerto Bello fairs had ceased to exist by the middle of the eighteenth century. The interloping trade, which did not operate on any schedule, and the Spanish commercial reform of 1720, which allowed certain registered ships to sail from Spain directly to the western South American ports via Cape Horn, spelled the almost certain destruction of the fair organization. The last of the galleons appears to have reached Puerto Bello in 1737, and from that time on the number of ships reaching the port was insufficient to warrant the continuance of the fairs on their former scale. In 1754, when the Mexican *flota* was revived, it was decided not to reëstablish the galleons for Tierra Firme, and with the Spanish trade thus definitely diverted to other channels, the *raison d'être* of the fairs vanished.

6. Spanish Seamen in the New World During the Colonial Period

PAUL S. TAYLOR

Professor Taylor of the University of California, Berkeley, was one of the few scholars to heed the advice of Dr. Jameson that more attention should be paid to the people who went to Latin America. The ships that sailed to the New World were manned by "rough, hardy seamen who underwent untold hardship and suffering from unremitting battle with wind and wave, cold, exposure, starvation, disease, and death." It is a sober story, presented with skill and based upon a wide variety of interesting sources.

The Spanish mariners of the New World were governed by the laws of the Indies. Their conditions of service were perhaps more vitally affected by the manner in which masters of ships saw fit to exercise (or exceed) their authority. But beneath both enactments and arbitrary authority lay the *Consulado del Mare*, the maritime law at the basis of all legal relationships of the sea, just as the Common Law is at the basis of all our legal relationships on land. For this reason, an analysis of the customs of the sea, as contained in the *Consulado del Mare*, is especially valuable as furnishing a background for a sketch of the conditions of life among seamen of the colonial period.

The *Consulado del Mare* furnished the laws used by practically all the *Consulados* of Spain, which for three or four centuries were accepted

From Volume V (1922), pages 631–661.

as authority throughout the Mediterranean area. It also furnished the basis of the laws of Oleron of about the same period. The *Consulado del Mare* was compiled at Barcelona, in all probability, according to an eminent authority, "by the scribe of the Consular Court for the use of the Consuls of the Sea." The exact date of its origin is a subject of some disagreement. Perhaps the more general opinion is that the laws were compiled during the thirteenth century. This is the view of such men as Capmany, Vinino, and Meyer. Twiss, writing at a later date (1874), states that he "considers the assumption to be well founded that the Customs of the Sea in the form in which they have come down to us in the Book of the Consulate of 1494 were not compiled until some time after 1340 A.D." But regardless of the exact date of origin, it is known that the *Consulado del Mare* was the recognized maritime law of the South European countries for several centuries.

The *Consulado* mentions six modes of hiring mariners: (1) for the agreed voyage at a lump sum; (2) by the month; (3) by the mile; (4) at the discretion of the managing owner; (5) for a share in the freight; (6) for the right to load goods on their own account. The contract of hiring was entered into when the mariner's name was entered on the ship's register, or he had shaken hands with the managing owner, a ceremony as binding as if they had gone before a notary. In addition, an oath of loyalty was required from mariners and all who received wages aboard ship. Once the contract was made, the mariner could go nowhere except with the consent of the managing owner. And the managing owner, on his part, could not dismiss the mariner unless it was upon one of four conditions: (1) robbery; (2) quarreling; (3) disobedience, and then only upon the fifth occasion; or (4) breach of oath.

The mariner's duties comprised anything he might be ordered to do about the ship and its navigation. In the words of the *Consulado,*

. . . the mariner is bound in all things which pertain to the ship, to go to the forest and fetch wood, to saw and to make planks, to make spars and ropes, to bake, to man the boat with the boatswain, to stow goods and to unstow them; and at every hour when the mate shall order him to go and fetch spars and ropes, to carry planks, and to put on board all the victuals of the merchants, to heave the vessel over, to go and fetch spars and ropes, to carry planks, and to aid to repair the vessel, and he is bound to do everything to improve the condition of the ship and of all which belongs to the ship whilst he shall be engaged to the ship.

A passage rather curious from our viewpoint, but not from the mariner's, attests the fact that he was never free from duty for very long intervals:

A mariner ought not to undress himself if he is not in a port for wintering. And if he does so, for each time he ought to be plunged into the sea with a rope from the yard arm three times; and after three times offending, he ought to lose his salary and the goods which he has in the ship.

In those days, vessels were not always accustomed to draw up alongside of wharves, so the mariner must be willing to step into the water himself and carry the passengers ashore upon his back; and if he was not willing, he was bound to reimburse the passenger any loss he might incur.

In general, freight was the mother of wages. But the mariner was safeguarded against loss through unprofitable voyages, for the *Consulado* held that in the last resort, the ship was liable for wages, even to the extent of selling the vessel. One source of mariners is indicated by the following passage concerning wages:

. . . the managing owner may not diminish the wages of any one. And if a man is worth more than the managing owner believed at the commencement, he ought to increase his wages; for many men desire to leave a country, because they are not sufficiently appreciated, and in order to get away from it, sell their personal services at a cheap price.

But evidently all mariners were not so eager to escape from the country that they were willing to take low wages. For it is also provided as follows:

Here let us suppose that the managing owner of a ship agrees with a mariner, be he bad or good, skilful or unskilful, he has to pay him his wages, nevertheless under this condition, that if the mariner has represented himself to be a caulker or a carpenter or a mate, and the managing owner has hired him upon that reliance, if the mariner knows nothing, the managing owner of the ship or vessel is not bound to give him anything beyond what the mate and the ship's clerk adjudge upon their oath that he ought to have.

A mariner who shipped for wages by the mile was bound to go wherever the ship went, even "to the end of the world". But if he signed for a voyage, then he was bound only for the particular voyage agreed upon. And if the vessel should be sold before returning, it was the duty of the owner to provide him with a ship to return to his home port.

A customary scale of rations, enumerated in considerable detail, is called for by the *Consulado:*

. . . the managing owner of a ship or vessel, which is decked, ought to give to eat to the mariners on three days a week flesh-meat, that is to say on Sundays, Tuesdays, and Thursdays, and on the other days of the week porridge, and every evening of every day accompaniment with bread, and also on the same three days in the morning he ought to give them wine, and also he ought to give them the same quantity of wine every evening. And the accompaniment of the bread ought to be such as follows, that is, cheese or onions or sardines or some other fish. . . . Further the managing owner of the ship or vessel is bound to double the ration of the mariners upon the solemn feast days. Further, he ought to have servants to prepare the food for the mariners.

Compared to the sea code of the Hanse Towns (which authorized branding on the forehead), the penalty for desertion stipulated in the *Consulado* was mild. The mariner was bound to make compensation to the owner for all losses incurred as a result of the desertion, and in case he was unable to do so, he could be imprisoned until such time as he was able to pay. And mariners who took away a ship without the consent of the owner were similarly bound to make losses good, and could be imprisoned, and a demand made against them, "just as against persons who renounce their lord and dispossess him of his authority."

Discipline aboard ship was of course to be very strictly enforced. Necessarily much authority was left to the master, and the mariner must be extremely careful in his conduct towards him. A mariner who quarreled with the managing owner lost half his wages and the goods he had in the ship. And heavier penalties were exacted in proportion to the gravity of the offense.

. . . . And if he raises a weapon against the managing owner, all the mariners ought to seize him and bind him and put him into prison, and take him before the local authorities, and those who will not seize him ought to lose their goods and the wages which they will receive or ought to receive for the voyage.

Thus it was made the duty of the crew to assist actively in disciplining itself. But the paragraph of the *Consulado* which deals with the limits of the mariners' right of self defense, shows most clearly his real status aboard ship.

Further, a mariner is bound to bear with the managing owner of a ship, if he reproaches him, and if he runs to attack him the mariner ought to run away to the bow of the ship and place himself by the side of the chain. And if the managing owner passes the chain, he ought to run away to the other side, and if the managing owner passes to the other side, he may defend himself, calling persons to witness how the managing owner ought not to pass the chain.

The Seamen of the Explorers

Spanish navigators explored the west coast of America from the Horn to Alaska, and across the Pacific to the Orient. Their ships were manned by rough, hardy seamen who underwent untold hardship and suffering from unremitting battle with wind and wave, cold, exposure, starvation, disease, and death.

It was the policy of the king to allow none but Spanish mariners in the New World, for reasons of greater secrecy surrounding the wealth of his possessions. Nevertheless, it was found necessary to enlist foreign sailors, especially in the earlier expeditions, because native Spanish seamen were lacking. Thus Magellan carried besides the Spanish among his crew of 265 men, some 37 Portuguese, 30 or more Genoese and Italians, 19 French, and others were Flemings, Germans, Sicilians, English, Corfiotes, Malays, Negroes, Moors, Madeirans, Biscainers, and natives of the Azores and Canary Islands. In 1565 many Portuguese sailed to the Philippines with Legazpi and caused him considerable anxiety, because in view of the relations between the two nations, he found them not to be trusted. The sailors for the later expeditions up the California coast were most probably all Spaniards, or natives of the vicinity of San Blas, as in the expedition of Martinez.

In the main, the men seem to have served and sacrificed with great fortitude, if not always with obedience, thoughts of glory or love of adventure proving sufficient stimulus. Probably on such expeditions a sufficient number of volunteers could be found, if not all Spanish, then of other nationalities. At least the writer has found but one case of shanghaiing recorded—that of a man from the island of Teneriffe who was forcibly added to the crew by the order of Magellan.

The sailors were a rough class of men, intemperate (if the example of the seaman on Bodega's schooner who drank himself to death is at all typical of their love of strong drink), given to excesses when they went ashore, commonly afflicted with venereal diseases, irresponsible, and turbulent. They loved to gamble and to barter, even with the very clothes they wore. When Vizcaino issued out the extra supply of clothing at the request of his men, to protect them from the cold, he thought it necessary to issue at the same time an edict "to the effect that no one should gamble or sell them, under pain of death." Maurelle records that his men cut their shirts, trousers, and jackets into strips, and bartered these little rolls or bandages with the Indians. And Governor Fages of California ordered that no bales of goods should be opened until the San Blas vessels left port, to avoid the waste of clothing in barter with the sailors.

Mutinies were of frequent occurrence, especially in the expeditions which crossed the Pacific. Although seamen took part in these uprisings against authority, they were often led by men of higher rank, actuated by motives of jealous ambition, who found discontented elements in the crew ready to aid them. Thus, royal officials led a mutiny against Magellan, which he suppressed by executing the ringleaders. But a short time thereafter a second mutiny broke out. The crew of the *San Antonio* put their captain, Alvaro, in irons, and after many difficulties returned to Spain. Mutinies broke out in the expeditions on the Pacific sent out by Cortes. One of the ship's companies mutinied against their commander Hurtado de Mendoza, and returned to port. Another expedition came to an unfortunate end when Ximines, in 1534, killed his superior, Bercerra, and took command, only to be himself killed soon afterwards by Indians. In 1537 the explorer Grijalva was killed by mutineers. The crew of one of the ships of Loaysa, in the South Pacific, mutinied, throwing the captain and his brother overboard. Like most of the mutinous crews, they ran into difficulties. The ship went aground on an island and the crew were overpowered by Indians. Saavedra, crossing the Pacific from New Spain, found them, and brought the mutineers to justice. The Legazpi expedition to the

Philippines in 1565 also has its record of mutinies. On the first occasion Legazpi hanged four leaders, severely reprimanded others, and as for the rest, merely imposed the order that no language but Spanish be spoken. When a second mutiny occurred, two more were hanged. The *San Gerónimo*, sent to aid Legazpi, had similar experiences. The captain and his son were murdered by mutineers; and two of the latter were hanged following a second, and successful, counter mutiny.

This frequency of mutiny no doubt reflected somewhat on the severity of discipline aboard ship. The death penalty was inflicted for mutiny and other crimes, and at least threatened for lesser offenses. Bodega seems to have been a commander who treated his men with great consideration. When they became discouraged he gave them small presents, and in other ways stimulated their enthusiasm. He took all precautions he was able to against sickness and scurvy. Yet when two of his men voluntarily went among the Indians, intending to remain, but were made captives, causing Bodega much trouble in securing their release, the commander had them laid across cannon and each given a hundred lashes, after which he put them in irons. It was considered to be, and was made the duty of commanders to punish severely blasphemy, gambling, immorality, and other sins. Before departing on the expeditions, sailors were required to take an oath of loyalty to the commander that they would obey him and not mutiny, and they had to present a certificate that they had confessed and received communion. Of those who were enlisted for the voyages, not only their name, but their father's name and his place of birth were entered on the register, that their nationality might be known.

The explorations were hazardous undertakings. Nearly every expedition suffered losses from attacks by Indians when the crew went ashore for food, wood, and water. The navigation of the small craft required much labor and exertion of the sailors, especially when storms were encountered, which was often. The schooner *Sonora* in which Bodega conducted his exploration up the coast in 1775 was but 36 feet long, 12 feet wide, and 8 feet deep, and carried a crew of a pilot, boatswain, boatswain's mate, ten sailors, a cabin boy, and a servant. Not all the vessels used were so small, yet the best of them were not large, and afforded but poor protection to the mariners. Huge waves would come sweeping over the gunwales, carrying away everything above deck. On such a schooner as the *Sonora*, except in a calm, the sailors could not perform their duties on the ship without becoming thoroughly wet. Since they were used to a warmer climate, they suffered greatly from the cold of the northern latitudes. Their clothes became soaked by the rain and spray, so that in spite of the extra issue of clothing provided by the king, large numbers fell sick with severe colds contracted from fatigue and exposure. There were no conveniences for their care and protection, and few medicines. Consequently many seamen died, and the work of exploration was hampered accordingly.

The seamen's rations which Magellan supplied for his voyage included wine, olive oil, vinegar, fish, pork, peas and beans, flour, garlic, cheese, honey, almonds, anchovies, raisins, prunes, figs, sugar, quince preserves, capers, mustard, beef, and rice. Other Spanish explorers carried similar provisions, though probably none so complete a list. Martinez carried aboard his frigate to Nootka Sound some goats, hogs, cows and calves. But not all ships were so well supplied. Often the men were forced to go on short rations. For instance, Maurelle tells how he was obliged to reduce the allowance to five ounces of bread, three of pork, and two of beans, per day; and many cases were far worse than his. Even so, the sailors would generally have been adequately provided for, but for the spoiling of the rations aboard ship. Fresh food would not remain fresh long, but soon all became corrupted. The ships were dirty and swarming with vermin and rats which attacked the rations. On board Maurelle's ship the cockroaches reduced the biscuit to a powder, and bored through the water casks, letting the precious water run out. Often the seawater found its way into the provisions, and further damaged the food.

Under such conditions it was inevitable that disease, principally scurvy, should break out. Until almost the end of the eighteenth century no long expedition was free from the ravages of this disease. Scurvy and cold were the most powerful obstacles to Spanish navigation of the Pacific. The death list was large, chiefly among the crew, for the commanders were accustomed to take somewhat better provisions for themselves. Many of the diaries of the explorers tell of being forced to turn back because not enough well persons were left aboard to navigate the ship. Vizcaino, with his men dying of hunger, dared not stop to receive food from Indians who offered it, as he did not have men strong enough to raise the anchors.

It was not generally known until Cook's voyage how to prevent scurvy on a long voyage. Venegas tells how the crew of a Manila galleon were cured by eating "pitahayas, acid fruits, and fresh meat". Vizcaino records in his diary the efficacy of a "small fruit like agaves, called juicolystlis". Martinez knew somewhat better how to combat the dread disease. His list of remedies included "wild celery, greens, the soft tender shoots of the nettle, and various other plants whose taste is similar to that of the radish leaf in salad". But none of them knew how to provide for the time when the fresh provisions were exhausted, so scurvy long remained the chief hazard and cause of mortality of Spanish seamen.

The Seamen of the India Trade Route

Trade between Spain and America (called India in those days) during the colonial period was for the most part conducted by great merchant fleets, or *flotas*, convoyed by one or more vessels of the royal armada. This precaution was necessitated by the raiding of Spanish commerce by foreign buccaneers, for these ships carried the coveted treasures of New Spain, and of the Orient, brought to New Spain in the Manila galleons. For a short time in the middle of the sixteenth century, when danger seemed least, all restrictions upon sailings were removed, but in 1555 the *flotas* were restored. There were two main fleets, the one with ships for the Gulf of Mexico, the other bound for the ports on the north coast of South America. Vera Cruz and Porto Bello were the destination ports which served the Mexican and Peruvian trade.

Commerce with America was a monopoly in the hands of the merchants of Seville, Spain, organized into the *Universidad de los Mareantes*. This organization resembled the English gild merchants, in that boatswains, mates, and mariners, as well as owners, masters, and pilots, were included in the membership. The mariners, however, were not allowed to hold office, nor to vote, but received certain privileges, of which more will be said later.

There was much variation in the composition of the *flotas* and the size of the ships. Five hundred and fifty tons were decreed as the maximum allowed on the India route, but the difficulty of crossing the bar at San Lucar, in Spain, kept the usual size down to more nearly 100 or 200 tons.

The manning scale of vessels in the India trade fixed by the Ordinance of July 14, 1522, required that every vessel of 100 tons burden must carry at least fifteen mariners (or able seamen), 8 grummets (ordinary or apprentice seamen), and three ship's boys. In 1552 the scale was raised somewhat, and declared to be as follows:

SIZE OF SHIP	MARINERS	APPRENTICES	BOYS
100–170 Tons	18	8	2
170–220 "	28	12	4
220–320 "	35	15	5

The merchant ships went armed, even to the mariners and passengers. And it was required that all mariners in the India route should be trained in artillery practice and regulations, and be examined upon the results of their training.

Foreign mariners (except from the Levant) were prohibited from sailing in the India fleets. And on the other hand, because of the scarcity of Spanish seamen, Spaniards were forbidden to sail in foreign vessels, unless those ships should be in the service of the India trade, in which case they must be manned by Spaniards. The penalty for breach of this law was four years' service in the galleys. Only in case of absolute necessity were mariners to be enlisted in the Indies, and then, upon selection of the best by examination, only enough, and no more, were to be chosen.

When it came time to enlist sailors, the general (or admiral) set up his standard. To this standard men came to be examined, and enrolled if found fit. No one was to be shipped as an able seaman who had not served three years apprenticeship as a grummet. Sailors had to be between twenty and fifty years of age. Care had to be taken not to enlist passengers as mariners or grummets for this was a favorite method of evading the emigration laws; nor were mariners to be enrolled as soldiers, for the former were none too plentiful. On the ship's register was entered the man's name, age, identification marks, place of birth, and his father's name; also the man's rating, or capacity in which he was to serve, together with his rate of pay, and the day.

Sailors were bound to give security that they would serve and earn their pay, and take an oath of obligation. But his Catholic majesty Philip II, in 1582, decreed that no pay or rations were to be given a sailor unless he could produce a certificate from one of the religious that he had been at confession.

When a mariner was under contract to serve one master, it was illegal for him to contract to serve another. If he did so, the penalty was double the amount of salary he would have earned, and twenty days in prison. The master who enticed him away knowingly, was also punished.

In the middle of the sixteenth century a gild of merchants engaged in the India trade was organized in Seville. A little later a hospital was founded for mariners who fell sick from the India voyage, or working aboard ship. In 1569 the gild and hospital united as the *Universidad de los Mareantes*, with the all inclusive membership before enumerated. Certain privileges were granted to the *Universidad* by the king. Those which included the mariners are given by Stevens as follows:

. . . That two hundred Ducats per Month be distributed among the Sailors of every Galeon [and ship of the *armada* and *flota*], above their Pay, so that no one receive above four Crowns, and that all those who serve in the India voyage shall be rewarded according to the service they do. 8. That those who do not furnish good Provisions, for the Armada's and Flota's, shall be punish'd. 9. That the Admirals do not suffer the Sailors to be abus'd. 10. That Sailors serving aboard the Armada's and Flota's, be exempt from Town Offices, if they think fit. 11. That no Quarters [for troops] be taken up in the Houses of such as serve in the India Voyage. . . . That a Seaman, who has serv'd 20 Years, enjoy for ever after these Privileges, tho' he follow not the Sea.

Besides, mariners were free from arrest for debt. The royal arm also stretched out to protect the sailors from the extortions practiced upon them by the people of Vera Cruz. To check this evil it was ordered that prices should be no higher to men of the fleet than to the inhabitants.

Judge Peters in 1807 declared that the Spaniards were "the most unkind, and indeed unjust, to their sick mariners of any people; for they neither pay them any wages nor maintain them. . . ." The mariners of the India trade thus apparently had an advantage over other sailors of Spain, in that they were entitled to the privileges of the hospital provided by the *Universidad* at Seville.

The ordinary daily ration for each person in 1534 was one and one-half pounds of bread, two pints of drinking water and another for bathing, and two pints of wine. Salt pork, fish, beans and peas, oil, vinegar, rice and sometimes cheese and beef were also part of the ration. In 1665 the allowance in the Windward *Flota* was as follows:

Biscuit	24.0	ounces
Water	4.5	pints
Bocallao, or Poor-Jack	8.0	ounces
Beans and Peas	2.0	ounces
Oil	1.5	ounces
Vinegar	0.15	pint
Wine	0.75	pint

This was the ration for four days in the week. The other three, instead of fish, beans and peas, eight ounces of bacon, an ounce and a half of rice, and a small portion of cheese was substituted.

When rations were cut, sailors were entitled to an indemnification called "pinch gut money". In order to avoid the payment of this, if possible, the *Casa de Contratación*, or India House of Trade, issued this precautionary order:

. . . that provisions be not shortened without evident necessity, because it has happened that a great quantity of Provisions has by these means, been brought into Port, where the Bisket is sold for the fifth part of its value, which is a very great loss.

Until late in the sixteenth century at least, sailors were hired on shares. The owner of the ship and the sailors each chose a representative to make the settlement at the end of the voyage. The amount of the freight was computed. Then they deducted the amount paid for the convoy service, and two and one-half per cent for distribution as a bounty among sailors and grummets who had rendered extraordinary service. Of the remainder, two thirds went to the owner. The remaining third was apportioned among the crew on the basis of a whole share to each able bodied seaman, two thirds of a share to each grummet, and a fourth to each boy.

Later, sailors shipped for agreed wages, but seem still to have been allowed to carry a limited amount of goods as a private investment. To each mariner was alloted thirty-four jars of wine as his share, and to each grummet ten jars.

Sailors, grummets, and boys were entitled to four months' advance wages when enlisted. To prevent desertion, no pay was to be given in the Indies, unless a certificate could be presented proving that the seaman had remained on account of illness, or other legitimate excuse, which prevented him from returning on the same vessel in which he came. Among the crew of each vessel in the India trade, 200 ducats above the regular pay was to be distributed as a reward for meritorious service. If the men were not paid promptly within three days of when pay was due, the master was liable to arrest, and for each day's delay, every sailor was entitled to two reals, every grummet to a real and a half, and every boy, one real. The conditions of life aboard the India ships were much the same as elsewhere among Spanish seamen in the New World. The ships were filthy, crowded, often unseaworthy, and inadequately manned. The prevalence of shipwreck was frightful, and buccaneers abounded. The profits were between 200 and 300 per cent, but the casualties also were enormous.

The principal disciplinary offenses were blasphemy, gambling, immorality, desertion, and crime. It was forbidden for any sailor to go ashore at the Azores under penalty of 200 lashes and ten years in the galleys. Sometimes mariners deserted before the ships left Spain. But desertion in the Indies was the most strictly prohibited, as it was the more common also, since many came as seamen to evade the emigration laws.

Permission to go ashore in the Indies was hedged about with restrictions, and every effort was made to ascertain and punish such as planned to desert. Guards were posted on the Porto Bello-Panama road to catch fugitives. India officials and commanders of ships were ordered to do all in their power to apprehend and proceed against deserters, and those who gave them refuge. Some seamen who wished to remain in the Indies sought immunity from capture by flight to the altar and other sacred places. Thereupon the king promulgated a law against such immunity, and ordered that such deserters should be taken from the altar and returned to Spain.

These were the conditions under which Spanish sailors lived and labored. If Spanish officials complained of the scarcity of mariners, the cause of the scarcity is readily to be found in the conditions which prevailed in the calling.

The Merchant Seamen of the Pacific

The discovery of a return route from the Philippines to Mexico by Urdaneta in 1565 made possible for the first time the establishment of a direct trade route across the Pacific Ocean. A regular trade was soon opened between Manila and Spain, by way of Mexico. The Pacific commerce was restricted to one or two annual galleons sailing between Manila and Acapulco, in Mexico. These Manila galleons, as they were called, were fitted out at royal expense and commanded by a royal officer. In size they ranged from small pinks to galleons of 2000 tons, but the more usual size, when there were two annual ships, was not larger than 500 tons, carrying crews averaging about 115 men. The last galleon sailed from Manila in 1811, and returned in 1815. The commerce then fell into private hands, and the ports of San Blas, Guayaquil, and Callao were opened to engage in it.

There was some trade on the Pacific from the earliest days of the conquest, between Mexico and Peru, but it was restricted to an annual galleon, and during some periods, prohibited altogether. The annual supply ships from San Blas to Alta California were not for commercial purposes.

Both routes were insignificant in comparison to the Manila-Acapulco line.

The voyage to Manila ordinarily required from seventy-five to ninety days, but the return to Acapulco usually took from seven to nine months, owing to the necessity of sailing northward beyond the belt of trade winds into the westerlies. America was approached in the latitude of Cape Mendocino; then the galleons turned southward, and sailed along the California coast down to Acapulco. By a renowned traveler who made the voyage to Mexico in 1697, it was characterized as

the longest, and most dreadful of any in the world; as well because of the vast ocean to be cross'd, being almost the one half of the terraqueous globe, with the wind always a-head; as for the terrible tempests that happen there, one upon the back of another, and for the desperate diseases that seize people, in seven or eight months lying at sea, sometimes near the line, sometimes cold, sometimes temperate, and sometimes hot, which is enough to destroy a man of steel, much more flesh and blood, which at sea had but indifferent food.

The crews which manned the galleons were composed chiefly of Spaniards and Filipinos (Indians, as they were called). The Spaniards were the sailors, or mariners, corresponding to what we know as able seamen. The Indians were rated as common seamen, corresponding to a lower rating such as our ordinary seamen. Spaniards, too, sometimes sailed as common seamen, but their wage was very much higher than Indian seamen of the same rating. The difference in wage, however, was not based upon difference of ability, for the seamanship of the natives was universally accorded high praise. Viana's description is as follows:

. . . There is not an Indian in those islands who has not a remarkable inclination for the sea; nor is there at present in all the world a people more agile in manoeuvers on ship board, or who learn so quickly nautical terms and whatever a good mariner ought to know. Their disposition is most humble in the presence of a Spaniard, and they show him great respect; but they can teach many of the Spanish mariners who sail in these seas. . . . There is hardly an Indian who has sailed the seas who does not understand the mariner's compass, and therefore on this [Acapulco] trade-route there are some very skilful and dextrous helmsmen. Their disposition is cowardly, but, when placed on a ship, from which they cannot escape, they fight with spirit and courage.

Common seamen could be secured without difficulty, the natives being ready to volunteer in spite of the great risks and hardships of the voyage. But with many of them, shipping as seamen was merely the chance to escape from captivity or worse conditions in the Islands. Once in Mexico they deserted and remained there. With the Spanish sailors, conditions were somewhat different. Appeals were continually sent from Manila to the king, asking for more sailors, who were sent out from Spain to Mexico, where they boarded the galleon for the Philippines. And it was deemed necessary to provide additional payment for sailors, by increasing the allowance of goods carried as private investment, in order to encourage Spanish seamen to enter the Acapulco trade. In 1724 hardly one third of the men aboard the galleon were of Spanish birth. Yet notwithstanding the scarcity of Spanish mariners, foreign sailors were barred from the South Sea by royal decree in 1572.

The sailors of the galleons were a rough class of men, discontented, living hard, hazardous lives, and dying in poverty and discomfort. They were variously described by men of the time as "the poor sailors in the continual dangers of their fearful duty"; as "a class of men who lack pity, and have too much greed"; and as "an ungodly people, guilty of sins of the flesh as well as other offenses, who know naught except to commit offenses against those with whom they deal." Doubtless the descriptions fitted the subject. Los Rios submitted as one of his recommendations to the king

. . . That slave women be not conveyed in the ships, by which many acts offensive to God will be avoided. Although that is prohibited by your royal decree, and it is also entrusted to the archbishop to place upon them the penalty of excommunication and to punish them, this evil has not been checked; and many sailors—and even others, who should furnish a good example—take slave women and keep them as concubines.

The Indian seamen who deserted at Acapulco, although married in the Islands, did not hesitate to remarry in Mexico. On the *Espiritu Santo* in 1618, seventy-five Indians came as common seamen, but not more than five returned.

In the Philippines, the king encouraged the marriage of poor Spanish sailors with native women, and interested himself in the provision of dowries for the Indian women for this very purpose. His Catholic majesty also found it necessary to establish hospitals, and provide physicians and care for both Indian and Spanish sailors and seamen, whose poverty was such that they could not provide for themselves. Said the king in his instructions to the governor of the Philippines,

. . . I have been told that . . . both of them suffer extreme need; . . . Both classes die in discomfort, through having no building in which to be protected from the ravages of the climate, and through the lack of beds, food, medicines, nurses, and other necessities.

Such was the type, and status, of the men who manned the galleons.

Very early it was decreed that sailors and common seamen should be examined before enlisting to determine their fitness for the duties at sea. This proved to be necessary for the reason that often as many as half those listed as sailors on the galleon were not sailors at all, but persons who had secured the position through favoritism in order to gain passage, and to share in a profitable trade. And natives from the interior, ignorant of the art of sailing, were often enrolled and shipped by the factor.

The pay received by sailors in 1635 was reported to be 150 pesos per year and 30 gantas of cleaned rice per month for sailors; Spanish common seamen received 100 pesos and 30 gantas of rice; Indian common seamen received 48 pesos and 15 gantas of rice. In 1637 wages were higher, sailors receiving 175 pesos and common seamen 60 and one half pesos. Gemelli Careri in 1697 gave sailors' wages as 350 pieces of eight for voyage from Manila to Acapulco and return. Seventy-five pieces of eight were paid at Cavite as advance pay, which was customary; but to prevent desertion at Acapulco, and insure return to Manila, the remaining 275 pieces of eight were not paid until the return, for as Gemelli Careri said, "if they had half, very few would return to the Philippine islands for the rest".

But it was found that wages alone were inadequate. A royal decree had declared that seamen should carry no more boxes or clothing than indispensably necessary, for the reason that they unduly cumbered the ships. In the boxes of course was merchandise carried as a private investment. But officials in the Philippines protested that wages were insufficient incentive, that greater zeal and willingness to render loyal service would be secured if the men had a stake in the treasure ships, and that more Spaniards would be brought into the service of the Acapulco trade. Accordingly permission was granted to carry small amounts, the exact amount to be allowed being a bone of contention between Philippine officials, who sought to raise it, and Spanish officials, who sought to lower it.

But even with a fixed rate of wages, and permission to carry goods for investment on his own account, the pay of the sailor was by no means certain. In 1589 one of the Philippine officials wrote to the king of grave evils existing in this matter.

. . . They should be paid in Nueva España as this treasury is too poor. As the money for their wages must be sent, sometimes it is not brought, and at other times it is lost, thereby causing the sailors to die of starvation. Therefore the sailors serve half-heartedly, and desert; and there is great negligence in the dispatch of the fleets.

A decree in accord with the recommendation was promptly issued.

Wages were not paid in money, but by a warrant, or voucher, which was supposed to be convertible into cash—and was, but not when presented by the sailor. In 1621 the archbishop of Manila wrote to the king as follows:

One could not believe the injury that is done to the soldiers and sailors, and to all the wage-earners, by not paying the vouchers earned by their labor and sweat; and on the other hand, by buying these for much less than their face value. For, being rendered desperate, they sell vouchers valued at one thousand pesos for one hundred, and the lamentable thing is that, if they did not sell them, they would never be paid. Scarcely have they sold the vouchers when they are immediately paid, and the purchasers even take the poor wretches to the office of accounts, so they may be present at the payment, and that it may appear justified, by their saying that they did it of their own accord, for which they give a receipt. As it is the price of blood, and they see that others take that price, it is a grief and sorrow that cries to heaven for redress. . . .

Fifteen years later this flagrant evil was unabated, and corruption continued to hold full sway. In 1636 another letter to the king again recited the abuse as practiced by corrupt officials.

As for those poor men, they have not been paid in one, three, ten, or fifteen years. They sell their warrants during such times for the fourth, fifth, or sixth part of their face value; and many have been paid at one hundred pesos for one thousand. The warrants are bought by the servants of the auditors, royal officials, governors, and other ministers, and to them is paid the face value.

Besides the abuses which have been mentioned, the sailors were subjected to petty annoyances by the collectors of port dues at Acapulco, who, when examining the former's small chests and wretched belongings, "practice many extortions on them so that many refuse to return".

It is evident that the compensations of the sailors were uncertain at best. And when compared to the 100 to 150 per cent profits commonly made by the merchants, and the severe hardships, petty annoyances, and great risks undergone, one cannot but conclude that the sailors and seamen were but poorly recompensed for their indispensable services in a trade which yielded such enormous profits.

Discipline aboard ship was enforced with severity, though probably the Spanish ships of those days were not worse than aboard many American ships within the memory of men still living. Gambling, swearing and blasphemy, and immorality were all punishable, as of course mutiny, desertion, quarreling, and insubordination. Putting men in the bilboes, ducking them from the yard arm, keel-hauling, and the lash, were well known forms of inflicting punishment. When the sailors and seamen sought release from discipline by going ashore at Acapulco, and behaved as they pleased, the king extended the jurisdiction of the ship's officers to cover the time while they were in port.

Life aboard ship could not have been attractive, except for the glamor which has always surrounded going to sea. Ships in those days were the antithesis of cleanliness. Rats and vermin swarmed over the vessel. The most vivid account of the conditions comes from the experience and pen of Gemelli Careri.

. . . the galeon is never clear of an universal raging itch, as an addition to all other miseries . . . the ship swarms with little vermine, the Spaniards call Gorgojos, bred in the bisket; so swift that they in a short time not only run over cabins, beds, and the very dishes the men eat on, but insensibly fasten upon the body . . . there are several other sorts of vermin of sundry colours, that suck the blood.

Besides these discomforts, he, like others, complains of the "terrible shocks from side to side, caus'd by the furious beating of the waves". The galleons were always overladen with merchandise, and the decks were crowded with the chests of the sailors, hen-coops, and bales of goods. The very narrowness of the quarters was distressing, and on one galleon at least, led to civil war which was stopped only through the efforts of the fathers who were aboard.

Provision for rations aboard ship was most unsystematic and improperly attended to. In the first place, those who furnished the rations for the crew often put in food of poor quality. Then also, the passengers and religious, who were often numerous, consumed food provided for the crew. Stowaways were an additional drain upon provisions. So also were the slaves of the passengers and sailors, who in addition stole whatever food they could lay hands upon; for even the slaves who aided the sailors in their necessities were not provided for by the king's allowance of food and water. For these reasons the sailors had to spend their wages buying provisions for themselves and their slaves. This was often the cause of overloading the ships, and was responsible for failure to carry the proper kinds of food, because of which the Indian common seamen suffered most, since they were less used to provide for themselves than the Spanish sailors. The Indians were even permitted to die of hunger and thirst aboard ship for lack of adequate provision and care. The various messes aboard stocked themselves as best they could. Swine, hens, fruit, and an abundance of greens were put on the deck until the ship looked like a floating garden.

But these never lasted the entire voyage. If fish could be caught en route the passengers and crew were fortunate, for the food became corrupted, and the water gave out unless the supply could be replenished from the rainfall.

Gemelli Careri, who traveled as a cabin passenger, gives the most graphic account of the hardships and fare aboard the galleon. Eating at the boatswain's mess, he began with fresh fowl, but ere long he found himself eating the king's allowance of rations to the men, of which he gives us a description.

. . . At last he depriv'd me of the satisfaction of gnawing a good bisket, because he would spend no more of his own, but laid the king's allowance on the table; in every mouthful whereof there went down abundance of maggots and Gorgojos chew'd and bruis'd. On fish days the common diet was old rank fish boil'd in fair water and salt; at noon we had Mongos, something like kidney beans, in which there were so many maggots, that they swam at the top of the broth, and the quantity was so great, that besides the loathing they caus'd, I doubted whether the dinner was fish or flesh. This bitter fare was sweeten'd after dinner with a little water and sugar; yet the allowance was but a small cocoa shell full, which rather increased than quenched drought. Providence reliev'd us for a month with sharks and Cachorretas the seamen caught, which, either boil'd or broil'd were some comfort. Yet he is to be pity'd who has another at his table; for the tediousness of the voyage is the cause of all these hardships. 'Tis certain, they that take this upon them, lay out thousands of pieces of eight in making the necessary provision of flesh, fowl, fish, bisket, rice, sweetmeats, chocolate, and other things; and the quantity is so great, that during the whole voyage, they never fail of sweetmeats at table, and chocolate twice a day, of which last the sailors and grummets make as great a consumption, as the richest.

On solemn feast days an extra allowance of rations was served out.

An interesting custom, related by Gamelli Careri, of the Sailor's Court of Signs (held aboard the galleon when the first signs of approach of land appeared), depicts a happier side to the life of the sailors.

. . . A canopy being set up for the sailors court of Senas, or signs, after dinner the two Oydores or judges and the president took their seats, being clad after a ridiculous manner. They began with the captain of the galeon, chief pilot, . . . and other officers of the ship; and after them proceeded to the trial of the passengers. The clerk read every man's indictment, and then the judges pass'd sentence of death, which was immediately bought off with money, chocolate, sugar, biscuit, flesh, sweetmeats, wine and the like.

These payments seem to have satisfied a turbulent and not too well fed crew, who, were they not appeased, were ready to inflict the kind of punishments with which they were most familiar.

. . . The best of it was, that he who did not pay immediately, or give good security, was laid on with a rope's end at the least sign given by the president-tarpaulin. I was told a passenger was once kill'd aboard a galeon, by keelhauling him; for no words or authority can check or persuade a whole ship's crew. . . . The sport lasted till night, and then all the fines were divided among the sailors and grummets, according to custom.

This picture of the Court of Signs, and others of amusements for crew and passengers—cockfighting, plays, dancing, and other entertainments—show that there was a lighter side to the life of the sailor aboard ship. But for the viewpoint of today, the balance seems to have been all the other way.

His very calling was hazardous in the extreme. It was not at all uncommon for men to be washed overboard and drowned by the huge waves which at times swept over, and well-nigh submerged the small craft of that day. More than one galleon was wrecked and went down, or was driven back to Manila by storms with half the crew lost. Then, too, the galleons often sailed poorly repaired through the fault of the shore workers. Pirates of all nations were active in preying upon such rich treasure ships, and the sailors and seamen might at any time be called upon to defend the ship with their lives against capture by these buccaneers or sea-dogs.

A worse enemy of the seamen, particularly of the Indians, was the severe cold encountered on the voyage. They came from a hot climate, and when, without protection, they were exposed to the severities of weather in the higher latitudes, they died in large numbers. They used to come aboard the galleon without clothes, and until the king provided clothing to be issued them as a protection, they had nothing to shelter them. They had no quarters other than the deck, often. Navarrete, describing the situation aboard his ship which was "not convenient nor big enough to celebrate that high mystery" [mass], said: "We had hardly room to stand. No body could live under deck, it was so full of provisions and commodities. All men lay exposed to the sun and air."

So it happened that many were frozen to death, or died of exposure. The lot of the Indian seamen was especially cruel. As Los Rios said, they were "treated like dogs".

. . . They are embarked without clothes to protect them against the cold, so that when each new dawn comes there are three or four dead men . . . besides, they are treated inhumanly and are not given the necessaries of life, but are killed with hunger and thirst. If he were to tell in detail the evil that is done to them, it would fill many pages.

The Indians, however, were not the only victims of the cold, for the sudden changes of climate, and exposure to wind and rain worked great hardship among all on board, and was the cause of much sickness and death. The treatment of the sick was shamefully neglectful. Gemelli Careri relates the callousness of the captain of his galleon, whose personal profits from the single trip were, according to his own estimate, 25,000 or 30,000 pieces of eight:

. . . Abundance of poor sailors fell sick, being expos'd to the continual rains, cold, and other hardships of the season; yet they were not allow'd to taste of the good bisket, rice, fowls, Spanish bread and sweetmeats put into the custody of the master by the king's order, to be distributed among the sick; for the honest master spent all at his own table.

But the worst danger was from disease. For three centuries European navigators in the New World were afflicted with the scourge of scurvy and beri-beri, especially the former. It was Captain James Cook, the Englishman, who first proved the use of lime juice as an anti-scorbutic, and thus removed one of the greatest hindrances to exploration and maritime commerce. The Spanish navigators paid especially heavy toll to these diseases, the cause of which was lack of fresh provisions, or food containing vitamins. Again we turn to Gemelli Careri for a description of these perils:

. . . There are two dangerous diseases in this voyage, more especially as they draw near the coast of America; one is the aforesaid Berben [beri-beri], which swells the body, and makes the patient die talking: The other is call'd the Dutch disease, which makes all the mouth sore, putrifies the gums and makes the teeth drop out. The best remedy against it, is going ashore. This is no other, but the sea-scurvy.

The proportion of deaths among the crew and passengers was often enormous. For instance, on one vessel with 400 persons aboard, 208 died before Acapulco was reached. On another, the *San Nicolas*, 330 died. A voyage on which only three persons died was regarded as most "propitious". Probably extremely few, if indeed any at all, of the voyages from

Manila to America were made without suffering to a greater or less degree from the ravages of these diseases. And on most trips, the sufferings were terrible, and the death list very long.

Small wonder then, that from such a voyage, and such conditions, the survivors frequently preferred to desert at Acapulco (or California, when the galleon stopped there), rather than return to the Philippines. Wages were paid only in the Philippines, and bonds were required of sailors and seamen in the endeavor to check the large number of desertions in Mexico.

Such were the conditions which prevailed among seamen engaged in Spanish commerce across the Pacific, a trade which flourished for over three centuries.

Other Articles of Interest

Bandelier, Fanny R., ed. "The Bill of Fare on a Spanish Fleet, 1770." III (1920), 184–188.

Smith, Robert Sidney. "Shipping in the Port of Veracruz, 1790–1821." XXIII (1943), 5–20.
During the last thirty-one years of Spanish rule effective progress was made in the improvement of the harbor of Veracruz and in the handling of traffic passing through it. The text contains ten tables: I, merchant ships entering, 1790–1821; II, ships paying tonnage dues, 1808–1821; III, value of imports, 1807–1819; IV, merchant ships entering Veracruz, 1830–1845; V, ships entering from United States ports, 1799–1821; VI, value of imports, 1805–1820; VII, average tonnage of ships entering, 1790–1821; VIII, tonnage of ships entering from Spain, 1790–1821; IX, average tonnage of these ships; X, indexes of tonnage and value of imports, 1790–1821.

7. The Archives of the Indies
at Seville

IRENE A. WRIGHT

As the managing editor of *HAHR*, Dr. James Alexander Robertson, explained to the subscribers in the first number of 1926, "it has not been the policy of the *Review* to publish metrical matter." But he went on to remark, and readers who have worked in Seville will surely agree with him, that "the short contribution by Miss Wright that is given below is so true to the spirit of the Archivo General de Indias and expresses so well the vast sweep of the documents there conserved that it is thought no apology other than this statement is necessary." Miss Wright did research for many years in the Archivo and is now retired from the Department of State.

EL ARCHIVO GENERAL DE INDIAS

These are the Archives of the Indies!
Here—in these tall cases, built from marble floor
Toward domed, arched ceiling—
Here are stored, in blue-wrapped bundles, pack on pack,
The papers passed between old Spain and her far colonies.
These are the records of their government
From days when they were conquered, one by one,
Until those other, bitter days when, one by one,
In revolution they wrote "Finis" at the close
Of these colonial records.
These are the Archives of the Indies!

PATRONATO. DESCUBRIMIENTOS, DESCRIPCIONES . . .

Here are the records of discovery . . .
Out of the waters rise two continents and countless isles,
Taking slow shape through tales of strange adventurings.
Here gleam the phantom walls of Cibola,
And here, the Gilded Man who never was.
Yonder flows on without restraint Juan Ponce's spring of youth.
Here fancy finds a northwest passage through
To mines, spice isles, and monstrous mysteries.
These are the Archives of the enchanted lands
That lay beyond the Ocean Sea of prose reality.

FLOTAS Y ARMADAS

Fleets and Armadas . . .
Here—within these packs of yellowed papers,
Written neat, or scrawled "Off Cape Saint Vincent" as she rolled
On surges that have broken since upon the shores of bleak eternity,
Or done in the trim numerals of a cipher used—
Here are confined in this small space
The winds that swept the Spanish main, the broad South Sea—
The winds that blew from Cadiz to the Philippines
Through four long centuries!
Here never set the suns that shone,
The moons that shimmered white

Among the islets of the Caribbes.
Here howls the fierce typhoon—
The hurricane roars hoarse through chartless channels,
Thundering south, from Jacan to the Name of God,
A-shriek amid the cordage of lost galleons, ballasted with gold
And emeralds, pearls and dyewood from
Peru and Margarite and Mexico.
       "May God be pleased to bring them safe to port
          As your Majesty desires and Christendom hath need!"
Candles and prayers at vanished altars spent for goods and men
Rocked in the bottom of Old Ocean
Lo! These past four hundred years!
Here—the voice of guns!
Hawkins' and Drake's and doughty Baskerville's!
Pater's and Heyn's!
With Don Fadrique and a host
Of captains-general, admirals, and crews,
Avellaneda and that bold, fanatic, honest Astur, who
Slit Ribaut's throat in Florida: Pedro Menéndez!
How they sail yet upon this troubled sea
Of finite History!
How brave they sail!
How brave they sail through these old papers here preserved!
    These are the Archives of the Indies! These!

AUDIENCIA DE SANTO DOMINGO. FLORIDA Y LUISIANA

    Letters of Governors, Accountants, Priests,
Of Captains, Indian Chieftains, Wives!
Who reads these records through sees north to Canada—
That "Frozen Land"—and finds Marquette, canoeing south
On mighty waters of an unknown stream.
Port Royal, Charleston, Jamestown, Augustine—
Here their beginnings told.
Half hid in sand, there lies
The wreck of La Salle's ship.
Who reads, hears arrows whistle, feels the whir
Of good Toledo steel; sees Indians skulk,
Creeping at dawn to storm the palisades
Of unremembered posts on river routes and shores:
       "My Governor, send help! We are surrounded,
          Our munitions gone. Send help."—
Sweated and torn, it lay against the heart
Of a bold friar, acting courier—
A scrap of paper here, that cry

Rings down the centuries: "Send help! Send help!"
    These are the Archives of the Indies. This,
The earliest history of your Florida.

AUDIENCIA DE MEXICO, SANTA FE, ETC.

    Look South!
How pale against the dawning sixteenth century arise
The sacrificial smoke wreaths o'er those piles
Of Aztec shrines and Inca palaces!
See yonder west coast sweeping on
From Darien to the Horn,
The flames around the funeral pyre of martyr-missionaries sink
To glow of furnaces at copper mines.
Amid the jungle see those clearings spread—cane and tobacco,
Bait for pirate ships!
On plains above the coastal fringe
Horned cattle graze, and sheep.
Two continents and countless, nameless isles
In fabled seas.
That acrid smoke . . . borne from the guns, I think,
That Dewey fired . . . Sampson and Schley, at Santiago.
    These are the Archives of the Indies! These—
Ashes of empire!
Worthless! Bale on bale!
So much old paper—tied with dirty string!

Other Articles of Interest

Aiton, Arthur S. and J. Lloyd Mecham. "The Archivo General de Indias."
    IV (1921), 553–567.
    Detailed information for students in this archive.

Burrus, Ernest J., S.J., "An Introduction to Bibliographical Tools in Spanish
    Archives and Manuscript Collections Relating to Hispanic America."
    XXXV (1955), 443–483.
    Detailed description of archives in Seville, Madrid, Simancas, and other
    cities in Spain with bibliographical commentary and recommendations to
    students regarding their use.

Shepherd, William R. "A Reminiscence of Simancas." VI (1926), 9–20.
    Life in Simancas, far from supplies and creature comforts, is difficult but
    has its compensation for the historian. The local castle was converted by
    Charles V into a repository for public papers which now cover the history
    of Spain from the marriage of Ferdinand and Isabella to the career of the
    Count of Aranda.

CHAPTER THREE

VICEROYALTY OF NEW SPAIN

8. Civil Congregations of the Indians in New Spain, 1598–1606

HOWARD F. CLINE

Dr. Cline, director of the Hispanic Foundation in the Library of Congress, describes in this article the attempts made by the Spanish crown to bring together in towns the dispersed groups of Indians who had already been somewhat Christianized. About a quarter of a million Indians were resettled from 1602 through 1605, an operation which required considerable administrative skill and money, and the results of which were interpreted very differently by the viceroy and the ecclesiastics. This study, based on extensive sources, includes both facts about the project and an interpretation of what it accomplished.

One consistent strand of Hispanic imperial policy was the repeated attempt to civilize the native Indians by urbanizing them. Plans to this end were early announced and with varying results were tried from time to time throughout the colonial empire. The program of civil congregations in New Spain from 1598 to 1605 was a relatively late example of these persistent efforts to translate the ideal of urbanization into social fact.

Administratively the project differed from previous attempts in the area. Appointees of the viceroy rather than ecclesiastics or *encomenderos* were selected as the agents to perform the chore. It was an enterprise of the civil bureaucracy, and was patterned on an earlier (1569–1571) plan which had proved workable in Peru under the famed Viceroy Francisco de Toledo. He had reorganized or created native hamlets according to a standard plan. The object there, as in New Spain a generation later, was to reduce to town life the dispersed groups of Indians who had already been Christianized to some extent. For their more effective indoctrination and administration they were resettled into pre-planned and sizable urban communities.

Even from relatively early times in New Spain schemes to regroup native families had been in progress, primarily in the hands of the mendicant orders. As their influence and prestige waned, responsibility for extension of their activities passed into civil hands, and from 1592 to about 1595 civil authorities made a somewhat feeble pilot effort. It was abandoned under ecclesiastical pressure. The vigorous prosecution of a revived re-settlement program launched by Gaspar de Zúñiga y Acebedo (a viceroy more commonly known by his title of Conde de Monterrey), and termi-nated by his successor, the Marqués de Montesclaros, is the enterprise dis-cussed below. Its broadest chronological brackets are 1595 to 1606.

In 1934 a pioneer study by Lesley B. Simpson exposed for the first time many features of these civil congregations. The present essay is com-plementary to the information presented by Simpson. New materials have come to light which clarify some topics sketched by him, especially minor revision of chronology, and which suggest that a quantitative analysis of the congregations might fruitfully be attempted. As a preliminary step toward the prime object—to analyze the magnitude of the congregation activity—a summary of the congregation enterprise as a whole is sketched.

Chronology of the Civil Congregations, 1598-1606

As an episode, the congregations under Monterrey and Montesclaros had a number of rather clearly defined phases. The first of these was a survey phase which ran from 1598 through 1599. This was followed by an interlude of debate and planning that ended around 1602 or 1603. From 1603 through 1605 came an operational phase, when Indians were actually moved from one area to another. For a short time thereafter formal at-tempts were made to keep Indians in their newly created villages, but by 1607 legislation permitted them to return to their old sites by special vice-regal permission. The timing of these separate activities is of particular significance here, since the quantitative estimates of how many Indians were involved rest in part on firm establishment of elapsed time and costs con-nected with it.

The surveys which preceded actual congregation were a costly and extraordinary endeavor. From 1598 through 1599, the Conde de Monterrey acted on crown orders by creating special missions to view the Indian com-munities which were deemed likely candidates for resettlement and at the same time to evaluate the potential sites on which they might be placed. Simultaneously about thirty of these survey teams were sent into the field for these purposes; nearly all the missions were formed in September, 1598. The viceroy sent them into Indian areas inhabited by docile natives. A helpful map of the communities thus surveyed has been prepared by Simpson. An unusual figure, Francisco Domínguez, had prescribed the com-munities and provinces to be visited. Among his many talents, Domínguez was a cosmographer by profession, unemployed but highly recommended by the Audiencia of Mexico in May, 1594. He had been in New Spain since 1571 and had prepared special maps from time to time. Thus from the very outset the civil bureaucracy, headed by a technician, was responsible for administrative decisions, without reference to the clergy.

Each commissioner-judge who headed a survey team was provided with a staff and a set of carefully worded instructions. A notary, a constable, and a locally hired interpreter helped him carry out his duties, as defined in the instructions. Seemingly one set of regulations was primarily for public consumption; for when it became apparent in November, 1598, that all the prescriptions they set forth would delay the survey task, a number of items which demanded reports on how administrative reforms were working among native groups were omitted from the public instructions. A shorter set of articles, a gloss or clarification of the public orders, modified them at important points, especially where the former took a strong tone concerning property interests of Spaniards. The Conde de Monterrey quite obviously and properly sought to avoid lengthy lawsuits which might impair the success of the projected congregations. When ecclesiastical writers charged the commissioners with corruption and collusion with *hacendados*, they apparently took the public instructions at face value, unaware of the secret orders under which the judges operated.

Both public and private instructions stressed the close liaison that was expected between the survey judges and the ecclesiastics in charge of the Indian parishes. After the civil judge had gathered a large body of designated demographic and geographic information, and had prepared a detailed map of the area outlined in his commission, he was ordered to prepare a joint recommendation with the minister: they were to decide which native families were to be reduced to village life, how many villages would be needed, and where they should be placed. Seemingly a rather elaborate mechanism of regional boards was set up to adjudicate disputes between civil and ecclesiastical authorities, each seating the bishop of the diocese and civil officials. Contemporary church sources are contradictory as to whether decisions consistently favored one or the other group's recommendations. Indians themselves had a voice in the matter, and there is considerable and indisputable evidence that where their petitions did not contravene the basic decision to congregate them somewhere, their suggestions as to sites were heeded.

The Conde de Monterrey had hoped that surveys would have been completed by spring months of 1599, in order that transfers of population could be made at the least inconvenient part of the rural agricultural cycle. The task of surveying was in itself an enormous one, and lagged into the autumn season of 1599. So far as can be judged by the several reports of the commissioner-judges, most of them performed their duties conscientiously. Inevitably their recommendations brought forth protests from all sides, from vested interests, from the clergy, and from the Indians themselves. From 1599 through the whole congregation program, a part of the time was devoted to ironing out specific petitions in concrete cases in which one or another of these parties claimed that redress or change was in order.

More important in many ways was debate which followed the survey operation. Rather than centering on details of execution, it focused on the policy itself. The issue was whether congregations should be undertaken at all, whether their social cost might not be too high. Repercussions from the unsuccessful venture of 1592 were still resounding. Opinion among the clergy was not unanimous either in favor or in opposition. The content and duration of the controversies are not well documented. From a polemic letter to the king sent by the provincial of Dominicans in Oaxaca it seems apparent that resolution of the question of whether or not to proceed with civil congregations was still in the balance as late as April, 1601. With clerical opposition split, and on the advice of a learned junta, crown authorities decided to carry on the program of wholesale transfers. Preparations for it had been going on while controversy was in process.

As an executive agency to handle many of the details, a Sala de Congregaciones came into being. Its origins are somewhat obscure, but its functions were to supervise, direct, and coördinate the field operations, in the name of the viceroy. Its formal records begin with the words "Books of congregations commence on 12 September 1603" and the first entry in the one surviving volume of its activities appears under the same date. However, subsequent entries imply that earlier than September, 1603, some agency had been toiling away to meet and solve practical field problems. Possibly, and even probably, the General Indian Court had handled materials up to the definitive establishment of the Sala. The Conde de Monterrey and his predecessor had been tinkering and rearranging the business handled by the court. During the period of congregations, from at least April, 1603, (evidenced by a *post hoc* entry in the Sala's record), to early spring of 1605, the Sala was an important organ, and it continued in existence for some time after the major task of congregating the selected villages was completed.

The heaviest body of entries appears between 12 September 1603 to 30 December 1604. Fourteen entries are scattered over a long period to 9 June 1625, the final date. For the most part entries of 1603–1604, perhaps five hundred in all, reflect careful but bureaucratic decisions on a wide range of routine problems. On important matters seemingly the members of the Sala referred the case for final word directly to the Council of the Indies, but most often it issued the appropriate orders itself in the viceroy's name.

Thus for a period of about three years, from April, 1603, to April, 1605, teams of civil officials were engaged in moving Indians from their old sites to new ones. The new villages were usually those recommended by the original surveys, or when difficulties appeared, others designated by the Sala after a second investigation. This operational phase went on without interruption despite the fact that there was a change in viceroys.

Under normal practice, the Conde de Monterrey was scheduled to leave his office in the fall of 1602. In order that the congregations might be completed under him, his term was extended for a seventh year, but as we have seen, the undertaking was just about swinging into high gear by the close of his time extension. His successor, the Marqués de Montesclaros, arrived in New Spain in September, 1603, and apparently was installed in office by November. Monterrey was promoted to the Viceroyalty of Peru, but died in 1606, shortly after his appeal of a *residencia* sentence was favored at the king's court. The *residencia* findings were that he had squandered 200,000 pesos of the royal funds on the congregation surveys, and he was fined that amount. This sentence was reversed in Spain, and the fine cancelled. On his death in 1606, the vacancy in Peru was filled by the Marqués de Montesclaros, promoted from Mexico after a three-year tour of duty as viceroy. In his case, as in that of the Conde de Monterrey, Mexican Indians mildly astonished critics of the viceroys and their congregation program by almost unprecedented demonstrations of affection for the retiring officials.

Traditionally the congregations are linked to the name of the Conde de Monterrey, for it was he who initiated and planned the effort. But it is also important to note that the bulk of the actual execution fell within the term of office of Montesclaros, from 1603 through 1605. There was continuity of policy until a third figure, Luis de Velasco II, reappeared to take office as viceroy for the second time. In his previous term, 1590–1595, the civil congregations which he had launched were unsuccessful and the program was terminated. The same thing happened shortly after he assumed responsibility as successor to the Marqués de Montesclaros in July, 1607. By special viceregal permission Indians in congregations were permitted to return to their original homesites; one of these permissive cedulas is dated 5 December 1607, and possibly earlier ones were issued.

Within a very short time many of the newly created congregations disappeared, once legal sanction could be obtained and the policy of apprehending fugitives was reversed. Reports transmitted in answer to a long questionnaire of 1609 dramatically reveal how quickly traces of congregation efforts could be erased from among a group of related Zapotec villages in southern Oaxaca. The permissive legislation under Velasco II ushered in a long epilogue to the civil congregations program of 1603–1605. During it native villages responded in various ways to the release of pressures.

The epilogue to the congregations tends to form a topic in itself. Not all of the congregations disintegrated completely; instead, some took root. In other cases there was at first a rapid movement away from them but then a re-integration of the group at or near the congregation site, though without all the formal apparatus of urban living which the authorities had hoped to impose on them. San Pedro Yolox in the mountain Chinantec region of Oaxaca illustrates one kind of adjustment. Without difficulty a number of tiny hamlets were congregated into one town in 1603. Before the close of the seventeenth century, the one nucleus had divided into two and the modern pattern had emerged, relatively unchanged to the present.

At best congregations could not hope to freeze the human landscape into a static mold, and they did not. They did, however, change and rearrange the sixteenth-century map of the realm. At a single stroke, and within a few months, the policy erased hundreds of minor settlements; their names often are never again seen despite the fact that in ancient or early colonial history the settlements were of considerable importance. In some cases the new congregation was given the name of an older community; this confusion of sites is an annoyance to modern investigators.

Standing above these considerations as a salient consequence of congregations is a humanistic one. A considerable portion of the native population of early seventeenth-century New Spain had their lives drastically reoriented, and in some instances went through the almost equally disturbing experience of trying to re-create or revive an old pattern after it no longer existed. Some died in the process of congregation, or its allied consequences. How many Indians were affected? The remaining pages attempt to provide an answer.

A Quantitative Approach: Methods and Procedures

To date no critical examination of the quantitative aspects of the congregation policy has been attempted, chiefly for the reason that sources of information which might yield meaningful results are more than scanty; they are almost non-existent. Simpson remarked in 1934 that it would be interesting to know "how far the plan of the Count of Monterrey was carried out, but unfortunately the records of the great congregation are preserved only in scattered fragments." From them no tabulations can be made directly, or even sufficient tabulations which by extrapolation would provide defensible figures to answer some of the questions which arise. Such queries can be infinitely extended, but perhaps the major ones are, first, how many Indians were involved in the transfers and how great a proportion of the total native populations did they represent? Secondly, how many new villages were created, and how many old ones disappeared? Thirdly, how great was mortality among the natives transferred from their old habitats to the new villages?

From available materials, treated below, the first question can be answered in rather satisfactory manner. In much less complete manner, only part of the second can be postulated; an idea of the number of congregations undertaken emerges, but the methods employed can give no hint of the number of old places which were uprooted. Unfortunately, the statistical technique similarly fails to present any clear picture of the number of deaths consequent on congregations.

Since the sources are inadequate on which to build a direct approach toward the possible answers, a brief explanation of the indirect method seems essential. It is based on cost accounting. If we know how much the outlay for the congregation project was, and what it cost to congregate one unit—a tribute-paying native and his family—the quotient of dividing the former by the latter will, within statistical limits, be the number of tributaries congregated. By comparing this number with the total native population, the resultant percentage helps historical understanding by placing the operation in relative terms.

For our second question, if we can find out about how many tributaries were located in the average-sized congregation site, by dividing the number of tributaries congregated by this figure, a quotient will represent very roughly the number of congregations needed and accomplished. This figure can be refined even further by noting the relative distribution of a sample group of congregations whose size is determined by the documentary materials; by proportioning the total number of tributaries congregated according to percentages in the known sample communities, a probable array of some value is the result. By performing the operations just outlined come replies to our two main queries: How many Indians transferred? How many settlements created?

From the outset it should be perfectly clear that a high degree of precision is impossible. Neither the sources nor the procedures will support more than approximations, rounded-off administrative figures accurate to not more than two or three significant figures. These, however, are definite enough to indicate the limits within which the ultimate truth is likely to be found and on which tentative historical conclusions can rest. The quantitative conclusions appear in Tables 2 and 3, followed by a brief discussion of their meaning.

Establishment of the Quantitative Elements

To arrive at measurable results, a number of items must first be known. The following paragraphs establish, as far as possible, the cost of the congregations, the cost of congregating one tributary, the average size of a congregated village, and the various sizes of such communities. These are all unknown at the outset, but another necessary quantity, the total number of natives in New Spain, has received previous scholarly attention. From this base we can move toward fixing the elements from which our ultimate conclusions emerge.

Very recently, in 1948, Sherburne F. Cook and Lesley B. Simpson published a study of Mexican Indian population of the sixteenth century, latest of somewhat similar demographic inquiries. For 1597 they conclude that the total native group was approximately 2.5 millions of individuals, and that ten years later this figure had dropped to 2.0 millions. A qualified contemporary, Rodrigo de Vivero y Velasco, in writing an economic treatise corroborated the half million population loss in a decade, a 20 per cent decrease. In their investigations Cook and Simpson discovered that rather than five persons representing a tributary group, four was nearer the truth, so that in 1597 a population of 2.5 millions represented about 600,000 tributaries. Although this figure is somewhat higher than the 400,000 which *encomenderos* of that date believed was plausible, it will be used below to derive our first approximations.

The figure of 600,000 tributaries is fundamental to calculation of the gross cost of the congregation phase. The congregations were financed from funds provided by part of a special levy first placed on Indian tributaries under Viceroy Velasco II, a forced contribution of four *reales*. The Conde de Monterrey was authorized to draw funds from various sources to carry on congregations, but apparently found only the new Indian tax available. Under him and the Marqués de Montesclaros each salary voucher recorded in the *libro de congregaciones* bears the notation that it was approved and paid "from the *real* of the four of the new *servicio* that is applied and ordered placed apart for the expenses of the general reduction." From this it may readily be seen that funds for the congregations amounted to one *real* per tributary for the time the program continued. For the time being we must assume that no great accumulation of funds was available after the expensive surveys had been paid for.

It is not a difficult matter to convert into pesos of eight *reales* the amounts annually contributed by 600,000 tributaries toward the fund for their congregation. Such annual income amounted to about 75,000 pesos. Operations, as sketched earlier, lasted about thirty months, but to err on the conservative side, if the amounts appropriated over three years are taken as a base for further calculations, the aggregate total will be liberal. Over the period from April, 1602, through April, 1605, such a gross amount is a maximum of 225,000 pesos, the cost of congregating an unknown number of Indians. Thus our first new element is established.

Examination of historical records also places at our disposal the next needed item, cost of congregating one tributary. From the congregation log of San Pedro Yolox it appears that Alonso de Quiroz and his staff handled 101 tributaries and congregated them in forty-four days; the cost in direct wages was 396 pesos. Another log, for a different area with a different set of circumstances during a period some months later reveals the activities of another *juez*, Pedro de Cervantes, who congregated Tlanchinol. He employed a slightly larger staff, and they needed 270 days to relocate 657 tributaries in four congregations. The team drew ten pesos a day in wages, which mounted the total to 2,700 pesos. In the Yolox case the per tributary cost was 3.9 pesos, while at Tlanchinol it came to 4.1 pesos. Considering all the variant conditions between the two places and efforts, this striking likeness seems more than coincidence. For the present we must assume that the average cost of congregating one tributary was

4 pesos. This is undoubtedly a *minimum* figure; less efficient and smooth-running congregations probably cost more. But until more than the two congregation logs known to investigators are uncovered the four-peso figure must be used.

Less crucial in many ways to the historical conclusions and judgments about congregations, but included as a main focus of inquiry, is the average size of the villages created under the program. Again our data are incomplete, but a series of twenty-one villages, each of whose size is known, has a mean value of 338, plus or minus 145 tributaries. A few congregations were very small, like Yolox with 101; the largest for which information is at hand was Xuchitepec, with 836 families.

In this respect the mean or average size of communities is a somewhat unsatisfactory implement of analysis. It does indicate that in practice the new villages generally fell below the optimum size of five hundred tributaries originally envisaged by the Conde de Monterrey. Table 1 presents the distribution of the twenty-one known cases; the exceptional nature of Xuchitepec has been deemed sufficient reason for its deliberate omission from the first percentage column; omission of extremes is standard practice,

TABLE 1. *Settlement Sizes of Some Known Congregations, 1603–1605*

TRIBUTARIES IN UNIT COMMUNITY	VILLAGES		TRIBUTARIES INCLUDED (ACTUAL)	
	N	PER CENT	N	PER CENT
800 (751-850)	1		836	12
700 (651-750)	0			
600 (551-650)	1	5	608	8
500 (451-550)	3	15	1,522	22
400 (351-450)	4	20	1,613	23
300 (251-350)	4	20	1,227	17
200 (151-250)	4	20	796	11
100 (51-150)	4	20	501	7
0 (0- 50)	0			
TOTALS	21	100	7,103	100

ACTUAL ARITHMETICAL MEAN: 338
STANDARD DEVIATION: 145

here doubly justified by the historical data on this unusual congregation. Further research could well shade these figures in detail.

Quantitative Results and Their Validity

The items of information necessary to perform the operations proposed above have been sufficiently established to permit their manipulation. By simple arithmetic the first crude approximations in answer to the questions, How many Indians? How many congregations? can be extracted. With some idea of the magnitude of these, the results can be adjusted and corrected slightly to serve as base for some historical conclusions.

Among the first approximate answers is that the number of Indian tributaries transferred must be in the neighborhood of 56,200. The number is obtained by dividing the total cost of congregations, 225,000 pesos, by the average expense of congregating one tributary, four pesos. Multiplied by four, the number of tributaries reveals about how many individual Indians were re-located; the total, 225,000, is less than a quarter of a million. Taking the population figures for the whole native group as a basis for comparison, it would appear that around 9 per cent of the Indians were directly affected by the congregation program. Subject to the modifications suggested below, these results answer the first question: How many Indians?

From the data set forth, it would seem that the number of communities created or enlarged should lie somewhere near 166. If all congregations were "average-size" (338 families) this would be true, but their variance in size shows that there may have been as few as 115, or perhaps as many as 290. On the working hypothesis that the congregated Indians were distributed according to the sample group of Table 1, then the total number of congregations was about 177. The number of each of various sizes, as well as the information just outlined, can be recapitulated in tabular form (see Table 2 opposite).

In such form, the inductions above are illuminating but imply a degree of precision which the basic materials and method do not wholly justify. The dogmatic assertions which the figures represent necessarily must be liberalized so that they conform more closely to the fact that numerous minor doubts and assumptions entered into their formation. Statistically speaking, we can really only indicate the probable upper and lower limits of knowledge and signalize the mean or average as the most likely point; this should bear fairly intimate resemblance to data in Table 2 but is not necessarily exactly congruent. The final, corrected information will be tabulated as Table 3, the final quantitative conclusions. A discussion of the corrective considerations follows.

Since the cost of congregations forms the nub of the technique, it is examined first. For preliminary purposes we assumed that the *real* per tributary that formed the reserve pool out of which congregations were financed was built up and used from 1602 through 1605. An upper limit

TABLE 2. *Recapitulation of Uncorrected Quantitative Results*

Costs (in pesos of 8 *reales*)

Survey phase, 1598-1599 200,000

Congregation, 1602-1605 225,000

Population Affected

Tributaries congregated 56,200

Individuals congregated 225,000

Proportion of total natives of area 9.4%

Communities Created or Enlarged (Theoretical statistical pattern)

Total communities created 177

Distribution by size:

TRIBUTARIES PER VILLAGE	VILLAGES OF THIS SIZE
551 to 850	15
451 to 550	25
351 to 450	34
251 to 350	32
151 to 250	32
51 to 150	39

to the number of families congregated may be obtained if a slightly different approach is employed. For this purpose let us suppose that throughout the decade of congregation activity, 1595 through 1605, this contribution was accumulated and expended, ten years rather than three.

Had such a situation occurred, then our base is shifted slightly. With an average tributary of population of 500,000 during the period, annual revenue would amount to 62,500 pesos and the ten year accumulation would thus be 625,000 pesos. Less the expenditures for surveys, 200,000 pesos, the remainder, 425,000 pesos, is applicable to congregations. Divided by unit cost of congregating one tributary, the newly obtained result would suggest that as many as 106,000 families were congregated; for statistical purposes this rounds off to 100,000. This seems too high.

The more likely situation, however, is that any accumulation was exhausted by the Conde de Monterrey in surveys, else there would have been considerably less outcry at the time of his *residencia*: The records suggest that for surveys he did not use funds from the special Indian tax, but drew on other revenues authorized by the crown and that to quiet the criticism of such procedure after 1600 he was permitted to allocate part of the Indian tax. For purposes of calculation, then, let us assume this more plausible situation, that funds were accumulated from

1600. Still keeping 500,000 as the average tributary figure, five years of contributions (one *real* of which went to congregations) would amount to 312,500 pesos, permitting the relocation of about 80,000 tributaries. That seems an appropriate and defensible maximum figure, our upper limit.

At the other extreme, to get the least possible, there are various ways to view the data. One is to take at the face value the *encomenderos'* assertion of 1597 that only 400,000 tributaries existed in New Spain, and to assume that a 20 per cent drop to 1607 would provide an average population for the congregation years of 360,000. From the *real* appropriated for the reduction program, annual revenue would amount to 45,000 pesos. Over the thirty months of actual congregations, the funds would have been limited to about 100,000 pesos, sufficient for congregating 25,000 families at the going rates. This seems too low.

Bound by the same considerations sketched in the preceding paragraph, if the monies were accumulated from 1600, a total fund of around 200,000 pesos would have been available. At this point let us interject a new factor by assuming that rather than costing four pesos per tributary to congregate a group the actual figure may turn out to be nearer five pesos, wholly possible in view of some of the difficulties encountered in certain localities, at Nejapa, for instance. Bringing all these into a synthesis, the most probable minimum number of tributaries congregated would be about 40,000. This is the lower limit.

Since the number of tributaries congregated control the derivative data of percentages and distribution of community sizes there is no need to complicate matters further by discussion of their variance. What has been done is to suggest as an upper limit of the number of congregated tributaries at 80,000, and a lower limit at 40,000. Expressed mathematically that is equivalent to saying $60,000 \pm 20,000$, or that there is a margin of possible error in the calculation of 33 per cent.

To make matters slightly more coherent, Table 3 arrays the several alternative solutions to the original questions, How many Indians? How many congregations? in the nearest to final form that state of knowledge now permits. For purposes of deriving percentages the average total native population has been called 500,000.

Conclusions and Discussion

Little remains to be said beyond what Table 3 has revealed. If there is any validity to the approaches and technique employed, then it seems apparent that, at best, less than half a million and nearer a quarter million Indians were resettled from 1602 through 1605. This represents a rather small fraction of the known native families. The startlingly small scale of the congregation program perhaps accounts for the absence of much concern over it by all but a handful of contemporaries.

TABLE 3. *Summary of Quantitative Data for Congregations, 1602-1605*

	MINIMUM	MAXIMUM	MOST PROBABLE
Population Congregated			
Tributaries	40,000	80,000	60,000
Individuals	160,000	320,000	240,000
Proportion of total			
Indian population	8.0%	16.0%	12.0%
Congregations Created			
Total communities	125	249	187

Distributed by size (statistical pattern based on sample in Table 1)

		VILLAGES OF THIS SIZE	
551 to 850 tributaries	11	23	17
451 " 550 "	18	35	26
351 " 450 "	23	46	35
251 " 350 "	23	45	34
151 " 250 "	22	44	33
51 " 150 "	28	56	42

Perhaps the negative conclusions are most significant. The mortality attributed to congregations, a million people more or less, seems unquestionably too high. There is no way at present of arriving at a more correct figure. A second, and rather minor, negative conclusion is that the 3,744 *congregaciones* listed in the 1940 Mexican census are not the direct product of the congregation program of the Count of Monterrey and the Marqués de Montesclaros; they may have arisen either in the period tagged the "epilogue" above (after 1607), but more likely refer to a change of meaning in the word, as Whetten suggests.

The findings here do not make it possible to say whether the critics of the congregation program were correct or incorrect, but at least the figures give some measure by which to weigh the accusations. Subjectively we are about where we were before: writers of the religious orders perhaps justly stressed the bad effects, suffering, and fatalities which civil congregation entailed. Juan Solórzano, in a less parochial view, emphasized the social and cultural gains to the realm as a whole and to the surviving Indians. But in either case the evils or benefits affected a relatively reduced number of families.

Apart from minor rectifications of chronology, the investigation of the congregations program perhaps has added one new dimension to previous discussions by suggesting a re-assessment of the Conde de Monterrey. On the one hand he emerges as an administrator who moved toward his objective despite, rather than in ignorance of, the obstacles to resettlement. He is found writing about the criticism which will arise, and from what quarters; to the crown he presented the alternative of allowing a program of monastery expansion or congregation, a cheaper means to the same end, and politically more compatible with royal policies at the end of the sixteenth century. Apparently from the *juntas* he called most of the facts were at his disposal. Among them may well have been the situation this quantitative investigation has suggested: that, administratively considered, a minor fraction of the natives were involved, dwelling mostly outside the main lines of economic and social interest. It is of some interest to note that a charge voiced by his critics supports his skill as an executive; the friars were disturbed that the civil bureaucracy performed their task in exact accordance with instructions. Too strict obedience to orders is not a common indictment of the seventeenth-century viceregal establishment.

Although it seems evident that the congregation program contributed its bit toward the decline of population between 1597 and 1607, that falling away by as much as a fifth calls for further, separate, exploration. One thing is evident. A number of important social institutions were changing and crystallizing. Among them might be listed the altered labor relations, and shifting land-tenure practices. Rise of the *gañanes* to importance as a class of rural labor was paralleled by initiation of the *composición* device to quiet land controversies and to stabilize the hacienda system. Although gradually the labor situation is emerging into clearer focus, studies of land tenure are lacking or wholly inadequate; proper description of even one functioning hacienda through the colonial period or even for a part of it has not appeared to date. From chroniclers and from other sources it seems probable that the great cycles of hacienda formation in the seventeenth century followed rather than preceded the congregation program, with recurring waves of *composiciones* after 1638.

Examination of these and similar seventeenth-century topics should cast further light on what happened to congregated villages during their "epilogue." Fortunately, the neglected seventeenth century is gaining some adherents as a field of scholarly interest. Congregations, 1595 to 1605, stand squarely at the transitional point. They tended to sum up the past and forecast the future, as in New Spain proper they apparently closed the era of large-scale attempts at Indian resettlements, an activity thereafter relegated to the remote frontier margins.

9. Grain Legislation in Colonial Mexico, 1575–1585

RAYMOND L. LEE

This detailed account of a period of economic crisis is a good example of what might be described as a "mini-study," for its scope is limited to the decade when Mexican viceroys attempted by legislation to overcome the recurring shortages of the grain supply which had led to much suffering by the people of their jurisdiction. This viceregal campaign against hunger was particularly significant because the fundamental measures drafted continued to regulate the grain supply of the viceroyalty for the rest of the colonial period and set a well-defined pattern of state control. Professor Lee was on the faculty of Stephens College when he wrote this article.

One basic economic problem in sixteenth-century New Spain was that of securing an adequate supply of food for the colony. Widespread deficiencies in the grain supply were particularly common, occasioned by underproduction, unfavorable weather, hoarding, labor shortages, maldistribution, or by a combination of these factors. In periods of acute shortage the lack of grain became a threat to the entire colonial economy.

Such a period of crisis existed in the decade from 1575 to 1585, and during these ten years a comprehensive effort was made to solve the grain-supply problem by means of legislation. Under pressure of necessity, laws were enacted that dealt with both the contemporary emergency and causes of the recurring shortages. Fundamental measures were drafted that regulated the grain supply of the viceroyalty throughout the colonial period, and a well-defined pattern of state control emerged. Drastic price-control laws were issued; the labor supply of farmers was regulated; compulsory production quotas were fixed; tribute grain of the *encomenderos* was appropriated by the state; and, finally, an *alhóndiga* and *pósito* were established as institutions for the sale and storage of grain and flour.

The immediate cause of these legislative measures was a great plague and famine that swept over New Spain in the years following 1575. Although pestilence was commonplace during the first century of Spanish rule in colonial Mexico, the epidemic that struck during the last years of

From Volume XXVII (1947), pages 647–660.

the administration of Viceroy Martín Enríquez de Almanza (1568-1580) appears to have been particularly virulent. Zacatecas first reported the new plague in 1575, and during the hot, dry summer of 1576 it gained a momentum that carried it to all parts of the viceroyalty. The pestilence was confined primarily to the Indian population, entire towns being stricken with the violent headaches, fevers, and nosebleed that were characteristic of the epidemic. So universal was the scourge, according to one eyewitness account, that many died of hunger because of lack of attention, an entire family sometimes expired without receiving aid, and nursing babies were often found clinging to their dead mothers—the sole survivors of a family group.

Mexico City was especially devastated by the pestilence. As the epidemic continued, the orderly burial of victims in individual graves broke down, and great ditches were opened in which the dead were interred by the thousands. Temporary hospitals were erected after the regular institutions had been filled to overflowing, and *barrios* of the capital were divided between the different religious groups, so that no one might suffer from lack of attention. Although the pestilence had moderated at the capital by December of 1576, it continued in full force in the surrounding area and became more destructive in the bishoprics of Michoacán and Nueva Galicia. Throughout the next year the plague ranged over the face of Mexico, and only in the fall months did it spend itself, except for isolated sections of the country where it continued until 1582.

While the full extent of the pestilence cannot be assessed on the basis of the incomplete statistics that exist, it is nevertheless apparent that the life of the viceroyalty was seriously disrupted in every quarter. In a century noted for its terrible plagues the pestilence of 1575-1577 is, by common consent, acknowledged to have been the worst experienced in Mexico. The chronicler Torquemada asserted that a survey conducted by Enríquez disclosed that over two million of the natives had died, and, although this figure is undoubtedly much too high, the early historians are in general agreement concerning the relative intensity of the plague, which they rated as being more than twice as deadly as the serious epidemic of 1545. In February of 1577 the Dominican friars of the capital wrote that, with the pestilence still continuing, 600,000 of the natives had perished; Archbishop Pedro Mova de Contreras stated flatly in 1583 that more than half of the Indians in New Spain had died of the plague; in a letter of the same year the king mentioned a report that two-thirds of the natives had died.

If all statistics are suspect, it is nevertheless apparent that the labor force of the colony was seriously reduced. This fact was of continuing importance, since a permanent deficit in the labor supply was created that proved to be a retarding factor in the later economic development of New Spain. Those who returned to the colony after an absence found it difficult to believe their eyes. Formerly populous towns were now deserted, and fertile fields were abandoned. In his instructions to his successor, Lorenzo Suárez de Mendoza, Conde de Coruña, Viceroy Enríquez declared that workers for the essential industries had been provided only with great difficulty after the plague. Thoroughly alarmed by the disaster, the cabildo of Mexico City (which had formerly been an ardent advocate of forced labor) filed an appeal with the audiencia, viceroy, Council of the Indies, and the king, suggesting that the Indians be relieved of all forced labor except that on the cattle ranches and farms.

This concern of the cabildo was evoked by an immediate problem, for closely behind the plague stalked its familiar accomplice, famine. The heavy rains of 1577 and the shortage of labor in the agricultural districts combined to cause a crop failure in that year, and by 1578 the audiencia declared that the surviving Indians were eating the roots of trees and the herbs of the fields. Spaniards also suffered from the lack of provisions; the teamsters engaged in the Veracruz trade protested that there was no grain for their horses, mules, and oxen; wealthy traders attempted to reap a profit from the famine by cornering the short supply of grain. To combat this new threat the viceroy, audiencia, and Mexico City cabildo united their efforts.

The measures which they adopted were largely determined by conditions peculiar to Mexico. By 1575 the European grain crops of wheat, barley, rye, and oats had become firmly established in the colony. Wheat had succeeded particularly well in New Spain, and a great region about Puebla was devoted to its production. Between seventy and eighty thousand *fanegas* were annually harvested in the valley of San Pablo, while an additional ten thousand *fanegas* were produced in the adjacent area. The nearby valley of Atlixco yielded 80,000 *fanegas*, and Ozumba, seven leagues west of Puebla, was also an important producing center. Surrounding the capital were the wheat fields of Escapuçalco (modern Azcapotzalco), Tacuba, Tacubaya, Tepotzotlán, and Chalco. In those regions where irrigation was feasible two crops were raised each year, the first being sown early in the year and raised with the benefits of the spring rains, while the second was sown in the summer and irrigated. Maize was more universally distributed, the great bulk of the crop being grown on small native plots of land for which no records have survived. Royal tribute maize alone amounted to nearly 38,000 *fanegas* in 1571, while in the region of Toluca 150,000 *fanegas* were grown annually. The northern mining area, which was completely dependent on outside supplies, was provisioned from the Nombre de Dios region. By 1575, twenty thousand *fanegas* of both wheat and maize were grown here.

Despite this production there was a constant danger of shortages. The concentration of a large portion of the population in a few metropolitan areas, the lack of food in the mining towns, and the relative ease with which the supply of any grain could be cornered were all factors that made more difficult the task of distribution, price control, and stimulation of production which the authorities now assumed.

Early efforts of the administration to combat the grain shortage tended to follow the traditional methods adopted in case of famine. Price regulation of foodstuffs in Mexico had a history of fifty years behind it by the time of the 1576-1577 crisis, and it had been invoked in the case of grain as recently as 1573. Along these familiar lines the government at first attempted to relieve the plight of the capital. On May 6, 1577, the viceroy loaned the cabildo six thousand pesos so that it might purchase wheat at Atlixco, and on September 3 the audiencia enacted legislation requiring the Indians to make their tribute payments to their community treasuries in maize and wheat, rather than in money. Further to stimulate production each tributary Indian was required to farm a plot of land sixty feet square on which one of the two grains was grown.

When these measures failed to halt speculation and rising prices, the audiencia proceeded to enact legislation that fixed the price of maize throughout the colony. By an *auto* of June 3, 1578, the retail price of maize in the capital and Veracruz highway areas was pegged at fourteen *reales* per *fanega;* in the environs of Puebla the maximum price was fixed at twelve *reales;* and, in the remainder of the colony, the ceiling price was established at ten *reales. Corregidores* and *alcaldes mayores* were empowered to confiscate maize at these prices for distribution to the residents of their districts; sellers were forbidden to require or accept gifts from the purchasers; and tie-in sales were forbidden. This regulation became effective on June 22, but on July 12 it was amended by increasing the maximum prices in the mining towns of Zagualpa, Temascaltepec, Zultepec, and Pachuca from ten to fourteen *reales*, because of their isolation and need for supplies.

The preceding legislation was more far-reaching than any previous regulation of grain in the history of the colony, and for the moment it appeared to have solved the supply problem. These measures, combined with the good crops of 1578, forced prices down, so that by October 29 maize was selling below the ceiling prices. Unduly encouraged, the audiencia repealed its price-control law, only to discover that it had reopened the way for a return of speculation and soaring prices. A new law, hastily drafted and proclaimed on November 21, contained provisions covering the sale of wheat, maize, barley, oats, and rye. Aimed particularly at speculators, it provided that all pre-harvest contracts that had been made with farmers and *encomenderos* for the purchase of their wheat and maize were to be submitted to the *alcalde del crimen*, Hernando de Robles, for examination. Those agreements that involved quantities greater than that necessary for the provisioning of the purchaser and his household were to be invalidated. Bakers were required to furnish a statement of their daily production of bread, and excessive amounts of wheat and flour were to be taken from them. By another *auto* of the same date the earlier prohibitions and penalties against speculation in grain and flour were reënacted.

The cabildo, however, was not convinced that the foregoing regulations would solve the serious crisis that had arisen at the capital. After discussing the food situation with Viceroy Enríquez, they requested that the city be given the royal-tribute maize and wheat of the area for fourteen leagues around Mexico City at the prices secured at the royal auctions of 1575-1576. This request was granted by Enríquez on December 2, when orders were sent out to the treasury officials to deliver the royal-tribute maize of this region to the city at the base price of 1576, so that the cabildo might establish an *alhóndiga* and *pósito*. Three days later the audiencia extended its controls to include private-tribute maize. *Encomenderos* in the same fourteen-league area were required to keep records of the amount of tribute grain which they collected; the amount expended in provisioning their own households was to be recorded; the purchaser, price, and date of all maize sold was to be entered in their accounts; the conversion of tribute to goods other than maize was forbidden; all records were to be submitted to Hernando de Robles for review.

On February 7, 1579, the continued scarcity of grain caused the audiencia to take the next logical step. Two-thirds of all private-tribute grain in the fourteen-league area were confiscated for the *alhóndiga* and *pósito* at the 1576 base price. Thirteen days later the regulations were extended to an additional fourteen-league area for the provisioning of the mining towns, and a fifteen-day period was designated within which deliveries were to begin. This *auto* was resisted by the *encomenderos*, and on March 11 it was reënacted, with another fifteen-day period being allowed for compliance. A special administrator, Simón de Roca, was appointed to collect and sell this maize.

Farmers in the area surrounding Mexico City were brought into the new system of government control on December 12, 1578, when they were ordered to keep records of the wheat and maize that they produced. As a lever to force compliance, the government exercised its control over the labor supply of the colony. Each farmer was required to bring sixteen *fanegas* of wheat to the public granary at Mexico City under threat of having his Indian labor supply withheld. Indian farmers who sold maize in their homes were ordered to comply with the price ceilings that had been established; purchasers of maize in the Indian markets were to report full details to the nearest Spanish official, but the Indians were allowed to sell their maize freely at the capital, the other Spanish cities, and the mines without observing the maximum prices. In an attempt to end speculation completely further regulations were issued in late 1579. On November 10, bakers were forbidden to buy wheat or flour outside of the *alhóndiga*, and farmers were ordered to sell all of their grain in the same market.

Considering the difficulties under which the officials had labored in provisioning the capital, the *alhóndiga* was established very late in the

Mexican capital. In Spain such institutions had been founded before the discovery of America, and the city of Lima in the New World had an *alhóndiga* by 1557. Although the cabildo of Mexico City conferred with Viceroy Antonio de Mendoza about the establishment of such a market as early as 1537, it was not until the serious grain shortage of the late 1570's that this municipal institution was established at the capital of New Spain. With the approval of Viceroy Enríquez the first public market for grain was housed in a building that the city had purchased from Hernando Dávila, but in 1580 it was transferred to the old *casa de fundición* that the city had purchased from the government. On July 18, 1580, repair work on the latter building had been completed, and the city officials asked that the ordinances which they had drafted for the municipal grain market be confirmed. These ordinances, approved by Enríquez and his successor, Coruña, were confirmed by the king on March 31, 1583. They later became the basis for the section of the *Recopilación* devoted to this phase of colonial administration, and by a cedula of Charles II these statutes became the model for all New World institutions of a similar nature.

These ordinances provided that all farmers, teamsters, and others bringing grain into the city were to deliver it immediately to the *alhóndiga*. Farmers were to testify under oath that the grain was of their own crop, while teamsters were to present a statement from the justice of the town in which they had made their purchase, showing the point of departure, the purchase price, and the destination of their load. Any speculators or middlemen discovered in this manner were to be heavily fined. Maximum prices of the day in the market were to be determined by the first sale; grain held in the *alhóndiga* for twenty days was to be sold at current prices; all weapons were to be barred from the market; and the salaries of its Indian laborers were fixed by law.

The chief administrative officer of the market was a *fiel* who resided in the *alhóndiga*. He enforced the price regulations, kept the records of receipts and sales, and had general supervisory powers. To guarantee faithful execution of his duties he was bonded for four thousand *pesos de oro común*, his annual salary was fixed at 517 pesos, and he was forbidden to trade in grain. The market also had its *escribano*, appointed by the city council, who kept separate records of the receipts and sales of grain. Two *regidores* served monthly shifts in the market to hear and sentence all cases involving violation of the ordinances, but appeals from their decisions might be carried to the cabildo.

Bakers, who appear to have been among the most common violators of former regulations, were subjected to particularly stringent provisions. They were forbidden to have in their possession more than a two-day supply of flour, and they were barred from making any purchases in the market until after the prayer of the high mass. Purchases earlier in the day were reserved for residents of the city, the *alhóndiga* operating from 8 A.M. until 11 A.M. and from 2 P.M. until all transactions had been completed. The expense of operating the market was borne by the sellers. Each *fanega* of wheat and barley was taxed three *graneros de oro común* (eight and one-half *maravedís*), and an equal charge was levied on each *quintal* of flour.

During this same period the *pósito* or public granary was established as a companion institution of the *alhóndiga*. Designed to end the recurring shortages by accumulating surplus grain in years of plenty, the *pósito* was intended to supplement the benefits derived from the public market. On March 8, 1580, an ordinance consisting of twenty-nine sections was submitted by the cabildo to the viceroy, who approved it two days later. By these regulations the construction of barns and warehouses for the storage of grain in Mexico City and the Indian towns was authorized. At the beginning of each year a *regidor* and *mayor-domo* were to be appointed to administer the granary designated for wheat and flour, while two similar officials were to be appointed to supervise another warehouse which was to be established for maize.

Financial support for the *pósito* came from an annual rental of three thousand pesos which the city collected from twenty-nine stores that it owned on the *plaza menor* of the city. All purchases for the *pósito* were to be made by specially designated officials, and the administrators were to sell the contents of their granaries only after consultation with the cabildo. These administrators were also to make monthly inspection visits to their respective granaries. They were to examine the grain for any damage that it might have suffered from weevils, rats, or dampness, and they were made personally responsible for any damage that they failed to report. Separate strong boxes of three keys were established for the receipts from the *pósitos*, and these boxes were placed in the monastery of San Agustín, under the charge of its prior.

Particular provision was made for the Indians of Mexico City. Since they had provided the labor for the construction of the stores from which the city's funds for the *pósito* were derived, they were guaranteed one-quarter of all the maize distributed by the city. The Royal Hospital of the Indians was also to have its needs supplied. Moderate prices were to be enforced during years of scarcity by placing city supplies of grain on the market. In years of plenty the city purchases were intended to prevent low prices that might cause the farmers to discontinue growing grain and encourage sloth among the inhabitants. With minor revisions the foregoing ordinance was approved by the king of May 22, 1582, and it was received and amended by the cabildo on December 7, 1582.

Prior to this formal approval of the ordinance there was experimentation with the storage of grain. A silo was built on the Agustinian farm near Tlalnepantla in 1580, and 201 *fanegas* of wheat were placed in it to determine whether that grain could be stored from year to year. Although this wheat was removed, ground into flour, and sold in the *alhóndiga* less than six months later, the silo was refilled and the experiment was continued.

In this early period, however, little distinction was maintained between the public granary and the public market. Prices were high, the city lacked funds, grain was scarce, and most of the grain purchased by the city was immediately resold, without any attempt being made to build up a surplus by storage. The first administrator of maize in the *pósito* was Hernando de Rivadeneyra, an *alcalde ordinario* of the city, who held this office until 1584.

In all plans for the public granary and price control the royal-tribute maize played an important part. That in the fourteen-league area about Mexico City was regularly claimed by the cabildo, and, as the population grew, the council often asked for and received that of a twenty-league area in time of crisis. The tribute grain of the *encomenderos* was not requisitioned except in case of serious emergency, but this policy, established by Viceroy Enríquez, was also resorted to on occasion.

The extension of royal control over the tribute grain of *encomenderos* marked another step in the declining power and prestige of this group. Throughout the sixteenth century the feudal rights of the *encomenderos* were encroached on by the state, so that by 1600 they retained few of the prerogatives that they had enjoyed at the time of the conquest. The fixing of tribute payments by the state after 1536; the prohibitions on the conversion of tribute into labor in 1549 and thereafter; the complicated laws of succession that caused such grants to revert to the crown; the confiscation of their tribute grain at a price below that of the open market —all of these measures served to reduce the *encomenderos* to the status of private collectors of such taxes as the state permitted.

Despite the wise ordinances drafted for the public granary, what appears to have been a commonplace defect was present from the outset. In years of plenty the stores of the *pósito* were allowed to decline, forcing the city to build up its stocks in competition with private purchasers in years of scarcity. The connection between the granary and the royal-tribute maize created an interesting conflict. In the same years that royal income from this source would have greatly increased because of high prices, the city demanded and received this grain at low prices for its inhabitants. In reality the *pósito* and *alhóndiga* were thus susidized at royal expense.

Prices of grain in this period indicate the remarkable fluctuation that constantly threatened the domestic economy of the colony. In the early 1560's tribute maize commonly sold for two or three *reales* per *fanega*, but as a result of the *visita* of Gerónimo de Valderrama (1563-1566) the price was increased to five and six *reales* at the royal auctions. The official maximum prices for 1578, however, ranged from ten to fourteen *reales*, indicating that they had risen to much greater heights on the competitive market. In 1579 the price slumped to six *reales*, but by 1583 it had again risen to fourteen *reales*—an increase of over 200 per cent. At this point the new *pósito* entered the picture. Viceroy Coruña sold the city 13,660 *fanegas* of tribute maize from Cholula, Tlaxcala, and Huejotzingo at ten *reales* per *fanega*, with the provision that it be resold to the natives of the capital at the same price. At times these widespread price fluctuations caught the city unprepared after it had become an active trader in the market. In 1580 the cabildo bought two thousand *fanegas* of wheat at nineteen *reales* per *fanega*, only to have the price of bread pegged at four and five pounds for a *real* by the viceregal authorities. Caught in this declining market, the city ordered its wheat sold at the best possible price.

Of more value in the state's attempt to control the grain supply was the *alhóndiga*. The sale and purchase of all grain in a public market under municipal supervision gave the government an over-all control it would not have been able to achieve in any other manner. In the instructions left with his successor, Viceroy Enríquez declared that no other measure had been as effective in preventing fraud and speculation. Although the original *alhóndiga* was established at Mexico City, similar institutions were founded in the other municipalities with the passage of time. The *alhóndiga* of the capital, however, remained as the center of the Mexican system, and it played an important part in the economic life of the colony throughout the colonial period.

While the greater part of the legislation during this period was devoted to the production and sale of grain, other food was also subjected to minute regulation. The series of ordinances that were issued both illustrate the seriousness of the food crisis that gripped the capital and the all-inclusive measures that the government adopted to meet it. From 1577 to 1580 ordnances were drafted that regulated the production and sale of honey, eggs, poultry, cacao, peppers, tomatoes, and fruit. Prices were fixed, places of sale were designated, some attempts were made to stimulate production, and penalties for violations of the ordinances were established. The net result of these laws was state regulation of nearly every phase of food production and sale.

While the foregoing measures played a part in the government's food program, control of grain remained as its chief concern. At the close of this decade of famine and pestilence, several important developments stand out clearly. An acute crisis in the grain supply of New Spain had forcibly directed the government's attention to this phase of the colonial economy. During these ten years a great mass of legislation was enacted that regulated sales, stimulated production, channeled the labor supply, restricted speculators, and fixed prices. Two permanent colonial institutions for the control of grain, the *alhóndiga* and the *pósito*, were established in Mexico, and many of the later laws concerning grain were based on the legislative experience of this period. Although hunger was not permanently eliminated in the viceroyalty, the government explored many methods of control and correction, and some measure of success was achieved.

Other Articles of Interest

Carrera Stampa, Manuel. "The Evolution of Weights and Measures in New Spain." XXIX (1949), 2–24.
Units of weight and measurement in colonial Mexico, deriving from Spanish and Indian practice, were numerous and unsystematic. Cities and towns repeatedly sought to impose order in weighing and measuring, but the variety of precedents, the discrepancies of official standards, and deliberate disobedience created a chaotic confusion. No common unit underlay linear, areal, dry, liquid, monetary, or other kinds of measure. Tables supply relative or absolute values for a large number of terms.

Dusenberry, William H. "The Regulation of Meat Supply in Sixteenth-Century Mexico City." XXVIII (1948), 38–52.
Meat for Mexico City in the sixteenth century was provided by a contractor, its price being fixed by public competition. The city's cabildo opened bids near the end of each year and the successful candidate enjoyed a monopoly of the supply from Ash Wednesday until the beginning of the following year. The contractor's duties respecting costs, salaries, and inspection were specified in detail. Serious problems of sanitation arose, especially in the early period. Animals were frequently killed for hides alone, a practice that contributed to the shortage of livestock. Meat sales to Indians were limited or forbidden entirely during shortages. Many improvements appeared in the slaughtering industry toward the end of the sixteenth century.

Smith, Robert Sidney. "Sales Taxes in New Spain, 1575–1770." XXVIII (1948), 2–37.
Imperial promises to keep America free of sales taxes were abrogated for New Spain in 1575 with the imposition of the first alcabala. The tax was payable on sales and turnover of raw materials, consumer goods, chattels, and real and personal property with every change in ownership. Indians were nominally or partially exempted. The tax rate rose from two per cent in the late sixteenth century to eight per cent in the eighteenth century. Administration and collection were variously in the hands of the royal treasury, the municipalities, and the merchant guild, and were attended by numerous difficulties. Nine sales-tax farms were contracted for between 1602 and 1753, with a progressive increase in annual rent from 77,000 pesos to ca. 375,000 pesos. The visitor general José de Gálvez in 1765 was instructed to examine the alcabala with the object of raising revenue. He did introduce some controls to reduce evasion but admitted that there was no practical way to check the loss resulting from traditional waivers and reductions of rate. Gálvez arranged each case separately, renewing farm agreements in some instances and providing for direct administration in others.

10. Conquerors and Amazons in Mexico

IRVING A. LEONARD

Professor Leonard, recently retired from the University of Michigan, has been a productive "mestizo" scholar in the field of literary history because of his equal competence in literature and history. He has consistently emphasized throughout his fruitful career the importance of using literary sources, and has staunchly championed—along with such other historians as John Tate Lanning and José Torre Revello—the approach to the history of Spain in America which recognizes the basic contributions of the mother country rather than the "Black Legend" of Spanish dominion. The article reproduced below is an early but characteristic sample of his style and approach to Latin American history.

Many were the myths which haunted the minds of the Spanish conquerors and their contemporaries as they adventured in the New World so recently revealed by the epochal voyages of Columbus, but the one which perhaps most persistently possessed these heroes was the legend of the warlike Amazon women. Wherever expeditions moved among the myriad islands or in the vast reaches of the mainland the quest of these legendary viragoes was pursued. The instructions issued to the Spanish leaders and the contractual agreements between the conquistadores and their financial backers —for the conquest of the New World was largely a private enterprise, capitalistic in character—frequently included clauses requiring a search for these mythical women. Again and again the chronicles and documents of the period contain references to the alleged existence or actual discoveries of such female tribes, and similar reports continued well into the eighteenth century. Beginning with Columbus' account of his voyages and in the writings of Peter Martyr, the first of the historians of the New World, and of his successors, Oviedo and Herrera, as well as in those of first-hand chroniclers such as Pigafetta of Magellan's voyage, and particularly Carvajal, who recorded the famous odyssey of Orellana through the heart of South America, the widely advertised legend appears conspicuously. And many other explorers and adventurers of the sixteenth century and later, including Sir Walter Raleigh, have left testimony of their varying shades of conviction concerning the existence of the Amazons.

The myth of a tribe of warlike women goes back to ancient times

From Volume XXIV (1944), pages 561–579.

when the Greeks reported them in Asia Minor, giving this strange tribe the name of Amazons apparently because of their alleged practice of removing one breast to permit the freer use of the bow and arrow, their chief weapon. The story persisted throughout the Middle Ages, gaining force as such travelers as Marco Polo, Sir John Mandeville, Pedro Tafur and others publicized their journeyings into remote parts. These female warriors were also reputed to be found in Africa, their island home lying in a marsh not far from the boundaries of the inhabited world, and also on the west coast near Sierra Leone. But in all accounts the location of the Amazons is exceedingly vague. The older writers placed them anywhere between Finland and India, but with Asia Minor, however, continuing to receive the most votes. It was probably inevitable that the discovery of an unsuspected continent in the western seas should open to the credulous new and likely possibilities of locating at last these elusive females. It was Columbus himself who first aroused such hopes by asserting that a number of these Amazons hid in caves on some islands of the Caribbean from which strong winds had prevented his approach. And he was certain that still others of this race could be reached on the continental mainland by passing through cannibal country. Subsequent Spanish expeditions always seemed, somehow, just to miss discovering the realms of these strange tribes. Orellana, to be sure, was convinced that he had not only encountered some of these women, but that he had actually experienced their combative prowess. Hence, as the name of the mighty river of South America, of which he was the first European to navigate to its mouth, that of the Amazons in time replaced his own.

Although the legend was of long standing, as already indicated, its strong revival in the early sixteenth century and the universal belief in its validity among the Spanish conquerors roaming the New World suggest that some recent and particularly vivid reminder had brought the subject sharply to mind. The fantastic rumors, including those concerning the Amazons, which flooded Spain and Europe soon after the fateful voyages of Columbus, found some confirmation in the apparently sober and trustworthy *Decades* of Peter Martyr which appeared in print in 1516, and still further currency of the belief in the existence of warlike women was afforded by the Spanish translation, first published in 1521, of Sir John Mandeville's *Travels*, the very year that Cortés was achieving his spectacular conquest of the Aztec capital. Two years later there came from the press the official account of the circumnavigation of the globe by Magellan's expedition written by its chronicler and eye-witness, Pigafetta, who stated in the course of his narrative that, after touching Java

Our oldest pilot told us that there is an island called Acoloro which lies below Java Major where there are not persons but women, and that the latter become mothers by the wind. When they give birth, if the offspring is male, they kill it, but if it is female, they rear it. If men go to that island, they kill them if they are able to do so.

But it is doubtful if these historical works alone can account for the almost passionate conviction of early sixteenth-century conquistadores in the reality and the proximity of the Amazon women. Such respectable books were hardly read by the ordinary soldier if, indeed, they were known at all to him; the more literate of these adventurers were likely to be addicted to other and more popular forms of reading from which they undoubtedly derived some of their fantastic notions. Since the rise of the fictional romances of chivalry coincides with the dramatic Conquest of the New World and they reflect all too clearly the contemporary naïve acceptance of the marvellous, it is logical to seek possible sources of inspiration in this immensely popular literature which exerted so strong an influence on the thought and behavior of the time. This quest quickly brings one to the sequel of that famous work of fiction, *Amadis de Gaula*, which bears the title *Sergas de Esplandián* (1510) *(Deeds of Esplandian)* and was written by Garcirodríguez de Montalvo.

In this prolix account of the adventures of the handsome son of the great Amadis is intercalated the episode of Calafia, Queen of the Amazons, who resided with her followers on a craggy island significantly named "California." In the course of the first 122 chapters the narrative of Esplandian's exploits is carried forward to the time when the King of Persia, named Armato in the novel, invites all the pagan princes to unite with him to capture Constantinople from the Christian allies of its Emperor. The response is highly gratifying to the Persian monarch, for a mighty horde is assembled to pit its strength against the outnumbered Christians rallying about the Emperor. Conspicuous among the latter are Amadis and Esplandian. Strangest among the heathen cohorts of the Persian Armato is the tribe of Amazon women under Queen Calafia who came with their man-eating griffins from the "islands of California" to fight for the Turks. Chapters 157 to 178 are devoted largely to the intervention of the Amazons in the ensuing struggle, particularly the personal encounters of the female leaders with the Christian knights who fare badly at the hands of the so-called gentler sex. This success emboldens "Calafia, mistress of the great island of California, celebrated for its great abundance of gold and jewels," to challenge both Amadis and Esplandian to personal combat. As might be expected, the Amazon queen is overwhelmingly vanquished by Amadis' skill and Esplandian's beauty, and falls captive to these Christian heroes. Though enamored of Esplandian she philosophically acquiesces in his marriage to another and accepts Christianity, marrying a husband generously bestowed upon her by the ever considerate Esplandian. Thus the hateful Turk is deprived of a formidable ally and Constantinople is saved for Christendom.

The fact that the main story of Esplandian is resumed after this incident and, save for a brief reference at the end, Queen Calafia and the Amazons do not reappear has a certain significance. It suggests that Montalvo, the author, may have deviated from the original plan of the book and decided to capitalize on a recently renewed interest in an ancient legend. It is possible that while he was engaged in writing this tale there reached his ears an echo of Columbus' report of Amazon-like women on some islands past which he had cruised and of their alleged proximity to the "Earthly Paradise." The reawakening of this scarcely dormant myth in the guise of an item of news possibly offered the story-teller, alert to the latest sensation, a theme for an exciting episode which he embroidered elaborately in his sequel to *Amadis de Gaula*. Later, his readers doubtless believed that they found corroboration of the earlier rumors when they read the following passages in Chapter 157 of the *Sergas de Esplandián:*

> Now I wish you to learn of one of the strangest matters that has ever been found in writing or in the memory of mankind. . . . Know ye that on the right hand of the Indies there is an island called California, very close to the Earthly Paradise, and inhabited by black women without a single man among them, for they live almost in the manner of Amazons. They are robust in body with stout, passionate hearts and great strength. The island itself is the most rugged with craggy rocks in the world. Their weapons are all of gold as well as the trappings of the wild beasts which they ride after taming, for there is no other metal on the whole island. They dwelled in well formed caves. . . .

And the novelist continues with further details on the manner of living and fighting of Queen Calafia's warriors.

Some details offered in this quoted passage are worthy of note. For the first time the shifting locale of these battling viragoes is identified with the new-found lands of the Indies, though the hazy geography of the novel places Calafia's islands within reach of Constantinople and Asia Minor by sea. When Montalvo was writing, the belief was probably still held that Columbus had actually found a new route to the Asiatic mainland, the existence of the intervening continents still unsuspected. That Queen Calafia's subjects "dwelled in well formed caves" and that their island home was "on the right hand of the Indies and close to the Earthly Paradise" are further indications that the novelist may have derived inspiration from the great Discoverer's reports of his voyages. And from the meager details of the latter Montalvo perhaps fashioned his heavily embroidered episode, changing the name of her island abode from the ugly Matinino of Columbus' journal to the more glamorous and euphonious "California." As the fact of a new hemisphere, to which the designation Indies adhered, dawned upon the readers of Montalvo's popular work, the fugitive Amazons now seemed tracked to their lair. Moreover, the positive assurance that "their weapons are all of gold . . . for there is no other metal on the whole island . . ." made it certain that the physical discovery of their insular realm would bring to the lucky finder a fabulous fortune. Thus the imagination of Montalvo elaborated the "facts" that Columbus had reported and for the conquistadores the association of the New World, Amazons, and wealth became inseparable.

The phenomenal popularity of the first two romances of chivalry promptly produced a formidable crop of sequels, carrying the account through successive descendants of Amadis and Esplandian. The *Seventh Book* of this series bore the title *Lisuarte de Grecia* and is mentioned because Queen Calafia again emerges from her California isle and wanders through its pages, forming further coalitions in the vicinity of Constantinople, though now always on the side of the Christian knights. Thus, any readers who may have missed acquaintance with the Amazon queen in the *Sergas de Esplandián*, had an opportunity to meet her and receive assurance of the existence of her tribe.

At this juncture it is well to consider the dates of the various editions of these two novels which had revived the old legend in such a fascinating manner in order to appraise the possible influence of these tales on the Spanish conquerors in the New World. Present bibliographical knowledge is insufficient to establish definitely the year of the *princeps* of the earlier romances of the Amadis cycle. For *Amadis de Gaula* the 1508 edition is usually cited as the first, though it is likely that there were earlier ones. Similar uncertainty surrounds the *Sergas de Esplandián* to which the year 1510 is ascribed as the date of the first edition. This was printed by the Crombergers at Seville, a significant fact since it was from this river port that most of the conquerors embarked for their adventures in the Spanish Indies, and it was this printing house that held a monopoly of the book trade with New Spain. It is apparent, therefore, that Montalvo's novel with its episode of the Amazons was available a sufficient number of years before the spectacular conquests on the mainland for the Spanish soldiery to have read or heard about it. It is likely that various other editions appeared soon after 1510, though no data on them have yet come to light; however, there are clear indications of at least four new editions of the *Sergas de Esplandián* that were published during a spectacular five-year period of the Conquest: one in Toledo in May, 1521, one in Salamanca in 1525, one in Burgos in 1526 and another in Seville the same year. This was a fairly rapid succession of reprintings for its time—and probably there were others unrecorded—but more important is the fact that this five-year period coincides with that in which Cortés was conquering and overrunning the broad realms of Mexico; in all directions his lieutenants, as well as himself, were heading expeditions with instructions to locate the Amazons and other oddities along with gold and silver mines. And it was during this period that Cortés was reporting to his emperor, Charles V, in his famous letter-reports rumors of the existence in New Spain of tribes of warlike women.

The *Lisuarte de Grecia*, which again reminds readers of Queen Calafia and California, was evidently less popular than the earlier *Sergas de Esplandián* or, at least, fewer editions of it are known. The *princeps* appeared in 1514—also in ample time to influence the minds of the conquerors —and others probably followed, though only that of 1525, likewise printed by the Crombergers at Seville, is definitely recorded. While the references to the Amazons in numerous documents of this time and particularly the bestowing of the name "California" on the peninsula to the west of the mainland of New Spain point to the probable influence of these and other romances of chivalry, more detailed evidence is necessary before accepting this conclusion.

Most critics dealing with the chivalrous novels have commented on the tremendous hold of these fictional works on sixteenth-century readers, and occasionally one manifests a belief in some connection between these books and the deeds of the conquerors. One authority states that "the books of chivalry had their part in suggesting the heroic delirium of the Conquest" and elsewhere asserts that "it is well known that at that time the ballads of chivalry and novels of knight-errantry were on the lips and in the hands of the conquerors." Benedetto Croce avers from abundant documentation that *Amadis de Gaula* and similar novels were favorite reading of the Spanish soldiers fighting in the Italian Peninsula, which fact leaves little doubt that their companions-in-arms in contemporary America were also familiar with the same literature. As if to support this statement one of the foremost commentators of Cervantes' writings inserted an interesting footnote to the effect that twelve of Cortés lieutenants banded together like the "Twelve Peers" of chivalry, solemnly pledging themselves with the vows of knights errant "to defend the Holy Catholic Faith, to right wrongs and to aid Spaniards and friendly natives!"

But much more direct evidence of the reading of the romances of chivalry by the conquistadores is supplied by that prince of chroniclers, a soldier in the conquering ranks of Cortés army—Bernal Díaz del Castillo. In his famous *True History of the Conquest of New Spain*, a first-hand account of the Spanish campaigns though written many years after the events, which, in some passages, itself reads like a novel of chivalry, the soldier-author records the profound impression that the first glimpse of the Aztec capital in the beautiful valley of Mexico produced on the approaching Spanish troops.

. . . when *we* saw so many cities and villages built in the waters [of the lake] and other large towns on dry land, and that straight, level causeway leading into Mexico City, *we* were amazed and *we* said that it was like the enchanted things related in the book of Amadis because of the high towers, temples and buildings rising from the water and all of masonry. And some of the soldiers even asked whether the things we saw were not a dream. It is not to be wondered that I write it down in this manner, for there is so much to think of that I do not know how to describe it, seeing as we did things never heard of or witnessed before.

The mixed use of the first person pronouns in this passage is of particular note. Where the plural *we* is employed it clearly indicates that Bernal Díaz, in alluding to the comparison of the scene before the Spaniards with descriptions found in *Amadis de Gaula* and its successors, did not express himself in terms of his own reading alone, but was conveying an impression shared by his companions who were also familiar with these novels. As they pushed inland on their spectacular conquest these bold adventurers doubtless talked of Amadis and Esplandian, and as they marched along they reminded each other of incidents and scenes described in the novels they had read or listened to, eagerly projecting from their own minds into the exotic landscape about them the images evoked by their acquaintance with this literature of fantasy. And elsewhere the soldier-chronicler refers to a character in *Amadis de Gaula*, Agrajes, a name which became the synonym of a braggart in Spanish slang. These allusions to this romance of chivalry were plainly no literary affectation on the part of Bernal Díaz, whose entire narrative is characterized by its forthright and unvarnished style. Rather, they are the spontaneous and almost involuntary exclamations of one who is suddenly reminded of what he and his comrades had so often talked about. There can be little doubt then that he and many other followers of Cortés, either before embarking from Spain for the New World or after their arrival, had read more than one of the chivalrous novels then available, and it is altogether likely that copies of these fantastic tales, probably much the worse for wear, lay about the soldiers' camps and served to divert the more literate in the lulls between campaigns. In the famous chapter of *Don Quixote*, in which the luckless Sancho Panza is tossed in a blanket by the roustabouts at an inn, Cervantes offers a realistic picture of the reading of romances of chivalry in the sixteenth century by those of a social status similar to that of many of Cortés' soldiers. In the mouth of the innkeeper the great novelist puts the following passage testifying to the universal enjoyment of this form of fiction:

> I cannot understand how that can be for, in truth, to my mind there is no better reading in the world, and I have here two or three of them [novels of chivalry] with other writings that are the very life, not only of myself but of plenty more; for when it is harvest time the reapers flock here on holidays, and there is always one among them who can read and who takes up one of these books; and we gather around him, thirty or more of us, and continue listening to him with a delight that makes our grey hairs grow young again. At least I can say for myself that when I hear of what furious and terrible blows the knights deliver, I am seized with the longing to do the same, and I would like to be hearing about them night and day.

It requires little effort of the imagination to translate this picture from its rural, peasant setting to the camp of the doughty warriors of Cortés and Pizarro where "there was always some one of them who knew how to read." Surrounded by his comrades "thirty or more" and by the flickering camp-fire or in daylight this literate soldier read aloud the adventures of Amadis, Esplandian and the other ideal heroes. If the innkeeper listened with special delight to the "furious and terrible blows the knights deliver," the conquerors doubtless found their enthusiasm stirred even more by the glowing descriptions of the wealth of the fabled cities and of the mythical races inhabiting strange lands. The marvellous exploits and fantastic accounts of persons and places thus brought to the eyes and ears of the conquerors now encamped in the midst of an unknown continent could not fail to stimulate their already fevered imaginations and easily prepared their minds to accept avidly the wildest rumors of riches which were forever luring them on. Absurd notions thus generated were eagerly projected into the dim, remote regions lying ahead in this mysterious, new-found world, and anything was possible, even probable.

The conquerors readily found confirmation of their fiction-nurtured dreams through the poorly interpreted languages of the Indians who vaguely understood the questions put to them. These frequently fearful and bewildered aborigines, as a rule only too eager to be rid of the strange, white invaders and not wishing to displease them, customarily answered all inquiries in the affirmative. And some were shrewd enough to perceive that they could easily satisfy their interrogators by agreeing that whatever the latter sought, whether gold, treasure, fabled cities, or Amazons, it could be had by going only a "little beyond." To the excited Spaniards all information tending to corroborate their own thoughts and desires, was reliable; thus, with imaginations inflamed by books of chivalry and convinced that the enchanted places described in them surely existed in this newly found world, the hardened campaigners could whip up the flagging vigor of physical bodies and goad themselves on to deeds more stupendous than those of the gallant knights of fiction who offered them such fascinating models. To the quills of sedentary novelists in far off Spain, Portugal, and France the extraordinary epic of the conquests of Mexico, Peru, and other regions of the New World indeed owes no small part of its realization! But to turn back to the quest of Queen Calafia and her California Amazons.

Columbus' early references to Amazon-like natives in the Caribbean islands, later reiterated by Martyr in his *Decades*, seem, on the whole, to have excited slight interest in the Spanish settlers on Hispaniola, preoccupied in extracting gold and labor from reluctant Indians. Presently, however, curiosity began to develop regarding the shadowy mainland to the west and maritime expeditions skirted those shores. It was about this time that the *Sergas de Esplandián* and *Lisuarte de Grecia* with their episodes of Queen Calafia began to establish a hold on their readers, reinvigorating the age-old myth of the Amazons. The Governor of Cuba, Diego de Velásquez, looking for further conquests, turned his eyes westward, and organized several exploratory expeditions equipped at his own expense. The first of these took place in 1517, reconnoitering Yucatán from which it brought back reports of a large town and considerable wealth. The following year and under the same auspices Grijalva coasted the shoreline from Yucatán to Pánuco, picking up a modest sum in treasure. Juan Díaz, a clergyman, has left a report of this expedition which includes a detail of immediate interest. Writing in May, 1518, he states that "they turned back to the Island of Yucatán on the north side. We went along the coast where we found a beautiful tower on a point said to be inhabited by women who live without men. It is believed that they are a race of Amazons. Other towers were seen, seemingly in towns, but the Captain did not allow us to go ashore."

The long delay of Grijalva in returning, coupled with the impatience of the enterprising Governor of Cuba to learn the secret of the mainland, moved him to enter into an agreement with Hernando Cortés which was to result in the conquest of that vast region, though with little material advantage to Velásquez. Under date of October 23, 1518, the instructions to Cortés were drawn up. While the chief purpose of the new undertaking was ostensibly to search for the overdue expedition of Grijalva, detailed orders covering other and important aims were included. Of especial interest is the twenty-sixth item which, after cautioning Cortés to exercise great care in taking formal possession of all islands he may discover and in gathering all possible information regarding the land and people, states:

. . . and, because it is said that there are people with large, broad ears and others with faces like dogs [you are to find out about this] and also where and in what direction are the Amazons, who are nearby according to the Indians whom you are taking with you.

Here it is apparent that, only a few years after the first publication of the *Sergas de Esplandián* and *Lisuarte de Grecia*, Cortés and his financial backer, the Governor of Cuba, were definitely counting on the possibility of discovering, among other curiosities, a realm such as that of the California isle of Queen Calafia. That the Indians accompanying the expedition are cited as authority for this expectation need not be taken too seriously, for it is quite possible that the idea was merely a projection from the minds of Velásquez and Cortés resulting from recent reading or hearing which they unconsciously imposed upon the half-comprehending and over-awed Indians, who then returned it to the true authors. It could hardly be expected that two hard-headed businessmen such as the Governor and the future Conqueror would acknowledge the real origin of their belief—quite possibly a popular work of fiction—in a legal contract if, indeed, they were conscious of its source.

This *idée fixe* of the existence of a race of warlike women somewhere in the New World remained with Cortés and other conquerors all through their campaigns and subsequent explorations. Occasionally, even in legal documents there is unmistakable evidence of this fact. The earlier of the five famous dispatches of Cortés to Charles V deal mainly with a recital of the stirring events associated with capture of the Aztec capital. The stern necessities of war against a powerful and numerous foe and the quick manoeuvres to frustrate the efforts of rival Spaniards bent on supplanting him preoccupied Cortés too greatly for a methodical investigation of the secrets of the vast realm that he was subduing, and it is not until his *Fourth Letter*, dated October 15, 1524, that exploration tends to replace the swift campaign of conquest and more detailed descriptions of Mexican civilization are offered. Now, with subordinates heading expeditions in many directions to consolidate and extend his territorial gains, the old fables and legends claim greater attention. Perhaps by this time copies of the translation of Mandeville's *Travels* and of Pigafetta's report of the globe-girdling voyage begun by Magellan had reached the conqueror of Mexico and seemed to offer their testimony to the reality of a California race of Amazons described in the novels of Montalvo and others with which he was probably familiar. At any rate, it is clear in the *Fourth Letter* that Cortés was dispatching expeditions with instructions not only to search for the rumored treasure in the interior of New Spain but to solve the mysteries of its hinterland. While the diligent quest of gold and precious stones thought to exist in abundance there continued, the search for clues leading to the discovery of the fabulous kingdoms lying always a little beyond each horizon grew more intense. Chief among the latter objectives were the Amazon women, and again and again the proximity of their realm was reported. One of Cortés ablest lieutenants, Cristóbal de Olid, with twenty-five horses and about eighty foot soldiers had penetrated into the rugged region of Zacatula and Colima near the west coast of Mexico, and returned with a comparatively rich booty of pearls and an exciting report to the effect that only ten days' journey beyond where they had reached was an island rich in treasure and inhabited by women only occasionally visited by men and who disposed of the resulting male offspring with distressing dispatch. This and other reports moved the Conqueror of Mexico to comment in his *Fourth Letter* to the Emperor:

> In his [Olid's] description of these provinces there was news of a very good port on that coast, which greatly pleased me since there are so few; he likewise brought me an account of the chiefs of the province of Ceguatan who affirm that there is an island inhabited only by women without any men, and that at given times men from the mainland visit them; if they conceive, they keep the female children to which they give birth, but the males they throw away. This island is ten days journey from the province, and many went thither and saw it, and they told me also that it is very rich in pearls and gold. I shall strive to ascertain the truth and when I am able to do so, I shall make a full account to your Majesty.

Elsewhere in the same *Letter* Cortés reports that his lieutenant had seized "a woman whom all in those parts obeyed and everything quieted down because she sent to all the chiefs and commanded them to observe whatever was ordered in your Majesty's name, as she intended to do. . . ."

Now, indeed, the Spanish explorers were pushing closer to the "right hand of the Indies" where Montalvo had located the California island home of Queen Calafia's Amazons and, geographically, they were approaching the peninsula, long mistaken for an island, and destined to bear the name which the *Sergas de Esplanián* had advertised so attractively. So much importance did Cortés attach to the news brought by Olid that he not only passed it onto Charles V but he set about organizing another expedition which should push the exploration of the region beyond Colima to where the Amazon realm apparently lay. This momentous mission he entrusted to one of his kinsmen, Francisco Cortés, to whom he issued very detailed and specific instructions in writing. With twenty or twenty-five horsemen and fifty or sixty foot-soldiers, mostly bowmen and musqueteers, and two pieces of artillery he should find out the truth of the reports received "because," so ran the Conqueror's command:

... I am informed that along the coast adjacent to the towns of Colima there are numerous well populated provinces where it is believed that there is much treasure; also, that in those parts there is a district inhabited by women without men. It is said that, in the matter of reproduction, these women follow the practices of the Amazons described in the "istorias antiguas." To ascertain the truth of this and the rest related to that coast will be a great service to God, our Lord and their Majesties. . . .

Particularly significant in this passage is the clear indication of the Conqueror's interest in the Amazons and the fact that his knowledge of them was derived from his reading. It will be remembered that he was a man of considerable education, a former student of the University of Salamanca for two years. Despite his preference for action he had found time then and later for reading some of the "istorias antiguas" to which he refers in his instructions. The expression used was broad enough in his time to include the novels of chivalry as well as the allegedly more historical chronicles. The romances frequently contained the words *historia* or *crónica* in their titles and the looseness with which these terms were applied to both fictional and factual accounts produced confusion in the minds of general readers as to the nature of what they were reading; consequently, the more interesting they found a book, the more inclined they were to believe in its veracity. The sense of time as well as geography was exceedingly vague in the tales of chivalry and usually the action was placed "some time after the Passion of our Lord," hence sufficiently remote for these self-styled chronicles to be thought of as "istorias antiguas." Since the recognized histories contained scarcely less of the marvellous than the acknowledged romances, both were readily confused by the uncritical reader. Hence, in this reference of Cortés in his instructions, one may find confirmation of the assumption that the Conqueror of Mexico, like most of his literate contemporaries, was acquainted with the popular literature of the day, and in his allusion to the Amazons and their habits which both Montalvo, the novelist, and Cortés' own lieutenants reported as existing in this vicinity, it is fair to surmise that he, too, had dipped into the pages of the *Sergas de Esplandián,* one of the more fascinating "istorias antiguas."

Like most other attempts to track down the elusive Amazons, Francisco Cortés odyssey hardly measured up to the hopes of his illustrious kinsman. One incident of this expedition, however, suggests that he had encountered a situation with some points of similarity to that of Queen Calafia. Beyond Jalisco he had found an attractive district governed by a native woman during the minority of her son. The female chieftain hastened to invite the white warriors to her realm, welcoming them with ceremonial acts which included the erection of an arch bedecked with flowers and a hunting expedition by her followers who bestowed their game upon the vistors. The Spaniards were then permitted to witness some of the religious rites of the tribe at a pyramidal temple. After this function they were comfortably lodged in the queen's palace where their accommodating host thoughtfully provided women for the entertainment of the soldiers. Apparently, this feminine company did not enjoy the degree of pulchritude desired by the Spaniards and Francisco Cortés reported that he had sent these females away after due inspection and ordered his men to conduct themselves properly.

What further interest Hernando Cortés may have taken in the solution of the vexing Amazon problem is not clear, though it is likely that he did not abandon his quest at once. Soon after dispatching his *Fourth Letter* he set off on the ill-advised march to Honduras, absenting himself from Mexico City two years during which his affairs there suffered severely from the activities of his enemies. One of his most bitter foes was a certain Nuño de Guzmán, a partisan of Governor Velásquez with whom Cortés had been on bad terms since the founding of Vera Cruz in 1519. Guzmán had received jurisdiction over a broad strip of land called Pánuco northeast of Mexico City and extending indefinitely inland. Overlapping and conflicting territorial claims soon brought friction between adherents of both leaders, particularly during Cortés' long absence in Central America. Guzmán, too, had heard much concerning gold and jewels and rumors of Amazon tribes existing somewhere to the west, and he set out to penetrate the mystery. Cruel and unscrupulous by nature, he cut a swath of terror and barbarism as he swept through Michoacán and northwestward toward "the right hand of the Indies." From Omitlán, in the west, he dispatched a letter, dated July 8, 1530, reporting:

. . . The next day I made a procession with a Te deum. Thence I crossed the great river of the Trinitie, and the River full of Crocodiles, and there are many venemous Scorpions. Here was erected a Church and two Crosses. Azatlán is three days journey hence, where they prepared to give me battell. From thence ten days further I shall go to finde the Amazons, which some say dwell in the Sea, and some in an arme of the Sea, and that they are rich and accounted of the people for Goddesses, and whiter than other women. They use Bowes, Arrows and Targets; have many and great Towns; at a certain time they admit males to accompanie them, which bring up the males, and these the female issue.

From all the foregoing it is plain that a belief in the existence of Amazon women on islands somewhere along the northern mainland of the

Indies was firmly implanted in the minds of the conquerors and explorers from their first tentative skirting of Yucatán through the dramatic conquest and overrunning of the mainland. The preoccupation of these men of action with such a legend and their repeated efforts to locate these warlike women can hardly be attributed to the mere satisfaction of an intellectual curiosity regarding a strange human species. Possibly there was the unconscious drive of men, who had left their womenkind behind, to find their own psychological counterparts. A more impelling incentive for discovery, however, was the rich treasure, particularly gold, inseparably associated with these female warriors.

But what made the Spanish conquerors so certain that these Amazon women could be found in the Indies? And what convinced the Spaniards that the gold with them would be ample reward for their efforts to hunt them down? The words of Montalvo's novel come instantly to mind: "Know ye that on the right hand of the Indies" and "their weapons are all of gold and there is no other metal on the whole island." The great "South Sea" or the Pacific Ocean, extending far beyond the west coast of the mainland, doubtless surrounded these mystic isles, and the nearby peninsula, looking like an island and projecting like a finger into its blue expanse came, somehow, to bear the romantic name of California which Montalvo had designated as the locale of Queen Calafia and her colorful followers. To be sure, no documentary evidence thus far has been unearthed to establish definitely the connection between this novel of chivalry and the naming of Lower California, but by 1542, when the *Sergas de Esplandián* and *Lisuarte de Grecia* were still widely read, Juan Rodríguez Cabrillo made an historic voyage along that part of the Pacific coast of North America and in the log of his voyage he used the name *California* in referring to a portion of the coast skirted, thus indicating that the appellation was already a fixed one. Whether applied in derision or in earnest, the island realm of Montalvo's Queen Calafia seems surely to have bequeathed its name to an elongated strip of land, long mistaken for an island, lying approximately "on the right hand of the Indies"—proof positive that some conqueror or explorer who had glimpsed it was familiar with those exciting chapters of the chivalrous tale, the *Sergas de Esplandián*.

Other Articles of Interest

Bernstein, Harry. "A Provincial Library in Colonial Mexico, 1802." **XXVI** (1946), 162–183.
   A list of 394 titles in the library of José Pérez Becerra from the Archivo General de la Nación, Mexico, Ramo de Intendencia, Tomo LXVIII (1802–1806). The owner was administrator of the Guanajuato *aduana*. His collection consisting of over 900 volumes is one of the largest known.

Castanien, Donald G. "The Mexican Inquisition Censors a Private Library, 1655." XXXIV (1954), 374–392.
About 1,600 books in the library of Melchor Pérez de Soto were examined by the Mexican Inquisition and their titles recorded in 1655. Their owner, an architect arrested for sorcery and other crimes, possessed the most extensive private library known for seventeenth-century Mexico. It included fiction, poetry, classics, didactic literature, history, religious works, and works of other classifications. The corrector found eighteen that were to be withdrawn from circulation.

Leonard, Irving A. "A Frontier Library, 1799." XXIII (1943), 21–51.
A brief description and analysis of the library of Don Manuel Gayoso de Lemos, governor of Louisiana, 1797–1799, indicate the broad culture and catholic tastes of the owner. The auction record of the governor's books in 1799 shows a working library of a man of affairs—411 volumes, on military affairs, medicine, engineering, mathematics, navigation, jurisprudence, geography, travel, religion, history, philology, and belles lettres, many of which appeared in the Index. One hundred and seventy-three items are listed.

———. "On the Mexican Book Trade, 1683." XXVII (1947), 403–435.
The political and cultural nadir of Spain in the late seventeenth century was not immediately reflected in Mexico, its most favored colony in the New World. Mexico City was a great and flourishing city of some 400,000 persons. Much of its intellectual and cultural life centered upon the University, and the period is that of the poetess Sor Juana Inés de la Cruz and the scholar Carlos de Sigüenza y Góngora. The needs of a large book-buying public were met by book merchants, importers, and local printing establishments, of which probably the most prosperous was the house of the Heirs of the Widow of Bernardo Calderón. The variety of the Widow's stock is attested by an inventory of 1683, which includes religious writings, secular nonfiction, and belles lettres. The inventory refutes the assertions often made regarding the obscurantism of Spanish policy in the colonial importation of books.

———. "The Theater Season of 1791–1792 in Mexico City." XXXI (1951), 349–364.
Theater, dramatic forms, and list of plays performed.

Pasquariello, Anthony M. "The *Entremes* in Sixteenth-Century Spanish America." XXXII (1952), 44–58.
Farcical episodes (*entremeses*) were inserted in religious spectacles viewed at church altars or monastery schools in order to point moral lessons or to amuse the audience. Some performances, as that satirizing the alcabala in Mexico City in 1574, precipitated conflicts between church and state authorities. The entremeses of Fernán González concern domestic quarrels, concluding with a *loa* to the viceroy and expressing a moral. The secular farces, by which the church sought to win the people through an appeal to their festive sense, became unrestrained to the point at which the very churchmen who had encouraged them were compelled to turn against them.

11. The Birth of the Mestizo in New Spain

C. E. MARSHALL

Since World War II the complex history of mixed races in Latin America, and the profound effect of this intermixture on the nature and composition of the various societies as they have changed through the centuries since the conquest, have attracted the attention of more and more social scientists. Professor Marshall wrote the following pioneer article for the *HAHR* when he was on the faculty of the University of Utah. Using legislation and a variety of more intimate sources, he presents a solid and suggestive account of what actually happened in New Spain as the Indian, Negro, and white races began to mix on a large scale and thus began to create a New World society different from that of Europe.

No colonizing nation of modern times has had, perhaps, a more interesting and significant history than Spain in the new world. Protestant commercial England in the seventeenth and eighteenth centuries built up a largely self-sufficing economic empire. Catholic medieval Spain created an empire inhabited by races of many colors. In the English colonies of North America, the Indians were brushed aside by land-hungry settlers who quickly took away their land and shot down their wild game. In the Spanish colonies the fate of the natives was far different. For the Spanish conquest of America, somewhat like the Norman conquest of England, had as its unique result the essential fusion of conqueror and conquered in the creation of a new society. It is estimated that, at the close of three centuries of Spanish rule, the total population in Spanish America was 16,910,000. Of these 7,530,000 were Indians; 5,328,000 were of mixed blood; 3,276,000 were white and 776,000 were Negroes.

Obviously such a society did not come into existence full-grown like Athena from the head of Zeus. It certainly is not to be explained in terms of unrestrained economic exploitation and ruthless extermination of aboriginal inhabitants by colonizing whites. It was owing rather to complex religious, social, economic, political, and geographical factors which in Spanish America brought the Spaniards and Negroes into intimate contacts

From Volume XIX (1939), pages 161-184.

with the Indians, mitigated the asperities of that contact, and made the readjustments necessary to a new environment a relatively easy and natural process. To describe this process is not only to explain the origin of a new race of mixed blood and cast much light upon the history of modern Hispanic America. It is not only to write an important chapter in the history of those abiding phenomena which have occurred in more or less varied form wherever modern colonizing nations have come in contact with so-called "backward" races. It is, in its larger aspects, to tell a story which, in a world troubled by perplexing and thorny racial problems, should not be without much interest and some value. For the birth of the Mestizo was a most essential step in the creation of a society which, rejecting the doctrine of racial patriotism, bids fair with time to solve all racial questions as they were solved in southern Italy in the days of the Roman Empire—by the complete assimilation of cultures and amalgamation of bloods.

Illustrative of the manner in which racial fusion occurred to a greater or lesser degree throughout the Hispanic-American colonies is the manner in which it took place in New Spain. In 1803, the population of this colony was estimated as follows: 41 per cent or 2,500,000 were Indians of pure blood; 19.5 per cent or 1,200,000 were white; and 39 per cent or 2,400,000 were of mixed blood. The process of racial fusion initiated during colonial days grew apace in the era of national independence. In 1930, the Indians of the Republic of Mexico had increased to 4,620,880 but formed only 28 per cent of the whole; whites totaled 2,444,466 or 14.8 per cent; and the number of those of mixed blood had risen to 9,040,590 to constitute 55 per cent of the entire population. This social order and many of the major problems of modern Mexican life find their origin in the sixteenth century. In this century one is among the hills whence descend the rivulets which in succeeding centuries became the floods of high waters.

That miscegenation occurred on such a large scale in New Spain was owing in no small degree to a humanitarian spirit which found its roots in the tenets of the Catholic religion, the principles of Roman jurisprudence, the philosophy of natural rights, and the nationalistic pride in things Spanish which was developed to such an intensity by the struggles against the Moors and Jews in Spain. This spirit which was particularly strong during the first century of Spanish colonization impelled Spain to look upon the natives as beings to be converted and assimilated to Spanish civilization spiritually, culturally, and racially.

Even more decisive perhaps in moulding Spanish-Indian relations were the social and economic factors which determined the nature of the association between native and colonist. The great majority of Spaniards did not come to the new world to convert the native or to better their own economic condition by manual labor. The early Spanish settlers looked to the natives to produce foodstuffs and to mine gold. They soon discovered, however, that a people who could satisfy their few wants with two roots from the forest and a bit of wild honey made unwilling workers.

Hence the need for some system of enforced labor. Thus the colonists desired the incorporation of the natives into Spanish colonial life but on a definitely subordinate plane. They were to be made the hewers of wood and drawers of water for the Spanish settlers. Curiously enough, these economic needs of the colonist received a religious sanction when many colonial missionaries became convinced that their proselytizing efforts would prove futile unless the Indians were weaned from their primitive vices by profitable occupations and the influence of continuous contact with Spanish society. But this was not possible unless Spaniards made permanent settlements. And Spaniards would not settle in the Indies unless they were assured of an adequate labor supply to work the mines and to till the soil. It was this alliance of local interests and religious aims, that, from the colonial point of view, made the assimilation of the natives to Spanish society an economic necessity as well as a humanitarian desire.

Brought into intimate contact by religious zeal and economic interest, racial fusion of Spaniards and Indians was to a certain extent inevitable. There were many circumstances, however, which hastened the process and determined the manner in which it took place. First, the number of Spanish women in the colony during the early days of settlement was exceedingly small. The long and dangerous sea voyage together with the rigors of frontier life provided few inducements for the emigration of women. Then, too, the Spanish Crown, unlike the English Government a century later, absolutely prohibited the emigration of unmarried women to the Indies unless they were the daughters or servants of migrating families. Spain did strive, however, to promote the emigration of Spanish families and endeavored to prevent married Spaniards from going to the new world without their wives. By law, no married man was permitted to sail from Spain without his wife except by special permission of the crown. Even then the lady concerned was given the right to say whether she would go or remain. When this prohibition proved ineffective, laws were enacted compelling all Spaniards in the Indies with wives in Spain to return to live with their mates or post bond that they would send for them within two years. This law, too, was either deliberately ignored or evaded. Many colonists posted their bonds and then left the jurisdiction of the audiencia in which it had been given. Others with wealth and influence had little difficulty in securing exemption. Numerous attempts were made to secure the more efficient enforcement of royal will. They were largely unsuccessful, for the bishop of Mexico reported that in his bishopric alone there were some 500 married Spaniards who were living without their wives.

Although the crown failed to populate the colonies with Spanish families, it did succeed in preventing the emigration of its unmarried daughters. Few of the 300,000 Spaniards who left Spain to make their home in New Spain during the three centuries of the colonial era were women. Humboldt cited the fact that, in 1803, the European-born Spanish men in Mexico City outnumbered the European-born Spanish women ten to one as good evidence that few Spanish women came to the colony during colonial days. And it was owing to this "lack of marriageable women in the beginning", the viceroy, the marquis of Montes Claros, declared in 1607 that "the Mestizo and Mulattoes who are descendants of the conquerors are innumerable. . .".

The Spanish Crown, influenced by the example of the Portuguese in the east, sought in the opening years of the sixteenth century to protect the native women and prevent illicit relationships between Spaniards and Indians by revoking its earlier prohibition against mixed unions and actively encouraging the free intermarriage of the two races. This step was taken to promote the conversion of many natives to Christianity and Castilian ways of living and as a means of repopulating the islands where the aborigines had all but disappeared under the first impact with the Spanish colonists. In its policy of promoting racial intermarriage, the Spanish Government received the active support of the Church and the religious orders which were trying strenuously to teach the Indians the virtues of marriage and monogamy. The Franciscan and Dominican religious orders, indeed, wished to provide special inducements to Spaniards to marry Indian as well as Spanish women by giving such persons preference in a general and permanent distribution of lands and natives in New Spain.

Spanish Crown and Spanish Church were determined to leave no stone unturned which might induce the colonists to marry and settle down as permanent residents in the new world. Thus, the crown, supported by the great majority of colonial churchmen, went far to meet the demand of the pioneer settlers for economic security and social stability by ceasing its efforts to abolish the encomienda and declaring in 1536 that such estates might be inherited by female as well as male heirs for two and three generations. And in 1539, a royal decree provided that henceforth encomiendas should be given only to married men. All single men or women holding such grants were required to wed within a certain time or forfeit their estate. In like manner, the possession of a wife and family became an essential qualification for the office of corregidor and other important posts in the local government.

This official policy of encouraging matrimony was not without its results. Mixed unions became at quite an early date almost as numerous as Spanish men and women. In 1534, the Spanish town of La Puebla de los Angeles had a male population of eighty conquerors and vecinos. Of these thirty-eight had Castilian wives; twenty were married to Indian women; four had wives in Castile and eighteen were unmarried. Much later in the sixteenth century the population of the City of Antequera numbered some three hundred vecinos. While two hundred of these were married to Spanish women, there were about one hundred who had Mestizo or Mulatto wives.

That encomiendas and royal offices were too difficult to obtain and too profitable to the colonists to be lost for the want of a mate is only too evident. Giraldo Díaz de Alpuche, in the description of his encomienda submitted to the crown in 1573 cast much light upon racial conditions in New Spain when he declared that

some thirty years ago there was sent to this province royal ordinances decreeing that every encomendero of Indians should be married. As this land had only recently been conquered there were few women. Some married those who were here; others took Mestiza wives. Many could not find a wife and asked for an extension of time so that they would not lose the Indians who had been granted them in the name of the king. And I, to fulfil the said decree, married Doña Isabel, the niece of Montezuma, the great lord of Mexico.

This Indian wife had borne Díaz de Alpuche two daughters and one son. All three had married. One daughter was a widow with three children, two boys and a girl. The other daughter, whose husband was still living at the time, had two children, a boy and a girl. The son's marriage had been blessed with two offspring. Thus ten Mestizos had resulted in two generations from one mixed marriage.

The various lists of encomiendas in New Spain during the second half of the sixteenth century reveal that the case of Díaz de Alpuche was the case of many an encomendero in the colony. For instance, Doña Isabel, daughter of the Aztec Emperor, Montezuma, was taken to wife by Alonso de Gallego. Of this marriage was born a son, Juan de Andrada. Upon his father's death this Mestizo fell heir to the family estate while his mother took a second Spanish husband, Juan Cano. Of this second union was born a Mestizo son, Gonzalo Cano, who likewise became the possessor of an encomienda when his father died. Another daughter of Montezuma, Doña Leonor, was married to Christobal de Valderrama. When Valderrama died, his estate passed with the hand of his Mestiza daughter to Diego Arias de Sotelo. The famed mistress of Cortés, Doña Marina, after bearing him a son, was married to a Spanish captain, Juan Xaramillo. The result of this marriage was a daughter, Doña María, who inherited as her father's encomienda half of the province of Xilotepeque. Doña María married Don Luis de Quesada and in due time their Mestizo son, Don Pedro de Quesada, came into possession of this princely estate. Examples of this kind could be multiplied many times. And not the least significant aspect of the mixed unions just cited is the fact that in no case is the race of these men and women mentioned. The only clue to the race from whence they came is found in their given names. In English America, the romance of John Smith and Pocahontas grew into a tale to delight the hearts of American school girls. In New Spain, racial intermarriage became too common to elicit special comment.

Not only did Spanish colonists take native and Mestiza wives to secure offices and estates but few women of any race who possessed any property were without suitors for their hands. For example, the viceroy, Antonio de Mendoza, during his administration, had established a home for foundling Mestizas who by that time had become quite numerous "in order that because of their poverty and weakness they do not offend God. . .". Here these half-caste girls were reared in the faith and educated in Castilian ways. And it was reported to the crown that "many Spaniards, officials and other persons because they see them so well taught and educated in the ways of virtue ask for their hands in marriage. . .". The Spanish colonists may well have been interested in securing such model wives. But their matrimonial desires were in no wise diminished by the fact that it had become a practice for the viceroys to provide these Mestizas with dowries in the form of money from the royal treasury, corregimientos, or other offices. That the number of these marriages was far from being a negligible quantity is attested by the fact that Francisco Terrazas in listing the great drains on the revenues of the colony declared

then the great number of orphan Mestizas whom we raise and marry to Spaniards so that they will not be lost among the Indians take their good share. . . .

On the other hand, many marriages between Spaniards and maidens of Castilian birth were prevented by the circumstance that the young ladies had no dowries to offer a prospective husband. Numerous were the complaints of the colonists during these years "that they have at home marriageable daughters who are in want because they have nothing with which to marry". So serious a problem was this for many Spanish families that a considerable number of Spanish girls were placed in the home for Mestizas "for better instruction . . . until the time of marriage". At this time, they were, like the Mestizas, given dowries by the local government.

But Spain was not unmindful of the plight of its colonial daughters. Indeed, it was precisely because the crown desired to facilitate their marriage by assuring them suitable dowries that the eldest daughter, and failing such, the widow, was permitted in the absence of legitimate male heirs to inherit the encomienda of a deceased encomendero. Single female heirs were required to marry within one year after inheriting such an estate or, if they were minors, within a year after attaining their legal age. Although widows possessing encomiendas were not compelled to wed again, they were urged to do so and thus carry on the original intention of the crown. In 1552, the home government went still further and decreed that the eldest son or daughter who had fallen heir to the encomienda of the father should support the other members of the family. Especially should care be taken of the mother and sisters until such time as they might be safely and securely married. To many orphans and daughters of poverty-stricken conquerors government pensions were granted. Thus the two orphan daughters of Pedro Abarca, Ana and Beatriz Pérez de Abarca, were given fifty pesos annual pension until they reached the age of marriage. At that time they were provided with certificates declaring them eligible as daughters of a conqueror to receive annual pensions of 500 to 600 pesos. Wedding bells promptly pealed for both young ladies. To the chagrin of all concerned, however, a pension of only 150 pesos was given to each bride and resort was immediately had to suit at law.

Such governmental aid doubtless enabled many a Spanish maid to wed but the problem was by no means solved. The Franciscan friar, Hierónimo de Mendieta, was protesting bitterly in 1562 against the immorality and social disorders caused by the poverty which prevented some ten to eleven thousand "maiden daughters of Spaniards" in Mexico from marrying for want of dowries. He emphatically declared that there was as great a need for houses for Spanish girls as for foundling Mestizas and he added his voice to the many who were urging the strict and immediate prohibition of the continued immigration of poor people from Spain which was only intensifying this social problem. While the number given by the friar may be greatly exaggerated and may include as qualified members of what he called "the Spanish nation" all maidens not of pure Indian blood, there can be little doubt that by the second half of the sixteenth century there was a large number of women of Spanish blood in the colony whose marriage to men of their own race was prevented by lack of property and income. Indeed, as late as 1607, many Spanish women were being married with no more dowry or property than the prospects of a successful lawsuit involving their claims as alleged descendants of the conquerors and pioneer settlers.

Thus too much emphasis must not be placed upon the lack of Spanish women in New Spain as a major factor advancing the fusion of whites and natives. For there is little evidence to indicate that the fewness of Spanish women so influential in initating the process of miscegenation lasted much beyond the first few decades of the sixteenth century. This condition, indeed, is one which both the viceroy, the marquis of Montes Claros, and the historian, Juan de Torquemada, writing in the first quarter of the seventeenth century, describe as having existed "in the beginning" of the period of conquest and settlement. That by this time there was probably no great scarcity of Spanish women, especially those born in the colony, is indicated by the fact that in direct contrast to earlier practice "few Spaniards of honor" now took native wives. And in 1803, Humboldt found that while Spanish men of European birth in Mexico City outnumbered the women in the proportion of 100 to 10, the colonial-born women of Spanish blood outnumbered the men 136 to 100. In the cities of Querétaro and Valladolid the ratio was 133 to 100.

While the intermarriage of whites and Indians during the years under review was promoted and widespread, legal alliances between Spaniards and Negroes were neither encouraged nor frequent. Unions between Negroes and Indian women, were, however, quite numerous. The importation of Negro slaves was owing in no small degree to the desire of crown, humanitarian, and colonist alike to shift the burden of enforced labor from the backs of the natives to the stronger backs of the African blacks. Few of the Negroes brought into the colony during the early period were women. Racial fusion of Negroes and Indians like that of whites and natives was, to a great extent, inevitable. According to Humboldt, however, the blacks found great favor with the native women chiefly for psychological reasons. The Mexican Indian was serious, melancholy, and somber. Even strong drink failed to enliven his temperament. The African Negro was vivacious and cheerful. "This contrast", he says, "causes the Indian women to prefer Negroes, not only to the men of their own caste, but even to the Europeans".

Whatever may have been the basis for the preference of Indian women for Negro men, it existed and played an important part in advancing racial intermixture in New Spain. The viceroy, Martín Enríquez, wrote Philip II in 1574 that

The Indian women are very weak people and are easily led astray by the Negroes whom they prefer in marriage to the Indian men.

Negro men, however, had a more tangible, if not more practical, reason for desiring an Indian wife. By the laws of the colony the child of a Negro slave and a free woman was, like its mother, a free person. So numerous became the offspring of such marriages that the colonists, who were in constant fear of an uprising of the Negro population, were thoroughly alarmed. Enríquez pressed King Philip to have the pope prohibit the intermarriage of Negroes and Indian or Mulatto women or at least to issue an ordinance declaring that the child of a Negro slave by an Indian or Mulatto woman should be the property of the owner of the Negro. Although the Spanish Crown was apparently unwilling to adopt such extreme measures, it did order that Negroes be encouraged to marry members of their own race because it believed the offspring of unions between Negroes and Indians inherited the vices but not the virtues of the parent stock.

That racial intermarriage was an important factor in producing a race of mixed blood there can be little doubt. By far the greater number of half-castes in New Spain, however, were of illegitimate birth. As early as 1533, the offspring of the illegal unions which marked the paths of the Spanish conquerors and pioneer settlers had become so numerous that the government established in Mexico City a home of Mestizo boys and another for Mestiza girls. Concubinage early became and remained a widespread and common practice. Bishop Juan de Zumárraga wrote Charles V in 1529 that

many of those who have Indians have taken from the chiefs of their villages their daughters, sisters, nieces, and wives under the pretext of taking them to their homes as servants but in reality for concubines. . . .

This seizure and wronging of their women by Spanish colonists was, indeed, one of the most common and bitter complaints of the natives. It was undoubtedly one of the main causes of the bloody rebellion of the encomienda Indians in Yucatán in 1546. So incensed were the natives that they set out to kill all the Spanish settlers and all Indian women who had served them in any capacity. Among the latter were several hundred women who had served the Spaniards as domestic servants.

The Spaniards were dependent upon Indian labor to till the fields and to work the mines. They were, likewise, dependent upon Indian labor to knead bread and to take care of other household duties. Even monasteries found it necessary to call upon Indian women to bake the bread to feed the Indian children within their walls. As a result Spaniards, Negroes, Mulattoes, and Mestizos mingled together, often in one household. This must in itself have presented an unique spectacle. Its influence in promoting racial fusion is only too apparent. Thus, for example, the testament of the pioneer settler, Diego de Ocaña, continued the following provision regarding an Indian woman in his household:

Item: I say that I once had relations with the said Antonica, my servant, who bore a child Alosico. But she was ill-watched for she also had relations with an Indian of my household. However, judging by the color of the child, everyone declares that he seems to be the son of a Christian. It seems so to me, for it may be that he is my son; and since in case of doubt it is better to acknowledge him than to ignore him, I command my sons to bring him up, have him indoctrinated, and so do something good for him, for I believe that he is a son of mine, and not of an Indian.

The home government made efforts to eliminate such evils. It passed ordinances prohibiting the personal services by which the colonists impressed the natives into household service. Little change was effected. For example, in Yucatán, the need for domestic servants was so great that Licentiate Francisco de Loaysa, one-time chief magistrate of this region, permitted each encomendero to select a certain number of Indians to knead bread in the homes of the Spanish settlers. Such persons were paid wages and changed from month to month. The alcalde mayor, Diego Quixada, disapproved of this arrangement

because aside from being personal service there come many women without their husbands and maidens who do not use their persons well on the roads or in the houses of the citizens which contain Spaniards, Negroes, and Mestizos with whom they commit many sins. . . .

Royal decrees were issued prohibiting involuntary service even for hire. But this practice became widespread throughout the Spanish colonies. Many Indians, moreover, were only too eager to enter the Spanish households to escape the payment of tribute and personal services which were exacted of them in their tribal villages. Thus there grew up in the vicinity of many Spanish towns colonies of native squatters who had deserted their tribal surroundings to sell their services as domestics and day laborers to the Spanish residents.

In yet another way the tributes and personal services required of the natives promoted racial intermixture. During the early years of the six-teenth century no tribute was exacted of free Negroes, Mulattoes, and Mestizos. Neither were they required to work like the Indians. In an effort to place the natives more on a basis of equality with the other elements of the population, tribute was imposed upon such persons and royal officials were ordered to sentence all vagabonds to serve in the mines or to do other labor. But such laws were for the most part a dead letter and "from these abuses", declared Solórzano,

it results that many Indian women leave their Indian husbands and scorn and desert the children they have had of them because they are subject to tribute and personal services. They desire, love, and prefer the children they have out of wedlock of Spanish men and even Negroes because such children are free and exempt from such obligations. . . .

Significant as were these currents of racial fusion it was the economic and social maladjustment of Spanish colonial life which gave rise to vaga-bondage that swelled them to flood tide. No doubt many of the Spaniards who lived among the Indians were so domiciled of their own free will. No country in Europe was more noted for its beggars and vagabonds than sixteenth-century Spain. And there is little evidence that the social habits of the Spaniards who came to New Spain differed from those of their fellow countrymen. Bishop Zumárraga in 1529 informed the home government that

as these Indians are so submissive, it is an old custom of theirs to give food to the Spaniards who come to their village and to the Indian men and women whom they bring with them as long as they wish to stay. For this reason, there are many vagabonds with nothing to do who go from village to village with two or even three Indian mistresses and as many Indian men who serve them. These persons who thus wander about are principally the ones who do violence and commit robberies in the native villages.

On the other hand, vagabondage, oppression of the natives, and cattle-stealing so prevalent during these years were, like poaching in eighteenth-century England, methods by which men sought to obtain a living which they could not secure by other means.

The economic dependence of the Spanish colonists upon the natives which, during the early years gave rise to the encomienda, was made a constant feature of colonial life by a commercial policy which hamstrung colonial commerce and industry chiefly in the interests of a few Sevillian merchants. The Spanish system of annual fleets under convoy; the limitation of trade and commerce to a few ports in the colonies and to Seville and Cádiz in Spain; the prohibition of strict supervision of intercolonial and oriental trade paralyzed colonial trade and industry and made the colony almost entirely dependent upon European manufactured goods. Spain's inability to control the seas coupled with a rapidly rising price level ac-celerated by the flood of precious metals from America curtailed the amount and raised the prices of these commodities. The continual export of gold and silver bullion by the crown and Spanish merchants; the unfavorable balance of trade with the Philippines as well as with Spain; the numerous exploring expeditions fitted out in the colony; the difference in the value of money coined in New Spain and the mother country which caused the former to be rapidly withdrawn from circulation; and the inability of the colony to offset this lack of specie by the more modern business devices of paper money or credit deprived New Spain of the capital sorely needed for the development of its own resources. The absence of good harbors along the eastern coast and the necessity of using the particularly dangerous and unhealthy port of Vera Cruz especially handicapped trade and made the goods imported from Spain much less in quantity and much higher in price than those in the other colonies. The lack of navigable rivers and an adequate system of highways increased the cost of those goods which trickled through Mexico City to the internal provinces still more. Many parts of the colony, indeed, were unable to obtain goods at any price. The almost universal cry that "the cost of merchandise is greatly increasing and the land is suffering dire want from the scarcity and high price of goods" was the inevitable result of Spanish commercial policy which together with other factors prevented that diversification of colonial economic life which would in coming true have provided the colony better opportunities for supporting its Spanish population.

Meanwhile, the Spanish population of New Spain was increasing both by birth and immigration. The larger the family, the more effective was the argument of the colonist that both need and merit commended him to special consideration in the dispensing of encomiendas and royal offices. When Jerónimo López petitioned the king in 1543 for a better grant he took great care to emphasize the fact that he had a wife and eight unmarried daughters. On the other hand, those who emigrated from Spain were few in numbers. Spain's conviction that the safety of the nation and the souls of its subjects lay in maintaining unity of religious belief and its determination to secure to itself the economic benefits of its colonies led it to prohibit the emigration to the Indies of foreigners, Portuguese, Jews, Moors, unfrocked monks and nuns, and all those convicted of heresy by the Holy Inquisition. Its desire, likewise, to correct, as far as possible, the evil results of the conquest impelled Spain to refuse emigration permits to those Spaniards whom it suspected of being "enemies of work" and attracted to the Indies by the lure of easy wealth, government jobs, and native women. Although such prohibitions were often more honored in the breach than in the observance, they were effective in curtailing the number of Europeans who might otherwise have come to the Spanish colonies. It is estimated on good authority that, in the sixteenth century, the entire emigration from Spain to America did not exceed 1,000 to 1,500 yearly. The number of those who came to New Spain is uncertain. The first census report of New Spain which is at best only a rough estimate shows that the Spanish population about 1560 was scarcely more than 20,000. Eight thousand of those resided in Mexico City. By 1574, it was estimated that some 15,000 Spaniards now lived in the capital.

This increase seems small enough but to contemporaries it was appalling. The colony was not yet able to support its original population in comfort. In 1565, Martín Cortés wrote Philip II that

the Spaniards here in this land are multiplying fast and every year a great number come from Spain. As no one applies himself to work and the price of foodstuffs is greatly increasing there are numerous vagabonds. The viceroy himself told me that every morning in Mexico there arise eight hundred men who have nowhere to eat. They do not try to remedy this by having the Spaniards work or by punishing the vagabonds and thus there are many robberies in this land, especially livestock, so that no one is the master of his property. And what is happening now is nothing compared to what will happen in the future because, in addition to the great number of Spaniards, there are so many Mestizos and Mulattoes that they cover the land and these persons are naturally born with evil tendencies and they do the greatest harm to the natives.

To make matters worse, royal officials, during the administrations of the viceroy, Antonio de Mendoza, and his successor, Luis de Velasco, were particularly active in reducing the tributes in kind paid by the natives or commuting them into money payments and abolishing the personal services by which the natives were required to deliver foodstuffs to the Spanish towns. Such activities seriously reduced the food supply of the colonists and added to the burdens created by the Seville Monopoly and the rapid rise in the level of commodity prices which was taking place in New Spain as well as in the mother country. The effect of these conditions upon Spanish-Indian relations can scarcely be exaggerated. The screw, which an increasing price level and an increasing population, together with a shortage of foodstuffs and European goods, turned on the natives explains much that, heretofore, has been attributed simply to the wilful cruelty of the Spanish settlers. Thus, for example, the Franciscan friar, Motolinía, wrote the emperor, Charles V, in 1555 that

Throughout the land prices are high and there is a scarcity of foodstuffs which used to be plentiful and cheap. And although the people were poor they had something to eat. Now the Spaniards are poor and indebted and there are many idle people eager to seize the least opportunity in the world to rob the natives because they say the Indians are rich and the Spaniards are poor and dying of hunger. The Spaniards who have anything are trying to make their fortune and return to Castile in the ships that are sailing from here. Royal officials as well as merchants and rich men are going away laden with gold and silver and the poor remain in want.

It is undoubtedly true that colonists who scorned manual labor and haughtily informed the king that they had not crossed the sea to dig and plough were, in no small degree, responsible for their own plight. But it is likewise true that the maladjustment of colonial economic life prevented

New Spain from maintaining its non-native population and caused many to seek an escape from the pressure of economic forces by going native. In 1557, Dr. Santander, royal veedor, estimated the number of those without visible means of support at 4,000. Luis Maiban, in his census report of New Spain about 1560, placed the number at 3,000 and declared that

there are many Indian villages in which there are many Spaniards but which are not recorded here because they would take too much space.

Many of these persons found employment on the encomiendas as overseers entrusted with the task of collecting the tributes of the Indians and supervising the sowing and harvesting of their grain. Others made their living by rustling livestock or by "bootlegging" strong drink to the natives. Still others served as interpreters or, like "ambulance chasers" of the present day, were responsible for the great number of lawsuits brought into court by the natives. And many merely battened upon the Indians and aided the Indian chieftains in oppressing their own subjects.

The inevitable result of this widespread dispersal of Spaniards, Mestizos, Negroes, and Mulattoes among the natives was a great increase in the half-caste population. In 1571, the indignant Friar Hierónimo de Mendieta went to great lengths to point out the urgent necessity of expelling all Spaniards, Negroes, and half-castes of fourteen years and over from the native villages in order to prevent among other things, the numerous illegitimate offspring that came of such intimate racial contacts.

It cannot be said that the crown was lax in making attempts to eliminate vagabondage. Local authorities were ordered to expel all vagabonds from the Indian towns and force them to work in the mines or do other labor. Efforts were then made to segregate the Spanish, Mulatto and Negro vagabonds in separate villages where they were to be given lands, tools, seed, and whatever aid necessary by the government in order to enable them to become self-supporting. But the lack of adequate communications within the colony curtailed the area of effective administration of the local government. There was little to prevent Spanish Mestizo or Mulatto vagabonds from taking up their residence in the Indian villages remote from the center of control, off the routes of trade or far from the outposts of the religious orders. In such districts, these vagabonds were masters of all they surveyed. Nor was the local government able to act quickly enough to apprehend such culprits. Encomenderos had no civil or criminal jurisdiction over such persons and were without legal power to seize them when they came into their estates. Report of their activities had to be made to the government in Mexico City. By the time the royal authorities had sent out an official to apprehend them they had gone elsewhere. As a result, Licentiate Francisco Ceynos, one-time oidor of the audiencia of Mexico, declared that Spaniard, Mestizo, Negro, Mulatto, and Indian vagabonds whose numbers were "as numerous as the grasses and were increasing by leaps and bounds", were roaming the country without any other means of support than living off the Indians. Small wonder that Luis de Velasco advised Philip II to send this unruly element out of the colony on expeditions of explorations and conquest. The only alternative to this measure, he declared in despair, was to close the port to further immigration and ship the Mestizos and Mulattoes away to Spain. The conquest and settlement of Florida authorized in 1559 was in part designed to help solve this thorny problem. The resumption in 1563 of voyages of discovery and exploring expeditions prohibited in 1542 was in no small measure dictated by the doctrine that colonization was a cure for the social and economic ills of mother country and colony alike. Well might the crown have tried to hew rocks with oyster shells as attempt to eliminate vagabondage by such means! The continued drain of gold and silver from New Spain; the continued rise in prices; the continued reduction of native tributes and their commutation into money tributes; the continued effects of the Spanish monopoly made more oppressive by Spain's inability to control the sea lanes to its colony; and the continued increase in population intensified the very evils which the government was striving to eradicate. Vagabondage and the Mestizo were thus inherited together by later generations, for the sixteenth century saw the beginning and not the end of these social problems.

By the second half of the sixteenth century the lines of racial fusion were fairly well established. The first census report of New Spain which was taken about 1560 is little more than a rough estimate. Yet it reveals that the population of the colony was already composed of many races and many colors. The number of Spaniards according to this report was 20,211; Negro slaves were not far behind with 16,147; Mestizos totaled 2,445 and Mulattoes 1,465.

The number of persons of mixed blood accounted for in the census is undoubtedly far too small. No social phenomenon in the colony was more marked and more commented upon by contemporaries than that which Francisco de Navarro in a later day so aptly called "the notorious fecundity of the castes". The census taker, indeed, found it impossible to obtain any count or even an estimate of the Spaniards, Mestizos, and Mulattoes living on the cattle and sheep ranches or in the native villages. And it was especially in such places that so many of the half-castes took up their abode. Then, too, even at this early date, it was probably a difficult matter to distinguish between some Mestizos and Spaniards. The color of a Mestizo of the first generation was almost perfectly white. The Mestizo's scanty beard, small hands and feet, and a certain obliquity of the eyes betrayed his Indian blood much more than did the color of his skin. If such a Mestizo or Mestiza married a white, the offspring was scarcely to be distinguished from an European.

But taking the figures it sets forth as a basis for calculation, the total population of the colony, excluding Indians, was 40,268. Whites composed about 50 per cent of this number; Negroes 40 per cent; Mestizos 6 per cent, and Mulattoes 3.5 per cent. For better or worse colonial society had become a society of many colors—white, red, black and the varying shades produced by the intermixture of these races. As a society of color it was unique. As a society of smells it was stranger still, for the castes of Indian and African descent retained the bodily odors peculiar to those two races. And Humboldt is authority for the statement that the sense of smell of the Indian muleteers became so sensitive that in the darkness of the night they could distinguish between an European, an Indian, and a Negro. To the first they gave the name, *pezuña;* the second they called *posco;* and the third *grajo.*

Other Articles of Interest

Friede, Juan. "The *Catálogo de pasajeros* and Spanish Emigration to America to 1550." XXXI (1951), 333–348.
The *Catálogo de pasajeros* provides valuable but insufficient data for a study of Spanish colonists moving to America. It is unsystematic and incomplete, fails to treat unlicensed movements, and omits some pertinent and recorded material.

Mörner, Magnus, and Charles Gibson. "Diego Muñoz Camargo and the Segregation Policy of the Spanish Crown." XLII (1962), 558–569.

Neasham, V. Aubrey. "Spain's Emigrants to the New World, 1492–1592." (1939), 147–160.
Emigrants from Spain came to America from all parts of Spain, even from the Balearic and Canary islands. The theory that the majority emigrated from the south was opposed by Cuervo. Thayer y Ojeda expanded Cuervo's work, and finally Henríquez Ureña showed by extended researches that the proportions from northern and southern Spain were about equal. The present study analyzes emigration by province for the years 1509–1588 in a statistical chart. In the latter years the trend was toward southern emigration because of the concentration of activities at Seville, which sent most. Mining in the Indies drew emigrants from the mining regions, and areas near the court, where news of the New World arrived early, were inclined to greater emigrations than the remote provinces.

12. Social Structure and Social Change in New Spain

LYLE N. MC ALISTER

One indication of the new currents of thinking in the field of Latin American studies is the application of a sociological focus to the relatively well-known facts of history. In the present essay Dr. McAlister, director of the Institute of Latin American Studies at the University of Florida, concentrates on the society of New Spain. The bold generalizations and solid documentation of the article provide a stimulating combination for students who want to enlarge their view of the growth and changes in Spanish colonial life in America in the light of a related social science.

The purpose of this paper is to examine the social structure of New Spain using a conceptual framework somewhat different from those commonly employed and one which may be more useful for the explanation of certain historical phenomena. It does not purport to be a piece of "basic research." It is more properly a theory of social structure. The principle concepts employed are abstracted from infinitely complex historical situations. A number of observations made cannot be precisely documented; they are hypotheses which seem to "make sense" in the light of the author's reading and research. Hypotheses and substantiated observations, however, appear to fit together and to accommodate the known "facts." The concept of society is arbitrarily separated from that of the state and the latter treated only incidentally, although Spanish political thinkers did not regard such boundary establishment as either real or desirable, and the political role of estates and corporations is factored out. This procedure can be justified by regarding the state as "nothing more than the organization of all social forces that have a political significance . . . as that part of society which performs the political function." Conceptually, therefore, state and society may be distinguished one from the other and the problem of the relationship between the two, while real and important, is somewhat different from the one to be examined here.

A word is in order about terminology. Such expressions as social struc-

From Volume XLIII (1963), pages 349-370.

ture, social organization, social system, class, caste, and the like are used rather loosely by historians, so that confusion in terminology often produces confusion in ideas. On the other hand, sociologists and social anthropologists in attempting to define such concepts more rigorously have come up with so many conflicting "scientific" definitions that they have simply created terminological confusion at another level. The term "social structure" is here used in a nontechnical sense. It presumes that a society is made up of individuals grouped according to the possession of common interests, attributes, and qualities; that these groups are definable, and that they are related to each other in some definable, non-random order. Other terms commonly used in social analysis are either explicitly defined or, it is hoped, their usage is implicit in the context.

On the eve of the conquest of America, the constituent elements of Spanish society were groups and associations identifiable in terms of (1) ascribed functions and/or statuses, (2) systems of shared values, attitudes, and activities associated with the latter, (3) distinct and unequal juridical personalities expressed in general legal codes or special *fueros, ordenanzas,* and *reglamentos,* and involving some degree of autonomous jurisdiction. This society was conceived of in organic terms; that is, like the human body, its several parts were structurally and functionally interrelated and interdependent. The health of the body social depended on the vigor and proper functioning of the constituent organs.

The constituent elements of Spanish society fell into two logical categories: the vestiges of the medieval estates and functional corporations. The primary estates, noble, clerical, and common, had a functional derivation. Thus, in the High Middle Ages they were identified as *defensores, oratores,* and *laboratores.* Leaving aside the church for the moment, as between the two secular estates the function of warrior was assigned a higher social value and initially was completely identified with the nobility. Despite isolated voices upholding the dignity and value of production, it was commonly held that without the defensores, the other estates would fall victim to predatory forces and the social order would disintegrate. Function and its assigned social value conveyed social quality and status and conferred or withheld honor. Thus the bearing of arms was honorable while productive occupations—agriculture, trade, manufacturing—were dishonorable. Quality and honor, moreover, came to be conceived of not as individual attributes which could be acquired but as deriving from lineage. The military function of the nobility and derivative social quality and status were juridically recognized in the *fuero de hidalguía* whereby the noble was exempted from personal taxes and tributes (*pechos*); he could not be imprisoned for debt nor could his residence, horse, or arms be attached for debts, and he could not be subjected to judicial torture or to base punishment.

Within the primary estates, hierarchies of social rank existed. Thus the highest level of the nobility consisted of the grandees who were the social equals of the king. Below them ranked the rest of the titled nobility—

marquises, counts, etc.—and at the bottom of the pyramd of nobility was the mass of knights or hidalgos.

Coincidentally with the evolution of a hierarchy of estates and sub-estates, countertrends were deforming its structural purity. These had their origin in the growth of towns, trade, and a money economy. They assumed the form of increased diversification of function and the modification of the functional base of the secular estates. Within the common estate, an emerging group of merchants, bankers, and legalists (*letrados*) performed functions so indispensable to society and the state that they could not be denied social honor and status. In the case of mercantile elements, wealth could literally buy many of the attributes of social quality. Moreover, when city dwellers organized urban militia and the *Santa Hermandad* for their defense, and as the nucleus of a mercenary army developed in the fifteenth century, the nobility lost its monopoly on the role of defensor. At the same time, the pressures of a money economy reduced many of the lower strata of the nobility to indigency or compelled them into money-making activities. Hidalguía, furthermore, acquired an economic value. The hidalgo as distinct from the commoner (in this case identical with the *pechero*) was exempt from personal taxes or tributes, and pretensions to hidalguía came to be based not so much on aspirations to honor or status but on financial advantage. Conversely, the emergent bourgeoisie were anxious to acquire a social quality and status which could not be validated completely by wealth alone. Juan Huarte de San Juan describes these attitudes in his *Examen de ingenios:* "To be well born and of famous lineage is a very highly esteemed jewel but it has one very great fault; by itself it has little benefit . . . but linked to wealth there is no point of honor that can equal it. . . ." "Some" he adds, "compare nobility to the zero of the decimal system; by itself it is nothing but joined with a digit it acquires great value."

As a consequence of these complementary trends, the traditional hierarchy of estates and subestates became blurred at the point of contact between the lower nobility and the upper strata of the common order and a new sector emerged which combined the values and functions of the nobility and the bourgeoisie. Nevertheless the image of a society ordered on the basis of functionally derived social quality remained virtually unimpaired in the minds of Spaniards. Jurists and theologians might challenge the system on philosophical, religious, or logical grounds, but any popular opposition to it that existed arose from dissatisfaction of individuals and groups with their place in it rather than from a realization of its inequity.

Examined on another plane, the constituent elements of Spanish society were a multitude of functional corporations which included the army, merchant's guilds (*consulados*), artisan's guilds (*gremios*), municipal organs, the *mesta*, and the like, each with a special juridical status. The relationship between the estates and the corporations raises a number of conceptual problems, the most fundamental being whether they actually represented two distinct systems of social organization. Beneyto observes that the corporate theory supported the stability of social stratification in that "the status of the corporation has to correspond to the status of the individuals who enter into it," implying that the corporations were actually suborders within a stratified society of estates. However, a case for the coexistence of two social systems can be made on the following grounds: (1) Within the estates, the ordering came to be on the basis of social quality and status divorced from their original functional bases whereas the corporations were specifically functional in fact and by virtue of their formal *ordenanzas* and *reglamentos*. (2) The boundaries between corporations in contrast to those separating social classes were sharp and absolutely definable in functional and legal terms. (3) Although there was some general correspondence between the status of corporations and the individuals who composed them, it was often blurred. Thus, as suggested above, within the merchant guilds, the noble-commoner dichotomy tended to disappear, and the standing army which emerged in the fifteenth century contained men from all ranks of society although recognition of social quality was maintained in the wide gap that existed between the statuses of officer and enlisted man. (4) The corporations maintained a higher degree of internal discipline. (5) Among the several functional corporations there was no explicit hierarchical ordering. The social structure deriving from estates was stratified; that based on corporations was conglomerate. Although two systems existed, there was a significant intersection or interpenetration between them.

The church cannot be accommodated in either of the categories established above. Historically it was one of the primary medieval estates. It was also a functional corporation. Its position in the social order, however, transcended both. It was, in fact, a society in itself providing for all the needs of its personnel. It possessed its own social stratification grading downward from the prelates—archbishops, bishops, and abbots who were identifiable with the secular nobility—to the parish priests identifiable with the commoners. It also had a conglomerate structure whose components were "subcorporations" such as the regular and secular clergy, the military orders, the Inquisition and the universities, each enjoying a particular *fuero* or jurisdiction. Moreover, although in terms of historical experience, self-identification, and certain aspects of its juridical status, it was a Spanish institution, it was also but a branch of the church universal. In view of these difficulties, within the conceptual framework of this paper, the church can be more properly considered in terms of its constituent groups rather than as a social estate or as a unitary corporation.

At a time that was particularly significant for social formation in America, agitation against an eventual expulsion of Moors and Jews from Spain activated a latent element in peninsular social organization. The status-seeking Spaniard became almost pathologically concerned not only with establishing his *hidalguía* but also his purity of blood (*limpieza de sangre*). Indeed the two qualities became almost coextensive. The latter is overtly ethnic, but its basic derivation was religious. It signified a lineage of impeccable orthodoxy. Thus Pedro de la Caballería, a member of Ferdinand the Catholic's entourage and a well-known Jew, forged an *expediente* supported by testimony from eminent nobles, according to which his progenitors had been "*verdaderos cristianos viejos de limpísima sangre.*" The possession of such qualities or the lack of them influenced not only social status but corporate membership. Purity of blood was a condition of membership in artisan guilds, religious and military orders, municipal *consejos*, and for the award of university degrees.

The concepts of estate and corps were integral parts of the cultural baggage which Spaniards carried with them to the Indies. Social structure there, however, developed a character that differed from its peninsular prototype. This divergence derived from two powerful influences: first, the deliberate intervention of the crown in the process of social formation, a phenomenon which will be considered later in this paper; second, the survival of large portions of the indigenous population, the importation of substantial numbers of Negro slaves, and miscegenation involving the three races. The ethnic factor produced what colonial writers called a system of castes. The latter word, however, should be taken as the equivalent of the Spanish term *casta*. It did not denote a rigid, closed social system such as that associated with India. Various classifications of the castes appeared. In the early nineteenth century amateur anthropologists constructed elaborate taxonomies such as the following:

1. Spaniard with an Indian woman, *mestizo*
2. *Mestiza* with a Spaniard, *castizo*
3. *Castizo* with a Spanish woman, Spaniard
4. Spaniard with a Negro woman, *mulato*
5. *Mulata* with a Spaniard, *morisco*
6. *Morisco* with a Spanish woman, *chino*
7. *Chino* with an Indian woman, *salta atrás*
8. *Salta atrás* with a *mulata*, *lobo*
9. *Lobo* with a *china*, *gíbaro*
10. *Gíbaro* with a *mulata*, *albarazado*
11. *Albarazado* with a Negro woman, *cambujo*
12. *Cambujo* with an Indian woman, *zambaigo*
13. *Zambaigo* with a *loba*, *Calpa mulato*
14. *Calpa mulato* with a *cambuja*, *tente en el aire*
15. *Tente en el aire* with a *mulata*, *no te entiendo*
16. *No te entiendo* with an Indian woman, *torna atrás*

A simpler classification was commonly used which appears to be the basis of descriptions of "colonial society" in modern textbooks. The elements were:

Spaniard or white (European or American)
mestizo: various mixtures of Indian and Spaniard
mulatto: Various mixtures of Negro and Spaniard
zambo or zambaigo: Indian and Negro
Indian
Negro

For official purposes, particularly the assessment of tribute and military service, three primary groups were identified: Spaniard (European and American); castes (castas), that is, persons of mixed blood; and Indians.

Although such classifications were overtly ethnic they were strongly influenced by cultural factors. Thus, in fact and in law, "white" or "Spaniard" was practically coextensive with *gente de casta limpia*, a category which included not only persons of pure Spanish origin but mestizos and castizos who were of legitimate descent, free from the taint of Negro blood, and who "lived like Spaniards." The distinguishing feature of the castes was illegitimate descent or the suspicion of it and the possession of Negro blood or the suspicion of such a taint because of illegitimacy. The taint associated with the Negro derived from his supposed physical and psychological characteristics and his juridical status. His pigmentation and features were regarded as repellent; early colonial officials and chroniclers regarded Negroes and mulattos as *"viles, traidores, ociosos, borrachos,"* etc. They were the people most *"rastreros, pérfidos e inmorales de la humanidad."* As slaves or the descendants of slaves they were *infames por derecho.* As such they were forbidden to bear arms or to enter military service, they were excluded from the clergy and public office, and they were forbidden to intermarry with Indians or whites. In regard to the Indian group, it was composed of ethnic Indians and mestizos who were culturally Indian. In a curiously reverse sort of way, a Spaniard or white might be most accurately defined as a person who culturally and legally was neither an Indian nor a caste; an Indian was a person who was neither a Spaniard nor a caste; and a caste was an individual who was neither Spaniard nor Indian.

Aguirre Beltrán has developed the following method of classifying castes which explicitly recognizes cultural factors in their formation:

European: persons of pure European descent
Indians: ethnic Indians
Negroes: ethnic Negroes
Euromestizos: persons of mixed European and Indian origin but with predominantly European ethnic and cultural characteristics
Indomestizos: European-Indian mixtures but ethnically and culturally predominantly Indian
Afromestizos: Mixed bloods with a Negro strain

The several systems of classification described above may be correlated as follows:

Spaniards-whites	Europeans	gente de casta limpia
castizos	Euromestizos	
mestizos		
mulattos	Afromestizos	castes
zambos		
Negroes	Negroes	
Indians	Indians Indomestizos	Indians

(tributaries)

The question arises as to whether these ethnic-cultural groups constituted elements in a definable social structure. The system of castes was certainly a contemporary reality and its component elements were identified in the contemporary mind in a loose reputational way. It is a useful framework for descriptive purposes but it has a limited value for structural analysis. In the case of the elaborate constructions of the early nineteenth-century taxonomists, the types are too numerous to be manageable; they are difficult to identify with any degree of precision, and status distinctions among them are by no means clear. The same criticism is true to a lesser extent of simpler traditional systems and the typology of Aguirre Beltrán. Or perhaps it would be more accurate to say that there are not enough data available in a usable form to enable such groups to be identified and ordered in a scientific system. The trichotomy Spaniard—caste—Indian, however, presents fewer problems. It does constitute a social structure. Its elements are identifiable; they possess definable social and juridical statuses, and they exist in an ordered relation to each other. They represent an American system of estates which evolved in an *ad hoc* fashion out of New World circumstances without the support of any fundamental social theory.

The Spanish sector of the population, although of diverse social and ethnic origin, possessed a certain homogeneity deriving from its position as a conquering race and its assumed superior culture. Its identity was supported, moreover, by the possession of or pretension to limpieza de sangre and descent from cristianos viejos, qualities which were identified with legitimate lineage. Its superior status was also expressed in almost universal claims to nobility or hidalguía. Theoretically, this quality derived from two sources: lineage and royal concession, both subject to documentary substantiation. In fact, many Spanish families could claim hidalguía on one of these grounds. Some of the conquerors, first settlers, and later arrivals came from peninsular families of substantiated nobility. The crown also made concessions of hidalguía to Mexican families, although rather sparingly. From the outset, however, the conquerors exhibited a sharp consciousness of nobility deriving not from lineage or royal concession but from a sense of personal excellence, from glory in deeds of valor done during the Conquest, and from a pride in noble action. It was such sentiments that moved Pizarro to claim that the Conquest created a new nobility. These feelings became diffused through the entire Spanish population and led the Council of the Indies to declare: "It is undeniable that in those kingdoms [in America] any Spaniard who comes to them, who acquires some wealth, and who is not engaged in a dishonorable occupation, is regarded as a noble." Alexander von Humboldt went even farther. "Any white person," he wrote, "although he rides his horse barefoot, imagines himself to be of the nobility of the country." Nobility, in fact, became largely an officially recognized individual and social state of mind. The concepts of Spanishness, whiteness, limpieza de sangre, vieja cristianidad, and hidalguía tended to become coextensive and together formed a system of values and status determinants clearly identifiable with a major social sector. These qualities were recognized in law, particularly in exemption from tribute, and the hidalgo-pechero dichotomy was thus preserved in the New World. The white or Spanish component of society was the American counterpart of the noble estate of Spain.

The place of the castes in the Spanish concept of a hierarchically organized society is rather difficult to define. Their existence was deplored. They really were not supposed to exist. In the eyes of most of the white population they were lazy, vicious, irresponsible, and a threat to social and political stability. Yet they formed a large proportion of the artisan and laboring population of the viceroyalty. As infames por derecho and as payers of tribute they possessed a juridical status or personality and a social status universally recognized and defined by reputation. They constituted a common estate deformed by New World circumstances.

In regard to the Indian, universally minded jurists and theologians argued for the equality of the Spaniards and the indigenous population, but from the outset of colonization a wide chasm yawned between the two races. The Indians existed as conquered people, the Spanish as conquerors. The Spanish became the employers and exploiters of labor, the Indians the hewers of wood and the drawers of water. Profound cultural differences existed between the two peoples; the Indians refused to live like civilized people, that is, like Spaniards, and were regarded by the latter as *rústicas* or *miserables*. Thus, the indigenous population acquired a dependent if not an inferior status which was juridically recognized. In the Laws of the Indies, the Indians were regarded as perpetual minors and wards of the crown and were placed under the tutelage of royal officials in *corregimientos*, of individuals and corporations in *encomiendas*, and of the regular ecclesiastical orders in missions. In recognition of their vassalage, they were required to pay tribute; they were forbidden to dress like Spaniards, to ride horses, or to bear arms. On the other hand, they were conceded privileges and immunities which in effect constituted a fuero. Official lay and clerical protectors oversaw their welfare; they had access to special tribunals such as the *Juzgado de Indios;* they were exempt from the direct jurisidiction of the Holy Office and from various taxes such as the *alcabala* and *diezmos.* Although functionally they were commoners, they were juridically distinct from the castes and constituted a peculiarly American estate.

The three primary estates contained internal stratifications based partly on ascribed status deriving from lineage, degree of whiteness, and nobility, and in part from status acquired through wealth or royal favor. Within the Indian component, the upper stratum consisted of a nobility whose rank was inherited from the preconquest *caciques* and confirmed by the Spanish crown. This group was juridically identified with the white nobility in that it was exempt from tribute and from legal inhibitions imposed on the general Indian population but it remained culturally Indian. At a lower level were the notables who occupied posts of distinction in Indian communities, while the base of the pyramid consisted of the mass of the indigenous population.

Within the white estate there existed a group which might be described as an upper nobility. Initially this was comprised of the conquerors who by virtue of their feats of arms regarded themselves as a new nobility. Immediately below them came the first settlers whose excellence derived not from martial exploits but from merits acquired in the initiation of colonization, the occupation of new territory for the king, and the founding of towns and cities. These two groups were rewarded for their eminent services by encomiendas: that is, grants of Indians from which they were privileged to extract labor and/or tribute. During the seventeenth century they tended to fuse and together were called by jurists, *beneméritos de Indias.* Initially the encomendero class gave indications of evolving into a military nobility along lines reminiscent of the emergence of the Spanish nobility in the Middle Ages. The encomienda initially displayed distinctly feudal features, particularly in its military aspects. In effect the crown and the encomenderos were parties to a feudal contract. The former granted the encomienda as a benefice, while the latter acknowledged vassalage, swore fealty, and were obligated to be ready with arms, horses, and retainers to fight the enemies of their lord. In order to fulfill this obligation, they were required to reside in the province in which they held their encomienda; in case of absence—for which permission was required—they had to appoint a champion (*escudero*); if a minor inherited, his guardian or tutor appointed a champion; if an encomienda passed to a woman, she was required to marry within a year so that her husband could fulfill the military obligations entailed. The army of encomenderos resembled the feudal host and was the principle reliance of the crown for defense of the viceroyalty up to the last quarter of the sixteenth century. Thus operations against the Chichemecas in New Galicia in 1541-1542 were conducted largely by encomenderos. Some ten years later when Viceroy Velasco requested assistance from the crown for operations against rebellious Indians, he was told that the responsibility lay with the encomenderos because "the encomiendas are rents which His Majesty gives to the encomenderos because they defend the land."

The emergence of a military nobility from the encomienda system, however, was prevented by several factors. In the first place, the encomienda proved to be unsatisfactory as a military institution. The encomenderos were a restless lot and, despite repeated prohibitions, abandoned their provinces for the lure of new conquests. Moreover, they displayed a marked reluctance to engage in organized campaigns, particularly if these were distant from their city and of long duration. As a result, during the last part of the sixteenth century the burden of defense was shifted to regular troops and to a citizen militia drawn from the white population in general. The sons and grandsons of the conquerors failed to perpetuate the martial spirit of their ancestors. Although the trappings of military service—titles of rank, uniforms, and military honors—were eagerly sought after, they were honorific in character and were not associated with attraction to a military way of life. At the end of the sixteenth century, old soldier Bernardo de Vargas Machuca lamented that although the military profession was the most honorable and sublime of all the arts, it had fallen into disfavor and there were few citizens who would not smile at the thought of a career of arms. A century later, Viceroy the Marquis of Mancera complained about the disinclination of the Mexican nobility for military service.

A second factor which inhibited the development of a powerful upper nobility in the Indies was the opposition of the crown. The encomenderos, whose mentality was essentially medieval, aspired to combine encomiendas with possession of land and jurisdiction to create seignorial estates, but the crown insisted on keeping grants of land and grants of Indians separate; it refused to grant Indians in perpetuity and, except in rare cases such as the Marquisate of the Valley of Oaxaca and the Dukedom of Atrisco, it denied seignorial jurisdiction to encomenderos. In the reforms of the 1540's, the latter were prohibited from extracting personal services from their charges and allowed to collect only tribute.

Thus the beneméritos became pensioners of the crown, a tamed nobility without any real vitality. Essentially they were dilettantes. They adopted the dignified mien and deportment of the noble estate. Among themselves and in their intercourse with other social sectors they insisted on being addressed as hidalgo or caballero. They eagerly sought titles of Castile and habits in the military orders of Spain. Their reading consisted of books of noble deeds and pious works and they displayed an extreme religiosity. They were vain, sensitive, disdainful of the mechanical and commercial arts, and addicted to luxury and ostentation. Perhaps their most distinguishing characteristic was an exaggerated sense of honor, a term not translatable in bourgeois concepts of rectitude, strict accounting for responsibility, moral conduct, and the like, but as self-esteem based on status. The meaning is more precisely conveyed by the Spanish word *pundonor*.

The formation of an American structure of estates was accompanied by the transference and florescence of the functional corporation along with its legally defined responsibilities, privileges, and immunities. The church came with the Conquest and during the sixteenth century most of its major subcorporations, the university community, the Holy Office, the secular and regular orders, the cathedral chapters, and the like became constituent parts of Mexican society. The municipal corporations likewise followed the Conquest. A permanent army appeared in the latter part of the century. The consulado of Mexico City was chartered in 1592, and most of the artisan guilds made their appearance in the late sixteenth and early seventeenth centuries.

As in Europe the relation between the estates and corporate structure was complex. On the one hand, following the medieval prescription, there was some correspondence between the two. Theoretically, *casta limpia* was a requirement for admission to all the corporations, and in practice the white element monopolized the consulado, the miner's guild, the officer corps of the army, the university community, and the higher levels of the ecclesiastical corporations. However, the reluctance of whites to engage in dishonorable occupations complemented by the economic aspirations of the more enterprising castes and Indians led to the admission of large numbers of non-whites into the craft guilds. They were also enlisted in the army and found their way into the lower levels of the church, particularly the secular clergy. Following the peninsular pattern there was an interlocking of class and corporate organization.

The preceding analysis of social structure employs a reputational or subjective method. That is, it is based on the way people of the time conceived of and defined their own and others' role and status. Colonial Mexican society may also be examined objectively; that is by assuming the position of an outside observer and by means of objective criteria dividing a society into groups, classes, or strata. Thus, a modern class system—upper, middle, and lower groups—based on the ownership and use of property may be discerned. The upper class consisted of the owners of haciendas and estancias, mines, textile factories, and mercantile establishments, and the upper levels of the bureaucracy and the clergy. At a point not clearly definable, this sector graded into a middle class composed of retail merchants and shopkeepers, the more substantial artisans, professionals, owners of small and middle-sized ranchos and mines, managers and salaried employees of rural properties, mines, and workshops, and lower ranked ecclesiastics and bureaucrats. The lower class comprised less affluent shopkeepers, peddlers, and artisans operating outside the guilds; servants, laborers, and a mass of landless, propertyless, and jobless idlers and vagabonds. Such a classification presents serious difficulties. Given adequate data on distribution of wealth, income, occupation, and the like, it might be practicable to analyze colonial social structure in terms of economic classes. The value systems commonly associated with such sectors, however, were lacking or at best rudimentary. Miners, merchants, and artisans might be functionally bourgeois but their mentality was not. Until the very end of the colonial period at least, they continued to think of social role and status in terms of nobility, titles, honor, and corporate membership, although in the case of the Spanish upper classes wealth reinforced nobility and vice versa.

The lower classes can be roughly identified with castes and Indians. Functionally they formed a proletariat. No class consciousness, however, existed within either element or linked the two together. A wide gap separated the rural Indian peon and the urban mulatto shoemaker. Their placement in society did not derive ultimately from economic function but from ethnic and cultural qualities recognized in law. Economic classes can probably be best regarded as an incipient situation and as a concept which can best be used for studying social development over a period extending beyond the colonial era rather than for the colonial period itself.

The social organization of New Spain was complicated by a peculiarly American cleavage which cut across the white estate and the corporate structure in general. This was the sharp status distinction between the European-born and American-born Spaniard, between criollo and *gachupín*. This schism originated within the first generations of Spaniards in the New World. The conquerors, first settlers, and their descendants deeply resented latecomers, both private citizens and crown appointees, who competed for the royal favors which they regarded as rightfully theirs. The new arrivals, on their part, resented the arrogance and privileges of the beneméritos. Original resentments were deepened and elaborated in subsequent generations. The peninsular Spaniard in common with his northern European contemporaries deprecated colonials as culturally and even biologically inferior. They were unenterprising, unreliable, and frivolous. The creole regarded the gachupín as common, pushing and, except for the higher levels of the church, army, and bureaucracy, as socially inferior. He resented the preemption of the choicest benefices in church and state by the European Spaniard despite the strict legal equality of the two groups. But he was embittered above all by the fact that the status conveyed by "born in Spain" was forever beyond his reach. Yet there was a certain ambivalence in the creole attitude. While he maligned and condemned the gachupín, he envied him because his lack of extended contact with Indian or Negro gave him a better claim to limpieza de sangre, and he eagerly sought marriage alliances with the European, even the most common, to reinforce his family lineage.

Some observations may now be made on the related problems of social cohesion, social control, and social change. The hierarchical society continued to be thought of in organic terms. Its component parts were supposed to be mutually interdependent, interacting, and together forming the functioning body social. In fact, however, the parts exhibited a strong compulsion toward autarchy. Juridically, each to some extent was a separate entity, a state within a state. Each was wrapped up in its own affairs and interested only in its own welfare, its privileges, and its immunities, all of which had to be defended jealously against similar aims of other segments. There existed no common values, interests, or objectives. There were Indians, castes, nobles, soldiers, priests, merchants and lawyers but there were no citizens. In the terms of Ortega y Gasset, it was an invertebrate society.

This society was held together by a combination of a number of circumstances. Among them was inertia. A society of estates and corporations was in the natural order of things and until the latter part of the eighteenth century there was no serious protest against a social system based on juridical and social inequality. Social unrest took the form of drives to improve the status of the individual and the group, not efforts to change the system. The hierarchical order was supported through the virtual monopoly of arms, wealth, prestige, and authority by the white nobility. Until the very end of the colonial period, its existence was encouraged by the crown as a means of social and political control. In an opinion of 1806, the Council of the Indies stated:

It is undeniable that the existence of various hierarchies and classes is of the greatest importance to the existence and stability of a monarchical state, since a graduated system of dependence and subordination sustains and insures the obedience and respect of the last vassal to the authority of the sovereign. With much more reason such a system is necessary in America, not only because of its greater distance from the throne, but also because of the number of that class of people who, because of their vicious origin and nature, are not comparable to the commoners of Spain and constitute a very inferior species.

The crown contributed to the creation and maintenance of the system in various ways. It was the "head" of the body social. It was the ultimate author of legislation defining the status of each estate and corporation. It had at its disposal the means of compulsion: the bureaucracy, the ordinary courts, the military, and the police. It was also the ultimate source of privileges and favors; it conceded land, monopolies, titles, honors, and offices. It reconciled class and group conflicts; it was the supreme court of appeal. As the final arbiter it checked and balanced the powerful centrifugal forces which were a constant threat to social stability. Perhaps most fundamental was the crown as a mystique and a symbol. Américo Castro observed that the people of Spain and Spanish America were united by a principle external to them, a mystical faith in and loyalty to the symbol of the crown. This faith was "an anchor of salvation, as was religious faith . . . ." "The monarchy . . . , especially from Ferdinand and Isabella on, appears surrounded by Messianic prestige." Bad legislation was not the fault of the king; he was inadequately informed. Wrong decisions could not be attributed to him; he was improperly advised. The hostility of creoles was directed against Spaniards, not the crown. Revolts and riots were not against the king but against his servants. The monarch might be a weakling or an imbecile; his servants might be ridiculed or even defied; his laws could be evaded, but the crown as a symbol was sacrosanct.

The church was an active partner of the crown in maintaining social control. It wholeheartedly supported a society of hierarchies and privileged classes both on doctrinaire grounds and as a beneficiary of the system. It employed directly to this end its control over education, its vast resources of moral suasion, and its temporal wealth. It upheld, moreover, the role of the crown as the ultimate temporal authority and as a symbol of Spanish Christianity.

Mexican colonial society has traditionally been viewed as static and ponderously stable, an interpretation epitomized in the expression, *la siesta colonial.* Traditional history has it that this structure was abruptly fractured by the Wars of Independence producing a half century, more or less, of anarchy. In fact, from the moment of the Conquest it was characterized by continuous although unspectacular change. The formation of the castes and the creation of an American system of estates was certainly an evolutionary if not a dynamic process. In the preceding pages reference has been made to qualities of flexibility and openness which characterized social stratification. Within certain limits upward and downward mobility existed. Castes with luck, enterprise, or official favor might and did become whites, while whites through misfortune or mismanagement might sink into the lower estates. A similar mobility appears to have existed between castes and Indians. Bagú emphasizes the miscibility of the colonial social system and particularly stresses the instability of the "middle classes." Adverse regulation, misfortune, lack of enterprise, or alcoholism constantly submerged artisans and shopkeepers into the mass of the indigent poor. Substantial changes in the character of the upper nobility also took place in the seventeenth and eighteenth centuries. In rural areas the nucleus of a new elite appeared, the masters of the great haciendas and estancias. Some of its members derived from the old encomendero nobility but others were American and European Spaniards who were rewarded for services to the crown by grants of land. Although some of the beneficiaries came from titled families and others subsequently acquired titles, the new upper nobility was primarily a nobility *de hecho* rather than *de derecho*. Titles simply confirmed a status derived from the ownership of latifundia. In contrast to its attitude toward the encomienda, the crown permitted and encouraged the growth of the hacienda as an instrument of economic development and social control. The strength of the hacendado group was consolidated by the entailment of its estates. By preserving indivisible family patrimonies, entailment established a family lineage through which status could be transmitted.

The growth of a landed aristocracy was paralleled by the development of a mercantile patriciate in the cities of the viceroyalty. This element derived in part from the old *morador* class; that is householders (*vecinos*) of the sixteenth century towns who were not among the privileged few receiving encomiendas and who generally lived by trade or manufacturing. It was augmented by second sons of encomenderos and new arrivals from Spain who entered commerce. The concentration of trade in a few cities, and monopolistic privileges conceded to merchant groups encouraged the accumulation of mercantile fortunes by a relatively small number of families. The mineowners who accumulated great wealth through the exploitation of Mexico's silver resources constituted a related group. The possession of great wealth conferred influence and status, much to the disgust of the old encomenderos. "Those who yesterday operated shops and taverns and engaged in other base occupations," wrote one disgruntled benemérito, "are today placed in the best and most prized positions." Mercantile and mining fortunes were recognized or perhaps it would be better to say exploited by the crown through the concession of titles of nobility. These were granted with increasing frequency in the latter half of the eighteenth century.

At the same time that new elite elements were emerging, the economic base of the encomenderos was deteriorating. In the seventeenth century there was a strong trend toward reversion of encomiendas to the crown while those remaining in private hands were subjected to new fiscal exactions. The lot of the bulk of the encomenderos is described by Guillermo Céspedes:

With such a small sustenance, the more tenacious of the beneméritos—converted into social parasites—composed accounts of the merits and services rendered by their distinguished ancestors, and swarmed the antechambers of the viceroys to beg *corregimientos, tenientazgos, alcaldías,* or any other bureaucratic post befitting the glory of their lineage. Their pride of caste, exacerbated by their economic difficulties would not countenance any occupation or employment other than waiting patiently for a shower of royal favors. They looked down on the newly rich, emerged from the "ashes and soot of the stewpots," and particularly on the hateful and wealthy merchants and on the *chapetones* who came from Spain to enjoy benefices in the governmental bureaucracy. They continued their addiction to pious works which revealed to them a God by whose inscrutable designs the grandsons of the conquerors lived on the verge of starvation. Some even reached the point of asking if they were suffering punishment and penance for the blood which their heroic ancestors shed during the conquest.

With the abolition of the encomienda system in the early eighteenth century they finally disappeared as a class.

A certain coalescence took place in at least a peripheral way among the various elements of the colonial elite. The more enterprising encomenderos managed to escape the general decadence of their class. Some managed to retain or acquire landed estates. Others, forgetting their class pride, married into the aristocracy of wealth or entered commerce themselves. Such concessions although distasteful were not degrading since commerce at the wholesale level had become officially and socially honorable. Among the other groups, wealthy merchants and miners employed excess capital for the purchase of rural estates, and needy hacendados contracted marriage alliances with willing merchants and mining families.

During the eighteenth century and particularly its later four decades social change was accelerated by the interaction of multiple influences including population growth and progressive miscegenation, expansion of areas of settlement, economic development and the increase of wealth, fiscal, administrative, and military reforms, and infiltration of egalitarian doctrines from abroad. Among the whites, new opportunities appeared to acquire wealth and improve social status. Creoles found additional avenues for social advancement in the officer corps of newly organized regular and militia regiments while the castes through enlistment in the army achieved exemption from tribute and acquired status through the possession of the *fuero militar*. In general there appears to have been a further blurring of the line between white and caste. Official documents and legal formulae of the last half of the eighteenth century frequently employ expressions such as *que se tenga por español* or *recibido por español* when referring to mixed bloods, and euphemisms such as *pardo* and *moreno* were increasingly used in place of Negro and mulatto. Aguirre Beltrán quotes contemporary sources to the effect that all those who were not clearly Indians or of *color achocolatado* were said to be and were considered as Spaniards. Indeed, identifications based on place of birth and ethnic origins tended to be replaced by others expressing only social quality. In the service records of militia and regular officers in the 1770's, under *calidad* are found the terms mestizo, castizo, pardo, *español europeo* and *español americano*. By 1806 these were largely replaced by such identifications as *noble, ilustre, conocida, distinguida, honrada,* and *buena*. Without renouncing its support of a stratified society, the crown attempted to ameliorate some of the more obvious—and more troublesome—inequities. The new army had an explicitly stated secondary aim of providing honorable and status-conferring careers for creoles in the officer corps and castes in the ranks. Titles were conceded with greater frequency to creoles, and the castes could achieve legal whiteness by the purchase of cedulas called *gracias al sacar*. Moreover, a cedula of February 1, 1795 dispensed pardos and *quinterones* from the status of *infame*, authorized them to contract matrimony with whites, and permitted them to hold public office and enter Holy Orders. The castes also found advocates among the whites. Viceroy Croix believed that their superior physiques, amenability to discipline, and inclination toward military service made them better soldiers than the effete and prideful whites. Lucas Alamán, who was certainly no egalitarian, rated them as the most useful part of the population and reported that the only time that Matías Martín de Aguirre, a European Spaniard and deputy to the Cortes of Madrid in 1821, rose to speak was to deliver a eulogy of the mulattos who had served in the royalist armies.

There appears also to have been some erosion of the bases of the corporate social structure. During the reign of Charles III, direct and indirect efforts were made to restrict or to level or to rebalance the power and status of traditional corporate groups. The principal device was the limitation of privileged fueros and the renovation and extension of the royal or ordinary jurisdiction. Crown policy was most striking in the case of ecclesiastical corporations. The royal patronage was extended, the ordinary ecclesiastical fuero was restricted, rights to church asylum were limited, the power of the Holy Office was circumscribed, the Society of Jesus was expelled from Spain and the empire and the famous *amortización* of 1804 struck at the pious foundations. In New Spain there appears to have been both an absolute and relative decline in the power and prestige of the ecclesiastical establishment as a whole. The reglamento of free trade of 1778 was a blow to the power of the consulados and at the same time the state loosened the restrictive practices of the artisan guilds. In New Spain an increasing volume of trade and manufacturing was conducted outside the guild system. One striking and consequential exception to these trends must be noted. At the same time that the status and power of other corporate groups were being subverted, the metropolitan and colonial armies were not only strengthened and reorganized, but their fueros were extended, their prestige enhanced, and their morale cultivated.

In summary, three general and interrelated observations may be made. First, a close look at New Spain on the eve of independence reveals a gradual erosion of a social structure based on estates, corporations, and juridical inequality, and outlines, at least, of a new system based on economic class. Perhaps the most apparent manifestation of the latter phenomenon was the growing strength of the mercantile "bourgeoisie" and the emergence of an entrepreneurial sector among the textile manufacturers of Valladolid, Guadalajara, and the Bajío. Second, the velocity of change was insufficient to accommodate severe tensions within the social order, principally the stored-up resentments of the lower estates and the frustrations of the white creoles. The former exploded in 1810, the latter boiled over in 1821, and the two combined fleetingly in the latter year to produce political independence. Third, the hierarchical colonial society survived the break from Spain with some reordering of its components, but with the disappearance of the symbol of the crown as an instrument of social control, its invertebrate character became fully emergent. It required nearly one hundred years for the formation of a juridically egalitarian society and the creation of a new social myth as an instrument of cohesion.

Other Articles of Interest

McAlister, Lyle N. "The Reorganization of the Army of New Spain, 1763–1766." XXXIII (1953), 1–32.

Prior to the Seven Years' War the obligations of military service in New Spain were largely theoretical, and the armed forces—regulars and militia—were small in number and imperfectly trained and armed. Lessons of the Seven Years' War prompted a new military program, under the command of Juan de Villalba y Angulo, the result of which was a thorough-going enlargement and reorganization of military forces. The basic structure and procedure of the military were fixed by 1766 in a form that would persist through the remainder of the colonial period.

Fisher, Lillian Estelle. "Manuel Abad y Queipo, Bishop of Michoacán." XV (1935), 425–447.

---

13. Music in the Cathedral of Mexico in the Sixteenth Century

LOTA M. SPELL

The study of Latin American history should not be confined to such topics as conquistadores, Indians, municipal cabildos, the Church, or economic matters. The transference of culture from Europe and the influences which led to a new and different New World culture constitute a basic theme in Latin American history. Yet only a few scholars, such as Mrs. Spell and Professor Robert Stevenson, have addressed themselves to the task of tracing the history of one of the most widely cultivated arts in colonial Latin America—music. Mrs. Spell offers in this article a carefully concentrated account of the important position music held in the life of sixteenth-century Mexico City as the records relating to the cathedral reveal it. The work is based upon manuscript sources and other rare materials.

Within three years after Europeans secured control of the Valley of Mexico in 1521, the rubble of the pyramidial *teocalli* on the vast Main

---

From Volume XXVI (1946), pages 293–319.

Plaza of the Aztec capital had been converted into a small parochial church in which Christian services were held for the conquistadores, and before seven years had passed the Emperor Charles V had dispatched to the New World a stern Franciscan to become the Bishop of Mexico and to make of the parochial church a cathedral. But so greatly did the emperor feel the immediate need of a spiritual mentor for the Europeans and of a protector for the new heathen subjects that the bishop-elect, Juan de Zumárraga, sailed before being consecrated.

After weary months of ocean crossing and days of steep mountain climbing, Zumárraga found himself in the Aztec capital—an island city high among snow-clad peaks—but again among brethren of his order, for some Franciscans had been in Mexico for five years, teaching and trying to Christianize the youth of the only highly civilized people then known in America. On the western edge of the section of the city that Hernán Cortés had set aside for the Spanish inhabitants, only a few blocks from the Main Plaza, a Franciscan monastery had been built; there the bishop-elect established his headquarters and began to study the problems of his diocese. About him he found a native society composed of a cultured aristocracy, of laboring classes, and of slaves—all controlled largely by the handful of Europeans who had conquered them. Zumárraga had the Indian chiefs of the region called together and assured them, through Fray Pedro de Gante, the Flemish schoolmaster who had acquired their language, that he had their interests at heart and had come to help them; he also made friends with the Indian boys, largely sons of chieftains, who were being taught Spanish, reading, writing, and music in the school that had been established in the Franciscan monastery. When he attended the service in the chapel of San José that had been set aside for them, he marvelled at their musical ability and at the progress they had made in absorbing a type of music entirely foreign to their own. For the Aztecs had long employed music in many aspects of their life—in recreation, in industry, in war, and in religious rites, especially in their temples when human victims were being sacrificed— but they knew only percussion and wind instruments, their pitch range was limited, and they had not developed any form of musical notation.

As Zumárraga went about the city, he realized that he had come to live in a region wonderfully blessed by Nature; but his church—the primitive structure that faced west on the plaza, toward one of Cortés' palaces— seemed miserably small and rude, even in contrast with the monastic chapel he had left at Abrojo, in Spain. There was space enough for a magnificent edifice, and visions of a cathedral like that in Seville, of which the Mexican church was a dependency, rose constantly before him. With time, he resolved, it must be built. At least he could have at once music as good as the Indian chapel had. Chants of a Christian choir must supplant those the Aztec priests had intoned while hearts were torn warm from human bodies to be offered as sacrifice to the gods.

Many helped the bishop-elect in those early days. Fray Pedro, the

Fleming who directed the Indian school, assigned a group of boys to serve him as choristers. Their further instruction in music was placed in the hands of Canon Juan Xuárez, who came in 1530, but Fray Pedro and Arnaldo de Basatzio taught them Latin in order that they might sing the service understandingly. An organ was then in use, and the organist was paid fifty pesos annually. Indeed the services in the Cathedral of Mexico were comparable in some respects with those in the Cathedral of Seville. Even in the early years of the bishopric Zumárraga was not ashamed of the music. Among his first purchases for his church were "four large choir books with notes for the singing of the service, and missals and large breviaries for the choir."

The interest of Zumárraga in the music of the church was evident throughout his incumbency, even though it was merely a detail in the general program. He recognized the unusual results achieved with the Indian boys and appreciated their musical ability. As early as 1531 he joined with others in vouching to the king for their ability to sing plain chant and polyphonic music: in a letter dated June 12 of that year addressed to the Consistory at Tolosa in 1532 he called special attention to the singing and music script of the boys in Pedro de Gante's school. While in Spain, to which he was recalled to explain the difficulties between the civil and ecclesiastical authorities in Mexico, he begged the Council of the Indies to provide choir books of plain chant and missals for the chapels of the friars, since the native boys taught by them were very capable in ecclesiastical song. Pedro de Gante certainly considered them competent to serve in the cathedral, for he wrote the king, who was his kinsman: "Y sin mentir puedo decir harto bien que hay buenos . . . cantores que podrían cantar en la capilla de V. M. tan bien, que si no se vee tal vez no se creerá."

Since the diocese of Mexico was a dependency of the archdiocese of Seville, many of the customs and practices of that cathedral, including the use of the Mozarabic liturgy, were slowly instituted in the humble church. The cathedral service involved music of two types: plain chant (*canto llano*), distinguishable from modern music both by its basic scales and the irregular accents derived from the text, which sufficed for simple churches and services; and measured music (organ-song, *canto de órgano*), recognizable by accents at regular intervals, which was usually employed at least for portions of the service on Sundays and feast days. The ranking musical director was the precentor, a dignitary of the cathedral chapter, who was responsible for the training of the choristers in chanting and the direction of all concerned with plain chant. The succentor was his assistant and substitute, upon whom much of the training of the choristers devolved. The chapel master, even if a cleric, was seldom higher in rank than a prebendary but was required to have extensive technical musical training and experience; he taught and directed all measured music, which included all polyphonic, composed musical settings and songs needed, and rehearsed the choir for the elaborate services of great feast days. Among the types of music then much cultivated in the cathedral were *chansones* or *chanzonetas*, popular songs adapted to sacred texts suited to such occasions as Christmas and Easter; and motets, polyphonic compositions in which the tenor usually had the principal part, often marked by the recurrence of some rhythmic or melodic figure but limited to one or a few words, while each of the other singers sang a different text.

At Seville a choir school was attached to the cathedral; there a group of boys called *seises*, as there were at first only six, were given their living, clothing, a good general education, special training in music and dancing, and a small salary, in return for their services as choristers in the cathedral. To preserve the beautiful soprano voices, some of the boys were castrated. They were expected to dance before the altar on high feast days, to take part in playlets, and to form their own choir for *chanson* singing. It was clear that the Aztec boys could be similarly trained, for they were unusually gifted musically and skillful, graceful dancers; besides, the Spanish residents had growing sons who could render such service. But before Zumárraga could foster such a school or any other institutions to disseminate European culture among the new subjects of Spain, he found himself in open conflict with civil officials who refused to recognize ecclesiastical rights or privileges. They even forcibly removed from the monastery two clerics who were being held under episcopal jurisdiction, executed one, and cut off a leg of the other. Zumárraga then felt that the climax had been reached. With the friars and their pupils he withdrew to Tezcoco and placed the capital of New Spain under interdict.

When news of the situation in Mexico reached Europe, the bishop-elect was recalled, but before he left, the provisional charter of the cathedral, dated May 1, 1530, had been received; and on May 26, 1532, the income was officially budgeted to cover the salaries of dean, six canons (one of whom, Juan Xuárez, was acting as chapel master), three curates, the succentor or assistant precentor, the organist, and four altar boys, all of whom were already functioning. They continued to perform their duties during his absence, as did the choir. Once in Europe, Zumárraga told his own story; in time he was exonerated and ordered to return to his post —with increased authority, for he had meanwhile been consecrated. He came back intent on a better choir; for his church he brought various music books, both plain chant and polyphonic, processionals, and psalters. The choir that greeted him had already won such general approval that when the first viceroy was to be welcomed to the city both the "cantores e música" of the cathedral were engaged by the city council to furnish "songs and music and playlet" and were rewarded by that body with seventy pesos, which were paid to Canon Xuárez for distribution among them.

When one of the canons was dispatched to Spain in 1536 on cathedral business, he was authorized to secure from the Cathedral of Seville a very good copy on parchment of the latest version of the psalter and other portions of the service, regardless of expense, and to request that the salary of the organist be increased—since a competent organist was very essential to the solemnity of the services, and none could be secured even for double the sixteen pesos specified in the provisional charter. The canon also secured an order that the schoolmaster, who was being paid fifty pesos annually by the crown to instruct both Spanish and Indian boys, include the choristers among his students without charge. Both requests were granted, the annual salary of the organist being raised to forty pesos.

Two years later the books from Seville arrived, and a contest was instituted to discover the best calligrapher available. To Padre Juan de Avecilla went the honor of making copies—in exactly the size and style of note and script—of the dominical, the offertory, and the kyrie. With these the permanent choral library of the cathedral was begun; and the ceremonies, both when the bishop wore pontifical robes and otherwise, were largely fixed for succeeding years by the copy of those of the Cathedral of Seville made by its choirmaster. These were the customs followed also by the provincial cathedrals as they were established.

In 1537 the permanent charter for the cathedral arrived, but since the dignitaries were appointed by the king and diocesan funds were limited, chapter organization was slow. At the time the charter was issued only five of those provided for had been appointed, but among them was a precentor, who was required to be a doctor and expert in music, at least in plain chant. His duties consisted of singing, teaching correct singing, and conducting personally all that concerned chanting. The first to hold that office in the Cathedral of Mexico was Cristóbal de Pedraza, who was appointed before July, 1533. In 1536 he was given a commission which took him back to Spain, and while there he located a printer with a press and even music type who was willing to go to the New World. Some three years later he was tendered the bishopric of Honduras. As a substitute, the treasurer, Rafael de Cervantes, enjoyed the emoluments of the position for some time; but in 1540 Diego de Loaisa assumed the duties of the precentor. On February 1, 1538, at a salary of seventy pesos, Canon Xuárez was officially made the chapel master, whose responsibility it was to sing and teach measured and polyphonic music.

While choirboys had been serving in the cathedral since before 1530, the available cathedral records of those years make no reference to them by name. Following Spanish precedent, official appointees were chosen from poor boys of Spanish blood; they were given daily instruction in plain chant and measured music. Their salary was twelve pesos a year, and after they began to serve as singers their cassocks were given them. They were expected to take part by turns in all the ceremonies of the church, both inside and outside the cathedral; especially were they to be a feature of all processions, whether of festival or mourning. The first Spanish choristers cited by name are Bartolomé Mexía, who began serving on February 1, 1538, and Francisco de Santa María, who began on the first of July of that year. Diego Agurto was also admitted; and shortly among others were Gabriel Ramos, the son of the organist Antonio Ramos, Francisco de Soto, Andrés Vizcaíno, Juan Muñoz, Juan Baptista, Francisco de Banegas, Diego de Olvera, Benito García, and Diego, the "son of Logroño," a Spanish cathedral-trained singer, at one time the assistant precentor.

Many of the chapter members proved themselves disposed to dissensions; at times the friction between prelate and capitularies rose to the danger point. The absence of members from the services and the type of music to be rendered provoked differences. Although the charter authorized a chapter adequate to ensure a dignified cathedral service, the funds in the early years did not permit all the appointments. Some of the limited number did not know plain chant, and since many were continually absent, the bishop felt that substitutes should be employed in an effort to maintain cathedral standards. In writing Charles V of his difficulties with the chapter members, Zumárraga asked for authority to deduct the salary of absentees and therewith to pay substitutes. Singers not provided for by the charter were each being paid thirty pesos annually. Zumárraga explained further that the chapter had been using organ music in the services; in explanation, and as grounds for continuing the practice, he contended that such music made up to some extent for the missing voices. He urged the need of elaborate and beautiful music in the churches, for experience had shown that the natives, themselves very musical, were thereby highly edified; friars who heard their confessions had reported that conversions were much more readily effected by music than by sermons. Indians would come a great distance to hear impressive music; they worked hard to learn it; and they succeeded amazingly well. These facts in themselves, he argued, were sufficient ground for singing the services with all possible solemnity.

In this view, however, some of the members did not concur. They argued, for instance, that the masses provided for by the charter need merely be said, and not sung, since the text read "to be said solemnly." On another occasion when five players came to assist in the services, the bishop insisted that the chapter members join with him in paying them; to this some objected, but they agreed on receiving the extra pay which accrued from absences. The matter of the masses was settled by a royal decree that masses be sung as the bishop wished and that able temporary substitutes for absent members be employed. Zumárraga's action in excusing from matins, except on high feast days, all chapter members except the succentor and the one whose weekly turn it was to serve was also approved. In 1542 the king was asked to appoint Bartolomé Sánchez a prebendary, since he had been acting as succentor without remuneration. Additional instruction under Pedro de Campoverde was provided for the choirboys by the chapter, but in the absence of special funds for the purpose, that body decreed on January 2, 1543, that four of the twelve pesos paid each boy were to be given the instructor, and this sum supplemented by six pesos from the funds of the church. But after the return of that personage to Spain two years later, the deductions from the boys' salaries ceased.

It happened so frequently in the early years that the singers left the cathedral to accept more remunerative employment, especially in the provincial churches, as soon as they were sufficiently trained to be of any real service, that the chapter required each boy on accepting appointment as chorister to agree to remain nine years. This put the choir on a more permanent basis and the results of the new system were shortly apparent.

Among the boys who served faithfully were three sons of the conquistador Portillo, whose widow lived near the cathedral. These were Esteban, Pedro—who was known as Garcés de Portillo—and a younger boy, Francisco. So highly were their services esteemed that when the mother threatened in 1548 to move to Puebla because she had no house to live in, the chapter assigned her one belonging to the Hospital del Amor de Dios, and the members took up a collection among themselves to pay the rent for a year. The church was well rewarded for this action, as both the elder boys proved not only efficient choristers but became high officials of the cathedral and the university—Esteban becoming rector of the latter, treasurer of the cathedral, and an inquisitor.

Repeated efforts had been made by Bishop Zumárraga to secure authorization for the erection of an edifice in keeping with the importance of Mexico City as capital of a great viceroyalty and headquarters of the many religious orders at work both in North and South America. But the episcopal revenues did not suffice for such construction, and the many calls upon the royal treasury for funds for other purposes precluded aid from that quarter. When the first summons to the Council of Trent reached Mexico in 1537, and it was decided that the bishop could not leave his duties to undertake the long trip, he appointed four representatives to present a report on ecclesiastical conditions in New Spain and various requests, among them a pressing appeal that provision be made for the erection of a cathedral such as Mexico deserved—"like that of Seville and no smaller." The size and bareness of his church were a continual source of humiliation to Zumárraga. But before more than the preliminary steps toward construction were taken, his earthly work was finished. Recognition of the progress achieved led to the establishment of the archbishopric of Mexico in 1547; notice of his elevation in rank reached him in 1548, but he was never to receive the pallium. Instead, the body of Juan de Zumárraga was laid to rest in the primitive cathedral he had tried so hard to provide with appropriate services, music, and furnishings.

The foundations of a cathedral choir had, however, through his efforts, been laid. Chapel master and schoolteacher had been provided to supervise the education of a small number of boys who devoted their best efforts to the production of dignified cathedral music. A European organ bought at the bishop's expense in Seville and a capable organist contributed to the solemnity of the services, and other instruments were at times called into use. While the chapter members were by no means all musicians, there were among the number some good voices and some conscientious souls who faithfully fulfilled their choral duties to the limit of their ability. Hand-wrought choir books and stalls contributed to the glorification of the God of the Christians. The Latin love of beautiful music in the service of the church had been stimulated by the Indian enthusiasm for the art.

During the next five years in which the chapter directed the affairs of the cathedral, there was certainly no improvement in its music, if we may judge from the letters of Alonso de Montúfar, the first to preside over the archbishopric. He reported that two of the canons were dead and two others, as well as several minor officials, absent. The problem of supplying able substitutes, which Zumárraga had faced earlier, was a serious one. Montúfar found the salary scale of his chapter members low and the cost of living high. Indeed, the salaries paid in the provinces were so much better in proportion that "los tañedores" (the instrument players) and three or four very good singers had left for other places, as was the case of one of the canons. The newly established university (1553) contributed little toward the improvement of these conditions, since music was not included in its curriculum. It did, however, offer singers the opportunity for professional education, of which the Portillo boys, among others, were taking advantage.

In spite of many discouragements, the archbishop set vigorously about instituting reforms. In 1555 he called a church council with the hope of unifying the program of the church. Among the decrees of that body concerning ecclesiastical music were a few that affected the cathedral choir and its members. Chapter members who abbreviated any portion of the service were made subject to a fine. Boys preparing for ordination were required to be fourteen years of age and to know Latin, but choristers and acolytes with two years' service were exempted; for epistler, boys were required to sing plain chant to the extent required to serve in a church, to understand what they sang, and to have mastered the breviary. Indians were forbidden to say mass or the hours, but were permitted to teach the catechism; clerics were prohibited from singing secular songs in public and from attending bull fights; especial emphasis was laid on the prohibition of songs by Indians unless approved by those able to understand them; texts must be censored to eliminate profane subjects, and dancing must be restricted to the hours between mass and vespers. All books were to be subjected to censorship, whether imported or printed in the country.

The cathedral choir was a subject of deep concern to the archbishop. Canon Xuárez, who served a quarter of a century as chapel master, was replaced in 1556 by Lázaro del Álamo "atento a su buena habilidad y que lo hará muy bien y a pro y servicio desta santa iglesia." Álamo was a native of Espinar in the bishopric of Segovia, where he and his brother Hierónimo had served during their boyhood as *seises* in the cathedral; later they studied at the university of Salamanca, where the chair of music, established in 1255, was usually held by distinguished men. Álamo did improve the music of the Cathedral of Mexico and secured more choir books from Europe; in return, he was given a gratuity in 1557 and later was promoted to a canonship. The musical qualifications of most of the capitularies continued low; but the members complained to the king that the archbishop appointed some that did not know how to sing and paid them more than those who did. As precentor, Loaisa was still serving; as succentor Pedro de Logroño, whose bass voice and musical skill had won for him, many years before, a recommendation to the Indies. In 1559 the number of choristers was increased to twelve, and among them were the only two sopranos, sons of Miguel de Eçija, whose beautiful voices made them objects of great attention. These were Serván Rivero and Alonso (Vásquez) de Eçija. They probably received early and special training from the chapel master who lived in their home. Both were frequently rewarded with gifts, and in 1566 the salary of Alonso was increased from thirty-five to forty pesos, as he was "bueno, virtuoso, y pobre." So popular were both boys that many people thought that without them there was no singing.

The work of the choirboys was not limited to the confines of the cathedral; they were required to take part as a body in religious processions and in other events of a civic or religious character. These included the procession and festivities of Corpus Christi Day and the annual procession on St. Hipólito's Day (August 13, the anniversary of the day on which the conquest of Mexico City was effected) in which the archbishop was accompanied by the choir, "tubis, fistulis, cettaris et omnibus aliis musicorum generibus"; for this service, the city regularly paid the choir thirty pesos. Among the events of 1559 were the ceremonies commemorating the death of Charles V, which had occurred in the previous year. The details of the work of the choir on that occasion give evidence of the state of cathedral music in Mexico at that time.

These ceremonies took place not in the primitive cathedral, whose roof was much too low to permit the erection of as lofty a funereal monument as the viceroy desired and whose location was too near the viceregal palace to permit of a long procession, but in the Indian chapel of San José, since its vast patio could serve as a site for the monument and could accommodate the large number who would attend. The entire chapel was draped in black, and special pews were designated for high officials and dignitaries. Around the archbishop's pulpit, placed near the main altar, were seated the chapter and choir of the cathedral and the four hundred priests who participated. At the vigil service, which was preceded by a procession, two hours long, from the Main Plaza down San Francisco Street to the monastery, the chapel master formed two choirs for the invitatory; one sang *Circumdederant me* and the other the psalm *Exultemus* in a contrapuntal setting of Cristóbal de Morales. After the cope bearers sang the antiphon and the first psalm *Verba mea auribus percipe, Domine,* the succentor joined them while the friars and clergy followed as a chorus; then the choristers sang the antiphon in contrapuntal form. The second psalm, *Domine ne in furore,* was sung in plain chant to the middle of the verse; to this the choirmaster and choristers replied in a four-voiced setting composed by Álamo. After the *Pater noster* of the bishop at the main altar, *Parce mihi* was sung in a contrapuntal setting of Morales, as was the *Qui Lazarum resuscitasti* after the second lesson. While the procession formed, the cope bearers sang *De profundis;* the response *Libera me* followed. To the final prayer of the bishop, after he and all his attendants had ascended the funereal pile, the singers responded with due solemnity. The next day, after the procession, mass was sung in a five-voiced contrapuntal setting; and, after the bishop preached, a motet to the following text:

> Nunc enim si centum linguae sint, Carole Caesar,
> Laudes non possem promere rite tuas:
> Qui reges magnos multos valdeque potentes,
> Fudisti summo et auxiliante Deo.

A psalm, as the procession formed, and the responses completed the service. Clearly works of the greatest polyphonists of that day were sung in the Mexican church only a few years after they were known in Spain, and the choirmaster was expected to, and did, compose original settings of portions of the service as the occasion demanded.

Regulations for improvement of the choir continued to be formulated during the next decade. On October 8, 1560, the three masses provided for by the charter were again ordered sung; the chapel master, on penalty of a fine of six pesos, was forbidden, on May 2, 1561, to attend funerals with the choir; sending a chorister out, speaking to one, or crossing from one side of the choir to another during a service were forbidden on October 3 of that year, as were, on December 3, 1566, succentor and singers from accepting any outside employment which would necessitate absence from their prescribed duties. All choristers were required, by act of the cabildo on the seventh of the next January, to take part in processions with the chapter and to sing polyphonic music with the chapel master; and during Lent, at a sign from the precentor, they were to stop what they were singing and proceed to the hymn *Vexilla Regis,* according to an order of March 29, 1569. In all the matins of the Easter service the chapter members were required to join in the Invitatory; in other matins to the first Nocturne; and when in honor of Our Lady until the "Gloria." Particularly did the archbishop stress the obligation of chapter members to learn to sing at least "capítulo, oración, lección, prefacio, gloria, credo, oración dominical, ite missa est, benedicamos domino, gradual, responsorio, aleluya, introito" and also antiphonal verse. If they did not learn plain chant within a year they forfeited one-tenth of their stipend; after the lapse of one year, one-eighth; and each succeeding year a correspondingly larger proportion.

In 1562 Loaisa was succeeded as precentor by Rodrigo de Barbosa, a man in his fifties, a doctor in theology of Salamanca, but Álamo continued as the chapel master and composed the music for the motets, carols and *"chanzonetas"* sung on high feast days, usually with texts written by local poets. One of these was Juan Bautista Corvera, to whom the archbishop sent requests through Álamo for poems for Christmas, Easter, and Corpus Christi Day. Corvera also wrote playlets; one, in particular, in which three shepherds and three shepherdesses took part, was very favorably received by both the archbishop and the viceroy, who were present at its performance. Another poet was a chaplain in the cathedral, Juan Pérez Ramírez, son of a conquistador and born in Mexico in 1543, who was being paid in 1569 fifty pesos, in addition to his regular salary of one hundred, for writing the texts of the plays and chanzonetas "para el ornato de la dicha iglesia y culto divino."

The qualifications of the chapter members and choir are set forth in a report made by the archbishop in 1570. The cathedral was still the structure completed in 1525; Barbosa was officiating as precentor; Lázaro del Álamo, "muy diestro en la música y buen eclesiástico," was the chapel master; and among the canons were Diego (López) de Agurto, one of the early choirboys, and Juan de Oliva, who had spent twenty-two of his fifty-eight years in Mexico and had been given his canonship by Montúfar as a reward for his fine contrabass voice and good service. The cantors included Canon Serván Rivero, "buen cantor, diestro en música," with a salary of two hundred pesos; Bartolomé Franco, a twenty-four-year-old native of Mexico, at 150 pesos; and Alonso de Eçija, "diestro en la música . . . y buena voz," who was receiving a salary as *racionero*. Among the other singers were Pedro Baptista, a Spaniard twenty-three years old who had been in the country only five or six years, and Juan Fernández from Olvega, near Tarragona in Aragon, each with a salary of one hundred pesos. Esteban de Portillo, the former choirboy, had received his doctorate from the university and was now acting as *visitador* of the diocese; among his duties was that of finding out whether any of the ecclesiastics went through the streets at night playing guitars or singing *"villancetes"* or were interested in women to the extent of holding their hands in public or giving them rides on mules or horses. Another singer, one of the much-needed sopranos, was Ventura Xixón, who was given a salary of one hundred pesos.

Although Archbishop Montúfar was not a man of the highest intelligence, throughout his incumbency he sought to improve the general conduct and musical attainments of his chapter, and he was clearly interested in encouraging promising local singers. After he became mentally incapable of performing the duties of his office, Bartolomé de Ledesma acted until Pedro Moya de Contreras, who was sent to Mexico in 1571 as inquisitor general, was made bishop-coadjutor. The vacancy in the post of chapel master caused by the death of Lázaro del Álamo was filled by Juan de Victoria, a native of Burgos, who had come to Mexico around 1567 and given evidence of competence.

In 1573 Moya de Contreras was named to head the archdiocese and that year the cornerstone of the great cathedral which was to face south on the Main Plaza was laid, but not until 1623, when one portion, the Sagrario, was opened for services, was the original chapel demolished. Slowly during that half century, by the side of the primitive structure, rose the massive walls of what was to be long the greatest cathedral in America.

But Moya de Contreras did not wait until after his consecration, which took place in December, 1574, to begin reorganization of the choir, which then consisted, in addition to chapter members, of the chapel master, organist, and twelve choristers. With that event in mind, he appointed Manuel Rodríguez, perhaps the famous organist, to form an orchestra of secular players; and in October Bartolomé de Luna was made its director at a salary of two hundred pesos. Canon Oliva was delegated by the chapter to take charge of the instruction in "*son*" and "*cantar*" and also of the Indian reed players three times a week.

Certain events which occurred in connection with the consecration of the archbishop bring to light other activities of the cathedral choir. On the day of consecration, December 5, and the day he received the pallium, the eighth, two plays were performed by the choristers under the direction of Juan de Victoria. The first of the plays, *Desposorio espiritual entre el pastor Pedro y la iglesia mexicana*, symbolizing the spiritual union of the archbishop and the church, was the work of a cathedral cleric, Juan Pérez Ramírez. Among the interlocutors were the Mexican Church, Faith, Hope, Charity, Grace, Peter the Prudent, Divine Love (a singer), shepherds and shepherdesses, and a chorus. The shepherds came on the stage singing, alternating with the shepherdesses, and from time to time the chorus chimed in with selections from the Psalms and the Songs of Solomon. Dame Love appeared singing "Whosoever shall seek me, shall find me;" then the wedding took place in song, the singers and Dame Love singing the ritual alternately. After the singers finished "And those whom God hath joined," the playlet concluded with a dance. The second play, by a theological student—Fernán González de Eslava—was on the same subject; but a farce between the acts delighted the public as greatly as it increased the animosity between the viceroy and archbishop which had been manifested on more than one occasion since Moya de Contreras came upon the scene as inquisitor. For in the course of the efforts of a collector to collect the alcabala tax, he tumbled several completely nude children out of bed, much to the amusement of the audience. But since this sales tax was about to be imposed for the first time in Mexico, the portrayal of a merciless collector and the sufferings of his victims went home. The viceroy, as the head of the civil administration authorized to collect the tax, saw in the performance only an intent to create trouble and bad feeling, and retaliated by reminding the archbishop that a decree existed prohibiting performances of any play without advance civil approval. He also ordered the arrest of

Juan de Victoria because he had given the play with the choirboys; of González de Eslava, because he was supposed to be the author of the farce; and of the mulatto who acted the part of the clown. Victoria was held in jail a few days and the others for over two weeks, in spite of the efforts of the archbishop to secure their release.

Such performances by the choirboys in the cathedral and other places were neither exceptional events nor was the performance in the cathedral the only presentation of the playlet of Eslava. It was given the next day in the monastery of San Francisco and had been requested by the convents of Regina Coeli and La Concepción, but these performances, as well as those of three other plays scheduled for the following Sunday, were canceled as a result of the viceroy's communication.

The viceroy had evidently also complained to the council that the archbishop was not filling the positions of cantor and chorister through competitive examinations, as required by law or European precedent, or with viceregal approval; for early in 1575 the new archbishop was explaining how difficult it was to secure capable singers at all, since the small salaries had no appeal, and it was more a matter of begging singers to accept positions than of requiring them to go through a process involving much red tape, which they certainly would not do.

In a later letter he describes frankly and in some detail the singers among his chapter members. Alonso Granero de Ávalos was the precentor. Canon Diego López de Agurto, now forty-six years old, has served in the church since childhood, yet "es hombre sin letras y apenas sabe leer. Muestra poco entendimiento y mal asiento de juicio, ynquieto y vano, y distraido en negocios de mugeres." Serván Rivero, twenty-four, is a skilled musician, but "sabe poca grámatica y no ha hecho fruto entre los Indios . . . no ha perseverado ni dado buena quenta." Bartolomé Franco, also a twenty-four-year-old native of Mexico, is a contrabass. Pedro Garcés, a moral man, honest, quiet and peaceful, with a university degree, fluent command of the Mexican language, and highly skilled in music, has grown up in the service of the church, served as prebendary and succentor many years, and now, at the age of forty-three, still has a good voice. The Aragonese Juan Hernández, who has been in Mexico some eight years, is a skilled musician with a good voice, by which he won a place as cathedral cantor; he is a graduate of the University of Mexico in canon law; of fair ability, moral, well inclined, and deserving of advancement. Juan de Salcedo, a thirty-year-old native of Mexico, has taken a degree in canon law and taught four years in the university—"es de buena habilidad y memoria: a estudiado y travajado con necessidad y virtud, tiene presteza y facilidad en la lengua y a sido algo infamado della, no sé si con verdad; al presente parece tener más reposo; es libre y orgulloso algo arrogante, a sido siempre recogido y honesto; merece que V. M. le haga merced." The archbishop's favorite appears to have been Alonso de Eçija, then thirty—skilled in music, possessor of a good voice, and succentor. He also mentions, among the clerics of his diocese, Diego de Olvera, one of the early choirboys, now forty-three: "bachiller en canones, buena lengua mexicana, a sido cura entre yndios más a de diez años, no ha tenido buen govierno en su persona, y a sido preso por desatinos que ha hecho con colera; de un año á esta parte parece que está mas asentado; está al presente en Huehuetoca."

During the early part of the first year of his incumbency as archbishop Moya de Contreras made further progress in the organization of the choir. De Luna, the director of the orchestra, was given a joint appointment with Francisco Covarrubias, Miguel de los Reyes, and Bartolomé de Sayavedra at a thousand pesos annually. In May a sackbut player, Pedro de Rivas, was added to the trio; and on May 20, 1575, Hernando Franco was given the position of chapel master. Although it has generally been assumed that Franco was a native of Mexico, he was born in the village of La Serena in the vicinity of Alcántara. He had known Álamo, the former chapel master, some thirty-three years before in Espinar, where the Álamo family lived for many years, and had come to Guatemala as choirmaster with the *oidor* Sedeña, who had later brought him to Mexico. Franco composed many works, some of which have survived. The vocal scores range from four to eleven voices, each treated very simply, but with some inspiration in spite of the simplicity of the Gregorian melodic line. Unless manuscripts of Álamo come to light, it is probable that Franco is the earliest cathedral composer in America whose works are in part extant.

By the end of 1576 there were many vacancies in the cathedral chapter. Two canons, Cervantes and Oliva, were dead; Luis de Villanueva had married; and their places were still unfilled.

Before this time local presses had begun to supply the liturgical books needed by the church. Music printing had been seen as a necessity even by the first precentor, Pedraza, but not until a quarter of a century after the conquest did the first volume containing printed notes appear in the *Ordinarium* of the Augustinians, 1556. The next volume to contain printed music was the *Manuale sacramentorum* (1560), and a *Missale Romanorum ordinarium* followed in 1561. The recommendations of the Council of Trent necessitated a revision of the text of the *Manuale* of 1560; this was issued in 1568. The adoption of a revised breviary (1569), missal (1571), and calendar by papal decree sent the earlier editions of these works to the scrap heap. Besides, news reached Mexico of the papal restriction to Rome of the printing of the new missal; then orders came to booksellers to clear their shelves of all liturgical books and turn them over to the archbishop to be destroyed, and notice that neither liturgical texts, Bibles, nor New Testaments were to be sent to the Indies unless approved by the Council. By 1573 Philip II had extracted from the pope authorization for printing liturgical works in his own realm, but he reserved the exclusive right both in printing and selling them in all the Spanish lands to the Hieronimites, who were then building the Escorial, and to Mexico went a provision, dated December 1 of that same year, ordering that no more breviaries, prayer books, or hours be published there.

But it so happened that in 1572 when Pedro Ocharte, one of the leading printers in Mexico, was arrested by the Inquisition for some slighting remarks about the pope for having issued such decrees, he had on his presses a volume of passion music, an antiphonal, and several other works of a liturgical character ordered either by the archbishop of Mexico or the bishop of Michoacán. While under indictment and thus barred from business, the passion music was finished by another printer and copies delivered to the bishop of Michoacán, but the revisions in text and music adopted in Rome necessitated further changes in the unfinished antiphonal. When cleared by the Inquisition in March, 1574, Ocharte applied to Moya de Contreras for permission to issue the *Gradual*, which was already on the press. This was granted on May 28, 1574, but not until December 22 of the next year was he able to secure authorization for publication from the viceroy, the printing having proceeded before securing it. That type had been set even earlier than March, 1574, is shown by revisions, which are clearly visible, made in accordance with Tridentine decrees first by the cantor Juan Hernández and later by Alonso Eçija, then succentor of the cathedral, for Eçija states in his approbation that he has corrected both the sanctoral and the dominical in accordance with the new Roman missal. Among the changes on title page and colophon made necessary by the time intervening between the original type setting of the *Gradual* and its issuance were the name of the pope, the title of Hernández, who had secured the degree of bachelor of canon law on May 25, 1574, the issuance of the new Roman missal, and the name of Ocharte, who returned in 1574 to the printing business, the name of the sponsor, and the date. Four different graduals bearing the imprint date of 1576 are now known, but two lack title page and colophon. That one was purchased by the cathedral is evidenced by an entry in the cabildo minutes of February 12, 1577, in which "se mandó dar libranza de 40 pesos de tepuzque á Pedro Ocharte impresor de libros por un Antifonario para esta Santa Iglesia." Although Mexican printers were authorized by royal decree to issue liturgical works after 1573 only with the approval of the Hieronimites, there is no evidence in the 1576 *Gradual* that such was secured. The second part, the *Psalterium amphonarium [sic] sanctorale, cum psalmis et hymnis, positis in suis locis propriis, uniuscujusque diei festi totius anni, nunc primo cun licentia excussum*, did not come from the press until 1584, after the reformed calendar had been made effective in Mexico, and the third part, the *Antiphonarium*, was not issued until 1589. All are typographically impressive works, especially for sixteenth-century Mexico. In large folio, the music is printed in two colors, and many elaborate woodcuts serve as initial letters. In the 1589 copy now owned by the University of Texas are many marginal manuscript notes, some relating to the organ accompaniment. Not until 1582 did shipments of European printings of the *Nuevo rezado* reach the Mexican cathedral, but within the next few years thousands of copies, many the gift of the king, were received by the archbishop, church dignitaries, and royal officials. In one shipment of forty boxes of books to Mexico City, passed by the censor on October 3, 1584, there were

> 10 Horas Dominicales. 4° becerro.
> 10 Arte de Canto llano. 8° badana.
> 3 Psalterio dominico de Choro [Venecia] grande becerro.
> 2 Breviario dominico. 6° badana.
> 2 Missale dominico. F° becerro, badana.
> 4 Diurnal dominico. 32° Venecia becerro.
> 1 Ordinario dominico. 4° badana.
> 13 Catecismo del Papa. 8° Plantino badana.
> 196 Biblios de Vatablo. Fo. becerro de los grandes.

It was fortunate that the new books were supplied free to the cathedral, for after work on the new structure started in earnest, the funds of the church were largely devoted to its erection. As a result, the poverty of the governing body was such that on July 3, 1582, it was decided that salaries of singers and musicians must be reduced, and they were notified that if they wished to continue serving they would have to wait for payment until funds were available. All refused, and there was no music until the archbishop late in August induced them to return to their posts. Slowly other subjects were included in the curriculum of the choristers; instruction on the organ was offered; and before many years a product of the school was employed as an organist, but at a smaller salary than was ordinarily paid, since he had received his training at cathedral expense.

The third church council which met in 1585 reaffirmed many of the earlier regulations relating to church music and made some more stringent. None were to be admitted to minor orders unless they had mastered the rudiments of ecclesiastical song, nor were to be promoted to a subdeaconship unless musically proficient. The chapel master must teach *canto figurado y contrapunto* and at such a time as not to interfere with the lesson of the succentor in plain chant. If a wrong note was sung by the choir, the chapel master was to be penalized. *Canto figurado* was required on Easter, "mas a las maitines el cantico *Benedictus,* alternados con el organo los versos, con aquella diferencia de música que se llama fabordon." During Lent, the *Salve regina* was to be sung; at Christmas, Epiphany, Ascension Day, and at the birth of the Virgin, *canciones devotas;* and on Palm Sunday and during Holy Week, the first Lamentations and the other specified offices. The chapel master was not to confine the choir to singing his own compositions but was to encourage the singing of works of the great masters.

An unpublished catalogue of the choral library of the cathedral in 1589 shows that the works of Guerrero, Morales, Victoria, Orlando di Lasso, and Palestrina were all represented; of Morales, both the requiem mass and two other masses are listed. There are also many volumes of *chanzonetas*, of motets, and of works by the various chapel masters. Choristers continued to take an active part in many functions outside of the cathedral. In 1578 the cathedral choir participated in the week-long ceremonies connected with the arrival of certain relics donated to the Jesuits by marching in the processions with the archbishop and chapter, and stopping to sing at various street intersections where arches had been erected, some of which served as altars. At one, while the procession halted to read the inscriptions, the choir sang a carol in praise of martyrs. On the fifth day of the celebration, in a religious *sarao* given by the College of San Miguel, choristers figured as a chorus of angels, while two instruments introduced their solemn, graceful dance. The presentation of the College of San Pedro and San Pablo opened with a dance by eight boys, and in conclusion the choristers sang *Pacem meam do vobis*.

The dramatic performances of the choir continued to be an event of the celebration of St. Hipólito's Day, and for this effort they received payment from the city. No less important was their contribution on Corpus Christi Day. In 1594 they were ordered given twenty pesos for the dance and play they gave, but a few days later the amount was increased to fifty pesos. They were also given a hundred pesos for many years for furnishing vocal and instrumental music after mass on the Sunday following Corpus Christi.

One of the most solemn occasions in which the entire cathedral choir and chapter participated toward the close of the century was that on March 1, 1599, when commemoration services were held for Philip II, who had died the preceding year. The general plan of forty years earlier was followed, but the officials of the Inquisition were in charge and the services were held on the plaza and in the church of Santo Domingo. We are told by one of those officials that the first psalm was rendered in organ-song in a very slow and sustained time with admirable harmony and balance of the voices, for, in addition to being carefully chosen, they were tripled in number. After the two choirs of clergy sang in plain chant, the antiphon was rendered in organ-song, and the first lesson entoned on the pitch of the first psalm. After the vigil service, the choir moved to the vicinity of the funereal monument and sang the response *Ne recordais* with unusual sweetness and unity of voice. In the absence of an archbishop, Juan de Cervantes, the presiding dignitary of the cathedral, officiated; then the *Requiescat in pace* followed.

By the close of the sixteenth century the cathedral choir had come to take an active part in the religious and social life of the capital of New Spain by singing in the services in the cathedral, by participating in processions, by themselves constituting a choir for the singing of *chansones* and carols on high feast days, and as singers, actors, and dancers in dramatic performances in the cathedral, the various convents and monasteries, and the viceregal palace. The boys were given systematic daily training in both chanting and contrapuntal music under the direction of capable precentors and able chapel masters—who composed original settings of many portions of the service, carols, and motets, as well as the incidental music for the playlets. That they knew and appreciated the works of the greatest polyphonists of their day is shown by the presence of such works in the choral library of the cathedral before 1600. While the regular number of choirboys seems to have remained officially at twelve, the choir was increased to triple that number when the occasion demanded, and the singing of chapter members was improved in both volume and quality. The primitive native-built organ was replaced by one imported from Spain and played until near the end of the century by Spanish organists; the native players who contributed the early instrumental music were increased in number and in the variety of instruments played, until by 1575 the cathedral boasted an orchestra of no mean proportion for that day. Clearly the beginnings and development of cathedral music in America can profitably be studied in the records of the Cathedral of Mexico, the greatest in the New World during the sixteenth century.

Other Articles of Interest

Stevenson, Robert. "Music in Quito: Four Centuries." XLIII (1963), 247–266.

———. "The 'Distinguished Maestro' of New Spain: Juan Gutiérrez de Padilla." XXXV (1955), 363–373.
Gutiérrez de Padilla in the seventeenth century essayed the principal musical forms of the Spanish baroque and demonstrated a developed capacity for musical composition. Details of his biography are documented from the Puebla Cathedral Actas Capitulares.

SPANISH SOUTH AMERICA

14. Intendants and Cabildos in the Viceroyalty of La Plata, 1782–1810

JOHN LYNCH

In the present study, Dr. Lynch of the University of London provides a detailed account of the way in which the port city of Buenos Aires established itself as the leader among the municipalities of the Viceroyalty of La Plata during the closing decades of the colonial period. This analysis of the often tense relations between the crown-appointed intendants and the municipal cabildos, whose members represented largely local interests, rests upon manuscript sources, and demonstrates how the Ordinance of Intendants of 1782 helped to invigorate the municipalities.

In December, 1807, the cabildo of Buenos Aires, conscious of the prestige it had earned in the recent defence of the region against the British expeditions which had invaded the Río de La Plata, petitioned the crown to grant it the title of "Defender of South America and Protector of the Cabildos of the Viceroyalty of La Plata." The petition was written by its legal adviser, Mariano Moreno, and the eloquent document which he submitted to Madrid contained a remarkable request by the cabildo to act as the recognized leader and mouthpiece of the other cabildos of the viceroyalty, the channel through which they could direct their complaints to higher authorities.

We learn by bitter experience in these dominions the constant practice followed by governors in general of humbling and depreciating the cabildos. Ignorant of their noble origin . . . they openly boast of vilifying them, and there is hardly a governor or subdelegate who does not consider it a supreme demonstration of his authority to scorn and despise the cabildos.

An earlier criticism of the treatment accorded to the cabildos in the era of the intendants had been made by Viceroy Croix of Peru in 1789 when he argued that the intendants had completely alienated the municipalities by an intolerant intrusion into their affairs. These assertions were echoed by later writers, and historians have generally agreed that the centralization of authority imposed by the Ordinance of Intendants, whatever its results at the level of efficiency, was a retrogressive move from the point of view of municipal self-government. The administration of public works and even of justice, it is argued, was almost completely assumed by the intendants, while the financial autonomy previously enjoyed by the cabildos was radically diminished by the complex exchequer system which was now established.

But even if it is granted that the great reforms of Charles III gave the intendant the initiative in town government, it does not follow that he took this initiative from the cabildos, for he could not take what they did not have. By the beginning of the eighteenth century the heroic age of the cabildos was a thing of distant memory in all parts of the Spanish empire, and not least in its southernmost provinces. The days when the cabildo of Buenos Aires could offer vigorous and successful opposition to its governors were over. Theoretically the legal position of the cabildos was well defined. The city appointed its judges, administered its property and exercised its moderate local functions. But in practice the legal theory was infringed by the very authority which was supposed to maintain it. By law the election of *alcaldes ordinarios* had to be submitted to the confirmation of viceroys, presidents, governors, or *corregidores*, who were ordered not to hinder the free election of any cabildo members either by interference or by influence. Governors, however, abused this right of confirming elections by using it as opportunity to revise or annul them, and they even adopted the habit of filling vacancies directly by their own appointments. In 1706 the cabildo of Buenos Aires complained to the king that Governor Maldonado had filled six vacancies in this way. Another governor, Valdés Inclán, dissatisfied with the legal municipal elections, appointed his own *regidores* without even consulting the cabildo, and in spite of a royal resolution sustaining the rights of the cabildo he threatened to fine those councillors who resisted him. The practice of sale of office completed the ruin of the municipal system and, in the words of a modern historian, "undoubtedly contributed to the apathy and incompetence of municipal government in many of the towns of the Indies." In Buenos Aires the proprietary councillors formed the majority of the cabildo and this was precisely the faction which allied itself to the governors. At the same time exchequer officials, in direct defiance of all the laws, frequently got themselves or their friends elected to cabildo offices. The abuses became so extreme that the governor of Buenos Aires in 1739 requested the king to abolish altogether the elections of alcaldes in Santa Fe, Corrientes, and Montevideo, for the meager functions they performed did not justify the electoral disputes which they caused.

A vigorous policy could not be expected from such bodies. Even in their modest local functions—the administration of their funds, public works, price regulations, inspection of prisons—their authority was subordinate to that of the governor. It was no part of the policy of an absolute monarchy to nurture vigorous municipalities, and neither in fact nor in theory was independence countenanced. The legal role of the cabildo was that of a counsellor:

> It is only to give its advice to those who have the supreme authority, and it has neither power nor competence to order or determine or put into execution its opinion or deliberations, but has to refer all these to the corregidor . . .

This dependence on higher authorities induced a subservience and inertia that can be read in every line of the minutes of the cabildos. The cabildo of Santiago del Estero frequently received messages from the governor of Tucumán ordering a certain line of action, and invariably these directives were received with submission. Its *actas capitulares*, barbarously written, are full of the most humdrum routine such as prison inspection and license granting, and are often brought to a fruitless close with the monotonous formula "and there being no business to attend to . . ." Any fundamental work, such as the reconstruction of the town reservoir, would take years to accomplish, and Santiago suffered from periodic shortages of water between 1748 and 1778 precisely because problems of this magnitude were so dilatorily tackled. In Buenos Aires, it is true, the cabildo showed a spasmodic energy in looking after the interests of its citizens. It often bestirred itself over food supplies, but it was powerless to regulate them on its own and needed to seek the co-operation of the governor to enforce decisions. Even in Buenos Aires, however, initiative was the exception, passivity the norm.

The fatal condition of the cabildos can be traced to two basic causes: they lacked any firm basis of popular representation, and they lacked adequate financial resources. The direct intrusion of governors in municipal elections has already been noticed. This burden was, if anything, increasing on the eve of the intendant system. Moreover, the viceroy was reaffirming in unambiguous terms his right of confirming elections, and assuring similar rights to his subordinate governors. But the oligarchic composition of the cabildos themselves was an even greater drag on municipal development. There were not infrequent complaints that the councillor class was itself "fixing" elections. Any ideas the cabildos had of changing the electoral system were liable to be retrogressive. The cabildo of Buenos Aires, for example, would have liked more than the three proprietary regidores which it already had. But there was no incentive for citizens to buy the office, for in return for sacrifice in time and money there was no prospect of their lining their own pockets from the empty municipal coffers. It was suggested, therefore, that those regidores who were elected should be elected for a term of six years, and that the alcaldes should be allowed re-election before their first term of office had been judged in residencia. The idea was submitted to the governor, and there it died a natural death, but the incident shows that, far from desiring a greater representative character, the cabildos of this period were actually inclined to make themselves a closer oligarchy than they already were.

They were also losing what little control they had over their own membership. A governor could in theory and often did in practice suspend a councillor whom he considered guilty of a civil misdemeanor. This was unquestioned. But the cabildo had long enjoyed the right of granting its members licenses of leave of absence of up to one year or even longer with the approbation of the governor. This right was used without challenge throughout the first half of the eighteenth century, but it was summarily rejected by a *real provisión* issued by the Audiencia of Charcas in 1774, which prohibited any cabildo member from taking leave of absence without the express license of the governor or of the audiencia.

The cabildos might have been able to withstand this increasing pressure on their position had they enjoyed a strong economic foundation, but lack of any financial influence was itself probably the most fundamental cause of their sterility in this period. The poverty of the cabildos was endemic. What income they had was limited to the *propios*, or rents from municipal land and property, and a few local taxes derived from the granting of licenses of various kinds. Direct taxation could only be imposed for some specific public object, and was limited to 55 pesos except by consent of the audiencia, which could raise it to 200 pesos; otherwise the approval of the crown was required. In 1708 the revenue from the municipal propios of Buenos Aires amounted to no more than 320 pesos a year. By 1751 this had increased to 844 pesos, but as the procurator pointed out, this was still an inadequate fund for local government, and in February of that year the cabildo requested the Council of the Indies for permission to extend rentable land. By a royal cédula of 1760 authority was given to charge five pesos on all built-up sites on the common ground in the city. But to go ahead and collect it was another matter. The cabildo had to make repeated requests to the governor to issue the necessary order to implement the cédula, but such was his unconcern that it was 1766 before the first rents were collected, and for many years their collection was surrounded with difficulties and hindrances. Further propositions were made by the cabildo to increase its propios, but royal permission was difficult to obtain. Meanwhile municipal activity was brought to an almost complete standstill. In February 1768 the cabildo was still lamenting its notorious lack of funds, "since with the *arbitrios* which it now has it can hardly cover the bare and essential yearly expenses." Eventually it was reduced to asking for voluntary contributions from citizens. The response was not very promising, and in December 1777 it asked the viceroy for a loan of 8,000 pesos to cover various expenses, but met with a refusal. A similar tale of poverty emerges from the pages of the council meetings of the cabildo of Santiago del Estero, and the story can be implemented from the records of other provincial cabildos. In the province of Tucumán the *sisa* tax was never fully paid before 1783. The yearly income of Mendoza from propios in the third quarter of the eighteenth century was only 400 pesos, that of San Juan 200, while San Luis had none at all. In the province of Cochabamba in Upper Peru only the cabildos of Cochabamba and Mizque possessed propios and arbitrios; other towns were completely devoid of this income.

Financial control means little when there are scanty finances to control. But not only was municipal revenue meager, its appropriation was for the most part prescribed. The very management of their own funds was so hedged around with restrictions that it is impossible to speak of the "financial autonomy" of the cabildos in the period before the intendants. Without previous consent of the audiencia or of the provincial governor, extraordinary appropriations or assignments of wages from revenue were limited to the minute figure of 3,000 maravedis. Governors were quick to pounce upon any deviations from this law. When the cabildo of Buenos Aires appointed a paid archivist in April 1772, assigning him 200 pesos a year, the governor decreed that it was legally incapable of disposing of its own funds in this way, and the cabildo had no alternative but to submit to the law.

The picture presented by the cabildos in the third quarter of the eighteenth century was not, then, an impressive one. An occasional cry of protest indicated that a flame of independence still flickered, but it was a cry of despair and signified impotence. It can be read in the words of the cabildo of Santiago del Estero:

> We debated the best way to seek a remedy against the despotisms of the chiefs of this province and their absolute government, the outrages they inflict on officials and other subjects . . . their complete immunity from punishment . . .

They decided to complain to the king through their attorney in Madrid, and no more is heard of the matter. Three years later, in 1776, the cabildo of Asunción del Paraguay submitted a long list of complaints against Augustín Fernando Pinedo, governor of Paraguay, accusing him of oppression, nepotism, maladministration of royal revenues, private commercial activities and many other crimes. But Gálvez, the Minister of the Indies, did not offer an opinion, and it was not until 1785, that is precisely in the period of the intendancies, that the complaints against Pinedo were really entertained. While Santiago and Asunción were complaining of despotism, from Upper Peru came a faint plea for more government. In 1781 the cabildo of La Plata petitioned the crown to move the seat of the viceroyalty there because of the lack of government in the province and its propensity to disorder, so great was its distance from Buenos Aires. Not surprisingly, the request was coldly received in Madrid where it was pointed out that the president of the audiencia had adequate authority for dealing with the problems of Upper Peru.

Any evidence of strength or independence on the part of the cabildos was abnormal and ephemeral. Yet twenty years later, between approximately 1800 and 1810, in almost all the main cities of the viceroyalty of La Plata vigorous cabildos were in conflict with the local political authorities and challenging them on many issues. Sometime between the 1770's and the end of the century the cabildos found a new lease of life. This coincided precisely with the period of the intendancies.

It is true that the centralizing policy pursued by Charles III and his ministers did not augur well for the cabildos. The municipality of Buenos Aires showed an evident desire to share in the increase of political powers assigned to the area with the creation of the new viceroyalty in 1776, a desire which was encouraged by Cevallos, the first viceroy, who relied on the support of the cabildo for initiating his new policy, and who responded completely to its demands for freer commerce. But five years' experience under Superintendant Fernández, before the Ordinance of 1782 inaugurated the full intendant system, dashed any hopes the cabildo may have had of the arrival of a new period in municipal government. Fernández kept cabildo activity carefully confined, as one example will show. There was in Buenos Aires a war fund amounting to more than 25,000 pesos and used for maintaining three militia battalions in the province. This fund was administered by the exchequer, but it had originally been collected and managed by the cabildo of Buenos Aires. When Fernández heard that the cabildo was pressing the viceroy to return the fund to its jurisdiction, he immediately sought confirmation from Madrid of his own exclusive control of this revenue as head of the exchequer in the viceroyalty. This was assured him by royal order of March 9, 1779.

The cabildo of Buenos Aires had political as well as financial pretensions. In April 1778, claiming to speak on behalf of all interests and classes in the city, it uttered a genuine cry of distress at the impending departure of Viceroy Cevallos to whom it attributed all the recent progress made in the affairs of the province, and implored him to remain in office while an extension of his appointment was sought from the crown. This representation was made after the publication of the appointment of Viceroy Vertiz and was therefore interpreted in Madrid as an affront to the prestige and reputation of the new viceroy and as setting an extremely dangerous precedent. Superintendant Fernández was instructed to examine the minutes of the cabildo and take note of all the events of the incident and the names of the members who were its promoters. As a result of Fernández's enquiry and advice two councillors, Judas Josef de Salas and Bernardo Sancho de Larrea, were banished to the Falkland Islands for a year after which they were to reside in Mendoza, while the other nine cabildo members who had signed the representation were prohibited from exercising office for seven years.

The cabildos, therefore, had no reason to welcome any extension, still less formalization, of the intendant system by the Ordinance of Intendants of 1782. Yet it was obvious that they themselves were incompetent to deal with the type of administration which local government was lacking and which the new system was meant to supply. The colonial municipal oligarchy treated and resolved the affairs of the city according to the same criterion as they dealt with their own personal affairs. But with the extension of commerce and increase in population this simple domestic machinery was no longer adequate to cope with the new administrative problems which were arising, nor were merchant-councillors competent to resolve them. The time had passed when they could miss sessions because there was nothing to do. Building, public works, hygiene, finance and justice were all clamoring for prompt attention and needed a treatment for which the cabildos had no precedent and their members no skill. This is the context in which the intendancy system must be judged. In view of the evidence showing the legal and practical weakness of the cabildos on the eve of the intendancy system, it is unreal to consider the problem in terms of local institutions being absorbed by centralizing officials. The criterion of any judgment on the cabildos in the new era will be whether the intendants made the cabildos more active and whether they allowed them to co-operate in the work they were doing.

It has been maintained that the cabildos lost part of their authority because the alcaldes and regidores appointed by them had to be confirmed in office by the intendant. In fact there was no substantial change. By the Laws of the Indies the ultimate authority for confirmation of municipal elections was the viceroy. This law was expressly annulled by the Ordinance of Intendants, and the power of confirmation was reserved exclusively to the intendants who were to ensure that "the said offices be assigned to individuals who are judged most suitable for the fair administration of justice and for the proper security of the revenues of my royal treasury . . ." This sytem operated until 1787 when by royal cédula of November 29 it was annulled and the right of confirming the election of alcaldes ordinarios was restored to the viceroy. In cities where there were audiencias, and for fifteen leagues around them, the president of the audiencia, was to confirm the alcaldes in office. In small towns viceroys could authorize intendants to do this with subsequent central confirmation. But whatever changes were made the cabildos themselves neither lost anything nor gained anything from the point of view of legal rights.

In practice, however, there were far less abuses under the new régime. Between 1784 and 1789 the intendants of Salta regularly confirmed the elections in Santiago del Estero without any intrusion. In 1790 the intendant annulled the election of Juan José Iramaín as junior alcalde on the ground that he was already subdelegate of exchequer and as such was precluded from municipal office by the Ordinance of Intendants. He ordered the cabildo to make a new appointment, which was done without demur and this time approved. In the event of a disputed election the cabildo of Santiago would voluntarily offer the case for solution to the intendant. In general the intendants only cancelled elections on strictly legal and not on political grounds. For example, Intendant Rodríguez of Córdoba approved the 1806 elections in Concepción except that of Josef Francisco Tisera as alcalde ordinario on account of the distance he resided from the city and of the fact that he had a tobacco *estanco* which would suffer from lack of attention—to the detriment of the royal revenue. The cabildo agreed without comment and proceeded to elect another alcalde whom the intendant confirmed in office. In fact whenever royal authority was brought to bear on cabildos in these matters it was likely to be in the interests of purer elections; a residencia on councillors of Santiago who had served between 1778 and 1790 disclosed that some regidores were very susceptible to bribery and would sell their votes to aspirants to office. Punishments in these cases varied from deprivation of votes to monetary fines.

In Santiago any diminution of the already weak representative basis of the cabildo came not as a result of pressure from the intendant but on the initiative of the cabildo itself. The traditional electoral procedure in Santiago was as follows: at the end of the year the cabildo met to choose six citizens "of education and intelligence" who were admitted to the council to assist in the election of the new cabildo. This system was followed until 1786 when, on the pretext of avoiding dissension which the admission of citizens was alleged to cause, the existing cabildo omitted this first stage and itself made the elections for the following year. This procedure was then approved by the intendant. On the other hand, when in 1797 Intendant Sobremonte created the town of Concepción del Río Cuarto and endowed it with a cabildo he did this in a more democratic manner than earlier founders of towns had followed. Instead of founding the cabildo by direct appointment, Sobremonte authorized the citizens themselves to make the first elections, and instructed his commissioners only to supervise. His two commissioners summoned the most suitable and substantial citizens on January 1, 1789; the latter elected the regidores who in turn chose the alcaldes.

But it was the cabildo of Buenos Aires which maintained most vigilance over its own composition, and came to resent interference not only from the intendant but also from higher political authorities. In the elections of 1788 it elected Manuel Antonio Warnes as senior alcalde. Superintendant Sanz approved all the other appointments but annulled that of Warnes and ordered the cabildo to make another one. Sanz's real objection to Warnes was personal dislike combined with a political distrust of what he called his "*espíritu revoltoso.*" The cabildo, however, would not retreat, and appealed to the audiencia which upheld its election and confirmed Warnes in office. In the election of 1792 it was Viceroy Arredondo who forbade the election of Warnes, but this was on the legal grounds that there was a law suit against him, and although the cabildo protested vigorously it had to obey. Nevertheless, it carried its protest to the Crown and received a royal cédula of December 24, 1795, disapproving of Arredondo's exclusion of Warnes from the elections as being against the spirit of the municipal ordinances of Buenos Aires.

At the same time the cabildo was securing more control of its own members. A royal cédula of May 8, 1789, conceded to the cabildos the privilege of hearing renunciations of office. When, therefore, Martín Alzaga, procurator-elect for 1790, obtained exemption from office from the viceroy, the cabildo of Buenos Aires insisted on its rights and enforced his acceptance. On August 21, 1794, Benito González de Rivadavia, regidor and *depositario general* of the cabildo of Buenos Aires, was exiled by the Audiencia of Buenos Aires to Córdoba. On the 22nd the cabildo protested that he had been banished on no more specific ground than that of public security, and, what was more significant, that no notice had been given to the cabildo on a matter affecting its own members: in particular it was complained that Rivadavia had been forced to leave without giving an account of the municipal deposits he held. These objections were made to the viceroy, who was supporting the action of the audiencia, and were continued unremittingly—three representations were made between August 22 and September 3—until the viceroy issued an order on October 26 authorizing the return of Rivadavia so that he could give an account of his deposits to the cabildo.

While the cabildo elections were subject to less intromission by higher authorities during the first stages of the intendant period, their financial basis was also becoming more secure. It is true that the Ordinance of Intendants circumscribed the already slender control they had over their own finances. These were now subject to inspection by the *Junta Superior de Hacienda* in Buenos Aires which could ask the intendants for information concerning municipal finance and communicate its measures to them through the account-general of municipal finance, who was also secretary of the junta. The intendants were instructed on taking office to ask each of the cities and towns within their jurisdiction for an exact account of their funds and of the municipal taxes. From this information the intendants were to draw up a provisional ordinance for municipal finance and submit it to the Junta Superior which in turn was to report it to the Crown. A municipal junta was to be established in each Spanish colonial city and town for the control of financial matters; this was composed of the senior alcalde ordinario, who was to preside over it, two regidores and the procurator-general, but it was supposed to be a distinct body from the cabildo which was forbidden to interfere with it in any way. The business of the junta was to conduct the sale of offices connected with municipal finance, and lease the town revenues to collectors. The intendants were to supervise the proceedings of the municipal juntas in order to prevent abuses, though if the juntas had any complaints against the intendants' measures they could appeal directly to the Junta Superior. In the smaller divisions of the provinces the subdelegate had much the same supervision over municipal finance as the intendants had in the provincial capital.

The financial authority of the cabildos was circumscribed to this moderate degree not from any conscious anti-municipal policy, but simply in the interests of greater efficiency and by the creation of a more detailed administrative machine. They were not completely deprived of financial powers. The cabildos chose from among their own members the two regidores who were to serve on the municipal junta, and the alcaldes were already cabildo appointees. The rule of submitting the accounts to the cabildo was adhered to. In a small town like Santiago del Estero the two bodies were virtually identical and the cabildo simply turned itself into the finance committee for certain purposes:

We the cabildo . . . having assembled as president and members of the municipal junta of propios and arbitrios of this city to treat of matters pertaining to it, determined to consider the business of bringing the taxable wine-stores at the disposal of this city up to the number of eight . . .

It is clear in fact that the cabildo of Santiago considered its own interests and that of the junta identical, and, far from regarding it as a rival, it was as ready to defend it as it was to defend itself whenever there was unwarranted interference on the part of the subdelegate.

By the new system the interests of efficiency were better served than they had previously been. At the same time the most important single fact in the life of the cabildos in this period was the increase in their funds. This can be ascribed in many cases precisely to the activity of the intendants. The quickest results were obtained in Córdoba and owed their existence to Intendant Sobremonte, who was able to report in November 1785:

The propios of this city have risen in the past year to 1040 pesos: the year previously they only amounted to 525 pesos. And according to what I have proposed to the Junta Superior for their increase, sufficient quantities can now be assigned to meet its needs, to complete the municipal buildings and other useful and decorative works.

He also had proposals for increasing the propios of the other towns of his province. His methods did not involve any spectacular creation of new taxes but simply a more thorough collection of existing ones, a thing which the cabildo had never been able to accomplish on its own. By this method he was able to triple the propios of Córdoba in his first five years of office there. The result in practical terms was seen in the new growth of public building in Córdoba.

Buenos Aires had completely outgrown its financial resources, and there the situation required not only a rigorous collection of existing taxes but also the creation of completely new ones. Superintendant Sanz spared no pains to increase municipal revenue. He kept the cabildo on its toes by periodically demanding a statement of revenue accounts. And soon after he took office he requested a formal statement from the cabildo containing its precise requirements in matters of taxation. This was the opportunity the cabildo had been waiting for all during the century. In a long and far from clear report the cabildo outlined its needs: new taxes amounting to more than 11,000 pesos were proposed and a substantial increase in existing propios were suggested. The proposals were considered by the Junta Superior, presided over by the superintendent, and on February 29, 1788, it conceded new taxes on a scale which the cabildo had been demanding in vain for years. Authority was granted for taxes on hawkers' stalls, gaming saloons, weights and measures and at an increased rate on built-up areas on the common land. Twenty-two taxable wine stores were added to the eight which were already assigned to the cabildo, at the rate of 25 pesos each one. Moreover, the Junta Superior tackled the chronic inability of the cabildo to collect its own taxes by prodding it to a stricter sense of duty in this respect. For instance, it demanded an explanation from the cabildo for its failure to collect the duty on the *Corredores de Lonja* (a sort of merchant exchange) to which it had been entitled ever since the foundation of the city.

It was not a tale of unrelieved progress. In January 1792 at the instance of certain citizens the viceroy suspended the tax on occupiers of common-land, in spite of a strong protest from the cabildo. On February 17, the cabildo was driven to ask the viceroy for a further increase of propios and arbitrios, but the financial support they had enjoyed under Superintendant Sanz was not so assured after the suppression of the independent superintendancy in 1788. Nevertheless, the increased taxative powers conceded by Sanz in the 1780's gradually began to bear fruit, and the funds in the municipal treasury steadily rose:

YEAR	PESOS	REALES
1798	9668	3
1799	15298	4½
1800	10674	1¾
1802	15903	¼
1805	23431	1¾

But the new municipal prosperity was not shared by every town. The story of Santiago del Estero continued to be one of crippling poverty. When the cabildo was organizing road repairs and improving the town hall for the viceroy's visit of inspection in 1789, it had to report that there were no funds available for this work from the regular municipal revenue. Santiago still suffered from what the intendants in Buenos Aires and Córdoba were trying to reform—an inability to collect its own taxes and control its own collectors. The senior alcalde for 1788 did not collect the propios for that year, so that in 1789 the cabildo had to inform the intendant of Salta that it had nothing with which to defray the expenses of public administration ordered by him. The inference to be drawn is that only the immediate presence of the intendant in his provincial capital was sufficient to stimulate the cabildos and that the others fared ill under the subdelegates.

Revenue in Potosí was in a much healthier state. In April 1787 the town propios had a fund of 7,960 pesos. In 1788 the annual revenue was 2,139 pesos from the sisa tax and 2,314 pesos 2½ reales from the propios. In all, therefore, the municipal treasury was in possession of 12,413 pesos 2½ reales. To put this income to profitable use Intendant Pino Manrique, in consultation with the cabildo, proposed to the Junta Superior in Buenos Aires a scheme for investing it in a public store, which would relieve the town of the necessity of buying its most essential foodstuffs in so-called *canchas* at exorbitant prices. This sort of financial activity was authorized by the Ordinance of Intendants. But in spite of the repeated applications of Intendant Pino Manrique, the Junta Superior took no resolution on the matter, and he was forced to report the situation to the home government. The result of his complaint was a salutary devolution of power. By royal cédula of September 14, 1788, it was decided that in order to avoid such delays to useful projects the investment of municipal funds in all the colonies should in future be made on the proposal of the intendants of the cabildos, and with the approbation of the audiencia, to which, and not to the Juntas Superiores, the proposal should be submitted.

With the validity of their elections more assured, and their finances clearly if fitfully improving, the cabildos entered upon a period of greater activity in public administration. The initiative generally came from the intendant, but this was not a question of removing the faculties of the cabildo; rather was it the necessity of making them do things which they should have done before but had neglected. In January 1779, for example, Superintendant Fernández made the cabildo of Buenos Aires undertake an inspection of weights and measures in the interests of the consumer. This task had of course always been open to the cabildo but only now was it undertaken. Superintendant Sanz pushed the cabildo along even more vigorously, consulting it on various points of public interest, and inviting a profusion of reports on matters such as the regulation of supplies and prices, public works, taxes, rights of citizens, and economic affairs. Meanwhile the cabildo pursued its own work of inspection in the service of the public, but there were many instances where by the nature of things it could not act alone but needed the assistance of higher political authorities. That assistance was generally forthcoming, and the vigilance of the cabildo would be implemented by a proclamation from the superintendant or the viceroy. In March 1791, for example, the cabildo of Buenos Aires informed the viceroy that many ranchers were slaughtering infected cattle for consumption and requested a prohibition of this activity. Arredondo issued a proclamation ordering the ranchers to take adequate precautions and detailing the *ministros de los corrales* to undertake inspections.

But this mutual co-operation between cabildo and governor did not extend to every branch of municipal administration. It did not extend to town planning and public works. By an order issued in agreement with the viceroy on February 14, 1785, Superintendant Sanz removed all competence from the municipal officials in matters of street regulation and public building, and reserved all executive power in these affairs to himself and his officials. His motives were greater efficiency and speed, and he specifically maintained the right of the cabildo to give advice and to put forward ideas. When the superintendancy was suppressed in 1788 the viceroy did not go back on this order, and he himself assumed the faculties of the superintendant. But the concentration of work was too much for him, and it was inevitable that the cabildo's own *diputado de policía* (generally the third regidor) should in practice assume more power in this field. But this could not make good the need for a full-time official in charge of public works. Consequently, on August 1, 1799, the viceroy appointed Martín Boneo *intendente de policía* in Buenos Aires, subject to the viceroy and charged with street registration, enumeration and censorship, duties which were later extended to more general public works. He soon came into conflict with the cabildo when he requested that its mayordomo should be placed at his orders and disposal. The cabildo bluntly refused and carried its point. But its real objection was the very principle of the new establishment, and it was not slow to carry its protests to the viceroy. The viceroy supported the intendant and reported to the government that he was doing useful work. Meanwhile the cabildo obstructed Boneo's work and appealed to Madrid with such success that a royal cédula of January 16, 1804, ordered Boneo to resign his post and return to Spain, singular evidence that South American cabildos were not without influence in the metropolis. The viceroy replaced him by Antonio de las Cagigas. The cabildo now implicitly recognized that a full-time official in charge of public works was essential, for it reported to the viceroy that it had no objection to this appointment, but insisted that the appointee "ought to proceed in his commission with the intervention and knowledge of this illustrious cabildo or of the *junta municipal* . . ." Its persistence was rewarded, for it was now allowed to appoint two councillors to audit the income and expenditure of funds destined for public works, and Cagigas had to regulate his account with them. Even in the sphere of public works, therefore, the cabildo was never completely excluded in this period. Furthermore, growth of business was shown by the fact that it had to decide in January 1790 to increase its meetings to two each week.

The history of Córdoba under the rule of its first intendant, Sobremonte, reveals a similar tale of invigoration and mutual co-operation. Until the arrival of Sobremonte, the cabildo consisted of eight members. He enlarged it to twelve, and initiated a subscription among members, heading it himself, to pay for repairs to the town hall. Drawing on his experience as viceregal secretary under Vertiz in Buenos Aires, he instituted the system of *comisarios de barrios;* six of these were appointed by the cabildo from among the citizens to see to the execution of orders for the improvement of the city, police and security, control of beggars, and traffic supervision. Already in 1786 the cabildo was remarking on the zeal of the new intendant. Sobremonte worked well with the municipality, which in turn gave support and co-operation. Through the initiative of Sobremonte, the cabildo contracted with the *hacendados* of the province to supply an adequate amount of meat every year at fair prices, free of alcabala and all other taxes.

In the neighboring intendancy of Salta del Tucumán a similar effort on the part of the intendant to stimulate municipal activity can be discerned, though the plans were less well defined and the policy was less vigorous. In December 1785 the intendant requested from the cabildo of Santiago del Estero a report on its various activities. The cabildo was apparently becoming more conscious of social problems in the town, and was developing a scheme of poor relief, the details of which are not clear. Two years later the intendant requested the remittance within two months of statistics of the size of the town, its population and racial composition, its agricultural and mineral products. Without waste of time, the cabildo collected and forwarded the required information. Thus in their task of collecting data and information for submission to Spain, the intendants had to seek the collaboration of the cabildos. In turn, the intendants passed on general news and information to the cabildo, which was thus the means of distributing to the people constitutional and political news from Spain. And for all the predominance of the intendant in the economic affairs of his province, the cabildo of Santiago could still look after its own economic interests: in January 1786 it forbade the export of grain from the district because of the bad harvest.

The cabildos themselves were not slow to show their appreciation of the intendants, and during the first fifteen years of the regime there flowed from the municipalities an impressive stream of eulogies of their political superiors. The cabildo of Mendoza described Sobremonte as its *"nuevo fundador,"* and in August, 1788, sent a long and glowing account of his services, requesting from the Crown his retention in office, "because his extraordinary activity and tireless zeal combined with his integrity and enlightened political ideas have contributed advantageously to the general prosperity, progress and administration of these remote and loyal dominions." In 1790 the cabildo of Córdoba decided to send a testimonial of Sobremonte's merits and services to the king. The good impression left by Sobremonte lasted long. When he was appointed temporary viceroy the cabildos of Córdoba, San Juan, Mendoza, and San Luis petitioned the Crown to confirm him permanently in office. And even after his conduct during the first British invasion of the Río de la Plata in 1806, when he not only failed to organize the defence of Buenos Aires but also deserted his capital, the cabildo of Córdoba defended him in a message to the king dated August 29, 1806.

In 1789 the cabildo of Salta del Tucumán reported on the good services of Intendant Mestre in all branches of government, and asked the king to prolong his term of office. Particular praise was given to his completion of a "magnificent town hall" and its division into decent and comfortable offices where the alcaldes and other officials could work with proper formality. The cabildo of Potosí reported on the new system of government in 1786, and, in terms disappointingly vague, declared that the intendancy system had had beneficial results in restoring public peace, stimulating industry, and formulating new municipal legislation. Special praise was given to Intendant Pino Manrique's administration in public works, commerce, mines, and exchequer. The cabildo was of the opinion that only the intendancy system had been able to provide a strong government in unruly Potosí. In 1793 the cabildo of La Plata informed the Crown of the good services of President-Intendant Joaquín del Pino, his zeal in reorganizing the hospital and personally visiting the sick, his reform of prison conditions, his efforts to promote public works, and his success in increasing royal revenues.

The cabildo of La Paz showed a particular readiness to support the intendancy system, and was in fact concerned that it was not operating to full advantage in this distant province. The cabildo was quite alive to the fact that what La Paz suffered from was a lack of permanency in its governors: there was a continual change of appointments, and no intendant completed a full term of office. In 1795 La Paz was enjoying the rule of a temporary intendant, Fernando Soto, a naval captain and a man whom the cabildo considered intelligent, experienced, and well versed in the affairs of the province and of the viceroyalty. So concerned was the cabildo to retain his services that it offered 25,000 pesos to the Spanish treasury for the war fund on condition that Soto's appointment be confirmed and prolonged. In August of the following year the cabildo sent a further and more substantial account of Soto's administration and renewed its previous request and offer. It was supported by the Audiencia of Charcas, but it failed to move the home government. Nevertheless his successor, Intendant Burgunyo, also earned the support of the cabildo and its gratitude for an increase in municipal revenue.

The cabildo of Asunción del Paraguay forwarded in 1798 a long report on the services of Intendant Rivera, whom it described as a "prudent and zealous governor," and supplied a detailed account of his administration and policy in military, frontier, Indian and financial affairs, concluding with an appreciation of his régime in no uncertain terms.

This reaction of the cabildos of the viceroyalty of La Plata to the activity of the intendants could be supported by an even more striking body of evidence from the viceroyalty of Peru. In 1786, for example, the cabildo of Lima submitted a report on the work of the superintendent and on his treatment of the cabildo which is convincing both in its generalizations and its particulars and which augured extremely well for future co-operation between the two bodies. Grateful testimonials came also from the cabildos of Huancavelica and Arequipa.

A cabildo which criticizes intendants is likely to be giving its real opinion when it praises them, and thus these testimonials are convincing precisely because they are not indiscriminate. The very cabildos which praise the intendants with whom they can work, do not hesitate to protest against those whom they oppose. In the 1780's and 1790's esteem and co-operation was the norm. But in the first decade of the 19th century in almost every part of the viceroyalty of La Plata the cabildos were at loggerheads with their intendants. The revival of political consciousness and public spirit which was evident in the municipalities in this era was then turned against the intendants who had helped to nurture it, or rather against their successors. This apprenticeship in opposition was in turn an invaluable preparation for the approaching revolution for independence. The change from collaboration to distrust was due to two causes. The quality of the intendants appointed to the colonies declined in proportion as the quality of patronage in Madrid declined: the difference between Sobremonte and González in Córdoba is the measure of the difference between the government of Charles III and Gálvez and that of Charles IV and Godoy. More-over, encouraged by their association with the work of the intendants and by the respect with which the early intendants treated them, the cabildos became more sure of themselves and began to resent the tutelage of their superiors. Anxious to control the funds which the intendants had made possible and to direct the work which the intendants had initiated, they reacted against their masters and began to claim more share of local government.

Hostilities in Chuquisaca began as early as 1796. In November of that year the cabildo submitted to Madrid a lengthy complaint against what it described as the violation of its authority and usurpation of its jurisdiction by President-Intendant Joaquín del Pino, whose conduct it had commended only three years previously. Pino was in fact a fair-minded administrator, and in this case the initiative came from the cabildo. It protested that its right of appointing the town doctor had been violated by the intendant, who, with the support of the fiscal of the Audiencia of Charcas, Victorián de Villava, had removed its nominee and appointed his own. In the sphere of public works the intendant had rejected a contract given by the cabildo to one of its regidores for the repair of a bridge at an estimate of 500 pesos, and commissioned a contractor of his own choice at 600 pesos, which the cabildo considered an exorbitant charge on the town funds. Generalizing from these and other particulars, the cabildo made an eloquent appeal for independence and municipal liberty, for free-dom of votes and acceptancy of majority decisions, ending with the remark: "We now feel that the city is no longer represented in its cabildo but in the vote of the fiscal and the will of the president."

The cabildo asked the crown for a judgment, and a royal cédula of September 15, 1787, requested the Audiencia of Charcas to collect information and forward its opinion. The audiencia accepted the intendant's case that he had authority in matters of public welfare, and judged that the complaints of the cabildo were unjustified. It would be a mistake to regard the attitude of the cabildo in this case as entirely progressive, or the result of the intendant's policy entirely oppressive. The cabildo regretfully reported that its authority and prestige had suffered so much from these rebuffs that the offices of regidores could no longer find purchasers and had consequently depreciated greatly in value. Thus there were no longer any proprietory councillors, and they all had to be elected annually. The intendant had unwittingly liberalized the municipal régime but the cabildo of Chuquisaca was quite unconscious of the irony.

In Córdoba the happy period of co-operation between intendant and cabildo came to an end in 1798, when a series of electoral disputes between cabildo and the temporary intendant initiated a period of administrative sterility. The situation worsened with the arrival of the new intendant, José González, a man of choleric disposition and domineering temperament. He was sworn into office on December 4, 1803, and one of his first acts was to demand that all the records of the municipal archive should be copied so that he could be precisely informed about the privileges of the cabildo. The latter considered that its province was being invaded and yielded with such reluctance that the intendant dropped the matter. A few days later the cabildo took the initiative and demanded that the intendant pay the 10,000 pesos security to which he was bound by the title of his appointment. Gonzáles retorted that "it ought not to waste the precious time of its sessions in useless affairs." Nevertheless the cabildo stuck to the point and informed the viceroy repeatedly until by September 1805 the intendant had fulfilled his obligation.

In a note of June 11, 1804, González informed the cabildo that it was "no more than a representative economic body, incapable of determining anything itself without the intervention of the governor." The reply of the cabildo was to draw a comparison between the régime of Sobremonte and the present state of affairs. But there was no improvement under the next intendant, Gutiérrez de la Concha, who took office on December 28, 1807. An immediate election dispute ensured that for the whole of 1808 the cabildo was dominated by a party hostile to the intendant. This feud was nourished by an excessive legal formalism and petty disputes over public ceremonial and precedence which were a perennial breeding ground of bad feeling in Spanish colonial society, especially in the small isolated communities of the interior. Then, in the elections of January 1809, the two cabildo nominees for senior alcalde and procurator were refused confirmation by the intendant who appointed others in their place. In the subsequent appeal the cabildo's case was defended by Mariano Moreno, then a lawyer in Buenos Aires and relator of the audiencia. He declined to labor the point that a majority vote decided municipal elections and that this obliged the superior authorities to confirm the choice of the cabildo unless there were legitimate legal objections, and went on to argue that "the most precious prerogative of the cabildos is the private right of electing the councillors who are to compose it," a privilege too important to remain exposed to capricious usurpation or to a "stroke of despotism."

Comparable tension also existed in La Paz, where the genesis of the revolution of 1809 which deposed the intendant lay mostly in cabildo activity. La Paz was in a state of unrest from 1805 onwards, and this became more acute in the early months of 1809 when news arrived of revolutionary developments in Buenos Aires. In March the intendant reported that the cabildo had been occupied in secret nocturnal sessions. Simultaneously the Spanish authorities started squabbling among themselves. Dávila, the temporary intendant, accused the inspector of the exchequer in La Paz, González de Prada, of engaging in subversive activities and of planning, in conjunction with certain members of the cabildo, to remove Dávila from the intendancy and substitute himself. These assertions need not be taken at their face value: it was probable that Dávila was trying to hide financial mismanagement or even peculation, and resented the inspection of González; the latter denied the charges and claimed that they arose out of personal malice. But the latent hostility between intendant and cabildo is obvious, and the cabildo was able to take advantage of the evident disunity among the authorities. After the events of May 25 and 26 in Chuquisaca where the audiencia deposed the intendant, the conspirators came out into the open. Under the direction of a mestizo soldier, Pedro Domingo Murillo, the commandant of the fort, the revolutionaries deposed the intendant and the cabildo took charge of the government in La Paz. Later it constituted itself as a junta, under the presidency of Murillo. The insurgents tried to clothe the action of revolt in loyal terms. On September 16 the cabildo wrote to the viceroy affirming their loyalty to him and to Ferdinand VII, and assuring him of the continuation of municipal government. Then, calling itself a representative junta, the cabildo initiated proceedings against Intendant Dávila before the audiencia of Charcas in order to clarify the events of the insurrection of July 16, and to affirm its loyalty. But this maneuver made little progress, nor did the representations deceive anyone in Buenos Aires. The viceroy advised the cabildo of La Paz to maintain government until the arrival of a new intendant and meanwhile to restore the ministers whom they had deposed. But this advice was simply a cloak for more violent action. The viceroy of Peru sent an army against the insurgents; by the end of October the junta was overthrown, and Murillo and his companions were put to death without mercy.

But the most vigorous defence of municipal liberty and opposition to arbitrary government came from the cabildo of Buenos Aires. Relations between the viceroy and cabildo deteriorated precisely under the régime of Sobremonte, whose character and behaviour underwent a strange metamorphosis after his appointment as viceroy in April, 1804. The part played by the cabildo in the critical events of the summer of 1806 when Buenos Aires was invaded by a British expedition, and its role in the reconquest, gave it a moral ascendancy over the viceroy which it was able to turn to good account. The viceroy refused to confirm the elections of 1807, arguing that in the critical circumstances of another imminent invasion experienced councillors should remain in office yet another year. The cabildo rejected this argument and appealed to the audiencia; as Sobremonte was nowhere to be found at the time the audiencia confirmed the elections within two days, and the viceroy sent a lame approval later. Sobremonte's answer to the British invasion of the Río de la Plata was to collect the treasury and make for Córdoba on the pretext of going to raise troops. In 1807 he was arrested by deputies of the cabildo of Buenos Aires near Montevideo and detained in a monastery in Buenos Aires. He was then deposed by the cabildo and the audiencia, and the latter was left temporarily as the depositary of royal authority.

Meanwhile the cabildo's denouncement of maladministration became more and more outspoken. Already on July 3, 1806, it had written to its attorney in Madrid reporting Sobremonte's conduct in the early period of the crisis. Then in secret dispatches to Madrid in May and July 1807 it instructed its attorney to impede the appointment of Santiago Liniers, the hero of the reconquest of Buenos Aires, as viceroy, for it considered him ill-suited for the command of the viceroyalty. In a representation to the government dated September 13, 1808, it requested the appointment of a worthy viceroy, and stated its conviction that

> Corruption in all departments of government has arrived at its extreme. . . . Justice is administered without any subjection to the law; administration knows no rules; the exchequer is managed without economy and with criminal indolence; . . . for many years America has had to suffer corrupt and despotic leaders, ignorant and venal ministers, inefficient and cowardly soldiers.

The vigorous example set by Buenos Aires in these years appealed to the other towns of the viceroyalty, and a growing consciousness of their rights and duties radiated to the other cabildos. Buenos Aires came to be regarded as a leader and protector in municipal politics. When the cabildo of Asunción del Paraguay planned to form a constitution for itself modelled on that of Buenos Aires, and submitted its scheme to the audiencia, the latter requested the cabildo of Buenos Aires to furnish a copy of its ordinances and constitutions for its information. In December, 1805, the audiencia ordered the cabildo to submit a similar record to the municipality of Córdoba. In April 1807 the cabildo of Asunción was in conflict with the newly appointed temporary intendant of Paraguay, and naturally sought the patronage of the cabildo of Buenos Aires for its appeal before the audiencia. For their part almost all the cabildos in the viceroyalty, and many beyond, rallied around Buenos Aires with generous gifts of money in 1807 for the repulse of the British invasions. By now the metropolis was conscious of its ascendancy, and in December 1807, in requesting the title of "Defender of South America and Protector of the Cabildos of the Viceroyalty of La Plata," it posed as the leader of municipal life in the viceroyalty, the benefactor who could help its poor neighbors, "the organ whereby the complaints of the cabildos reach Your Majesty and through which they receive Your graces." Buenos Aires was already prepared for its role in the revolution of independence.

15. Colonial Tucumán

MADALINE W. NICHOLS

Until 1776 when the establishment of the Viceroyalty of La Plata shifted political and economic power to Buenos Aires, a much more important center of Argentina was Tucumán, hundreds of miles inland. Dr. Nichols sketches with a quick and sure hand the life of the Spanish settlers, the Indians, and the commerce of this region, from the time when the conquistadores rode down from the Peruvian highlands in 1535 until the end of the sixteenth century.

When the Spanish conquistadores rode down from the Upper Peruvian highlands and toward the region of the great Argentine plains, they came upon Tucumán, a pleasant and indefinite land. Its very name was of dubious meaning. Tucumán may, indeed, have been the "land where the cotton grows", or the Incas may have used the term merely to designate "a land to the south, in the little-known part of the world". But one thing now seems certain. Since the land had been named Tucma long before the birth of its famous Indian chief, Tucumanhao, historians have decided that while that particular Indian may have been named after his land, the land was *not* named after him.

The boundaries of our Tucumán were even more uncertain than the origin of its name. Not only was there an unfortunate lack of precision in their original delineation, but during the course of history those limiting lines expanded, contracted. The extent and location of Tucumán became a matter of date.

The earliest reports seem to locate the land in the mountain and valley region east of the Andes and extending from present Jujuy to San Juan. The Incas stretched this Tucumán until it became their vast southern dependency between the eastern and the western boundaries of the Paraná-Plata rivers and of the Andean chain. Early Spaniards at first applied the name of Tucumán only to the eastern plains of the present province of Santiago del Estero; then, being acquisitive by nature, our Spaniards added to this Santiaguan Tucumán the land of the present provinces of Cajamarca, Rioja, Tucumán, Córdoba, Salta, Jujuy, and a part of the Chaco. This great hinterland province was colonial Tucumán. After the creation of the viceroyalty of Buenos Aires in 1776, the Chilean province of Cuyo—comprising the modern Argentine provinces of Mendoza, San Juan, and San Luis—was added to Tucumán; six years later the resultant new province was split into two divisions, which became the intendencies of Córdoba del Tucumán and Salta del Tucumán. Only with the period of Independence was the term Tucumán applied to the region immediately around the city of that name—the modern Argentine province.

In the course of history, then, the term Tucumán has been applied to the whole central and western part of the present Argentine Republic as well as to that republic's smallest modern province and to its capital city. For the purposes of this paper, the region considered will be that of colonial Tucumán. The period covered will be the sixteenth century time, when Indian and Spanish civilizations clashed and the great hinterland provinces came into being.

Colonial Tucumán slid off from the high plateau of Upper Peru. In the northwestern part is the barren puna of Jujuy and Salta, a continuation of the plateau land of the desert of Atacama and of southern Bolivia. From this puna, descend broken mountain ranges, paralleling the Andes and dividing western Tucumán into a series of fairly evenly spaced mountain and valley lines which run north and south, and which mark roads for travel and settlement. As one looks at these broken mountain lines on a map, they can be visualized into stepping stones, decreasing gradually in height as the mountains lumber down into the plain. Or, again, our mountain lines may be seen as a series of parallel folds in the earth's crust, marking lines of tectonic force and backing up the mighty Andes in the crush of a continent against a stiff Pacific basin. East of this succession of mountains and valleys are the plains, with their sub-tropical forests, to the north; the great saline desert in the center, where Santiago, Cajamarca, Rioja, and Córdoba dip down to meet; and the pampa grass lands to the south.

In general, the slope of the land is a slow one from the northwestern highland southeast to the Plata Basin. This is the course marked by the three rivers which survive to reach the sea—the Bermejo in the north, the Salado in the center, and the Tercero or Carcarañal or Amazonas in the south. The Dulce, Quarto, and Quinto also seem to have headed for the Plata system, but they died in lagoons on their way. For this land is bad for rivers. In the west, melting snows run into salt hollows where they are burnt up by desert heat. The climate of the whole region is comparatively dry. The land slant is so gradual that a river must run with many a turn and twist; heat and winds, together with the distance to cover before reaching the sea, increase the hazards from evaporation. When the rains do come, rivers swell rapidly, tear away soft clay or sandy banks, broaden their beds, decrease their depth with new sediment deposits, make evaporation dangerously easier. Again, the soil is porous, and a river may even disappear in it entirely.

The vegetation of this great area falls into four main classes, which are determined not so much by latitude as by altitude or by the rain supply. These four classes are desert, "monte" vegetation, pampa, and sub-tropical forest. On the high northern puna of Jujuy and Salta is the cold desert country; down out of the high altitudes, still close to the western Andean rim, is the hot land, desert, save in valleys watered by little streams from mountain snows; and the broad gash of the great saline desert lies through the center of the country from Rioja to Santiago. The "monte", or scrub vegetation, is found in the rather dry strip which includes central and western Córdoba, central Santiago, central and eastern Tucumán, and north into the province of Salta. This vegetation line runs generally from southeast to northwest. Again, this vegetation is to be found in those valleys of the western provinces of Cajamarca and Rioja whenever there is enough moisture to defeat the desert. The tropical forest luxuriates in the rains caught by the eastern slopes and lowlands of Jujuy and Salta, and in the Chaco. The pampa grass lands extend into south and eastern Córdoba.

Into this Tucumán, with its diversity of pampa, scrubby forest, desert land, and luxuriant sub-tropical growth—with its mountains, valleys, plains, and deserts—came meddling and inquisitive Spaniards.

The first of these was appropriately named César. Like his illustrious predecessor of the same name, he came and saw; he conquered at least to the extent of survival. Unfortunately, this Francisco César seems to have been an unlettered gentleman and to have left no commentary on his adventures. This has led to a disconcerting multiplicity of accounts of his famous walk from the fort of the Holy Spirit (Sancti Spiritus) to Cuzco.

The story runs that when Sebastián Cabot came to the Plata region, he met two survivors of a still earlier expedition led by Solís. With Solís had been one Alejo García, who had ventured inland and reported of a land of fabulous wealth, with a white king. Cabot welcomed this news, and in 1529 he sent out an expedition to investigate it, as well as the possible existence of mines of gold and silver. This expedition was led by our Francisco César, who was accompanied by three or four or fourteen or twenty or thirty men. There is a similar diversity of opinion in regard to the route followed. One account is that César went west to the Andes and then north to Bolivia, reaching Cuzco at about the time when Pizarro, entering from the west, came to Cajamarca. A second version runs that César returned to report to Cabot after a journey to the Calchaquí valleys. Finding his leader gone and the fort destroyed, he again dauntlessly plunged into the wilderness, found a rich European city down in the Patagonian wilds near the lake of Nahuel-Huapí, and then followed the Andes north to Cuzco—a walk totaling some two thousand leagues according to the reckoning of the worthy Father Techo. A third version of the story, coming principally from declarations taken when Cabot was officially investigated, tells that the party of fourteen was divided into two groups, one of which just disappeared, possibly to Cuzco. The other group, composed of César and six companions, returned after a journey of some forty or fifty days, during which time they had supposedly been to the lake of Nahuel-Huapí. This account, though documented, is as improbable as the others.

There are misanthropic sceptics who speak of Andalusian imaginations and doubt even the existence of Francisco César—an attitude as negatively extreme as a positive belief in the extensiveness of César's travels and his loot of an emerald "the size of a half a moon". Obviously truth and fable mixed, but it seems fairly certain that a real César went west through southern Tucumán and quite possibly reached the plains of San Luis and Mendoza. When Diego de Almagro, the second Spaniard to invade Tucumán, passed through the country en route to Chile, he was heartily attacked by the Indians, and five of his followers were killed. In view of the fact that the initial Indian reaction to a Spaniard was one of amazed curiosity, the instantaneous hostility aroused by Almagro may well be indicative of the fact that at least news of César had spread through the land.

Almagro entered Tucumán in 1535. Three great roads from Cuzco to Chile lay open to him. One went through the desert of Atacama and along the coast. A second road, by the mountains, was shorter but far more dangerous, with paths only practicable at certain seasons of the year. It passed through the present provinces of Jujuy, Salta, Tucumán, and Cajamarca. Though his guide, the Inca Paullu, strongly advised the coast road, Almagro chose the shorter mountain road instead and followed the Incan advice only on his return trip, after he had learned wisdom. The third road between Cuzco and Chile turned aside from Almagro's inland route at Los Chichas.

In Chile, Araucanian Indian trouble led to Spanish requests for reinforcements from Peru and to increased traffic through Tucumán. Almagro's own journey through the land had left no personal trace save the highly irritated Indians waiting to greet any further Spaniards. By 1545, when Pedro de Valdivia wrote his first letter from Chile to the emperor Charles V, he reported that one Captain Monroy had returned from a recent journey to the northern supply base and that he regretfully noted "not having seen one peaceful Indian from Peru to here".

Yet the Indians of Tucumán do not seem originally to have been an unduly ferocious lot, despite the accounts of Spanish chroniclers. The Spaniards had really annoyed the Indians, disturbed their whole manner, and often even continuance, of life. Spaniards were unpleasantly insistent about making Indians carry things from place to place, and when urged to replace a life of comparative ease by one of hard labor, Indians quite naturally objected. True, there had been Indian family quarrels and the Lules were reported as eating up the Juríes, but the fact that the Spaniards were the chroniclers and that the Juríes were their friends may have colored this report.

When the Spaniards entered Tucumán, many of its Indians were reputedly going to school. The historian Garcilaso tells how Indian deputies had called upon the Inca Viracocha, begging annexation to the Inca Empire, and offering gifts of cotton, honey, wax, grain, fruit, and vegetables. In return they received school-teachers—the Peruvian *amautas*, or those wise men who should teach the new subjects the religion and laws and customs of the empire, together with such practical skills as those of irrigation and agriculture. Apparently, the only districts actually occupied by the Incas were those of modern Jujuy, Salta, Cajamarca, Rioja, San Juan, and Mendoza—the lands of the Diaguitas. These Diaguitas, while overpowered, nevertheless kept their language and never were entirely submissive. The conquest was a political and military matter involving the collection of tribute, rather than one of colonization and the replacing of one culture by another. However, by the time the Spaniards arrived, the Inca's subjects had been trained in many an art, as evidenced by archeological remains found in the region. The period of the Incan occupancy was reported to mark one of the best of all possible governments.

Tucumán was a land of diversity of Indians as well as one of diversity of landscape. While many of its tribes frequently changed their territorial boundaries, in general, it may be said that Diaguitas lived in the mountain valleys to the west, the Comechingones in Córdoba, the Lules in north Tucumán and on the Salta plains, the Juríes in Santiago and west Tucumán. The Calchaquíes were merely the more annoying of the Diaguitas, if one spoke from the Spanish point of view. Of these main Indian cultures, that of the Diaguitas was of greatest importance.

The Diaguita culture problem involves a nice balance between the question of the possible existence of an autochthonous civilization and that of one originating in Peru. Anthropological experts seem to be in disconcerting and discouragingly unanimous disagreement on the matter. Traces of Tiahuanaco culture, a pottery motif similar to that found at Recuay, Tupí-Guaraní influence in the use of a certain tiger motif and in the manner of construction of tombs, note of definitely Incan influences—all have been stressed. Since there seems to be no proof of the racial mingling of the Diaguitas and the Incas in the period immediately before the Spanish invasion and since it is doubtful whether the imposing archeological remains in the Calchaquí valleys belonged to the comparatively simple Diaguitas encountered there by the Spaniards, the general consensus of belief is in some early lost culture, influenced by diverse foreign elements. Involved is the fascinating possibility of an early culture sweep from the east to the west and north. The Diaguitas, with the imposing prehistoric ruins of their land and the evidences of their skill in weaving, ceramics, and basketry, still invite investigation.

As a people, the Diaguitas occasioned many a Spanish description. In general, a Diaguita was of so fierce an aspect that he caused terror and horror. He wore his hair long, unbraided; in the woolen band around his head were stuck brightly colored feathers. He stained his forehead with black, down to the eyes, while the rest of his face was painted "with a thousand colors". He was corpulent and of terrible aspect. From the level of his eyebrows down to his waist hung two scarlet bands made of wool. His arms were bare save for circlets of bright rose-colored wool. Sandals were on his feet. Both men and women wore a shift which came down to their feet; this was girded up when they were about the business of hunting or war or any other kind of travel. A Diaguita never laid aside his bow or the quiver with its fifty and more arrows. He had the reputation of being brave and of having skill in shooting Spaniards.

Just as the Diaguitas were of greater courage than the other Indians, so were they of greater understanding. They formed towns, lived by agriculture and skilful irrigation; obeyed a local chieftain, provided that he was strong enough to force that obedience. They were clever in weaving and in the use of vegetable dyes. They made baskets and beautifully decorated pottery; they worked in gold, silver, copper, tin, and bronze. In all, they were described as being "of more reason" than the Indians of the plains. These Diaguitas of the western valleys were important in the lives of the Spanish conquistadores because they so often brought those lives to an untimely end.

In pleasing contrast to the Diaguitas, the Juríes were the most properly submissive Indians of the land. Yet, despite Spanish friendship, the descriptions of the Juríes are none too flattering. The men dressed lightly in ostrich feathers and the women in some very little blankets woven of straw and wool. The main item of Jurí diet was fish, caught in a most individual way. An Indian would tie a cord about his waist and throw himself into a river. After a long while he would rise to the surface, with six, eight, and more fish hanging from his belt. "These he must have caught in some caves". Since they had so much fish to eat, the Juríes did not bother much with other food. However, they did have maize and frijoles and many manner of roots, such as the yucca. There were algarroba and chañar trees, and the land abounded with game. Honey, wax, sisal, rosin, and many dyes were to be found. In the midst of this plenty the Juríes had become lazy "by nature". In other respects, too, their characters were not above reproach. They were drunken like the rest, and worse. They made very potent, badly smelling chicha from the algarroba. They were great thieves and went abroad with bow and arrows, not only through fear of the tigers, but in case they might find people to assault. They did not hesitate to shoot a traveler to get his blanket.

At the time of the coming of the Spaniards, hostile Lules were reported as keeping the Juríes well corraled in forts made of stakes. Miguel de Ardiles, reporting around 1567, emphasized Jurí affliction. "Had it not been for the favor of the Spaniards at this time, undoubtedly the Lules would have brought them to an end." A desire to escape from such enemies probably accounted for Jurí fondness for Spaniards.

The Lules were nomads, in from the Chaco land. They had been highly successful in making a living from hunting, theft, and cannibalism. With the coming of the Spaniards, this happy state of things was ended; and such Lules as escaped the newcomers, hastily made their way back across the Salado River to their Chaco refuge land and independence. Those who did not escape went sorrowfully to work.

South of the Lules and Juríes were the peaceful Comechingones, who lived in Córdoba. In 1572, Don Gerónimo Luis de Cabrera wrote his report upon their land, where he was planning to found a city. In the neighborhood he had computed some six hundred little Indian towns, composed of from ten to forty houses, and each containing four or five families. These houses were necessarily large; for example, ten Spaniards with their horses hid in one of them, when ambushed for a skirmish. They were low, and at that, half their height was under ground. The purpose of the excavation of these cellars was for shelter in the cold weather and because there was a scarcity of wood in some places. The towns were circular in form and protected by hedges of prickly trees and thistles, as a military defense. Cabrera computed a total of some 30,000 Indian inhabitants.

Most of these Indians were clothed in beaded woolen shifts or in beautifully worked skins. They wore feather and metal ornaments. They busied themselves in agriculture, raising maize and frijoles. They also ate the fruit of the algarroba and chañar, the edible roots of the land, and the plentiful game for which they hunted. Differing from other Indians, the Comechingones were not interested in intoxicating corn liquor. A curious custom of theirs was reported, however. They made a powder from the cebil tree and "drank it through their noses".

While the Diaguitas, Comechingones, Juríes, and Lules were the main tribes of Tucumán, on the eastern and northern boundaries were many tribes that frequently came visiting. The Abipones were to the east and north of Córdoba; in the Chaco were Mocovíes, Tobas, and Chiriguanos; on the northern highlands were Humahuacas and Atacemeños. Of all these Indians, the Chiriguanos became the most annoying. As late as 1586, however, the northern Indians seem not to have been too hostile to the Spaniards of Tucumán. They would come in from their land beyond the Bermejo River and bring feathers, skins, honey, and wax to trade. The skins were of deer and of the little mountain cats.

Considering the land of Tucumán as it was when the Spaniards came, it may be said to have been well populated by comparatively peaceful and happy Indians. With the exception of the newly invading Lules, those Indians were agricultural and sedentary. Their towns were well placed, with a nice regard for such essentials as the water supply on which soil fertility depended, nearness to natural food supplies, ease of defense and of communication. In lands where there was rock, the houses were built of stones and arranged in villages of the kind of which Quilmes was typical. On the plains of Tucumán, Salta, and Santiago, houses were mere brush shelters. In Córdoba, a wood covering of a dugout seems to have been typical.

Writing at the end of the sixteenth century, Father Barzana left a general description of Tucumán. The land was reported as fertile. The algarroba furnished the basic food supply. It was also used in the unfortunate manufacture of a drink "so potent, that never are there more deaths and wars than during algarroba time". There were many kinds of fruit trees; sugarcane grew wild in the woods of Tucumán; there was an abundance of honey, varying in taste in accordance with that of the different kinds of bees which gathered it; game was plentiful. Agriculturally-minded Indians added to this natural food supply their crops of corn, frijoles, etc. Tucumán was a land "of much food".

Indian life was not without amusement. All our Indians of Tucumán were reported as "greatly given to singing and dancing, and so insistently, that some stay up all night, singing, dancing, and drinking". Notably would the natives of Córdoba, after having worked and walked all day, dance or indulge in chorus singing the greater part of the night. The big events of the year were the tiger- and lion-hunts, after which, gathered about their fires, Indians would tell tales of the apparition of mysterious, unknown Things; of strange cries heard in the woods; of black magic; of birds that lure unwary travelers to misfortune—a whole Indian lore.

Population figures for Tucumán have been consistently indefinite. Father Barzana admitted that he was unable to make any accurate estimate, but that "if Spanish thirst would allow the Indians to multiply, they would be innumerable".

Into this happy Indian land came Spaniards. They planted cities over its landscape; introduced animals and crops that changed its vegetation; and they changed the Indian language, dress, religion, and modes of life. Spaniards also busied themselves in fighting heartily with each other. The very fact that they were in Tucumán was indicative of the belligerency of their characters, for Diego de Rojas in 1543 led on the first *gran entrada* those soldiers who were regarded as a menace to the peace of Peru. Tucumán entered Spanish history either as a place through which one must pass in order to get to some other place, or as a place in which to dispose of potential trouble makers.

Despite the disreputable character of the Rojas expedition, it was of geographical importance through the very extensiveness of its travels. Starting for Chile, it abandoned all such thoughts after meeting wily Indians who had learned that the way to get rid of Spaniards was to mention gold in other and distant lands. The Indians had also aroused a spirit of rivalry by exhibiting certain "Spanish chickens" reputed to have been brought from an eastern country where Spanish men were presumably finding wealth. The Rojas party immediately crossed the Andes and began its wanderings all over Tucumán. They toured the Calchaquí valley, the eastern plains, the Córdoba mountain region; finally they came to the Paraná. On its bank they found a cross with the sign "Carta al pie", and digging, there was a letter left by Irala, who wrote of Asunción and how passing Spaniards might get there! At this point, the party was undecided as to further procedure, but having killed the leader who had been unwise in his opposition to the majority will, they returned to Peru. Reports of wars and hope of consequent booty there hastened them on their way.

From 1546 to 1549 Peru was busy with civil war. Only when this unpleasantness was over did the authorities of Peru again think of Tucumán as a place where ex-soldiers might profitably be employed. Juan Núñez de Prado led this second expedition. He was assigned to the Jurí lands of Santiago.

The Juríes welcomed Spanish military aid against their local enemies. Moreover, they were told that an Indian who put a cross on his house could count on freedom from any unreasonable Spanish molestation. But presently there came into the land a second band of Spaniards who ignored the mystic symbolism of all the little crosses on Indian homes, who robbed in hearty Spanish fashion, and who killed all objectors. Francisco de Villagrá, badly off his route to Chile, was attempting to annex Tucumán to the jurisdiction of his commander, Valdivia. Núñez de Prado too hastily attacked Villagrá. He was defeated, and only after persuasion would he consent to believe that he was in Valdivia's jurisdiction and not in his own. Though allowed to continue in the land as a deputy ruler, it is interesting to note the haste with which he resigned that position and moved his little town of Barco out of the horrid Valdivia jurisdiction as soon as Villagrá had departed. Valdivia's fourth and fifth letters to Charles V, however, give a different interpretation of events:

> Him [Prado] la Gasca gave a commission, to go and settle a valley he had heard of, called Tucumán, and he founded a town, calling it the city of El Barco. It would seem that when the said deputy Villagrá was going along 30 leagues away from El Barco, for he was thus ordered by the said President in Los Reyes, this Juan Núñez de Prado, with mounted men, fell suddenly at night on Villagrá's camp, firing muskets, harassing and killing soldiers and calling out: "Viva el rey y Juan Núñez de Prado". His reason . . . was to scatter those men, if he could, and take them for himself . . . and to play such pranks as they had been wont to do in those provinces. After steps had been taken against this, Juan Núñez de Prado, of his free will and without compulsion, gave up the authority he held, and which the President had given him, saying he could not maintain that town, and the cabildo and townsfolk asked of Francisco de Villagrá, since it fell within the bounds of this government, to take it under his care, and in my name to administer it, that it might be maintained and kept in being; and he . . . put it in your Majesty's name under my protection and shelter. . . .

After Villagrá's departure,

> One "Juan Núñez de Prado" laid waste the town of El Barco which the said Villagrá had fostered in your Majesty's name and . . . went off to Peru, hanging an alcalde. . . .

The passage of Villagrá through Tucumán had been unfortunate. It had necessitated the removal of the Spanish town; it had commandeered many necessary Spanish supplies; vitally important soldier settlers had been induced to leave for Chile. Moreover, after noting Spanish weakness, the Indians turned against their former masters, burned their crops, and sought a general revenge for Spanish insults. Hunger, fear, lack of discipline, discontent grew. Barco was moved again, in a hope of Indian escape; settlers despaired and grew to dislike their Núñez de Prado cordially.

At this period there came to Tucumán the most remarkable man of its history, and one who was to control its destinies for a period of approximately twenty years. From 1553 to 1572, Francisco de Aguirre either ruled Tucumán in person, or someone ruled it for him while he was collecting supplies and straightening out his many personal difficulties with the Inquisition. It was under Aguirre that Santiago, Argentina's first permanent town, was founded and that systematic expansion began. Settlers were collected, supplies shipped in, Spanish livestock and crops introduced. In 1554, five brave warriors ventured through the hostile Indian lands to Chile to escort back the equally brave padres who were to supervise the spiritual salvation of new little Santiago. By 1556, trade with Chile and with Peru had begun. Tucumán was exporting honey, wax, cotton, and dyes; it imported clothing, livestock (horses, cows, goats, sheep), plants, and seeds.

While a hardy conquistador and a practical administrator, Aguirre was unfortunately indiscreet. Such statements as "One did far more service to God by creating Mestizos than the sin thereby involved" made good copy for the Inquisition. Though twice taken to Peru to make a proper explanation, Aguirre was finally released and pardoned. However, as it was felt that his presence and that of his enemies in the same province would mean civil war and as settlers were too precious to be wasted, the old conquistador was retired to Chile.

After Aguirre, leading governors of sixteenth century Tucumán were Gerónimo Luis de Cabrera, the inefficient Gonzalo de Abreu, and the very bad Hernando de Lerma. It is typical of Tucumán's history that Cabrera was murdered by Abreu, who, in turn, was tortured and murdered by Lerma. Lerma was so thoroughly unsatisfactory that he was forcibly removed by the audiencia even before the completion of his term of office. Then came the good governor and colonizer, Juan Ramírez de Velasco. The century ended with the comparatively obscure Hernando de Zárate and Pedro de Mercado de Peñalosa.

Through this century of colonization and settlement, it is interesting to trace the Spanish plan behind Spanish rule and occupation of the land.

The first purpose in entering Tucumán had been to get rid of possible trouble makers or to give a suitable reward to faithful supporters of the Crown. An economic emphasis was given to the subsequent strategic and political occupation of the land by an interest in eastern expansion with the establishment of a river port which should make possible direct trade from Peru to Spain by way of Tucumán. In contrast to these plans for eastern expansion was the stress upon the assurance of the conquests already made and of safe communication between Peru and Chile. However with Cabrera and his foundation of Córdoba and the river ports—San Luis on the Paraná and Santa Fe—the idea of eastern expansion for the purposes of trade finally gained the ascendancy and pointed the way to the eventual realization of the viceroyalty of 1776 two hundred years later.

Not only was there a Spanish plan behind the conquest as a whole, but the location of individual towns was well considered. Spanish cities might fail temporarily, but a new town rose upon the ruins of the old in emphasis of the fixity of Spanish purpose. Barco I (1550) became Cañete (1559) and San Miguel (1565) and modern Tucumán (1683). Similarly Nieva (1562) led to San Francisco de Alava (1575) and then to Jujuy (1593). San Clemente II was followed by San Clemente III (1577) and then in the same valley, though not on the same exact site, came Salta (1582). In 1591, new Rioja was founded near the ruins of Londres I (1558) and Londres II. Near Barco II (1551) was founded Córdoba de Calchaquí (1559) which in turn was followed by San Clemente I (1562) and then Nuestra Señora de Guadalupe (1631). Barco III (1552) became old (1553) and then modern Santiago del Estero (1554). In 1609, Talavera de Esteco (of 1567) merged with Madrid de las Juntas (of 1592) to become Talavera de Madrid, but only to disappear in the earthquake of 1692.

Yet though a cool Spanish plan for conquest and the organization of settlement might well be of fundamental importance, there were other reasons for the ultimate success of the occupation. These were both romantic and economic. The first led to a rapid and thorough reconnaissance of the territory; the second led to permanency and controlled the growth of settlement.

The romantic reason for the exploration of Tucumán was the determined Spanish search for a "lost" land. This "land of the Cesars", named after Francisco César, Tucumán's first pioneer, but really having nothing to do with him, reputedly lay somewhere to the south. It was a lost kingdom of shipwrecked Spaniards, who were popularly supposed to have attained wealth in the wilderness and to be longing for Spanish comrades to share it with them and to join them in Catholic fellowship. There was, of course, many a version of the story, but the remarkable thing about it was its potent influence on men's lives. Political, military, and religious leaders either went looking for these Spanish Cesars, or made extensive plans to go, or sent their subordinates. Witness after witness was solemnly examined, and whatever information he might give was forwarded to

Spain. Bishops and viceroys sent Indian letter-carriers wandering out into Patagonian wilds with messages to the Cesars written in many a language, just in case these lost brother Spaniards might have forgotten their own. That the Cesars and their land were never found did not affect the importance of the geographical knowledge resultant from the search.

Economic law regulated the land gained by military conquest and organized with a view to political control. Roads were opened through Tucumán and over these roads went trade. As early as 1586, Portuguese merchants were reported in Santiago del Estero, "selling the things that they have brought". Presently, this eastern trade progressed to an extent alarming to the monopolist control of Spanish merchants, led to Spanish restrictions despite American protests. By the end of the sixteenth century Tucumán had theoretically settled down to a languid economic existence under the control of Lima, but practically, that life was far from being as languid as it seemed. Spain had required the impossible. The money of Potosí and the raw materials of the inland cities of Tucumán moved down to the coast, there to be exchanged for the manufactured necessities smuggled in by enterprising Dutch, English, French, and Portuguese. The urge to live united Tucumán with the Río de la Plata. Settlers might officially and humbly beg for the means of survival, but whether granted or no, they availed themselves of those means. The two regions were interdependent. And growth of settlement obeyed economic law.

Spanish colonial life in Tucumán centered in the basic unit of the Spanish system of occupation—the Spanish town. Such a town was built in strict occordance with definite specifications prescribed in the laws of the Indies. One began with a rectangular central square. Around it were located the church, the jail, the cabildo or town hall, and the lots for convents and for the principal citizens. From this central square, straight streets divided the surrounding land into the rectangular lots which were apportioned to the settlers. Then there came an open space of three hundred paces, left for defense purposes, and fortifications of stockades and trenches. Outside the walls were the grazing and farm lands. After marking out their town, the settlers planted crops and built their homes. These must "be of one form, for the sake of the adornment of the town". Each had several patios and a corral; it was backed against its neighbor for purposes of mutual protection. Walls were of adobe; roofs of straw or palm. Later, cornices were attempted, floors were paved, walls whitewashed, and rejas of turned wooden bars reminded the settlers of their native Spain.

To found a town, one must first collect thirty qualified settlers— men who possessed a minimum fixed amount of property, including a definite number of cattle. But additional settlers were badly needed. The land itself might be good, but men must work it and defend it, and honorable governors must administer it and "not turn their interest to pleasure, and drawing their salary, and plundering their land, leave it forlorn". A settler's lot, however, was none too happy. He lacked the proper tools with which to work. He was badly in need of clothing and even of food. For example, poverty in Talavera was such that settlers ate horse and dog meat, or sold their Spanish clothing in exchange for food and then imitated the Indian dress of deerskins or ostrich feathers. One has to imagine a conquistador dressed in ostrich feathers to get a proper perspective of colonial conditions! Again, Spanish settlers frequently died from Indians, as well as from hunger, for Indians were "a warlike, astute, and devilish people who fought beastially to defend their land, in their desire to cast the Spaniards out of it".

The Indian trouble was a serious matter in Spanish settlements; in fact there was a proverb which ran "Sin indios, no hay Indias". Here the Indians referred to, however, are not the Indian warriors on the outside, but the Indian laborers within the Spanish colonies. This Indian factor conditioned the progress and even the life of the colonies. Unfortunately, Indians ran away or were stolen or died. They, themselves, fled to desert or mountain regions where it would be hard for Spaniards to find them, or passing merchants stole them and drove them away to do the work in other lands. Governor Lerma officially countenanced a wholesale destruction of Tucumán's native population by allowing the Indians to be driven away like cattle and hired out or sold in Chile and in Charcas. Eight thousand Indians were reported to have disappeared in this way alone. Each Spaniard conquering expedition was fatal to the health of thousands of Indian burden bearers, and there were many such expeditions. Almagro alone is said to have left a "one hundred league empty land behind him, all sown with frozen dead Indians". As a result of this destruction of the native population, not a fourth part of the Indians who had been in the land at the time of the Inca were left by 1560. Repartimientos of thirty thousand had supposedly been reduced to two thousand. However, the land was far from deserted. Population figures given for 1584 report in Santiago del Estero 48 Spanish *vecinos* and 12,000 Indians; San Miguel had 25 *vecinos* and 3,000 Indians; Córdoba, 40 *vecinos* and 18,000 Indians.

Governor Juan Ramírez de Velasco's report of 1586 is an excellent official portrayal of sixteenth-century conditions in Tucumán. The governor had found five towns in his land—Santiago, San Miguel, Talavera, Córdoba, and Salta—though the last was called a town merely out of courtesy. Two of the governor's main problems were the need for more settlers and for more livestock. As one means of meeting the first issue, Velasco was busily finding husbands for more than two hundred maidens, daughters of conquistadores, "who had no other help save that of God and Your Majesty", as the governor wrote to the king. He reported,

I have married off ten, and some with two or three repartimientos. Two results have been obtained, which are: marrying these poor girls, and increasing the number of settlers, for from one, two will be made.

He planned to marry two dozen more to the soldiers of Salta, and the rest would be attended to in the very first town that should be founded. Velasco also called the king's attention to the disgraceful stealing of the Indian population to be sold in Potosí or Chile in exchange for Spanish clothing and other luxuries. To climax this indignity offered to the poor Indian, the governor noted that he was not even given *alpargatas* for his weary walk to slavery in Chile or Peru.

Ramírez de Velasco was also interested in economic matters. There was need of an increase in the livestock of Tucumán. Owing to the carelessness of early governors, the respectably sized herds of cattle, horses, goats, and sheep of earlier times, had been lamentably depleted. And the high prices of commodities from Peru were distressing. A yard of cloth cost thirty pesos, a pound of soap three pesos, four horseshoes cost six pesos, and a quire of paper, three.

In contrast to these unhappy circumstances, the governor noted that while, to date, no gold or silver had been found in his land, yet there was great news of such mines in the hostile Indian country. Also he had news of a land of the Cesars. It lay between Chile and the northern sea, and behind Arauco. North and south, it extended some 350 leagues, from Córdoba to the strait of Magellan. In it were many people and much gold. If it is the king's will, as soon as Ramírez de Velasco has settled the Calchaquí and Salta valleys—a matter of a possible two years—he will organize a party at his own expense and conquer this rich land for his king. In return, may he please have the title of adelantado of that land, a tenth part of the Indians who shall be conquered, and two robes of the order of Santiago—one for himself and one for his oldest son?

Summarizing, then, the changes wrought in sixteenth-century Tucumán, one may say that Spaniards have come in, have founded their monotonously geometrical little cities, have introduced their Spanish animals, trees, food crops, and weeds. By the end of the century, the Indians are far fewer in number than they were at its beginning, and those still surviving have changed their mode of life. If properly submissive, Indians now live where they can most efficiently work for Spaniards. They speak Spanish or, at the worst, Quechuan, as these languages have become generalized and replaced the pleasing individuality of dialect of pre-conquest times. Indians now wear more and a different kind of clothing. Strange new items of food have been added to their diet. Indian economy has been badly upset.

The main work of the conquest in Tucumán is over. To be sure there are hostile Indians on the frontiers, but the land itself is safely occupied. Spanish colonial life will develop slowly. Religious orders will build their houses; the land will become more extensively cultivated; livestock numbers will be increased; new industries will develop; new settlers come. Eventually there will come a conflict between the arbitrary economic control of the region from a Peruvian base and the economic interests of the land itself. When Buenos Aires and Argentina's economic interests win, the new viceroyalty of Buenos Aires will be created and Argentina will at last turn its back upon Peru and face the world trade markets to the east. For two hundred years Argentina was Tucumán; with 1776, Argentina begins to be Buenos Aires.

Another Article of Interest

Tapson, Alfred J., "Indian Warfare on the Pampa during the Colonial Period." See pages 239–257.

16. The Encomienda in Paraguay

ELMAN R. SERVICE

Professor Service, an anthropologist on the faculty of the University of Michigan, brings to the following analysis of the encomienda in Paraguay the techniques of his discipline and delineates the unusual circumstances in this isolated region which produced one of the most racially amalgamated and culturally integrated societies in Spanish America.

In the Spanish colonization of the New World, the *encomienda* system and the mission system were the two most important means of institutionalized control of the native population, especially during the early years of the colonial period. Sometimes side by side, competing, sometimes widely separated and alone, these two types of agencies each succeeded in varying degree, and by varying methods, in bringing the New World natives into a place within the orbit of Spanish colonial society. It seems probable that the several kinds of Spanish-Indian relations which were implicit in these institutions may help to account for certain features of subsequent cultural developments in particular regions of Spanish America, and to some extent, for some of the cultural and racial distinctions which exist in our own day.

The *encomienda* system, as it operated in certain areas of the New World, has been described in some detail by modern historians. With respect to Paraguay, however, it is the mission organization of the Jesuits

From Volume XXXI (1951), pages 230–252.

which is the best documented colonial institution, and which has even been the subject of many popular works. The area of primary Spanish settlement in Paraguay, however, was the region around Asunción, and from here the *encomienda*, rather than the Jesuit missions, rapidly extended the area of Spanish control over the aborigines throughout the whole central region. The later Jesuit "state" of thirty mission towns was situated mainly in the Alto Paraná basin, a region remote and nearly inaccessible from central Paraguay, where the nucleus of the later nation of Paraguay was in the process of formation. It is the purpose of the present paper to offer some data descriptive of the Paraguayan *encomienda*, and to suggest a few of the possible long range effects implied in this type of Spanish-Indian association.

The *encomienda* system of exploitation and control of indigenous populations which the Spaniards employed in different parts of the New World was general in conception and intent. Since the laws regulating this institution were promulgated by the Spanish king and his Council of the Indies, they were usually formulated to apply to all of the Spanish possessions in the New World. They were, however, often modified in practice by local conditions of geography, kinds of available wealth, and type of native population. Exceptions in the application of these rules in Paraguay, as compared to other areas, emphasize and make explicit those features which were unusual in the relationship of Spaniards and Paraguayan Indians in the early colonial period.

At the time of the first Spanish exploration of the La Plata region, Guaraní-speaking Indians occupied a large area extending from the Atlantic coast westward to the Paraguay River, covering much of the present-day Brazilian state of Rio Grande do Sul, Paraná, Misiones Territory in Argentina, and virtually all of Paraguay east of the Gran Chaco. This part of Paraguay and the Alto Paraná basin to the east were occupied almost exclusively by Guaraní.

Guaraní culture was roughly similar to the generic culture type called "Tropical Forest" in the classification used in *The Handbook of South American Indians*. Subsistence activities were based on widespread tropical forest agricultural techniques. There was no irrigation nor fertilization of cultivated fields, so that every two or three years the fields were abandoned in favor of more productive virgin areas. The usual tropical foods were grown, sweet manioc and maize being the important staples. Several kinds of sweet potatoes, beans, peanuts and pumpkins were also cultivated. There were no domesticated animals, with the possible exception of the Muscovy duck, and meat was therefore obtained by hunting such animals as the tapir and deer. Fishing and gathering wild forest products were important supplementary activities. The digging-stick was the basic agricultural tool, and the bow and arrow the important hunting weapon. As with most tropical forest peoples, the women concentrated on horticultural labor, the men on hunting and warfare.

Villages were usually composed of large thatched communal buildings, each housing the several families which formed one patrilineal lineage. Often a whole village consisted of a single house. Each of these units had a headman or chief, and if the village were composed of more than one lineage, these chiefs may have been subordinate to a village chief. The Guaraní headman's power over his kinsmen was quite limited compared to that wielded by chiefs in the higher cultures of the Andes and circum-Caribbean areas, for Guaraní society was not class-structured with an hereditary hierarchy of chiefs whose authority extended over great numbers of conquered or federated villages. This feature was to be an important determinant of the type of Spanish control system, for the Spaniards could not simply replace the top-level native rulers and govern through an intermediate bureaucratic class. Control had to be immediate and specific, reaching the individual Indian, in contrast to the situation in Peru and Mexico.

There is evidence, however, of a status system which suggests an incipient trend in the direction of socio-political classes. The chief's crops were planted and harvested by the members of his community, and, additionally, chiefs or important people commonly had plural wives or concubines, the number of which corresponded roughly to his prestige. The lack of political power of the leaders continually impressed the Spaniards, who often referred to the general anarchy and lack of authority.

The original expedition of Spaniards to the La Plata region was inspired by false beliefs that the region was very wealthy in gold and silver. This was the great Mendoza expedition which was a powerful force in its time, but was so reduced by hardship and battles with Charrúa and Querandí Indians near Buenos Aires and by subsequent losses suffered in various attempts to reach Peru via the Gran Chaco that those who finally formed the settlement near Asunción, even when reinforced by the remainder of the garrison from the original settlement of Buenos Aires, numbered altogether three hundred and fifty Spanards. The first and only important reinforcement the colony ever received was that of Cabeza de Vaca's group, which brought the greatest number of Spaniards to about six hundred. This was a small number of soldiers for the huge area they hoped to dominate. Asunción was a thousand miles from the mouth of the La Plata and much of the intervening area was populated by hostile tribes. The fort at Asunción was especially threatened by a great number of enemies in the nearby Chaco. It is plain that the Spaniards would have been in a strategically untenable position had the Guaraní of Paraguay proper also been at war with them, for under these circumstances it would have been more difficult to conquer and rule than in a region of relatively united "empires" like Mexico and Peru.

It was, perhaps, entirely fortuitous that just as the first group of Spaniards arrived in the vicinity of Asunción, in 1537, the agricultural Guaraní, who were hard-pressed by warlike Indians of the Chaco, preferred to welcome the newcomers as potential allies rather than enemies. The Spaniards, who had already suffered grievously from Indian warfare, formed an alliance with certain Guaraní chiefs and built the fort at Asunción. Asunción soon became the Spanish headquarters and base from which further explorations were made in search of the fabulous "Sierra de la Plata." The Spaniards were now settled in a region where the Indians were friendly, and useful, and they took great care not to "violate the customs or wound the sensibilities of the Guaraní."

During the first twenty years of the settlement at Asunción, the assignment of lands and establishment of *encomiendas* was not considered, because the Spaniards still hoped to find gold and silver mines, or Indians with treasure, and had no intention of forming a permanent settlement. In the absence of *encomiendas*, the Spaniards acquired large numbers of Guaraní women, who served not only as wives and concubines, but also as servants and food providers. The relatives of these women also helped provide food and labor for the Spaniards in the same way that they customarily provided for their own chiefs. The Guaraní apparently considered this situation a normal consequence of the alliance.

Numerous coöperative military expeditions were carried out during the first years of the settlement. Under Spanish leadership, the Guaraní won a number of victories over their Chaco enemies, the Guaycurú and Payaguá tribes. Spanish prestige grew as a consequence of these military victories, and the Guaraní contributed very large contingents on subsequent expeditions to the west. This kind of military coöperation and the acceptance of Spaniards as in-law relatives with the status of chiefs was of utmost importance in determining the character of the later, permanent colonization of Paraguay.

This rather casual adaptation of the two peoples to each other was typical of the pre-*encomienda* periods, and has often been considered one of the most notable aspects of the early colonial period in Paraguay. In later times the *encomienda* system appeared, and was a more characteristic Spanish institution, but the concubinage-kinship-labor pattern was never entirely replaced, and it imparted its flavor to the whole subsequent history of Spanish-Guaraní relations.

In 1556, in accordance with a crown order, Governor Irala divided the Indians in the vicinity of Asunción into *encomiendas*, and turned the attention of the colonists from the fruitless search for wealth to the task of permanently settling the land. This new orientation resulted in the rapid extension of the *encomienda* system to new areas of Paraguay, and even to parts of present-day Argentina, where new Spanish towns were established as well. Santa Fe, Corrientes, and Buenos Aires, and Santa Cruz, in what is now eastern Bolivia, were all founded within thirty years after the original *encomienda* grants, and so were many villages in Paraguay proper. Most of the Paraguayan settlements were not created to be populated by Spaniards but by *encomienda* Indians. A total of thirty-eight of these towns were formed, and many of them are still in existence in modern Paraguay.

This expansion of colonization which began after the issuance of *encomienda* grants in 1556 was made possible by the increasingly important role of mestizos. The number of original peninsular Spaniards in Paraguay had diminished greatly in the second half of the sixteenth century, but there had been a great increase in the number of their mestizo sons and daughters as a consequence of the extensive polygyny of the conquistadores and the Guaraní women. Santa Fe was founded by nine Spaniards and seventy-five creoles, and Buenos Aires by ten Spaniards and sixty-three creoles. A great many sources from the latter half of the sixteenth century indicate that the mestizos not only greatly outnumbered the Spaniards, but held offices and *encomiendas* and were already displaying a very independent attitude toward Spanish rule. Several scattered rebellions were already called *comunero* movements and presaged the revolts which in later years culminated in the independence of the Latin American states.

The transitional period following the 1556 grants involved the formation of new *encomiendas* in remote areas, and the adaptation of Irala's decrees to the already existing patterns of Spanish-Indian relations which we have described as characteristic of the pre-*encomienda* period. By about 1580, or one generation later, the colony had taken on the most important local characteristics which were to influence the adaptation of the *encomienda* Indians to Paraguayan colonial life. By this time, the influence of the earlier patterns and the exigencies of economic life had developed two quite separate types of institutions of Spanish-Guaraní association—the *originario* and the *mitayo encomiendas*—which retained their stability for the remainder of the colonial period.

The rigid royal laws relating to the *encomienda*, which did not take account of cultural and ecological differences in the various areas of Spanish settlement, were never entirely enforced in Paraguay, despite repeated attempts by several governors to create a system which would conform to crown intentions. As we shall see, some of the laws which had originally grown out of the crown's experience in the West Indies, Mexico, and Peru had unforeseen consequences in Paraguay, while others had to be modified or disregarded.

The *encomienda* laws most generally ignored in Paraguay were those designed to prevent unpaid, unregulated exploitation of the labor of the natives. The restrictions on Indian labor had been judged by the Spanish crown and its advisers to be the most important means of preventing the rise of a powerful feudal class in America and of protecting the Indians. The frank violation of this prohibition was always one of the characteristics of both the *originario* and *mitayo encomiendas* in Paraguay.

There were many factors in the Paraguayan situation which may have been responsible for this practice, but the most direct and influential imperative was the nature of the Paraguayan economy. Lack of mineral wealth, isolation, and limited commerce meant that Guaraní labor-power was exploited in terms of a subsistence economy, and that tribute of money, agricultural produce, or a native trade ware could not develop in place of labor services, for there was no export market of any importance. Documentary evidence clearly demonstrates that this situation continued from Irala's time throughout most of the colonial period. Irala's ordinances of 1541–1547 indicate that all trade was by barter of produce within the colony. Wages were paid in corn, beans, manioc, etc., and once Irala tried to institute knives as a standard of value. López de Velasco, observing the period 1571–1574, reported:

... todos tienen lo que han menester para su mantenimiento y sustento, aunque ninguno rico de moneda, porque no la hay en la tierra: sus haciendas son todas la crianza y grangerías del campo ... no hay mercaderes porque no hay puertos a la mar; las comulaciones se hacen en una casa pública, donde pone cada uno lo que quiere trocar en poder de un corredor, puesto por la ciudad, y allí acuden los que quieren feriar por otras; porque no hay moneda, sino sean unas cuñas o hachetas de hierro de siete onzas. ...

Ramírez de Velasco, in 1597, and Ruiz de Montoya in the early seventeenth century also wrote on the poverty and nature of the barter economy. Similar comments are available from other writers during the seventeenth century, and the famous Dobrizhoffer, referring to the middle of the eighteen century, said,

... money is used very rarely, if at all, its place being supplied by the exchange of commodities, as among the ancients ... the want or ignorance of metals may be reckoned amongst the divine blessings and advantages of Paraguay.

The poverty and scarcity of markets, which reduced the colony to a barter economy, helped bring the Spaniards and Indians into a symbiotic relationship in subsistence activities and were, therefore, very important in promoting the mixing of the two cultures. The limited economy also had the effect of reducing the great gulf which has always existed between the philosophy and attitudes of Europeans and American Indians in economic matters. In other parts of Latin America, the profit-seeking motives of the Spanish entrepreneurs as opposed to the native conception of production-for-use was, and often still is, an important factor inhibiting a mixture of the two cultures. In Paraguay, circumstances never permitted the growth of a class of traders and financiers whose interests and ideals would necessarily be opposed to the Indian viewpoint. The Spaniards in Paraguay were, truly enough, the exploiters, and the Indians were exploited, but as this occurred within a subsistence economy, it was a situation at least comprehensible to the Indians, and probably even a more acceptable one than it might have been under the conditions of a commercial economy.

In addition to these economic characteristics, the adaptation of the Spanish conception of *encomienda* to Paraguay was also affected by such factors as the previously mentioned simplicity of Guaraní socio-political structure and the lack of large population centers when contrasted with the native "empires" of Mexico and Peru. To these must be added the important circumstance that the *encomiendas* were not established in a formal sense until the Spaniards and Indians had already undergone a period of about twenty years of expedient, informal adjustment during which the newcomers acted as allies rather than as conquerors of the Guaraní. As the settlement at Asunción gradually came to be regarded as permanent, the original system of year around personal service by the "harems" of Indian women and their relatives came to be regarded as an *encomienda*, and was called the *encomienda originaria*. This *originario* had such a firm basis in Paraguayan life that, despite the crown's attempts to limit or abolish it from time to time, it remained a characteristic of Paraguay throughout most of the colonial period.

The more formal *encomienda* created by Irala's ordinances of 1556 was used to extend Spanish control to villages of Indians in areas at some distance from Asunción. This latter system was called the *encomienda mitaya* because the Indians were brought to Asunción periodically as laborers, hence *mitayo* after the *mita* or *corvée* labor system of Peru. Certain main features of both the *originario* and *mitayo* were influenced by the factors outlined above. The specific differences between them will become apparent below where each type of *encomienda* is discussed separately.

The *originario* was not created by decree but was merely the gradual institutionalization of the Guaraní customs of polygyny and kinship obligations. As Diego Téllez Descobar, a contemporary of Irala, stated:

Hera la costumbre de los yndios de la tierra servir a los Xpianos y de darles sus hijas o hermanas y venir a sus casas por via de parentesco y amystad y ansi heran servidos los Xpianos porque tenian los Xpianos muchos hijos en la gente natural de aquella tierra y a esta causa venien los yndios a servir como a casa de parientes y sobrinos.

Statements from the most reliable chroniclers of the period from 1579 until about 1630 indicate that out of the total population of about four thousand people in Asunción, there were about ten women to every man, and the ordinances of several governors during this period indicate that Guaraní women were continually taken from the *mitayo* pueblos to augment the *originario*. Successive decrees of Governors Irala, Ramírez, and Hernandarias, and of the royal inspector, Alfaro, made in the years 1556, 1597, 1603, and 1611, respectively, attempted to limit the practice of procuring women from the Indian villages. The fact that they all prohibited the same acts seems sufficient indication that the laws must have been ineffectively enforced, and additionally, most of the decrees describe the situation before prohibiting it. For example, Governor Ramírez state:

Iten por que en el sacar serbicio los encomenderos an tenido deshorden y mediante ella los pueblos de sus encomiendas estan disipados y sin aber en algunos dellos muchachos ni chinas por haberlos sacado para su serbicio personal/

hordeno y mando . . . que ningun encomendero saque para serbicio personal ninguna india que sea casada por el notable daño que recibe particularmente teniendo hijos.

Specific details are lacking on the manner of life of the *originarios,* but there is evidence indicating that these Indians were regarded as permanent residents of the homes and *estancias* of the Spaniards. Some of the *originarios* were simply domestic servants living all the time at the residence of the *encomenderos* in the Spanish towns. Other whole families of Indians lived as permanent laborers on the outlying *estancias* and farms of the *encomenderos,* and were often passed on in inheritance with the land they worked.

As might be expected, the few sketchy descriptions of life in the *originario* vary, picturing it as either heavenly or hellish. It is difficult, and probably profitless, to attempt to make a judgment—probably some Indians were well-treated and others were not. Writers were partisan in their defense or opposition to the system because the question of personal servitude of Indians was full of political significance. It is notable, however, that Francisco de Alfaro, visiting inspector (*veedor*) of the crown, and great opponent of the *originario,* indicated that he did not believe that the Guaraní considered themselves victimized. One of his ordinances which sought to end labor service and substitute tribute in its place also mentions the difficulty involved:

Porque los más de los indios, en la Visita que he hecho, especialmente en esta ciudad de la Asunción, dicen que no quisieran tasa; unos, ó los más, porque no saben lo que es, aunque se les ha procurado dar á entender: otros, porque son pobres; otros, porque dicen que ellos sirven cuando quieren y como quieren, y les dan alguna gratificación los españoles: otros, que vienen á ayudar á los españoles no á título de tasa y servicio, sino como á parientes.

The hours and days of work were apparently regulated only by the "*originario*" *encomendero's* own desires. For example, Ramírez de Velasco stated:

Y porque en esta gobernacion no ay horden ni tasa en el travajo de los indios y los dichos encomenderos se sirben dellos con gran deshorden ocupandolos todo el año y avn los dias que la santa madre iglesia manda guardar los hacen trabajar en sus labores y grangerias ansi en sus pueblos como en las cibdades que estan pobladas de lo cual rredunda notable daño y disminucion de los dichos naturales. . .

Alfaro's decrees summarily attempted to abolish personal service altogether and substitute wage labor in its place, so we cannot compare his ordinances with the others on specific points. That labor was regulated mostly by the whim of the *encomendero* is indicated by the fact that the regulatory ordinances were repeated so often as correctives that they must have been ineffective.

There was little real attempt to indoctrinate the *originario* Indians to the extent the crown considered necessary. We have seen that it was common for the Indians to work on fiesta days and Sundays. Ramírez de Velasco attempted to remedy the lack of religious instruction by ordering that each *encomendero* should have on his estate two native boys and two girls who knew the doctrine in order that they teach the *originario* men and women who were to be brought together each night to hear evening prayers. Alfaro also indicated his dissatisfaction with the failure of the Spaniards to indoctrinate their Indians. One of the factors related to this state of affairs was the notable lack of clerics during the whole period from the conquest until the arrival of the Jesuits. In fact, this is suggested as one of the reasons why the Jesuits were finally asked to come to Paraguay.

The Spanish settlers of Villarrica and Ciudad Real in the Paraná region also had Guaraní Indians in *encomienda*. The little evidence available suggests that the *originario* system there was like that of Asunción, except that more Indians were involved and that the poverty and lack of religious instruction were even more notable. The royal cosmographer, López de Velasco, writing of the period 1571–1574, said that Ciudad Real "tendrá ochenta ó cien vecinos españoles, casi todos con indios de repartimiento, que había muchos en aquella comara . . ." Ruiz de Montoya gave Villarrica "130 hombres, tenia en su jurisdiccion nueve pueblos de indios de que se sirvian." Vásquez de Espinosa visited Paraguay in the 1620's and described Villarrica as follows:

. . . in that wretched country, with the extreme poverty of the Spaniards living there, they have no priests to administer the Holy Sacraments, and so they are like savages without a country, never hearing Mass, and their children go seven or eight years without being christened. . . . The Spaniards living here are so poor that their only clothes are of cotton and they wear palm-leaf hats, for no Spanish merchandise ever gets here, and they have nothing with which to buy any.

The *mitayo encomienda*, unlike the *originario*, extended Spanish influence to Indian villages which were far from Asunción and brought Indians who had been relatively untouched during the exploratory phase of the colonization into a regulated colonial system. The *mitayo* Indians retained the integrity of their society longer than did the *originario* Indians because they still lived together and tilled their own village lands, so that their culture was altered less as a result of breakdown than of slower modification. Although the *mitayo* system allowed the Indians less independence than the crown desired, the Indians were, nevertheless, more protected than in the *originario* system.

The *mitayo encomiendas* were not large at the time of their inception in 1556, and they became even smaller as the Indian population declined during the first hundred years of the colony. Irala stated that twenty thousand Indians were placed in the first *encomiendas*, divided among "320 or more Spaniards." This would be about sixty-two Indians per Spaniard, though they were not apportioned equally. There was a storm of complaints about this, the original colonists feeling that the Indians were too few to be divided among so many *encomenderos*. There are references to two epidemics which killed great numbers of Indians, one in 1558 or 1560, and another in 1605-1606. By the time of Alfaro's ordinances in 1611, many documents stressed that the *encomiendas* often had less than ten Indians.

The usual crown policy that *encomiendas* were to be held for only two generations was not observed in Paraguay, so this cannot be considered a cause of the diminution in numbers of *encomienda* Indians. Alfaro and the Council of the Indies attempted to establish this rule in Río de la Plata in 1611, but although it was observed in Buenos Aires, Santa Fe, and Corrientes, it never was in Paraguay. The right of the first *adelantados* to grant *encomiendas* was retained by subsequent governors, and even Philip II gave permission to Governor Ortiz de Zarate in 1579 to regrant *encomiendas* and also to grant them for three generations.

The small average size of the *encomiendas* helps to explain why *encomienda* labor was always used instead of tribute; there were simply not enough Indians from whom to collect tribute in any substantial amount. It is also probable that the small number of Indians per *encomienda* was a circumstance which contributed directly to their acculturation. As the proportion of Indians to *encomenderos* grew smaller, the amount of personal control over individual Indians increased; Spaniards and Indians were in closer and more immediate contact. There seems to be no evidence that the size of the Indian villages decreased, so some may have been combined as the general population declined—thus more *encomiendas* and more *encomenderos* appeared in each village. This would increase the amount of Spanish influence in each village, or at least contribute to the disruption of native village organization. Alfaro remarked this situation in an illuminating passage:

Aunque yo quisiera hacer tasas para cada pueblo en particular, no he podido hasta el presente por las razones referidas: porque en cada pueblo hay indios de diferentes encomenderos: que los más tienen tan pequeño número, que no son de consideración. Porque aun en esta ciudad de la Asunción, cabeza de la Gobernación, hay muchos que no tienen á diez indios de reducción. Y he visitado pueblo que, aunque era bastante para doctrinante, hallé indios de cinquenta encomenderos.

The Guaraní, in their aboriginal condition, lived in extended family groups in small villages which shifted their location every few years. One of the important effects Spanish control had on their culture was the change induced by grouping them into larger permanent villages, "reducing" them to easier control and indoctrination. López de Velasco described Paraguayan *encomienda* villages of 1571–1574 as follows:

Estan todos en pueblezuelos de á de doscientos o cien vecinos y á menos, en unas casas o bohíos grandes hechas de paja, de cuatrocientos ó quinientos pasos de largo, donde cada uno tiene su rancho: estan todos encomendados en repartimientos, sin haberles declarado cosa ninguna que hayan de tributar, y así sirven á sus encomenderos por sus tandas en hacerles sus labores y grangerías.

By 1620, some of the towns seem to have had larger populations. Vásquez de Espinosa lists the following Indian villages and their populations: Elita, 500 Indians; Yaguarón, 400; and Yutí, 600.

The Spaniards' control over the settlement pattern of the Indians must have been fairly complete, for they often arbitrarily moved whole villages. R. I. Cardozo describes how four *encomienda* villages were moved long distances as the Spanish town of Villarrica was moved in 1575. Similar movements of other *encomiendas* also occurred. According to Azara, Ipané, Guarambaré, Atyrá, Tobatí, Yutí, Loreto, San Ignacio-Miri were all relocated at one time or another. These, incidentally, were all among the largest and most important of the *encomienda* villages.

Spanish control of the daily life of the village Indians was also considerable. The authority of the *encomendero* was virtually unhampered, as the crown laws which were supposed to limit his prerogatives were largely ignored in Paraguay. Additionally, the Paraguayan *encomendero* customarily placed Spanish administrators, *pobleros* or *mayordomos*, in residence in the villages to rule the Indians. These men apparently had considerable authority and freedom of action. Repeatedly, ordinances by Ramírez and Hernandarias complained that they misused authority, kept Indian girls in concubinage, and set a bad example in general. Alfaro, of course, tried to abolish *pobleros* altogether, as their use conflicted with law. The Indian officials who actually should have been in charge of the villages had little power. Except for the native chief, or *cacique*, there was not even a legal provision for Indian town officers until Governor Hernandarias attempted to institute *fiscales* in 1603, and Alfaro, in 1611, required that Indian officials be appointed after the Spanish pattern.

We may expect that certain aspects of aboriginal village life were altered in the interest of efficiency of control by the *encomenderos* and local administrators. As examples, we may cite ordinances 1 and 15 of Irala's *encomienda* rules which stated that the Indians were to remain permanently in their own villages, and that the *encomendero* did not have rights to the land of his Indians, nor could he interfere with its use. This rule was general in Spanish America, and grew out of the problems the crown faced in protecting the Indians of Mexico and Peru, regions of dense aboriginal population and large permanent towns. There, the greatest disruptive effect occurred when the scarce and valuable Indian lands were encroached on by Spaniards, and when the Indians were dislodged from their towns. In Paraguay, however, there was plenty of cultivable land, thus there was no necessity to dislocate Indian villages by progressive encroachment. On the contrary, the aboriginal Guaraní practiced a shifting agriculture which involved periodic relocation of their villages, so that as the Spaniards enforced stability of Guaraní villages, they interfered with aboriginal techniques of land use. Thus, ordinances which, when enforced, tended to preserve aboriginal village and land systems in Mexico and Peru, had the effect of altering them in Paraguay.

Ordinance 15 specifically changes one aboriginal custom by ordering that on the death of an Indian husband, his wife, or wives, (and children, of course), must continue to occupy the house of the deceased, instead of returning home to her consanguineal family "as was the ancient custom." Like the previously mentioned ordinances, it seems likely that this one was enforced, as the *encomendero* would naturally be loath to lose any of his Indians as a consequence of such an "ancient custom." It should be noted here that it is a characteristic of primitive society that the unilateral consanguineal family is the stable unit through which property is inherited, and in which the security of the individual is provided through mutual aid; the conjugal relationship of men and women of different blood lines is a fragile one, and property is not inherited by the surviving spouse. The above ordinance, however, forces property to be retained by the widow, thus adding a characteristically European element to the Indian marital relationship. We might also expect that the Spaniards would discourage the aboriginal tendency toward easy "divorce," both for reasons stemming from Christianity, and for the practical necessity of maintaining permanence of residence among the *encomienda* Indians.

There were probably many other kinds of disturbances to the native village organization. Through the years, small *encomiendas* were probably combined occasionally or growing ones divided. Epidemics reduced some villages, and the depletion caused by the Spaniards' practice of taking away women must also have been disruptive. All of these occurrences would disturb the delicate balances of house size, population size, subsistence coöperation, and marriage customs, which keep a unilateral kinship group a smoothly functioning unit. Every disturbance would tend to strengthen the conjugal family at the expense of the consanguineal unit, which was larger, more complex, and thus less able to withstand strains.

Probably the most profound acculturative effects resulted from the use of the Guaraní as a labor force in the *mita*. Irala's ordinances of 1556 stated that the Indians were obliged to serve their *encomenderos* in building houses, repairs, agricultural work, hunting and fishing, or any other enterprises, and that they must obey in what they were ordered to do. The sole restriction on the amount of labor was that only one-fourth of the *encomienda* could be used at one time. If work were divided equally, therefore, an Indian was expected to serve three months of the year. The ordinances said nothing about age limits, nor did they forbid the use of women.

Subsequent evidence indicates that abuse of the Indians as laborers was characteristic of the early period. Governor Ramírez de Velasco, in 1597, expressly issued his ordinances to alleviate the hardships of the Indians, ordering that only one-fourth of the *encomienda* be used except during the grain harvests, when half might be used. Further, the labor force was to include men only, between the ages of fifteen and fifty.

Inasmuch as these ordinances were designed, as stated, to correct abuses, it can be argued that in Paraguay prior to 1597 the Indians were probably used as a labor force more than three months of the year, and that women, and children under fifteen, were probably also used at the convenience of the *encomendero*. The validity of this inference is strengthened when we consider the ordinances of Hernandarias, issued six years later. Governor Hernandarias, like Ramírez, complained of the "great lack of regulation in the treatment of the Indians." His ordinance 5 required that boys under fifteen, girls under thirteen and people over sixty should be exempt from work. Ordinance 12 provided that no more than one-third of the Indians of a village could be taken for the *mita*, except for the grain and grape harvest, when one-half could be taken. These ordinances are less restrictive than Ramírez' earlier ones. It seems reasonable to judge, therefore, that inasmuch as Hernandarias was trying to help the Indians, the actual situation must have been quite out of hand.

In addition to the general farm labor required of *mita* Indians, there were several more specialized tasks. Indian women, for example, were required to work four days of each week for ten months, spinning and weaving cloth for the *encomendero*. In regions where the *yerba mate* grew wild, Indians were employed intensively in the labor of cutting and curing it, and carrying it to market. The *yerba* was one of the first of the few cash crops ever developed in Paraguay, and it came to be Paraguay's most important commercial crop. Ruiz de Montoya, writing of the early years of the seventeenth century, notes that the lack of money in Paraguay caused *yerba mate* to become the principal medium of exchange. The transportation of products from the farms to the city markets was another usual kind of labor service. Apparently, the Indians were so commonly used as carriers that both Ramírez de Velasco and Alfaro saw fit to prohibit this practice, though Ramírez admitted that human carriers were necessary in the interior regions where carts were handicapped by lack of roads. Indians were also used as oarsmen for the river craft which carried cargoes between towns.

The farm labor of *mita* Indians under close supervision of the *encomendero* or Spanish *mayordomos* resulted in a blending of Spanish and indigenous subsistence items at an early date. Captain Martín de Orue described the products of Paraguay in 1573 as follows:

En esta ciudad y su tierra se da mucha comida en tal manera que casi todo el año se provee de la heredad, porque el Mayz se da dos vezes en el año de seys en seys meses y los tres meses de cada cosecha, despues que se comienza a comer está en el campo para amigos y enemigos de manera quel año aqui para lo de los bastimentos se puede dezir que no es mas que seys meses porque en la una cosecha se coxe mayz frisoles habas, calabazas melones mandulges, frutas de la **tierra** hubas higos granadas y algodon; hazese vino que en este año pasan de sys myll aRobas, y de cada dia va en alzamiento; el vino es bueno porque con cierto cozimiento que se haze dura un año y dos y mas. En los otros seis meses se coje mayz algodon batatas balucus mandoca que es grand bastimento ques aquella manzaçalque, que esto dura debaxo de tierra tres y mas años y puesto que todo el año se come y sacan mejor esta por el ynvierno y mas de sazon y frisoles que dizen tupis; y en este tiempo se hazen las cañas de azucar cada año sin Regarlas.

Most of the European garden vegetables apparently never found favor in Paraguay, even in modern times, although the country is well-suited to many of them, nor was rice adopted in the early colonial period. Wheat was necessary for the sacrament, but as daily fare it never competed with manioc. Sugar cane and citrus fruits, especially favored by the Paraguayan climate, were accepted almost immediately. Such domestic animals as chickens and pigs had become part of the Indians' diet as early as 1556, and were of great importance as subsistence items, for aboriginally most of the meat had been obtained by hunting. Horses and cattle, goats and sheep, were very useful and fitted well into the Paraguayan ecology. The use of these animals probably did not require the cultivation of feed since large areas of excellent pasturage were available all year, nor were the Indians crowded from their best agricultural lands by the herds, as in the Andes.

The addition of so many useful Spanish elements to the native inventory was undoubtedly of great importance. The new skills in agriculture and animal husbandry merged with the native technology, first among the *originario* Indians, and eventually in the *mitayo* villages, and resulted in a new and higher level of productivity. The introduction by the Spaniards of various domestic animals abolished the most important lack in the native food economy. Improved tools, transportation by wheeled vehicles, and the use of horses, burros and oxen, together with a more productive and secure food economy, permitted the larger and more stable population aggregates which were prerequisites for the effective participation of the Indians in Paraguayan colonial culture.

Summary

Guaraní aboriginal culture differed considerably from the Indian civilizations the Spaniards encountered in Mexico, Middle America, and Peru. The society was not politically unified nor class-structured, and the villages were small and only semi-permanent. This meant that the Spaniards could not simply place themselves in the position of the top-level rulers for purposes of control of the natives through subsidiary chiefs, but had to intervene in each village and personally force or teach the Indians to live in the required manner. The Indian *pueblos* had to be "reduced" to permanency and eventually to be made larger than the simple kinship units which had comprised the aboriginal villages. Such immediate control was accomplished by *pobleros*, who lived with the Indians, enforcing the changes which were to disrupt the native society.

Certain Guaraní customs remained, however, as characteristics of the colonial society. The most noteworthy of these survivals was the unusual role of Guaraní women in the *originario encomienda*. In aboriginal society women were the agriculturalists, and in the polygynous household of a man of the status of chief, the labor of the wives was augmented by that of their relatives. The adoption of this aboriginal pattern by the Spaniards is related to the fact that they did not subjugate the Guaraní, but instead found it expedient to adapt native customs to their own purposes in order not to strain the alliance with these Indians during the precarious early years. Status polygyny and women's agricultural role remained as features of the later colonial society, and even in modern rural Paraguay one may find traces of these customs.

Another circumstance which affected the relations of Spaniards and Indians was the isolation of Paraguay from the normal currents of trade with the other colonies and with Spain. For purely geographic reasons, communication was difficult, and additionally, Spain purposely subordinated the interests of the La Plata region to those of vested interests involved in the monopolistic trade to Peru via Panama throughout most of the colonial period. This isolation permitted Paraguay to develop rather independently and to regulate its *encomiendas* in its own way without much effective Spanish interference.

The absence of precious metals and other important marketable wealth contributed to Paraguay's commercial isolation, and the people were reduced to a barter economy. This had important consequences for the *encomienda* system, for there was no product of sufficient value to be used as tribute from the *encomienda* Indians. These factors also prevented the development of a large trading class and inhibited the spread of a money economy. The gulf between the normal European profit-seeking values and those of the Indians was probably not so great in the context of a poverty-stricken subsistence economy.

Another result of isolation and lack of Spanish interest in Paraguay was that the clergy were not numerous nor was the crown able to give them much political support. In most of the important areas of Spanish America, some of the clergy often exerted their strength against the exploitation of natives by lay Spaniards, and thus reinforced the crown policy of segregation of *encomienda* Indians from Spanish colonists. Church and state battles over control of Indians in Paraguay, however, were never an issue except as they concerned the fate of the Indians in the distant Jesuit missions. The influence of the Spaniards on the *encomienda* Indians was primarily secular.

Demographic factors were influential in determining certain characteristics of the colony. Few Spanish reinforcements ever came to Paraguay and soon the original peninsular Spaniards were so reduced in numbers that the non-Indian population was predominantly mestizo, and the remaining Indians were then subject to a dominant culture that was somewhat different from the original Spanish. As mestization increased, the number of *encomienda* Indians diminished. This contributed indirectly to a more rapid Indian acculturation, for as the *encomiendas* became smaller, control over them became more direct and personal. The small size of the *encomiendas* also helps account for the Spaniards' failure to substitute tribute for Indian labor.

All of the above-mentioned circumstances so modified the Spanish *encomienda* in Paraguay that the ruling population and the Indians were brought into closer personal contact than in the usual Spanish colonial systems. The *originario encomienda* Indians lived permanently on the lands of the Spaniards. They received no wages, but were supposed to be fed, clothed, and given religious instruction in return for agricultural work, herding, household services and child care. A large proportion of these Indians were Guaraní women, many of whom were wives and concubines of the *encomenderos,* and others were relatives of these women. Relationship ties of both consanguinity and affinity became an important aspect of the association of the *encomendero* and his workers, for aboriginal customs such as status polygyny, the role of women as agriculturalists, and kinship labor obligations were by this means incorporated into the colonial system.

The *originario encomienda* thus had an important role in the addition of many native elements to the original Spanish culture. The close, permanent association of the Indian laborers, servants, and wives with their masters resulted in the merging of native and Spanish ways in such matters as food, food preparation, and agricultural methods. As the mestizo products of *originario* polygyny became the basic "Spanish" population, perhaps certain other habits and customs were derived directly from association with their Guaraní mothers and relatives. The retention of the Guaraní language is an obvious example of this sort of cultural survival.

The *mitayo encomienda* derived from the Spanish legal conception of *encomienda,* but differed from it in several important respects. The Indians paid no tribute, but were used as an unpaid, part-time labor force which served the *encomendero* about one-third of the year or more. The rest of the year they lived in their own villages. In the absence of political unification in the native society, the Spaniards could not govern indirectly through native rulers, so it was necessary that these villages be ruled directly by the *encomenderos* or *mayordomos* who lived in them. Kinship ties, similar to those of the *originario encomienda,* were a part of the system of control, as the *encomendero* often took women as concubines from the *mitayo* group.

The *mitayo encomienda* altered Guaraní village life in many ways. Villages were made larger and more permanent, and the aboriginal political organization was quickly displaced by Spanish internal rule as powers of local chiefs were taken over by Spanish administrators. Indian marriages were stabilized, and the extended lineage unit was probably correspondingly weakened. The influence of the *mitayo* system was to modify the aboriginal village and kinship structure toward a Spanish type of town with emphasis on the conjugal family unit.

It would seem that one of the chief differences between colonization in Paraguay and in the more well-known regions of Spanish America was the rapidity with which the aborigines and Spaniards were amalgamated racially and integrated culturally into a self-sufficient society. The conclusion seems inescapable that an important factor in this process was the rather special nature of the Paraguayan *encomiendas*. The *encomienda* which often, in other areas, tended to isolate the indigenes from acculturative influences, seemed to have the effect in Paraguay of actually fostering the assimilation of the Indians into the new colonial culture. This unusual effect of the *encomiendas* in Paraguay was, for its part, a product of peculiar local circumstances which were quite different from conditions in Mexico, Central America, and Peru. These circumstances—the nature of Guaraní culture with its small unfederated local groups, commercial and political isolation from Spain, poverty, lack of clerical influence, and such demographic factors as the small size of the *encomienda*, and eventual predominance of *mestizos* over peninsular Spaniards—so altered the *originario* and *mitayo encomiendas* that the Europeans were brought into closer contact and interaction with the Indians than was general in Spanish colonial society.

Other Articles of Interest

Chamberlain, Robert S. "Simpson's The Encomienda in New Spain and Recent Encomienda Studies." XXXIV (1954), 238–250.
Review of the revised (1950) edition of Simpson's study of the encomienda and of recent contributions to encomienda studies by Silvio Zavala, José Miranda, and others.

Kirkpatrick, F. A. "The Landless Encomienda." XXII (1942), 765–774.

————. "The Landless Encomienda." XIX (1939), 372–379.

Rowe, John Howland. "The Incas Under Spanish Colonial Institutions."
Corruption in all departments of government has arrived at its extreme.
XXXVII (1957), 155–199.

17. Indian Warfare on the Pampa During the Colonial Period

ALFRED J. TAPSON

The dramatic conquests of Mexico by Cortez and of Peru by Pizarro have somewhat obscured the fact that Indians remained a threat to Spanish power in some parts of the New World throughout the colonial period. The skill and tenacity of the Araucanians in opposing the Spanish invasion in Chile are well known, but the resistance of the Indians of the enormous Argentine plains has been less widely recognized. Spanish colonists made so little progress in peopling the pampa that the boundaries of viceregal Argentina at the close of the colonial period were almost identical with those established by Juan de Garay in 1590. The following article sets forth the reasons why "a few annoying barbarians" could thwart the Spaniards for so many years and constitutes an interesting study in the little cultivated field of the military history of Latin America. Dr. Tapson is a member of the history department of the City College of San Francisco.

The Viceroy of the Río de la Plata was reminded in 1796 that the boundaries of his dominions, "because of a few annoying barbarians," were the same as those which had been secured in 1590 by Juan de Garay and sixty men. This charge was essentially true; expansion of white settlement into the Pampa was exceedingly slow during the colonial period. The lack of maps for the plains, the absence of economic incentive to expansion, trade restrictions placed on the area by the mother country, and the meager colonial population were all factors contributing to the lethargic European expansion into lands destined to become great pastoral empires. The prime cause, however, must be attributed to the "annoying barbarians"—the Indians of the plains who stubbornly refused to share their lands and cattle with the whites.

The terrain over which these natives ruled was itself an effective barrier to expansion. No European experience prepared the Spanish colonists for the "boundless monotony of the billowing grasses which greeted them on the Paraná-Plata shore." In only three areas did high ground punctuate the "flatness" of the plains: the Cordoban hills, rising to approximately five thousand feet; the highlands of Ventana of about the same height; and the

From Volume XL (1962), pages 1–28.

rocky outcroppings in the Tandil area with an elevation of about 1,600 feet. Several streams provided occasional variations in the landscape. The Río Negro and the Río Colorado, on the southern Pampa, flow from the Andes to the Atlantic. The abundant wood supply along the river banks, in contrast to the treeless plains, made this area the ultimate goal of all expansionistic activity to the south. These valleys are also of historical importance because they were the routes by which Chilean Indians made their way to the fertile plains of Buenos Aires. To the north, the Carcaraña, replenished by the waters of the Tercero and Cuarto rivers, flowed across the plains and emptied into the Paraná. Between these two river systems, the Salado struggled its way into the Bay of Samborombón, 150 miles southeast of Buenos Aires. The area along the banks of this stream, known as the Salado Slough, was a series of small lakes during the rainy season; at all other times, it was a line of swamps which acted as a cultural boundary between Indian and white throughout most of the colonial period. Although rainfall normally was adequate throughout the Pampa, much of the area was subject to occasional droughts which brought disaster to Indians and Spaniards and to the cattle upon which both depended. In general, water was more plentiful in the eastern plains of Buenos Aires than in the western interior provinces, a climatic factor which brought greater numbers of cattle, Indians, and settlers to the eastern sector.

The Indians who inhabited this region were from several tribes with very similar cultural traits. At the time of the conquest, the Querandí occupied an area between the mouth of the Plata and Córdoba. Between this area and the Río Negro lived the Puelches, while south of this river the Tehuelches wandered over the plains of northern Patagonia, occasionally spilling over into the Colorado River area. The Pehuenches, of historical importance because they controlled the passes through which the Araucanians of Chile entered the plains, occupied a small zone in the Andean foothills. All these inhabitants of the Pampa were nomadic hunters who existed on the meat of the guanaco, the rhea, the deer, and the otter. They practiced no agriculture. Prior to the arrival of the Spaniards, the Querandí supplemented their diet with fish from the rivers, but with the gradual European occupation of the river valleys they were forced to a complete dependence on the hunt for their existence. Since these Indians were usually on the move, their shelters were light and portable, consisting of rude half-huts fabricated from the skins of animals. Their clothing was also of the scant variety, a small apron of cloth and a fur robe providing the entire wardrobe.

The natives were brown in color with apparently no unusual physical characteristics. The Querandí were described as "taller than Germans but not as tall as the Tehuelches." The latter were reported by Magellan's men as giants of seven-foot stature, but their height appears to have diminished when observed by later witnesses. Thomas Falkner, a Jesuit missionary, acknowledged that these people were tall and described one chief as "seven feet and some inches tall; because, on tiptoe, I could not reach the top of his head." Falkner stated, however, that this height was exceptional and disclaimed any knowledge of the gigantic race of Indians allegedly inhabiting Patagonia. The Pehuenches were described as about "two varas tall" and were said to be more robust, more active, and stronger than any other Indians of the region.

There are no accurate figures on Indian population. Juan Díaz de Solís, the discoverer of the Río de la Plata, disembarked and was attacked by a great number of Indians who killed every man ashore. The natives must have been numerous, because the remaining Spaniards were so impressed by the hordes of Indians that they dared not leave their vessel to support their comrades. The fort founded by Sebastián Cabot in 1526 on the northern rim of the Pampa was attacked and destroyed by a native army reputed to number twenty thousand. In 1535 a settlement near the newly-founded town of Buenos Aires was inhabited by two thousand Querandí who were reinforced by four thousand more natives to do battle with the Spaniards. Later in the same year, an army estimated at 23,000 Indians assaulted the new settlement. The accuracy of these figures is doubtful, but

supposing even that the first explorers exaggerated the number of Indians, there is little doubt that the Pampa along the southern shores of the Río de la Plata and the western banks of the Paraná supported a dense population according to the conditions prevailing in aboriginal America. The military resistance of these people to Spanish invasion at the time of Spain's military vigor, not only by guerrilla warfare but promptly and directly by battle, again suggests an active and numerous people.

The plains to the west and south, however, were uninviting to the natives, and all evidence indicates a relatively small population in these areas. The highest estimate of Puelche or Tehuelche strength in the colonial period was ten thousand. In 1745, Falkner noted that the Pehuenches "although formerly very numerous . . . are now so much diminished as not to be able to muster four thousand men amongst them all." A British traveler of the early independence period estimated the total number of Indians on the Pampas at eight thousand. Whatever the actual numbers of Indians, it is certain that the myth of countless hordes of savages gained a firm hold on the imagination of white settlers in the region. Estimates ranged as high as 200,000. Fantastic as these concepts of Indian strength may appear in retrospect, they had a direct effect on the tactics and methods adopted by Spanish authorities to meet the native menace.

Although the sixteenth century was characterized by almost constant hostility between Spaniard and Indian, large-scale military operations were not usual. The tribes attacked convoys traveling to the interior, raided outlying estancias, and occasionally mounted an attack sufficiently large to cause the settlers substantial losses. But warfare, worthy of the name, did not generally prevail until the seventeenth century.

Once the initial settlements had been secured, the great advantage of the horse enabled the whites to maintain their precarious position on the Pampa. The changes which took place during the seventeenth century, however, provided the seeds from which generated the long struggle for control of the plains.

The horse provided the greatest single social and military transformation of the Indian character. Different tribes adopted the animal at different times. The Puelche and Tehuelche probably became equestrians in the late seventeenth century. In Chile, however, the Indians were using horses by the middle of the sixteenth century, and the Pehuenches must have been familiar with the animal shortly thereafter. From Chile the horse made its way, with or without rider, to the plains of the east. In the great grasslands, the horse found a situation ideally suited for existence and multiplication. Wandering Spanish cattle found the same happy grazing grounds.

Horse and cattle became the focus of Indian life. Prior to the equine invasion, the native was fleet afoot; he now became virtually helpless without his animal. From infancy he lived on a horse, and his legs became extremely bowed and all but useless. Nearly all his occupations and amusements were performed on horseback. At one time the Indian considered horseflesh his greatest dietary delicacy, but the economics of the situation forced him to utilize cattle as his primary food. There were too many cogent uses—transportation, trade, and war—for the horse. The complete dependence upon the horse for transportation and on cattle for food forced the Indian to resort to thievery, raids, or open warfare whenever these animals were in short supply.

The seventeenth century also saw a change in the ethnic pattern of the Indian of the plains. The Chilean Indians from the very beginning of warfare with the Spaniards adopted the tactics of their foes, and the horse played a highly important role in these tactics. To secure horses, a brisk trade developed between the Indians of the Pampa and the Araucanians—the former gave horses, the latter textiles or other articles of a higher culture. The Pehuenches were the intermediaries. Using the Pehuenche homeland as a base, the Araucanians gradually took over the greater part of the Argentine central plains. As early as 1708, Araucanian leaders attended a council of Indian tribes on the Río Quinto. A year later an expedition seeking salt to the south of Buenos Aires reported a vast number of "aucás" moving large herds of cattle and horses toward Chile. This removal of livestock from the plains was made a matter of official record in 1710 by the Cabildo of Buenos Aires. By 1725 the Araucanians were definitely established on the Pampa, and in the 1740's their language was reported to be the "most generally understood among the Indian population of the plains." The new environment transformed a settled people with an Andean culture into nomads who lived on cattle and pillage. This migration and cultural conquest brought greater unity and more dynamic leadership to the Indians of the Pampa.

The weapons and tactics of these Indians were well adapted to the type of warfare they waged. For close-in fighting, a small wooden cudgel with a sharpened point was effectively used until the beginning of the nineteenth century. The primary weapons, however, were the lance and the bola. The lances were usually from fifteen to eighteen feet in length and were handled with great dexterity. The bola, small weighted balls on the end of a leather cord, was the chief hunting weapon. The natives were extremely accurate with this missile and used it extensively to hamstring cattle and horses. If it were impossible to hurl it, they used it as a club. The boleadora, a longer, heavier weapon operating on the same principle, was also a part of the Indian horseman's equipment. Although the Indians of Chile first used firearms shortly after the European conquest, the natives of the Pampa did not make extensive use of them during the colonial period. In the mobile warfare against the whites, native weapons were quite as effective as those of their opponents.

The Indians rarely made a frontal assault on a fortified position; they never dismounted. Whether the operation was a large-scale attack on a town or a small raid on an outlying estancia, they utilized much the same methods. All operations were planned. The warriors usually assembled at a considerable distance from the objective; from this point, scouts were sent to reconnoiter the proposed line of march, the state of the frontier, the condition of enemy horses, and other items of interest. On the reports of these advanced patrols, much of the success of the undertaking depended. Closer reconnaissance of the objective was made after nightfall. The main body united at a pre-selected point, and when all contingents were ready, the leaders reviewed, briefed, and exhorted their men. In the approach to the battle positions, the Indians rode by night to prevent dust clouds from revealing their presence. The individual fighter's chief concern during the march was the selection of a good mount for the critical period ahead. Normally, he did not utilize his best horse until the raid was about to begin.

The Indians attacked just before dawn, approaching the objective at full gallop and uttering loud shrieks. The assault was rapid and furious. If the opposition proved stronger than anticipated, the raiders withdrew and seldom returned to the fight. The first wave of the assault had the mission of setting fire to buildings. If those within rushed out, they were killed or maimed by lances. If possible, the women were captured; the men, whether they resisted or not, were killed. The main purpose of all raids, however, was booty in the form of horses and cattle. One special group of the force was always assigned the special mission of gathering animals and driving them away from the scene of hostilities. Pillage of all installations was usually complete. In retreating from a raid, the natives divided into small groups to make pursuit more difficult.

The hatred between Indian and frontiersman on the Pampa was intense. A prevalent Indian maxim was "Spare an enemy today, and he will cut your throat tomorrow." The attitude of the gaucho is well illustrated by the following incident related by a traveler on the plains:

I asked the man how many prisoners had been taken in a fight with the Indians. He replied with a look I shall never forget. He clenched his teeth, opened his lips, and then, sawing his finger across his throat for a quarter of a minute, bending toward me with his spurs striking his horse's side, he said in a low, choking voice: "*Se matan todos.*"

It was in this atmosphere of reciprocal hatred that the war on the Pampa was carried on.

Throughout the seventeenth century there was no great economic incentive motivating the Spaniards to push their estancias into the uninviting Indian country. Nor did the natives have an impelling reason to attack the small white settlements since their European neighbors had little that the Indians could not obtain themselves. The abundant cattle and horses supplied food. Through the easy passes of the Neuquén region of the cordillera, the Indians traded cattle and hides to the estancieros of Chile and received the few items they needed in return.

Early in the eighteenth century, several important developments tended to throw the Indians and the colonists into closer contact. The discovery of salt beds southwest of Buenos Aires prompted expeditions to secure this necessary commodity. The procurement of salt was considered a public service, and the authorities gave these expeditions preferential treatment. The acquisition presented certain difficulties, and armed, well-planned expeditions were necessary to make the journey commercially profitable. By 1730, annual excursions were made to the salt beds in the heart of Indian territory.

The problems inherent in early cattle ranching were even more significant than the demand for salt. In order to obtain hides, grease, tallow, and to stock and re-stock their ranches, the cattlemen depended on the unbranded animals of the Pampa and made periodic forays into the plains. Originally these hunts were of short duration, but as the years passed it became necessary to cross the Salado and go farther into the plains to obtain animals. In 1723, the Cabildo of Buenos Aires noted that the only free bulls were to be found one hundred leagues from the city. "To obtain these," continued the minutes, "an expedition guarded by one hundred men is necessary." The entrance of the white hunting parties into these areas aroused native antagonism.

These expeditions were co-operative endeavors, the expense being shared by the ranchers of the district. The men chosen to take part were excellent horsemen who knew the frontier and were willing to face Indian hostility. By the eighteenth century, there was a nucleus of individuals who had spent a great part of their lives in the pursuit of wandering cattle; they knew the best waterholes, the most lucrative hunting areas, and the physical nature of the terrain along the Atlantic Coast and to the southwest of Buenos Aires. By 1714 the cabildo had reasonably accurate information concerning the territory near Tandil and Salinas, and one missionary-explorer mentioned that the region of the Mar Chiquita was visited prior to 1748 by these "rurales." These men were later utilized as scouts in military operations against the Indians.

If the whites became more interested in the land of the Indians, the reverse was also true. The easily-obtained food supply proved exhaustible, and the natives found it increasingly difficult to secure cattle. After 1725 the notes of the cabildo largely concern themselves with domesticated cattle or runaways. The cimarron had virtually disappeared. To the Indian this situation was little short of catastrophic, but he soon provided a solution. His supply of food depleted, he turned to the domesticated cattle grazing on the frontier estancias of his Spanish neighbors. His way of life continued; Spanish cattle satisfied his hunger quite as well as the wild variety, and his commercial contacts in Chile proved morally indifferent to the source of their purchases. The procuring of livestock was more difficult, but the Indian had improved his raiding capabilities by his mastery of the horse and the infusion of Araucanian leadership.

The diminution of free cattle was the fundamental cause of conflict, but actions by both whites and Indians tended to inflame the growing hostility. Indian raids of 1737 brought a retaliatory expedition by the colonists. Unfortunately, the retaliation vented itself upon an innocent tribe. This error brought severe Indian attacks on Areco and Arrecifes. To avenge these actions, Juan de San Martín, the frontier commander, led a strong force to chastise the responsible parties, but once again zeal for revenge outweighed better judgment. San Martín led his men in a vicious slaughter of the tribe of Calelían, a cacique who had formerly been highly co-operative. If an object lesson was intended, it failed. The tribes mobilized, and for the first time arose en masse against the whites. Thus were initiated the countless incursions—the dreaded *malones*—of the Indians. The frontier soon was a battleground covering one hundred leagues, and the lives and wealth of the estancieros were constantly in danger. The Cabildo of Buenos Aires was besieged with demands for action against the tribes.

The most usual reaction of the authorities to Indian attacks was to organize an expedition to take the field against them. There were literally hundreds of these punitive campaigns undertaken during the colonial period. They were seldom successful. Rarely did they have sufficient strength to achieve a decisive victory over the natives even when they were sufficiently fortunate to locate the guilty tribes. The Indians simply withdrew into lands they knew far better than their pursuers. Nevertheless, these expeditions gave the harassed estancieros a respite from raids by forcing the Indians to take refuge some distance from the frontier. The show of strength on occasion frightened some of the more docile tribes into peace overtures. A seven-hundred man expedition of 1739 achieved no distinction as a fighting force, but a year later three hundred Indians requested that they be located in a reduction. Under the leadership of two missionaries, Matías Strobel and Manuel Querini, the Jesuits were at this time undertaking the spiritual conquest of the Indians of Buenos Aires and had established a settlement at Concepción, near the mouth of the Salado. The Indian petitioners were located at the new mission.

After an Indian massacre of two hundred people at Magdalena in 1741 and another fruitless pursuit, the Spaniards determined to utilize further the talents of the Jesuits in an attempt to bring peace. Strobel was appointed chaplain of an expedition into Indian country which had the primary mission of negotiating a peace treaty with Cangapol or "Cacique Bravo," the acknowledged leader of the intransigent tribes. The sister of Cangapol, a neophyte in the mission, was used to effect an audience. The resulting parley found the Spaniards representing the reduced Indians as well as themselves. Considerable negotiation brought an agreement naming Cangapol the field commander (*maestre de campo*) of the highlands of Tandil and Volcán. In this capacity, he was to be the intermediary between Spanish authorities and the natives. He alone could give permission to any Indian to cross the Salado; he alone was responsible for return to the reduction of fugitive Indians, and he was to determine the punishment for recalcitrant natives. It was also to be Cangapol's duty to see that the missionaries were allowed to say mass to any Pampa Indians and to require his kinsmen to treat the priests with great veneration "as persons sent by God to show them the way to heaven." Although this treaty failed to bring order and peace to the plains, it was highly significant in that it established the Salado River as a recognized cultural and military frontier. Throughout the rest of the colonial period, the authorities largely expended their energies toward the defense of this line.

On September 16, 1744, the cabildo agreed to the feasibility of establishing forts along the Salado River, and an implementing committee recommended that these installations serve as headquarters from which reconnaissance parties could maintain constant surveillance of the frontier. In April, 1745, the cabildo authorized a daily wage for the men who would occupy the forts and named a field commander to inspect all installations. The financing of these projects, however, proved difficult, and it was not until 1751 that the needed revenue was obtained. The general economic level of the region was low and sources of taxation were few. Levies were finally made on salt gatherers and on farmers who brought their orchard crops into the city. In addition, a small levy was made on each head of family, and a sales tax was placed on leather goods and wine.

Three forts were established in 1752 at Luján, Salto, and Zanjón, each of which was to have "quarters for troops, a chapel, and lodgings for a priest." Apparently the planners had in mind some sort of a military colony since the establishments, in addition to being strategically placed, were to be located in "an area offering natural conditions of fertility so that the soldiers could obtain the necessities of life." Personnel to man these defenses was not easily obtained. Prior to this time, unpaid militia constituted the only soldiery available. Their recruitment was at the pleasure of the local authorities who usually exempted no one over the age of sixteen unless he was the sole support of elderly parents. The men served for a specific period of time, but the slightest infraction of regulations doubled their time in service. Juan de Martín had diligently attempted to forge these troops into an effective frontier force with some temporary success, but the dreary nature of the work resulted in low state of morale and a high rate of desertion. The men were not paid; there was no provision for the protection and subsistence of their families. Because of these experiences with the militia, the cabildo decided that a better military organization was essential.

By June, 1752, three companies had been formed and were garrisoned in the three forts in December. For several years these "blandengues," as they were called, remained under control of the cabildo, and complete records of expenditures, replacements, and other pertinent data were maintained. Unfortunately, the blandengues proved almost as ineffective as the militia had been. They were drawn from the same source as the unpaid troops, and the official status and uniforms given them did not alter their basic annoyance with military discipline. Their zeal varied directly with the promptness with which they were paid, and a chronic shortage of funds made this circumstance rare indeed. Desertion was still commonplace.

Upon his arrival in 1770, Governor Francisco de Paula Bucareli found the three companies of blandengues in a state of dissolution. Innumerable requests for military aid from the outskirts of his jurisdiction gave proof of the ineffectiveness of existing defenses. By the payment of salaries, some of which were twenty months in arrears, Bucareli managed to restore troops to the frontier forts. He then set out with energy and determination to bring peace to the harassed frontier areas. His task was lightened somewhat by a disastrous drought in the years of 1770–1771. Ranchers moved their cattle northward to more adequate pasturage, but the stock upon which the Indians depended for their subsistence was seriously depleted. Hunger accomplished what Spanish force and negotiation had generally failed to do—a number of tribes sued for peace.

The terms were harsh. Indian movement was severely limited, and their cattle could be brought to pasturage only with the express consent of the authorities. To contact the Spaniards, the natives were to approach along the Salinas-Luján road in groups of not more than six and were to be accompanied by an escort of frontier troops. Of greater importance was Bucareli's scheme to destroy Indian unity and make the more amenable tribes serve Spanish purposes. Each chief was held accountable for the suppression of uprisings within a circumscribed zone. If another group of natives wandered into this preserve, the responsible chief had the authority to confiscate the interloper's cattle or to take other reprisals by whatever means he deemed necessary. The governor hoped that these arrangements would keep peace within the Indian sectors or, at worst, give them the opportunity to destroy each other. Under the terms of the treaty, captive renegade Indians could be purchased for a fair price at Luján. This head-quarters was also to be the depositing place for the heads of those chiefs who refused to accept the peace terms. To provide an assurance of good will, the son of one of the prominent caciques was held hostage in Buenos Aires. Nine of the eleven chiefs agreed to these terms and promised to bring the other two into the fold or to punish them for their obstinacy.

The colonial authorities, however, soon found that there were flaws in these agreements. What action were they to take if the friendly tribes were defeated by the more intransigent groups? If the allied Indians did not dominate the plains, the entire treaty structure would collapse. As a result of successful Tehuelche attacks, several Pampa chieftains appealed to Bucareli for aid. The subsequent expedition significantly included 291 Indians and 231 whites, proportions not attained in previous campaigns. The column crossed the Salado, pushed deep into Indian territory, and soundly defeated several groups of obstreperous natives. It was evident that the "desert" could be penetrated by large military forces.

The success of this campaign indicates that the Indians were on the defensive and gives rise to speculation as to why Bucareli did not carry out extensive operations to sweep all hostile Indians from the plains. While it was relatively easy to launch a single expedition with a limited objective, it was a much more involved problem to prepare a strong striking force which could operate over an extended period of time and permanently police the conquered territory. There were no available reserves of men and supplies.

The inability to control large areas was illustrated in 1773 with the arrival of information from Chile that an Indian invasion from that area might be expected. Manuel Pinazo, the commander of the frontier, was ordered to take charge of defensive preparations, but he could not raise sufficient troops nor gather enough supplies to take to the field. He complained that he lacked cavalry, that the weather was not propitious, that rations could not be obtained, and that, inasmuch as there was not yet an overt act, warlike preparations were premature.

Pinazo's general attitude illustrates clearly the prevailing attitude toward the frontier problem throughout the seventeenth and eighteenth centuries. There was no urge to occupy and develop the land immediately adjacent to the south and west of the settlements. The unknown Pampa, the warlike Araucanians, the small population, the lack of funds—all these difficulties had to be overcome. The failure to conquer the Indians is attributable, not so much to the lethargy of the colonials, but rather to the world situation which at this time prevented the Plata area's economic development. The stifling restrictions on maritime commerce and on the trade with the interior prevented economic growth. To be sure, there was an extensive contraband trade with Brazil, with foreign powers, and with the Andean sections, but this traffic was illegal and could not be protected or encouraged by any local governmental actions. Traders traveling to the interior had to protect themselves from Indian attack; they were rarely given military escorts. The gradual rescinding of oppressive legislation in the eighteenth century and the great increase in contraband trade, however, brought a measure of prosperity to the Plata region. In 1778 Buenos Aires was granted the right to engage in commercial intercourse with other parts of the Spanish Empire. The region was granted administrative autonomy in 1776 through the establishment of the Viceroyalty of the Río de la Plata. In 1777 exports to the interior provinces through the port of Buenos Aires were finally authorized; the entire country could now take advantage of direct commerce with the outside world. To make full utilization of these new economic possibilities, however, the land had to be controlled and developed. The wealth was in the land, but the land was dominated in large part by the Indians. Thus the Indian problem became an important element on the agenda of the new viceroys.

The first year saw no major decisions as to the procedures to be followed on the frontier since Pedro de Cevallos, the first viceroy, was more occupied with the immediate problems of foreign war than with domestic questions. Certain stop-gap decrees, however, were issued. All inhabitants of the plains were to place themselves at the disposal of the military officials under penalty of six years' imprisonment and loss of their property. Increased military escorts were supplied for merchants who wished to travel to the salt beds. Some life was infused into the three small forts by making necessary repairs of these establishments.

Cevallos was convinced that the Indians could be brought under control by a concerted offensive launched with an army of ten to twelve thousand men. Royal approval for such an undertaking arrived as he was relinquishing the viceroyalty to his successor, Juan José de Vértiz de Salcedo. Vértiz was a creole and had served previously as governor of Buenos Aires. He was somewhat reluctant to carry out the project of Cevallos and created a council to study the feasibility of the plan. Prominent civil and military leaders, including those experienced in frontier fighting, were summoned to the conference. In the event that the junta decided in favor of an offensive, it was to draw up the necessary plans and determine the number of men, arms, horses, and provisions which would be required. The statement issued by this body clearly reveals the attitudes of the authorities toward the Indian problem at this time.

The junta did not share the optimism of Cevallos. There were serious doubts among the conferees as to the possibilities for success of any such expedition. To raise ten thousand men for this purpose would create a scarcity of labor and leave the "trades and agriculture" exposed to neglect. The greatest army which could possibly be assembled would comprise 4,800 men from Buenos Aires, 1,500 from Córdoba and Tucumán, and 1,800 from Mendoza, San Luis, and San Juan. The junta used these figures as bases for determining the quantity of other necessary items. The members of the junta stated their wholesome respect for the Indian as an antagonist with these words:

> The Indians form a nomadic body without definite habitation or location; they carry all their wealth and goods with them; they lack appreciation of comforts; their diet of mare's meat and other animals is foreign to us; they do not need fire in order to prepare food nor other provisions for their marches; they reside in the hills and in other hidden places; they travel by sterile and arid routes; their mastery of the elements we cannot begin to approach. The Indian knows the wide uncharted lands for which we have no accurate maps nor guides to give us even a moderate knowledge before we start to form any expedition.

The junta drew a pessimistic picture of the complicated logistical problems in launching such an expedition. If the duration of the undertaking was longer than four months, the required forty thousand horses would have to be augmented by an additional two thousand to replace those "tired, lost, dead, or runaways." The number of cattle needed for food would probably have to be doubled because of the loss of weight the cattle would suffer after two months. The estimated quantity of rations approached astronomical figures. A guard of five hundred regular troops would have to accompany the expedition to "assure the respect and subordination of the troops to curb desertions."

Even if these seemingly insurmountable problems could be solved, the junta doubted whether any beneficial results would be achieved by the expedition.

> If we encounter a party of Indians, nothing would come of it because one or two would be able to escape and carry the news to the other tribes. These would return to their hideouts in the hills and make useless our efforts. By effective retreat, denying access to water, they could occasion the ruin of our army.

For the foregoing reasons, the junta considered an offensive at this time highly impractical. It is apparent that the military leaders did not want to carry the fight to the Indian on his own territory; it also seems quite clear that the men making up the committee had no vision of the economic future of the southern plains. Their aim was not to expand the frontier, but to maintain it as it then existed. Their thinking continued to be defensive. They recommended that the existing forts be shifted to new locations and new ones created until such a strong belt of fortifications guarded the frontier that Indian raids would prove too costly for the tribes to undertake. The junta recommended the development of new lands and the building of new towns to create a greater frontier population which would be available to meet extensive Indian raids.

Vértiz accepted in principle the recommendation of his advisors and notified the king of his decision to abandon the proposed offensive. The frontier was to be secured through the medium of forts. Pinazo, the field commander, had been the principal proponent of this idea within the conference, but the practical work was entrusted to Francisco Betbezé, the artillery commander of the province of Buenos Aires. The latter undertook a thorough study of the old locations and the newly-proposed sites. His findings were presented to the viceroy with maps, illustrations, data on water points, pasturage, and other essential details, plus his conclusions as to the preferred locations for the actual forts. This detailed analysis recommended the maintenance of the established line with minor modifications. The present forts were to be repaired and new ones constructed.

At the energetic prompting of the viceroy, the plans were drawn, the materials secured, and the new structures completed in 1781. This Vértiz-Betbezé Line consisted of six forts located at Rojas, Salto, Luján, Monte, Ranchos, and Chascomús, and five outposts at Melincué, Mercedes, Araco, Navarra, and Lobos. A company of troops was permanently to occupy each fort while small detachments of from twelve to fifteen men were to garrison the intermediate *fortines*. Across the frontier of Santa Fe, San Luis, Córdoba, and Mendoza there was similar activity. The forts of Melincué, India Muerta, and Pavón were rebuilt to guard the approaches to Santa Fe, and reductions were established in Rosario and Coronda. In the province of San Luis, the fort of San Carlos was not providing adequate defense, and in 1779 a new establishment was constructed at Chañar, ten leagues south of the old site and thirty-six from the city of San Luis. This location had high strategic importance since it covered the general approaches to both San Luis and Córdoba. Córdoba had a frontier of seventy leagues, covered by a more extensive network of defenses than any other province. The fort at La Carlota, in the center of the provincial frontier, was the headquarters, and along the Río Cuarto were the outposts of Pilar, San Carlos, Reducción, San Fernando, and Concepción. West of La Carlota, other forts and outposts controlled the territory to the San Luis border; to the east installations were already established which tied in with the fortified line of the province of Buenos Aires.

What were the characteristics of these frontier forts? They were designed as simple refuges for troops who maintained constant vigilance over the surrounding territory. Although a direct attack was possible, it was generally believed that the natives would infiltrate through the intermediate areas. If the forts were subjected to direct attack, they would face light cavalry not equipped with heavy weapons. No heavy palisades were required to meet such a threat. It was also deemed financially imprudent to expend funds on the construction of installations which would probably have to be shifted from time to time. These factors combined to make the forts rudimentary in construction. If wood was available, it was utilized. In Santa Fe the installations were often mud huts, and many of those in Córdoba were of adobe and required "continuous maintenance to prevent their falling down." Although the Indians often attacked these forts, they rarely succeeded in destroying them.

The forts, although improved under the viceroys, were crude edifices. They formed a type of settlement, however, peculiar to areas under Spanish control and marked an official frontier beyond which only those who were optimistic enough to rely on friendly relations with the Indians dared to settle. Pioneering of this type was discouraged by the authorities.

The frontier soldiers who manned these lonely outposts were known as blandengues in Buenos Aires and Santa Fe, *partidarios* in Córdoba, and *enganchados* in Mendoza. These men were gauchos. When they entered the military service, they made few noticeable changes in their way of life other than the achievement of respect because of their uniforms. They were nurtured on the plains and were accustomed to a nomadic form of life. They were frugal beyond all imagination, a piece of meat to eat and a poncho to cover their bodies sufficing to support their existence. All were excellent horsemen and preferred the bola, the lance, or the lasso to firearms. On reconnaissance, they often reached Cruz de Guerra, thirty leagues from Luján and deep within Indian territory. The coming of the viceroyalty, however, found them all in a disorganized state because of factors previously mentioned. None of the groups in existence at this time received any formal military training, and the service had gradually degenerated to the status of part-time employment since the men were often released from duty during the months of March, April, November, and December. Shortly after taking over his office, Viceroy Vértiz augmented the number of companies to five, each consisting of one hundred troops. More significant, however, than the mere increase of personnel was the incorporation of the blandengues into the regular military establishments. The organization, known as the "*Corps of Blandengues of the Frontier of Buenos Aires,*" now had its own headquarters, and the commanding general was placed in charge of the entire frontier. The Cabildo of Buenos Aires urged the viceroy to approve leaders experienced in the type of life led on the frontier. "The people of the plains," said the cabildo, "are loath to submit to all the formal military rules." Vértiz acceded to these requests, and the blandengues were commanded by men of their own stamp.

In addition to regular troops, militia in the frontier areas were available for service. In the preparation of an expedition in 1784, the frontier commander forwarded the following information as to the number of militia available:

PARTIDO	TOTAL	MILITIA TO ACCOMPANY	EXPEDITION TO REMAIN
Arroyos	386	200	186
Arrecifes	242		241 (*sic*)
Areco	251	120	131
Luján	320	120	200
Morón y Matanzas	721	200	521
Magdalena	251	60	131 (*sic*)

By 1792, however, it was apparent that the militia was used mainly in the smaller intermediate posts while the regulars manned the larger installations. A report of that year indicated the following distribution of troops:

INSTALLATION	REGULAR	MILITIA
Ranchos	85	0
Chascomús	85	0
Monte	85	0
Lobos (Fortín)	0	16
Navarro	0	16
Luján	85	0
Areco (Fortín)	0	16
Salto	85	0
Rojas	85	0
Mercedes (Fortín)	0	16
Melincué (Fortín)	0	16

Normally, the militia were relieved every month and paid twenty reales for rations. It is difficult to estimate the actual number of soldiers at any one time on the frontier since there was never any relationship between the number who were presumed to be there by the authorities and those who were actually present. The rate of turnover was tremendous. Despite the royal decree of 1801 previously mentioned, calling for a force of 1,204 men on the Buenos Aires frontier, an actual count revealed only 483 men.

Although the men in the fort preferred to use lances, bolas, and lassos like their Indian enemies, the government usually supplied a carbine, two pistols, and a sword. Additional weapons were usually stored in a central fort and issued as required. Training in the use of arms and in general military tactics was prescribed for all units. The exact nature of this training is difficult to determine, for the reports of the inspectors are replete with such generalities as "The instruction is excellent," or "The troops obey their superiors," or the highly questionable statement, "The troops are satisfied with their salaries." It may be assumed, however, that some formal training was carried on within the forts.

The frontier soldiers refused to accept the discipline commonly expected of military units. When quartered in the forts, they were not divided into companies and slept in any particular location that seemed to suit them at the moment. The troops were so disorganized that orders had to be issued a day in advance to insure that every man received the necessary information. Much planning usually went into the preparations for a march. Once the movement was underway, however, the troops usually adopted any formation they desired. Each individual normally marched next to the cart in which his personal belongings were carried. When the column halted, the troops usually camped in a circular formation leaving the center free of impedimenta so that it could be used for an assembly place. Rope fences were erected to keep the cattle from straying. Duty as a sentinel was considered an insult with the result that this important mission was usually entrusted to the weakest and most poorly-trained soldiers. Reforms of any kind were derisively ignored by the troops. Even in combat the troops fought without order or cohesion and paid little or no attention to their leaders. The normal method of defense was to form a square with the infantry resisting Indian attack by fire while the cavalry attacked the flanks or rear of the enemy. Friendly Indians usually were assigned reconnaissance duties well forward of the main body.

Judged by any standards, the salaries of the soldiers were pitifully small. The commanding general of the frontier of Buenos Aires received 115 pesos per month; his second in command was paid eighty. From these lofty heights, the pay scale ranged downward to the private's salary of fourteen pesos in Buenos Aires and eight in Córdoba. Nor were the Córdoban authorities any more liberal with their high ranking officers since the commanders of the three main forts received but six hundred pesos annually. Out of these wages the men were expected to pay for their uniforms and to maintain their horses. In most instances rations were supplied by the government; the larger forts had a corral nearby to maintain a reserve of horses and to insure a future food supply.

The deployment of the frontier troops followed a simple pattern. From each fort, small detachments were sent out in each direction, and a systematic reconnaissance of a prescribed area was made. These parties normally spent eight to ten days away from their home station. There was little co-ordination between the forts in the early stages of this defensive development, and the Indians quickly took advantage of this weakness. Many small scouting patrols were ambushed, captured, or killed, and some time elapsed before their compatriots ascertained that they were missing. In the interim, the Indians attacked through the unguarded parts of the frontier. By the time the soldiers were aroused, they usually had no other alternative than a long, wearisome, fruitless search. To improve the coverage of the front, two-man teams came into general usage toward the end of the colonial period. Two pairs of men left each fort, one set riding to the east and the other to the west; at midday they met the scouts from the adjacent fort, exchanged verifications, and returned to their base. If the Indians had penetrated the frontier, the troopers learned the general axis of attack; one man returned, and the other set out to alarm the adjacent areas. Forces could thus be assembled quickly either to prevent the Indian from completing his raid or to cut off his retreat. In this manner, the frontier could be reconnoitered in a few hours. Moreover, since each commander was responsible for about twenty leagues of territory, he could soon become thoroughly acquainted with the characteristics of the terrain under his jurisdiction.

These defensive preparations, however, could have no permanent results unless they were supplemented by an advancing population. Thus the forts were made the centers of settlement, and the nucleus of the frontier population was supplied by the blandengues and their families. The plainsmen who had already settled in areas beyond the line of forts were brought back to the vicinity of the defenses, and the innumerable vagabonds of the Pampa, when apprehended, were forced to take up their abode near the new settlements. In addition to the above groups, a few colonists from Spain were distributed along the frontier. All were responsible for the defense of the zone in which they lived, and the death penalty was prescribed for those who failed to assemble at the fort on a given signal.

The new towns showed continued growth during the years of the viceroyalty. Chascomús had 374 inhabitants in 1781 and one thousand at the turn of the century; Luján showed a rise in population over the same period from 464 to 2,000. There was a distinct effort on the part of the authorities to make the new settlements as self-sufficient as possible; wherever the lands were suitable for agriculture, there was a sharp increase in the production of wheat and other cereals.

This fort-building program of the viceroys contained the Indians. The last major raid of the colonial era was an attack on Luján in 1780 in which over one thousand Indians took part. This was the last time an obvious union of tribes combined for warlike purposes. On the very day of this malón, several chiefs were in the process of negotiating treaties of "peace and friendship" with the officials in Buenos Aires. The parleys were broken off with the news of attacks on the frontier. Until the defenses were again completed, the viceroy decreed severe penalties for those who treated with any Indian tribe. The new forts were constructed, and the blandengues were reorganized by 1781. Late in that year, an attempted raid was beaten back with heavy losses to the Indians. A similar situation developed in the Córdoban sector where the Ranqueles constituted the major threat. Forceful action and swift retaliation for incursions eventually discouraged native attacks, and in 1784 twenty-one chiefs came to terms with the governor. Mendoza, with a mountain frontier to the west, made the Pehuenches faithful allies who discouraged their more recalcitrant cousins from committing overt acts. It is probable that the attitude of the Pehuenches reflected their fear of the disruption of their lucrative trade relationships between Chileans and residents of the Pampa. Whatever the reason, sufficient friendly forces were in the mountain passes to protect the flank of the entire viceroyalty.

The gradual stabilization of the frontier and the prosperity which ensued gave impetus to plans to advance the line of forts farther to the south. Several expeditions were dispatched to explore this possibility, the most noteworthy being the excursion headed by Félix de Azara. Viceroy Melo de Portugal felt that his predecessor had established the forts without accurate geographical knowledge. To gather data he assembled the most capable men in the Plata region under the leadership of Azara. After spending several months in an extensive study of the plains, Azara came to the conclusion that it was advisable to advance the frontier at once. Moreover, the explorer believed that the government should accomplish this expansion at one stroke and carry it clear to the Río Negro.

To the arguments that scarcity of water and construction materials would make such a project unfeasible, Azara answered that these same difficulties were inherent in the present frontier line. Furthermore, the islands in the Río Negro provided a potential supply of wood greater than the Salado area. What would be the results of such expansion? Azara maintained that

Control of the Río Negro would once and for all make the whites masters of the Pampa, for the Indians would dare not attack for fear of being cut off. Five thousand square leagues, capable of maintaining more cattle than the entire Banda Oriental, would be brought under control of the government. It would also make the viceroy immortal by pushing out the boundaries of his dominions which today, because of a few annoying barbarians, are approximately the same as those which Garay took with sixty men 216 years ago.

But once the preliminary frontier line had been established, the viceroys felt reasonably secure from attack. They were now willing to develop a peaceful and friendly relationship with the Indians. On a single occasion eighteen chiefs signed pledges not to violate the territory of the whites. There followed a long period of quiet in the province of Buenos Aires, and trade in skins, hides, and minor items developed between Indians and the settlers. The greatest single factor in the development of friendship was the use of gifts to the natives. Undoubtedly, the Indians used the whites for their own advantages, and the viceroy almost despaired of establishing a genuine peace because the natives only came to "pass an amusing time receiving gifts." Nevertheless, the system of rewards brought satisfactory results. The Indians who received meat, bread, tobacco, wine, clothing, and mares became the special friends of the authorities and were utilized as spies to obtain knowledge of the plans and movements of less amenable tribes.

In 1802 a military commander was able to report that the Indians "are very peaceful and there has been no incident for five years in which they have committed the least excess." A brisk trade grew with the Indians in the market place of Buenos Aires and other cities. In these towns certain locations were known as "corrals," where the Indians could come to trade and where they were certain to find buyers. This type of trade was advocated by at least one individual as a means of keeping the peace. Feliciano Chiclana pointed out that it was essentially the desire of the natives for trade which was responsible for the peaceful relations; the Indians wished to do nothing to break the flow of these products to their *tolderías*. Chiclana advanced the suggestion that the Indians be given a monopoly of the salt trade and provided with sufficient carts to carry out the project. By this means they would be provided with money to purchase articles they desired.

During the British invasions of 1806, the Indians did not take advantage of the weakened defenses to attack the frontier but did utilize the embarrassment of the government to seek new favors. Ten prominent caciques appeared before the cabildo and offered to raise twenty thousand men for the defense of the "Patria." Two others promised seven thousand troops, and still another, more conservative and seemingly more accurate in his statistics, stated that he had 2,872 warriors ready to take the field. All were wined, dined, and given the coat-of-arms of the city, but their offers were declined. The local leaders had no desire to see any such number of armed Indians within the environs of Buenos Aires.

The fighting qualities exhibited by the blandengues during this critical period did nothing to enhance their reputation. One hundred of the frontier soldiers were estimated to have engaged the British at Quilmes, the initial landing, but at the sight of the disciplined enemy they beat such a hasty retreat that they trampled neighboring troops and created a panic. The day following this debacle, Viceroy Sobremonte sent an emissary to the forts to urge all troops to come to the aid of the city, but the viceregal messenger found only cattle and horses dead from exhaustion—mute evidence of the speed with which the blandengues had fled.

Despite the occasional unheroic performances of the blandengues, they had made the frontier secure. Although raids along interprovincial roads by small bands of Indians were still prevalent, no great Indian combinations threatened the existence of the new settlements. This general peace, lasting until 1815, transformed the frontier area. Rural settlements developed on the edge of Indian country; the forts gave way to thriving towns. There was peace on the frontier, but it was the same frontier which, in the words of Azara, "Garay took with sixty men." It remained to be seen how the Indian would react when the frontier was pushed forward into his hunting grounds to meet the demands of an expanding European economy; it remained to be seen how the whites would face the Indian problem when they lacked a unified government. With these problems the viceroys were not to be concerned, for they were preoccupied with the waning Spanish power in the Plata.

---

18. Antonio de Ulloa

ARTHUR P. WHITAKER

This brief but substantial biography of one of the most representative figures of the enlightenment in Spain affords the reader an excellent insight into the career of a loyal officer of the crown who studied colonial affairs assiduously, served in important posts in Peru and Louisiana, and drew up with Jorge Juan one of the most discussed criticisms of Spanish

From Volume XV (1935), pages 155–194.

rule in America, the famous secret report of 1749, brought out in London in 1826 as the *Noticias Secretas*. Professor Whitaker, recently retired from the University of Pennsylvania after a long and fruitful career, has devoted a number of his many publications to studies of eighteenth-century Spanish America.

As a colonial and naval official, Antonio de Ulloa failed conspicuously in some of his most important undertakings and, though he was the author of several books, Fitzmaurice-Kelly's *New History of Spanish Literature* does not even mention his name. He is, nevertheless, a significant figure in the history of his age, which was the age of the enlightenment in Europe as a whole and of the Bourbon renaissance in Spain. Two of his books about Spanish America were widely read in western Europe during his lifetime and both of them, together with another work published posthumously, are still highly esteemed by historians; and an inquiry into the reasons for the repeated failures of this exceptionally intelligent and upright servant of the crown possesses interest for all students of the history of the Spanish empire. That no one has ever written a good biography of Ulloa is probably explained by his versatility, the wide geographical range of his activities, and the dispersion of the sources relating to his career. The present article makes no pretense to being definitive, but it is based upon a study of important manuscript sources and it gives, I believe, a better rounded and more accurate account of Ulloa's life than any that has been published heretofore.

Antonio de Ulloa was born at Seville, Spain, on January 12, 1716. About this time, there occurred two events which were to have considerable influence upon his career. Just before his birth the war of the Spanish Succession came to an end and a branch of the house of Bourbon was firmly established on the throne of Spain. The coming of the Bourbons opened up a long period of reform in the administration of Spain and its colonies and brought Spain back into the main current of European thought. Just after Ulloa's birth the monopoly of trade with Spanish America was transferred from Seville to Cadiz. The loss of the monopoly that had made Seville for nearly two centuries the commercial metropolis of the Indies did not bring about an immediate abatement of interest on the part of the Sevillanos in a region that had long been their peculiar province; but now that they were no longer the chief beneficiaries of Spain's venerable colonial system, they could regard it with more detachment and in a more critical spirit than formerly.

It is, therefore, not surprising either that many of Ulloa's activities, both literary and administrative, had to do with Spanish America, or that, both as official and as writer, he called attention to serious faults in the colonial system. The special character of the interests that he developed was also an obvious result of influences to which he was exposed early in life. His father was Bernardo de Ulloa, who gained some repute as an economist; his tutor, Fray Vázquez Tinoco, instructor in mathematics in the *colegio* of

Santo Tomás at Seville. To the former he doubtless owed his interest in the social sciences; to the latter, that in the exact sciences.

In 1729, he was sent to Cadiz to seek a place in the *Guardias Marinas*, a select corps recruited from the sons of the Spanish nobility and devoted to the study of mathematics, astronomy, and navigation. While waiting for a vacancy to occur, he sought to gain practical experience in navigation by taking service at his own expense in a fleet of galleons commanded by Manuel López de Pintado. The cruise lasted two years (1730–1732) and took him to America for the first time—to Cartagena de Indias, Portobelo, Havana, and Santo Domingo.

Admitted to the *Guardias Marinas* on November 28, 1733, he was almost immediately sent with a fleet to reinforce Naples; and he returned to Spain at the end of 1734 just in time to take part in a scientific expedition that was to give him occupation of one sort or another for the next fifteen years and enable him to make an enduring name for himself. Scientists were already agreed that the earth was not a perfect sphere, but there was no agreement as to whether the greater diameter passed through the poles or through the equator. The problem was one in which, as Ulloa subsequently expressed it, "not only geography and cosmography are interested, but also navigation, astronomy, and other arts and sciences of public utility". To settle the question the French Academy of Sciences decided to send one group of scientists to measure an arc of the meridian at the equator and another to make a similar measurement as near the north pole as possible. The only place on the equator where such an operation was then practicable was the Spanish province of Quito in the viceroyalty of Peru. Through the French foreign office, the king of Spain was persuaded to give his consent and promise his coöperation, but he did so on condition that one or two Spanish mathematicians should take part in the enterprise. This was readily agreed to.

The court finally decided to send not one Spanish representative but two, and the persons chosen for this difficult undertaking were the nineteen-year-old Ulloa and his friend Jorge Juan, who was his senior by only three years. Though both of them were members of the *Guardias Marinas* and therefore specially prepared for the kind of work they would have to do, their extreme youth makes one suspect that their appointment was obtained through personal influence. The suspicion is strengthened by the knowledge that their appointment was not made in the normal manner—that is, on the recommendation of the Consejo de Indias—but on the recommendation of the king's chief minister, José Patiño.

The king's consent to the French expedition was formally signified in August, 1734, and by the beginning of January, Juan and Ulloa had been chosen to accompany it; but, proceeding with its accustomed leisureliness, the court did not complete the drawing-up of their instructions until April 22, 1735. These instructions, consisting of ten articles, directed them to join the Frenchmen in Cartagena de Indias, take part in all their operations, record the results carefully, make plans of all the cities, harbors, and fortifications on their way, gather information about the soil, plants, industry, and people of the colonies, including the uncivilized Indian tribes, and make observations that would be useful for navigators. They were also instructed to use the scientific instruments belonging to the French members of the expedition until their own could be made and sent to them. Both were given the rank of lieutenant in the navy before their departure, and they were promised that, upon their return to Spain, the king would reward them according to their merits.

At the very outset they had a stroke of great good fortune. A new viceroy, the Marqués de Villagarcía, was about to go out to Peru, and room was found for the two young mathematicians on board the warships, the *Conqueror* and the *Conflagration*, which were to take the viceroy and his suite to Portobelo. As it happened, he was a man of good sense and education, and Juan, who traveled in his ship, seems to have made an excellent impression on him. This friendship was to prove invaluable to both Juan and his companion while they were at Quito; and it turned out that the protection of the viceroy was worth a good deal more to them then than was that of their friends at the remote Spanish court.

In Cartagena de Indias, they were joined by the much larger French party, which was headed by the talented scientists Godin, Bouguer, and La Condamine. Proceeding by way of Panama and Guayaquil, they reached Quito in 1736. So slowly did their work progress that Juan and Ulloa's part of it was not completed until 1744. There were many reasons for the long delay. Chief among these were the difficulties inseparable from the character of the country in which they had to work; the controversies with the local officials in which both the French and the Spanish members of the expedition became involved; and the war between Spain and England that broke out in 1739 and lasted until long after Juan and Ulloa had sailed for Spain.

No effort will be made here to describe the technical operations that quite properly occupied most of their time, or even to sketch in outline the story of the expedition. Both subjects are discussed in great detail in works published by members of the expedition upon their return to Europe. It is enough to say that the desired information was obtained and that Juan and Ulloa acquitted themselves most creditably, their zeal and ability soon winning the respect of the French members, who were at first inclined to regard the raw young Spaniards with contempt.

One incident that occurred soon after their arrival at Quito is worth relating in some detail, for it not only illuminates one side of Ulloa's character but also brings out in high relief some important aspects of the workings of the Spanish colonial system. That incident is the violent dispute that they had in 1737 with the president of the audiencia of Quito, Joseph de Araujo y Río. Though the cause of the dispute seems rather absurd to the modern mind, its consequences were almost fatal to our two young lieutenants, for it first imperiled their lives and then very nearly blighted their careers. It was the proud, high-spirited Ulloa who started the fight, and he started it because in addressing him President Araujo used the common form for you, *usted*, instead of the more honorific form, *usía*. Possessing a full sense of his importance as the son of a distinguished father, a member of the aristocratic *Guardias Marinas*, and an agent of the king in an expedition of international significance, Ulloa found such treatment intolerable. The character of his antagonist made the affront all the more galling, for it was notorious that Araujo y Río, who had only recently arrived in Quito, had brought with him a mule-train loaded with contraband goods which he was selling in flagrant violation of the laws he was sworn to enforce.

To suffer an indignity at the hands of such a man was more than Ulloa could bear. After trying vainly to get satisfaction in a more decorous way, he decided to beard the lion in his den. Going to Araujo y Río's house one morning, he pushed past the servants to the presidential bed chamber, gave the august occupant a piece of his mind, and returned home a happier man. When he was overtaken by an officer sent by the outraged Araujo y Río to arrest him, he refused to submit. Juan, who had also been addressed with the denigrative *usted*, supported him in his refusal. They argued that, in the first place, they were naval officers and as such acknowledged no superior in Quito, and that in the second place a mere president of an audiencia had no right to interfere with agents engaged in the performance of duties for which they were commissioned by the king himself.

Araujo y Río promptly sent an armed band to take the two insolent boys dead or alive. A skirmish ensued in which blood was shed and the president's men were worsted; and Juan and Ulloa succeeded in making their way into a church where they took sanctuary. Araujo y Río then threw a cordon around the building and prepared to starve them out, swearing—according to one reliable account—that he would put them to death as soon as they fell into his hands. Though they had many friends in the higher ranks of Quito society, especially among the Jesuits, these friends were powerless to protect them against the president, who was virtually a dictator, and things might have gone hard with them had not Juan slipped out of the church under cover of night and set out for Lima to seek the viceroy's protection. He succeeded to perfection, for he reached Lima safely and obtained an order from the viceroy directing Araujo y Río to let the two young men go on about their business pending the decision of their case by the court.

That, indeed, is the course that Araujo y Río himself decided to take as soon as he learned that Juan had escaped to tell his story to the viceroy; and since he had the privilege of direct correspondence with the court he now bent all his efforts toward turning it against his antagonists. The despatches in which he described how Juan and Ulloa were turning the whole province of Quito upside down by the example of their scandalous insubordination had the desired effect. At court, the case was handled by the Consejo de Indias. Already prejudiced against them because it had not been consulted about their appointment, that body recommended that Juan and Ulloa should be summarily recalled to Spain and punished according to their deserts; and, although after a long delay, the king decided to let them complete their scientific mission, he approved the recommendation that they should be punished upon their return to Spain.

Again good fortune, aided and abetted by the viceroy of Peru, came to their aid. The recommendation of the Consejo de Indias was made in March, 1738, the king's decision was embodied in a royal order issued in June, 1739, and in the same year the war of Jenkins's Ear broke out between Spain and England. Invading the South Pacific, the English attacked Peru. The two young naval lieutenants were now in their element. They possessed a far better knowledge of the arts of warfare and navigation than did most of the higher officials of Peru, and the viceroy gave them abundant opportunity to distinguish themselves. On two different occasions he employed them in important undertakings; they served him well; and he promoted them to the rank of captain, subject to the king's approval, and praised them highly in his despatches to the court.

After devoting the greater part of three years to the defense of Peru, they returned to Quito for a few months in 1744 to complete their scientific mission. That done, they prepared for the long and dangerous journey back to Spain, which they accomplished not by way of Panama, as they had come, but around Cape Horn. Since the war had disrupted communications between Spain and America and prevented the regular sailing of the treasure fleets, the king had given permission to four French ships from St. Malo to call at Callao for a cargo of two million pesos. Traveling separately for the better protection of the records of their work, Juan and Ulloa embarked in two of these ships, which sailed from Callao on October 22, 1744. Though Juan's ship was delayed at Valparaiso by an accident, he reached Spain first arriving at Madrid in January, 1746, after an adventurous journey that carried him to St. Domingue, Brest, and Paris. In the latter place he addressed the Academy of Sciences and was elected a corresponding member of that body.

Ulloa's ship—hopefully named the *Notre Dame de Bonne Délivrance*— and its two companions got safe past Cape Horn and the enemy-infested West Indies, but at a point just north of the Azores they were attacked by English privateers. Possibly because it was the smallest and presumably the least valuable of the three French ships, the *Délivrance* was the only one that escaped capture. With a wholesome respect for British sea power, its captain now decided to seek safety in Acadia. They arrived at Louisbourg in August, 1745, after a comparatively uneventful voyage, and as they entered the harbor "complacency and joy swelled every heart" at the sight of the French flags fluttering over the town. Complacency and joy soon turned to bitter disappointment, for, when it was too late to retreat, they found that the flags lied—Sir William Shirley with his doughty New Englanders and a British fleet had taken the place.

Again, however, fortune favored Ulloa. Though he suffered the annoyance of imprisonment and another postponement of his scientific and literary labors, he was well treated in Acadia and was soon sent to London. There he continued to receive generous treatment, met many distinguished scientists and writers, and was made a fellow of the Royal Society—a signal honor for an enemy alien. After a delay caused by the uprising in Scotland, the good offices of his influential friends enabled him to recover his notes and papers, which the admiralty had turned over to the East India Company. Returning to Spain by way of Lisbon, he arrived at Madrid in July, 1746, eleven years and two months after he and Juan set out from Cadiz for Cartagena de Indias.

II

Even if the comminatory royal order of 1739 had not been forgotten by this time, there was no disposition on the part of the court to carry out the threat it contained. In the course of the seven years that had elapsed since the issuance of the order many things had happened to reinstate Juan and Ulloa in favor. They had won high praise from the viceroy by their services in defense of Peru; they had been signally honored by two of the most distinguished learned societies in the world; Philip V., who issued the order of 1739, was dead, and his successor, Ferdinand VI., was no doubt glad to signalise the beginning of his reign by a conspicuous patronage of learning. At any rate, he gave instructions through his chief minister, the Marqués de la Ensenada, that the viceroy's promotion of Juan and Ulloa to the rank of captain should be confirmed and that they should write an account of the expedition and submit it for publication at government expense.

Though the account was not published until 1748, the writers were not responsible for the delay. Within two weeks after Ulloa's arrival in Madrid he and Juan submitted a detailed inventory of their papers and a sketch of the book that they proposed to write. It appears from this inventory that, although at the time of his capture at Louisbourg Ulloa had thrown overboard the manuscript of several sections that he had already written, all the original records of the expedition were preserved intact. They were, therefore, able to proceed with the labor of composition as soon as they received the necessary authorisation and to make such rapid progress that Juan's part of the book was completed by March 22, 1747, the first half of Ulloa's by June 29 and the second half by September 22 of the same year.

Then, however, the manuscript had to run the gauntlet of a long line of censors, and although their reports were altogether favorable, save for minor criticisms, it was not until June, 1748, that the last report was submitted. The manufacture of the book also presented difficulties that delayed its appearance. Suitable paper was found in Barcelona, and the authors finally decided to content themselves with the type available in Madrid rather than take the time to get a superior variety in Holland, as at first they planned to do. The problem of the engravings was not so easily solved. The only engraver in Madrid who could do the work wanted to take a year for only half of it, and the authors had to send their sketches to Paris, where all the engravings were made within three months.

At last, all these difficulties were surmounted and the book was published in 1748. It consisted of five volumes. The first four volumes, entitled *Relación histórica del Viage a la América meridional* and containing an account of the experiences of Juan and Ulloa from 1735 to 1746, together with a description of the people and places they saw, were written by Ulloa; the fifth volume, containing a technical account of the scientific work of the expedition, was written by Juan. The division of labor was a natural one. Ulloa was the better writer of the two, and his encyclopaedic mind and wide-ranging curiosity fitted him admirably for the writing of the general account, which, aside from its narrative of travel and adventure, contains observations on history, anthropology, geology, linguistics, morals, and many other subjects. In short, he not only wrote four-fifths of this coöperative work: he wrote the only part of it that ever interested the general public. It was also Ulloa who handled the financial accounts and saw the book through the press. And yet, since Juan had shared his labors in Peru, Juan's name appeared on the title-page of all five volumes; and, since Juan outranked him in the navy, Juan's name was printed before Ulloa's on every title-page.

The book did not disappoint the hope, expressed by several of those who read it in manuscript, that it would make a noise in Europe. That national pride had a great deal to do with the publication of it is apparent from all the records. In the opinion of one of the censors, the Marqués de la Regalía, the book would show the world "that the Spaniards have not lost either the appetite or the talent for great undertakings"; and another, the distinguished Jesuit scholar, Andrés Marcos Burriel, wrote,

This is one of the best and most useful books that have been published in our tongue; and I have no doubt that . . . it is destined to fulfil every expectation of the European public, to the great glory of the nation, of his Majesty, of the ministry, and of its authors. . . .

It was this thirst for fame among the literati of Europe that induced the government to draw aside the veil of secrecy with which it had hitherto sought to hide the Indies from the prying eyes of foreigners. The decision was made all the easier by the realisation that foreign interlopers had already penetrated the veil in many places and that in some respects other nations were better informed about the Indies than was Spain itself.

Distributed broadcast by the court, the book at once met with acclaim despite the fact that it was written in Spanish, a language not widely known in other countries even in learned circles. Copies for sale were distributed among the provincial intendants of Spain, and complimentary copies were sent to the kings of Portugal, Naples, and France, to the Royal Society of London, the French Academy of Sciences, and similar societies, and—as a gesture of triumph—to the French members of the expedition, Bouguer and La Condamine, whom Juan and Ulloa had beaten into print. Fathers Berthier and Clairvoix of Paris—the latter of whom was then engaged in writing his history of Paraguay—read it at once, praised it highly, and expressed the opinion that it would put the French associates of Juan and Ulloa to shame. As time went on, the solid merits and unique value of the book were more and more widely recognised, and ultimately the language difficulty was removed by its translation into German (1751), French (1752), English (1758), and Dutch (1771). The English translation, which was made by John Adams, passed through five editions (1758, 1760, 1772, 1806, and 1807), and, with a few omissions, it was again printed in 1813 in John Pinkerton's *General Collection of Voyages*. In the present article the title of the English translation, *A Voyage to South America*, is used in referring to the book.

As soon as this task was completed, Juan and Ulloa wrote another account of their observations which is comparable in scope and importance to their *Voyage to South America*. This is the confidential report which is generally known today by the title under which it was first published many years later, *Noticias secretas de América*, but which the authors themselves entitled *Discurso, y Reflexiones Políticas sobre el Estado presente de los Reynos del Perù.* . . . Containing valuable information about the military defenses of Peru and a frank revelation of many faults in the Spanish régime there—notably the venality of the colonial officials, the tyranny of the *corregidores*, the exploitation of the Indians by the village priests, the horrors of the *mita*, and the dangerous antagonism existing between the creoles and the European Spaniards—it was of course written for the eyes of the court alone. Not until nearly eighty years later did it become known outside of court circles. In 1826, David Barry, an English merchant of Cadiz, somehow got hold of a copy which he published at London, with some slight alterations, under the title *Noticias secretas de América*.

Quite naturally, the book is galling to Spanish pride, and historians of that country have tried in various ways to deprive it of its full effect. Rafael Altamira even went so far as to question its authenticity; and while Cervera and Ballesteros, after studying the problem more carefully than did Altamira, accepted the *Noticias* as authentic in most respects, they state their conclusions in such a way as to make it appear that the book does Spain a substantial injustice. They assert that, by changing a word here and there, Barry made the published version criticise the Spanish colonial system more harshly than does the original manuscript; that Barry was guilty of unethical conduct in publishing a confidential report; and that, even though the *Noticias* is substantially identical with the original manuscript, neither the one nor the other represents the views that Juan and Ulloa would have expressed if they had designed their report for publication. It is hardly necessary to point out that most historians would regard the confidential nature of the report as the best justification for publishing it and as the best guarantee of its fidelity to fact and of the veracity of its authors. We may readily agree with Ballesteros that a new edition, based directly on the original manuscript preserved in the Biblioteca Nacional at Madrid, should be published; but until that is done, it should be distinctly understood that there are no important differences between the published version and the original manuscript, and that the authenticity of the latter is not open to serious question. It seems to have been mainly the work of Ulloa, for it bears the stamp of the same encyclopaedic, inquiring mind that produced the *Voyage to South America* and the paper and handwriting bear a very close resemblance to those of other documents of the period of which Ulloa was unquestionably the author.

Some valuable information on this subject is contained in an autograph letter written by Ulloa in 1762 and recently discovered by the present writer. This letter, addressed to the secretary of state for the colonies, Julián de Arriaga, was written in reply to a royal order of 1761 directing Ulloa to make a confidential report on the conduct of the treasury officials *(oficiales reales)* of the province of Huancavélica, Peru, of which he was then governor. In the course of the letter, which described scandalous abuses committed by the treasury officials in connivance with their superiors at Lima, he said:

Part of what I have told your Excellency can be found, if it please you, in a confidential report on the civil and political government of these kingdoms [the viceroyalty of Peru] that I wrote in the year '48 or '49 by order of his Majesty and by disposition of his Excellency, the Marqués de la Ensenada, and which I filed in your ministry of the colonies, and I have no doubt that it is still there, for after your Excellency took over that office I one day found Don Francisco de Aosmendi reading it. In the part of this account that deals with the treasury officials, the irregularities in the administration of the exchequer [*Real Hacienda*] are noted; but since the experience that I had acquired at that time was not so extensive as that which intimate participation in the administration of the exchequer has given me, what I said in that account is only a very faint sketch of what actually happens.

This letter points to some interesting conclusions. In the first place, it proves beyond the shadow of a doubt that a confidential report on Peru was written by Ulloa in 1748 or 1749, and that that report discussed at least one of the subjects that are discussed in both the manuscript preserved in the Biblioteca Nacional and the *Noticias secretas,* and dealt with it in the same critical spirit. In the second place, the letter heightens the lurid effect of the *Noticias secretas,* for it shows that if the report of 1749 had been written from Ulloa's larger experience of 1762, he would have painted an even darker picture of the Spanish colonial régime than the one of which apologists for Spain are now complaining. In the third place, the letter shows that the report of 1749 was not pigeonholed and entirely forgotten, as is sometimes assumed, but that it was read by one of the officials of the colonial department some time after Arriaga took charge of it, which was in the year 1754.

Finally, the letter to Arriaga strengthens the assumption that the confidential report of 1749 was mainly the work of Ulloa, for Ulloa speaks of it as "the report that I wrote", not as "the report that Juan and I wrote". To be sure, Juan's name appears on the title-page along wth Ulloa's; but it also appears on the title-page of the first four volumes of the *Voyage to South America*, which were certainly written by Ulloa alone, just as Ulloa's name appears on the title-page of the fifth volume, which was written by Juan alone. In other words, the title-pages of the works that Juan and Ulloa wrote at this period are misleading; and if we are to determine which of the two wrote a given book, we must draw our conclusion from some other source than the title-page. In the case of the confidential report on Peru, the evidence we have mentioned, though not conclusive, points to Ulloa as the sole author.

III

Upon the completion of the report in question, Ulloa was sent to France and the Netherlands on a special mission that occupied him for the next two years and that ultimately carried him to Denmark and Sweden as well. His passport stated that he was to go to Paris to study mathematics, but his secret instructions show that his mission was part of a plan to promote the industry and commerce and strengthen the military defenses of Spain. His principal duty was to obtain informtion about the ports, harbors, roads, canals, and factories of France and the Netherlands, and to induce skilled workmen from those countries to emigrate to Spain. For this purpose he was to visit Toulon, Marseilles, Bordeaux, Brest, Rochefort, Lyon, and other cities, as well as Paris, and was then to proceed to the Netherlands.

He executed his mission to the complete satisfaction of the court. Going by way of Barcelona and Marseilles, he arrived in Paris in January, 1750. In the summer he visited Brest and other Atlantic ports of France. In February of the next year, the court wrote him that, since he had made so much progress and was needed in Spain, he should return as soon as he had visited the Netherlands; but he asked permission to include Denmark and Sweden in his tour and his request was granted. By December, he was back in Paris and early in 1752 he returned to Madrid. The results of his observations and inquiries were embodied in a series of reports that he wrote after his return. They contain a great deal of valuable information, and if the one that describes the roads of France were published, it would take rank with the well known work on the same subject that Arthur Young wrote a generation later.

Rejoining the *Guardias Marinas* at Cadiz, he remained there until 1757. During this period the court frequently consulted him about important projects, such as the founding of a museum of natural history and an astronomical observatory. In 1757, he gave up the naval for the colonial service, accepting appointment to a key post of great difficulty in Peru—the governorship of Huancavélica and the superintendence of its quicksilver mine. The post was an important one because that mine was the only one of its kind in America and was in normal times the sole source of supply of an article which was indispensable for the working of the rich silver mines of Potosí. The post was an extremely difficult one, partly because of the technical problem of maintaining an adequate volume of production in a mine that had been in operation for nearly two centuries, and partly because the miners and local officials were leagued together in a fraud ring that was apparently invincible.

The records suggest that Ulloa's old friend, Jorge Juan, who also was serving with the *Guardias Marinas* at that time and was frequently consulted by the court, had something to do with the appointment; but that it was made in recognition of his merits is shown by the memorandum of Arriaga's advice to the king in the matter. "It is very important," said Arriaga,

that an honest and intelligent person should fill this post, and in all the time that I have sought for such a person I have found no one who is better qualified for it than Don Antonio de Ulloa . . . of whom I spoke to your Majesty on a former occasion; and I now renew the recommendation, for I have been assured that he has made a special study of metals, mines, and construction, and he is most disinterested.

Ulloa professed to be not at all eager to make the change. Surrounded by his relatives and friends and with congenial work to do, he found life at Cadiz very pleasant. In prestige, he said, his present career in the navy was not inferior to the one offered him in the colonies. "It also has the advantage," he added, "that here I am free from many cares and from the vexations [*desazones*] that might unexpectedly occur in that occupation." If, as this passage suggests, the information about Huancavélica that he had acquired during his first residence in Peru caused him to view with some apprehension the prospect of governing that stormy province, he was soon to find out that his fears were only too well justified. But the larger salary —8,000 pesos a year instead of the 4,800 pesos that he was receiving at Cadiz —proved an irresistible bait, and he accepted. Perhaps the recent fall from power of his patron, the Marqués de la Ensenada, also disposed him to try his fortune in a new career.

Sailing from Spain at the end of January, 1758, he arrived in Huancavélica on November 2 and took over the government two days later. His first despatch to Arriaga, dated November 15, describes a clash he had already had with the miners, and the fight thus early begun continued with increasing bitterness throughout his administration. At first, he met with some success in his effort to introduce efficiency and honesty into the operation of the mine, the payment of cash advances to the miners by the government, and the repayment of those sums to the treasury; but he was doomed to failure by the collusion that existed between the miners and their abettors, who included officials, ecclesiastical as well as secular, both at Huancavélica and at the viceregal capital, Lima. The harder he strove to destroy the net of fraud that enmeshed his province, the more astutely did his powerful enemies move to checkmate him and bring about his ruin. Their influence was so widespread and reached into such high places that they were able to turn even the viceroy and the audiencia against the luck-less governor.

By May, 1762, Ulloa was confessing himself utterly exhausted and hopelessly beaten. In a letter in which he used the same word, *desazones*, that had betrayed his misgivings about the post at Huancavélica while he was still debating whether to accept it, he implored the court to rescue him from a situation made unendurable by the "vexations, mortifications, and rebuffs" that he was suffering. In August of that year, he wrote the confidential report on the misconduct of the treasury officials of Huancavélica from which we have already quoted. In another part of that report he said:

To remedy this situation is, if not altogether impossible, at least extremely difficult because of the way in which these abuses, as well as the people who are responsible for them, are linked together. The situation is such that the mine operators do their business under the protection afforded them by the bribes they pay the treasury officials; and I may say the same thing about the *corregidor*, the *arrendador de alcabalas*, the smuggler, and others. The treasury official in turn acts under the protection of judicial officials, of the subordinate officials of the viceroy's palace, and of the attorney general [*fiscal*]—and the office of the latter is a marketplace where he who has no substance to distribute is an object of contempt.

Even more serious charges appear in other letters, for he asserted that both the audiencia of Lima and the viceroy, Manuel de Amat, were actuated by dishonorable motives in their opposition to him. The audiencia, he said, hoped to discredit him in order to pave the way for a return to the system under which Huancavélica was formerly governed—that is, by rotating the office of governor and superintendent among the members of that tribunal, each of whom would enrich himself during his administration. As for Amat, he was angry because Ulloa refused to pay him the annual bribe of 10,000 or 12,000 pesos a year that he was accustomed to collect from the government of Huancavélica. There was probably some truth in these charges, for the viceroy and the audiencia, far from giving Ulloa the support to which he was entitled, issued a series of unjust and humiliating decrees that destroyed the last vestige of his authority over his unruly province; and it may be added that by the end of his term as viceroy, Amat's name had become a byword for corruption throughout Peru.

By the summer of 1763, Ulloa's complaints and prayers for relief, together with the vicious charges preferred against him by the viceroy—they included almost every offence from technical incompetence to embezzlement

—had moved even the leisurely Spanish court to action. A mass of documents relating to the dispute was collected and sent to Jorge Juan for his opinion. His report was favorable to Ulloa, whom he described as "certainly one of the most intelligent of Spaniards"; but he continued, no good purpose would be served by keeping him in Huancavélica, where he was at the mercy of his enemies. It was accordingly recommended that he should be recalled and employed elsewhere. On January 4, 1764, a royal order to this effect was issued; and since the court probably realised that his enemies in Peru would hold him there if possible, so that they might continue to persecute him, the order warned the viceroy that Ulloa's departure must not be prevented or delayed on any pretext whatever. Subsequent events showed that but for the peremptory terms of these instructions he might have been forced to spend the rest of his life in Peru contending on unequal terms with the officials, high and low, whose venality he had done so much to expose and—through no fault of his own—so little to correct.

This episode is a most significant one for the history of Spain's colonial administration. There was abundant evidence that Ulloa was in the right and that the administration of Peru was honeycombed with corruption. And yet the Spanish court was unable to sustain him; it was not even able to punish the corrupt squadron who were persecuting him for his honesty; the utmost that it could do was to rescue him from their clutches.

Toward the end of 1764, Ulloa, armed with the peremptory royal order of January 4, succeeded in shaking off his enemies and left Peru. Sailing from Callao to Panama, he proceeded thence to Havana where he had been told to await further instructions. Before these arrived, he wrote Arriaga signifying his readiness to continue to serve the king in America if that were necessary, but begging the minister to help him to escape from "these ungrateful climes". His Peruvian "Purgatory", as he called it, had left him with no desire to protract his stay in the brave new world.

Unfortunately, it soon turned out that the king did have need of him in America. Louisiana had recently been ceded to Spain by France and just at the time when Ulloa's recall from Peru released him for service elsewhere, the court was preparing to take possession of the new province. Perhaps because it was thought that his two-year residence in France and his eight-year association with the French academicians in Peru fitted him to govern colonists most of whom were French, or perhaps merely because he was available, the king appointed him governor of Louisiana.

The unhappy story of his administration is so well known that the details need not be repeated here. It should be pointed out, however, that while he again failed conspicuously, as he had done in Peru, this second failure, like the first, was due to circumstances over which he had no control. His own errors did not contribute to it in any important degree. The irritation caused by his unbending pride was a mere trifle in comparison with the hatred he incurred as the loyal agent of a power that the Louisianians cordially detested.

Commissioned in 1765, he went from Havana to New Orleans early in 1766. The troops and funds with which the court had provided him were utterly inadequate to his needs, and he was forced to leave the administration in the hands of the last French governor, Aubry, who henceforth governed the province in the name of the king of Spain. Though Ulloa warned the court time and again that the situation was an impossible one and that Spanish authority over the people of Louisiana could not be maintained unless he received heavy reinforcements, little attention was paid to his warnings, and the measures adopted at Madrid only made the situation worse. Their indecisive character kept alive the creoles' hope that Louisiana might yet return to the possession of France and thereby fostered the spirit of fractiousness that was already so strong in them; and the court's commercial decree of 1768 was the immediate cause of the rebellion that drove Ulloa out of the province in October of the same year. Aubry was probably right when he said that insubordination had reigned in Louisiana for ten years past and that the storm of 1768 was necessary to clear the air. Only by adopting a clear-cut policy and by supporting it with a sufficient show of force could the court have saved the situation; but that is precisely what it failed most conspicuously to do.

Though it must have been as obvious then as it is now that Ulloa was not responsible for the fiasco, it brought his career in the colonial service to a close. He was doubtless well pleased with this result. Had he not, even before he knew that he was to go to Louisiana, begged Arriaga to rescue him from "these ungrateful climes" of America? At any rate, after his expulsion from New Orleans he hastened to return to Spain without waiting to get permission from the court.

With the exception of one more unfortunate episode, the remaining twenty-seven years of his life were comparatively calm, happy, and uneventful. The court was apparently convinced that he had done the best he could in Louisiana, for he was permitted to resume his career in the navy, was soon promoted to the rank of *gefe de escuadra* (rear admiral), and continued to hold responsible posts to the end of his days. In 1777, he went to Vera Cruz in command of the last of the famous treasure fleets *(flotas)*. For once he was altogether successful, and at the end of June, 1778, this son of Seville brought back to the rival city of Cadiz a treasure that he described as the richest ever sent from New Spain to the mother country. We may note in passing that the court's solicitude for the safety of this fleet was partly responsible for its refusal to support the pro-American policy of France early in 1778 and for delaying Spain's entry into the war of the American Revolution.

In 1779, occurred the unfortunate episode mentioned above. Spain had by this time been drawn into the war with Great Britain, and Ulloa was given command of a squadron with orders to cruise between Galicia and the Azores. Upon his return from the cruise he was tried on various charges, the most serious of which were that he was responsible for the loss of a Spanish ship and for the escape of a fleet of British merchantmen which he should have captured. The court of inquiry gave him a complete vindication. There is an amusing but apocryphal story to the effect that he failed to fulfil the purpose of his mission because he was sailing under sealed orders and became so engrossed in the reading of a new scientific book that he forgot to open the orders until it was too late. A pretty story —but, if we are to believe the voluminous records of the trial, there is not a word of truth in it. There is no allusion to it in those records; on the other hand, the findings of the court of inquiry state that, far from being guilty of any neglect, Ulloa was entitled to reward for having done everything in his power to comply with his instructions in spite of most unfavorable weather and the poor condition of the ships assigned to him.

IV

After his return to Spain from Louisiana, he devoted a large part of his time to writing. His most important work of this period is his *Noticias Americanas* (Madrid, 1772), which should not by any means be confused with the *Voyage to South America* of 1748. The book published in 1772 is both briefer and more comprehensive than the earlier one, for, while it consists of only one volume, it deals with the whole of Spanish South America and the eastern part of North America; and it contains information about Louisiana and Florida and the quicksilver mine at Huancavélica that is not found in the *Voyage* and that was obviously gathered by Ulloa during his service as a colonial official from 1757 to 1768. The *Voyage*, moreover, is primarily a narrative account written for the purpose of advertising the part taken by Spain in the important scientific expedition of 1735–1744; whereas the *Noticias Americanas* is almost wholly descriptive and expository, and its declared purpose was to contribute to the progress of mankind by making an addition to man's store of systematic knowledge.

In view of the character of the book and of the fact that Spain's policy of shrouding the Indies in secrecy had already been abandoned with the publication of the *Voyage* a quarter of a century earlier, it is not surprising that permission to publish was given quickly and without hesitation. Ulloa submitted the manuscript to Arriaga who on April 3, 1772, sent it to the Consejo de Indias for action. Within three months after the *fiscal* of the Consejo received it he submitted a favorable report, and the book was published the same year. Again Ulloa was regarded as the champion of Spain in the intellectual lists of Europe, for the *fiscal* declared in his report that Ulloa had already given "repeated proofs of his erudition and critical discernment", and that this new book would save Spain from the common reproach among foreigners to the effect that, since the discovery and conquest of the Indies, it had never taken the trouble to inform the rest of the world about "the rare and precious things that they [the Indies] contain". This book did not share the popularity abroad of the *Voyage*, but it was translated into French and German and a second Spanish edition was published in 1792.

Ulloa was less fortunate with a survey of the navies of Europe that he submitted to Arriaga in 1773. He began writing it in 1755, was interrupted by his appointments to Huancavélica and Louisiana, and at last completed it toward the end of 1772. This time the *fiscal's* report was adverse. He criticised Ulloa's style on the ground that he used too many Gallicisms—a complaint that Spanish critics have frequently made against the writings of their compatriots. He dismissed as worthy of a philosopher rather than of a practical politician Ulloa's suggestion that, for the sake of economy, the European powers should reduce their navies to one-tenth of their existing strength; and he said he doubted whether the department of foreign affairs and the navy would consent to the publication of the book. The latter consideration was probably decisive, although Ulloa declared that his manuscript did not contain any information about the Spanish navy that was not already in the possession of foreigners. The license was not granted and the treatise was never published.

Ulloa continued in active service to the end of his days—at the time of his death he was chief of operations of the navy—but in the last twenty years of his life he did not write anything of importance. He was growing old; perhaps he was deeply discouraged over the rejection of his treatise on the navies of Europe; and perhaps his official duties and his growing family, to which he was devoted, left him no time for writing.

We know little about his private life. It appears that he was entirely dependent upon his salary save for his wife's dowry, which was probably not large. This may explain why, although his interests were scientific and literary, he devoted so much of his time to writing government reports, surveys, and similar documents, which might be expected to win him promotion and an increase in salary. His wife was Francisca Ramírez de Laredo, daughter of the Conde de San Javier of Lima. The marriage took place in Louisiana early in 1767. They had nine children, the first four of whom were born within a period of seven years. One of his sons, Francisco Javier de Ulloa, subsequently rose to the rank of admiral and was twice secretary of the navy.

A delightful sketch of his life at home was drawn by the English traveler, clergyman, and dabbler in science, Joseph Townsend, who visited him at Cadiz when he was some seventy years of age. "I found him perfectly the philosopher," says Townsend,

sensible and well informed, lively in his conversation, free and easy in his manners. Having observed at his door two soldiers mounting guard, I expected some pride of appearance, but I met with nothing like it. This great man, diminutive in stature, remarkably thin and bowed down with age, clad like a peasant . . . was sitting to receive morning visitors, in a room, the dimensions and furniture of which, for a few moments, diverted my attention from himself, the chief object of veneration. The room was twenty feet long by fourteen wide, and less than eight feet high. In this I saw dispersed confusedly, chairs, tables, trunks, boxes, books and papers, a bed, a press, umbrellas, clothes, carpenters tools, mathematical instruments, a barometer, a clock, guns, pictures, looking-glasses, fossils, minerals and shells, his kettle, basons, jugs, American antiquities, money. . . .

Surely not much money—rare coins, no doubt. Ulloa had neglected a golden opportunity to enrich himself in Peru, and if his wife ever possessed a great fortune it was gone now. His treasures were the fossils—"he shewed me a variety of seashells, collected by himself near the summits of the highest mountains in America"—the books, the antiquities, the mathematical instruments, that reminded him of a life well spent in the pursuit of knowledge. But he looked forward as well as back. A true philosopher in the eighteenth-century meaning of the word, he knew the uses of posterity; and he was wrapped up in his own posterity. Townsend found him "surrounded by his children, with the youngest about two years old, playing on his knee"; and he noted that one of Ulloa's treasures, "a curious mummy from the Canary islands", had served as a plaything for the children, who had "amused themselves by drawing its teeth, and breaking off its limbs". Ulloa's last book was entitled *Conversations with his three Sons in the naval Service*. It was published in 1795, and he died on July the fifth of the same year.

The foregoing account of Ulloa's public career suggests some of the limitations of the vaunted Bourbon renaissance in Spain, which was almost precisely coterminous with his life. It reveals the existence in three important spheres—the colonial administration, the court, and the navy department—of serious and long-standing defects which it was apparently impossible to correct even in that age of revival. The story of his sufferings in the purgatory of Huancavélica forms a melancholy footnote to the tale of iniquity told in his own *Noticias secretas*. His expulsion from Louisiana was clearly the result of the dilatoriness and ineptitude of the Spanish court; and yet his expulsion occurred almost a decade after the accession of Charles III., whose reign is generally regarded as marking the flood-tide of the Bourbon renaissance. Though his failure in his cruise to the Azores in 1779 was due in part to foul weather—the "wind and waves" of which Philip II. so justly complained after the defeat of the Spanish Armada, and which showed a strange persistence in destroying the best laid plans of Spain's naval strategists—it was largely owing to the miserable condition of the ships with which he was forced to make the cruise; in other words, to the same inadequacy of preparation that, ever since the time of Philip II., had made it so much easier for wind and waves to do their work of destruction.

Ulloa's writings form an important chapter in the history of another and a more edifying aspect of the Bourbon renaissance, the intellectual revival of the eighteenth century. His well written and widely read *Voyage to South America* provided Europeans with the first comprehensive and authoritative account of that region. The *Noticias secretas de América*, of which he was at least the joint and possibly the sole author, probably stimulated the reform movement already in progress at the Spanish court and is still one of the principal sources of information about Spanish America in the later colonial period. His *Noticias Americanas* is important not only because of the quaint and curious lore that it contains, but also because of the emphasis that the author places upon the value of a comparative study of cultures. And finally, following Menéndez y Pelayo, we may note that Ulloa belonged to the small and select group of practical scientists who brought about a notable revival of scientific studies in Spain. Among other things, he established the first museum of natural history in Madrid, and the first metallurgical laboratory; he brought from London to Spain the first scientific information about electricity and magnetism—information that he doubtless obtained from his friend William Watson; and Abbé Raynal rightly credits him with having given Europe its first knowledge of platinum.

His mind was neither bold nor original and, though he was a reformer, he was by no means a revolutionist. He believed in progress through enlightenment but he also believed that that progress would have to be gradual and very slow; and, unwaveringly loyal to king, church, and country, he was convinced that there was ample room for the process within the limits of the established order. It is significant that many of his friends and admirers were Jesuits and that he accorded the order sympathetic treatment in his books. It is also significant that, after discussing the problem of the development of different forms of plant and animal life from a common origin, he concluded that the problem was insoluble and that these developments were merely another evidence of the workings of an inscrutable providence. Here was no Lamarck or Darwin in the making.

Ulloa's liking for the Jesuits did not prevent him from finding people of a very different sort congenial. He was as much at home in the secular atmosphere of London and Paris as in the ecclesiastical atmosphere of Madrid; and, we may add, he was much more at home in all of those places than in America, which he found a fascinating subject for inquiry and speculation but not a desirable place of residence. He succeeded in doing something that only the rarer spirits can do, for, though he borrowed freely from abroad, he never lost his native character. Without ceasing to be a Spaniard, he became a cultured European; and that was no mean achievement for a Spaniard of his generation.

Aside from the translation of his books into several languages, there are other evidences of the recognition that he won outside of Spain. In 1747, the year before the *Voyage to South America* was published, Voltaire spoke of Spain as a country that had hardly any heroes and not a single writer. By the time he published his *Dictionnaire Philosophique* (1764) he knew that Spain had at least one writer, for he cited the *Voyage* and referred to its author as "le philosophe militaire Ulloa". In another work, published four years later, he again referred to Ulloa, this time as "si célèbre par les services qu'il a rendus à la physique, et par l'Histoire philosophique de ses voyages". A very different sort of person from Voltaire, but one who shared Voltaire's enthusiasm for enlightenment, also used the word "philosopher" in referring to Ulloa, who was to him an "object of veneration". That person was, of course, Joseph Townsend, whom we have just quoted. And several learned bodies—among them the academies of Stockholm and Berlin, as well as the Royal Society of London—honored Ulloa and themselves by electing him to membership.

Ulloa's writings breathe the spirit of didacticism that was characteristic of the literature of western Europe in that age; but his was a gentile didacticism. A fisher of minds, not of souls, he baited the hook of instruction with entertainment. The subtitle of his *Noticias Americanas* contains the word *entretenimientos*—entertainments, amusements—and he called the subdivisions of the book not chapters but *entretenimientos*. His avowed purpose, which was the same as that of many of his contemporaries in other lands, was to instruct by amusing.

He also shared the humanitarian zeal that was beginning to spread over Europe. In this respect, however, he showed himself not so much a cosmopolite as a follower of one of the best traditions of his native land; for his humanitarianism, like that of the sixteenth-century Bartolomé de las Casas, from which it stems, found its chief expression in an effort to ameliorate the wretched lot of the Indians of Spanish America. Though he might well have saved some of his sympathy for the downtrodden masses of his fellow-countrymen, we must do him the justice to repeat that the circumstances of his life fixed his attention, and kept it fixed, upon Spansh America rather than upon Spain itself.

There were large realms of ideas as well as whole physical continents that lay beyond the margin of his speculations; but within these limits, and in his own way, he did valiant service in the cause of justice and enlightenment. If some new Parrington should write a history of main currents in Spanish thought, Ulloa would surely occupy an honorable place in it.

Other Articles of Interest

Hanke, Lewis. "Dos Palabras on Antonio de Ulloa and the *Noticias Secretas*." XVI (1936), 479–514.
  Part I concerns the "pyramid controversy," a quarrel between Ulloa and La Condamine over the honor due to royal patronage. A lawsuit of two years ensued, then a period of five years awaiting the decision of the Council of the Indies concerning the erection of the pyramids of Yaruquí. Part II concerns whether Barry had a purpose in publishing the *Noticias Secretas*, which apparently came out as the culmination of a campaign of propaganda against Spain. Or was it just "snappy reading"?

Kirkpatrick, F. A. *"Noticias Secretas."* XV (1935), 492–493.

Whitaker, Arthur P. "The Elhuyar Mining Missions and the Enlightenment." XXXI (1951), 557–585.
The Elhuyar brothers, Juan José and Fausto, contributed to the scientific renaissance in Spain in the latter half of the eighteenth century as the discoverers of tungsten and as experts on metals. An official metallurgical interest was aroused in Spain in the late 1770's and early 1780's through an effort to produce better guns for the Spanish Navy. Juan José Elhuyar was sent to northern Europe in 1778 for training in the scientific manufacture of cannon. Two government financed chairs of chemistry-physics and metallurgy-mineralogy were established at Vergara, and the second of these was filled by Fausto Elhuyar in 1781–1782. Juan José Elhuyar's dismissal by the Navy Department was the direct cause of his mission to New Granada, at the same time that Fausto Elhuyar took charge of a mining mission to New Spain.

———., ed. "Jorge Juan and Antonio de Ulloa's Prologues to their Secret Report of 1749 on Peru." XVIII (1938), 507–513.

CHAPTER FIVE

COLONIAL BRAZIL

19. Padre António Vieira, S.J., and the Institution of the Brazil Company in 1649

C. R. BOXER

Professor Boxer of Kings' College, London, has produced a rich and remarkable variety of studies on the history of the Portuguese empire, including Brazil. He has contributed detailed monographs, editions of documents, bibliographical reviews, polemical studies, and numerous scholarly articles during the last thirty years. The following article, which examines the economic ideas and proposals of probably the greatest ecclesiastical figure in Brazilian history, is an excellent sample of his style.

"A Companhia do Comercio do Brazil, que restaurou Pernambuco e Angola, e deu cabedal ao reino para se defender, por ser invento e arbitrio meu me tem trazido à presente fortuna, quando se pudera prometer uma, muito avantejada e honrada, quem tivesse feito ao seu rei e à sua patria um tal serviço, sobre tantos outros em que tantas vezes, e com tão uteis efeitos, arrisquei sem nenhum interesse a vida."—*Padre António Vieira in a letter written to Queen Catherine of England, 21 December 1669, complaining of the ingratitude of the Prince-Regent, Dom Pedro.*

"Navios e mais navios é o que havemos mister. . . ."—*Padre António Vieira to the Marquês de Niza, 16 March 1648.*

Three hundred years ago, the national existence of Portugal and Brazil was at stake. This may not readily be realized today, when Brazil is the greatest nation in more than mere size on the South American continent, whilst Portugal possesses the third largest colonial empire in the world. But those who have more than a passing acquaintance with the history of the seventeenth century may remember that for fourteen critical years (1640–1654), Portugal's chances of survival as an independent nation seemed slim indeed, whilst there was a distinct possibility of Brazil becoming a Dutch possession, either in whole or in part.

The fall of the one would, in all probability, have involved the collapse of the other. Portugal could not carry on her twenty-eight years' war of independence against Spain (to say nothing of fighting Holland for most and Cromwellian England for part of this time) without the economic resources provided by her Brazilian "milch-cow"—as King John IV aptly if crudely characterized his most profitable colony. Conversely, Brazil could not indefinitely sustain her struggle against the stubborn Hollanders ensconced at Pernambuco, unless means were found to break the Dutch mastery of the South Atlantic Ocean (even if only temporarily), so that men and munitions from Portugal and slaves from Angola might provide her with the sinews of war and of agriculture. Whatever successes the patriots of Pernambuco might score against the Dutch ashore (and many hard knocks did they give them, as Tabocas and Guararapes testify), they could scarcely hope to capture Recife itself, so long as the Dutch were masters of the sea and could reinforce their beleaguered stronghold at will. So long as Pernambuco held out, a potential threat to Bahia existed, as the events of 1638, 1647, and 1649 clearly demonstrated. It was therefore essential for the safety of Brazil that Portugal should secure at any rate local command of the sea in defiance of the greatest maritime power of the age. The difficulties of such a reversal of roles will become apparent if we recollect the international situation in so far as it affected the Portuguese Empire at the time of the Congress of Westphalia in 1647–48.

This congress marked the close of two wars which had distracted Western Europe for generations. The Thirty Years' War in Germany, and Holland's eighty-years' war of independence against Spain, had both by this time lost their original *raison d'être* and had become even more futile and purposeless than most wars. Prolonged negotiations at Münster and Osnabruck between Spain and the Hapsburg Empire on the one side and Holland, France, Sweden, and their satellites on the other, finally culminated in the treaties collectively known as the Peace of Westphalia (January-October, 1648). Unfortunately for herself, Portugal's national existence was not recognized by this treaty, since neither France nor Holland was prepared to press the claims of their weaker ally against the adamant opposition of Spain. Spain's decision finally to recognize the independence of the United Provinces, which for over half a century had been an accomplished fact, was largely because she wished to divert against Portugal some of the veteran *tercios* fighting in Flanders, Germany, and Italy. Portugal's sole friend was France, who remained at war with Spain for another decade; but France was distracted by the *Fronde*, and Cardinal Mazarin was prone to ask more of King John IV than he was prepared to give him. The reborn nation's precarious position was characterized by Padre António Vieira, who pointed out that although the Portuguese monarch had sent a dozen ambassadors abroad since his coronation in December, 1640, and still had seven actually accredited to foreign countries, there was not (and never had been) a single ambassador resident at the Court of Lisbon. Moreover the pope had declined to recognize Portugal's independence, or even to fill the vacant episcopal sees in this most devoutly Catholic of all countries. The diplomatic scene showed clearly enough that the other European powers thought little of her chances of survival.

The Peace of Westphalia left things worse than ever from the Lusitanian point of view. Not only were Spain's hands freed to a large extent, but those of Holland as well. A ten-year truce had been concluded between King John IV and the States General in June, 1641; but it was ill observed beyond the Line, whilst Luso-Dutch relations in Europe were only occasionally correct and never cordial. Since Holland was far and away the greatest maritime power of the age (in some respects perhaps the greatest maritime power of *any* age), whilst Spain was still a formidable military power, the outlook for Portugal was dark indeed. She could only continue her struggle against Spain for so long as the maritime route to Bahia and Rio remained open for the sugar, tobacco, and other Brazilian products whose sale paid for the upkeep of the armies which held the Spaniard at bay along the frontier, and for the imports of corn from North Europe to feed her people. The Peace of Westphalia set free more Dunkirk privateers and the Zeeland corsairs *(kapers)* to attack Portuguese shipping in the Atlantic, already grievously harassed by the depredations of the Dutch West India Company's shipping.

How grievous these losses were, is apparent from a glance at contemporary sources, such as the Dutch chroniclers De Laet, Barlaeus, and Neiuhof, or from the correspondence of Padre António Vieira, one of the relatively few people in Portugal who was not only fully alive to the desperate nature of the situation, but had a concrete remedy to propose for it. On reading the numerous references to maritime affairs in the letters of this remarkable man—perhaps the greatest that Portugal has ever produced after Afonso d'Albuquerque and Luis de Camões—one is inclined to believe that the Portuguese navy lost a potentially outstanding admiral when the young Vieira took a Jesuit's *roupeta* at Bahia in 1623. Throughout his long life, Vieira evinced a remarkable grasp of the importance of sea-power, and he took an intelligent interest in the Anglo-Dutch wars which revolutionized naval tactics. He obviously knew a good deal about shipbuilding, for his observations on the relative qualities of Dutch, French, and Dunkirk frigates in 1647–48, reveal sound sense and acute observation. Had his plans for the building and purchase of a fine fleet of frigates been followed, Portugal might well have recovered more of her colonies than Angola and Pernambuco.

Portuguese shipping losses in the South Atlantic from 1621 onwards were colossal, but still trade with Brazil increased rather than diminished. This vital but generally forgotten fact speaks volumes for Portugal's resilience and powers of recovery. It is also the surest proof of the size of her merchant marine, usually stated to have wilted away during the "Sixty Years' Captivity" to Spain (1580–1640). In the first fifteen years of the "piratical" activities of the West India Company (1623–1638), no fewer than 547 laden Portuguese ships were taken by the Netherlanders. In the year 1633 alone, ninety Portuguese prizes fell a prey to Dutch corsairs in the Atlantic, and in 1647–1648, as many as 220 were lost. It is only when we realize that Recife used to load about 130 sugar ships annually (before its capture by the Dutch), Bahia about seventy-five, and Rio de Janeiro, twenty-five or thirty, that we can understand how Portuguese shipping could survive such losses. Obviously this strain could not continue indefi-nitely, even at an epoch when a small port like Vianna boasted of two hundred ships at sea, and the breaking-point appeared imminent in 1648. The Luso-Dutch truce of June, 1641, had brought only the most temporary relief, for as already mentioned, it was but ill observed in the Southern Hemisphere. Rudyard Kipling's aphorism about there being no Ten Com-mandments east of Suez was anticipated by Caspar Barlaeus, who quoted his countrymen in Brazil as saying that there were no sins on the other side of the Equator ("aan de andere zijde van den evenaar weet men van geen zonde"). Small wonder that the Brazilian sugar-planters ruefully termed themselves *lavradores de Olanda*, whilst Dutch defeats at the hands of the Pernambuco patriots ashore were largely offset by the prizes which the Hollanders secured at sea.

Seven years after the restoration of Portugal's independence and its formal recognition by Holland, things were as bad as ever they had been. Vieira wrote from The Hague in May, 1648, "a ship has arrived from Pernambuco bringing twelve Portuguese, masters and merchants of our ships captured there. They say that between the 1st January and the day they left, which was the 7th March, the Dutch captured twenty-two ships from Lisbon, Oporto, Vianna, and the Atlantic Islands [Madeira and Azores], Recife being full of their cargoes and supplies, to its great bene-fit." An officer in Admiral Witte de With's fleet which reached Recife at the end of March, 1648, gives a list of fifteen Portuguese prizes at the time of his arrival. He states that out of every six caravels which left Cape Saint Augustine (used by the Portuguese for the export of sugar from the hinterland of Dutch-held Olinda and Pernambuco) at least half were in-variably captured by the waiting Hollanders.

Vieira was at one time the protagonist of a scheme for the purchase of Dutch Brazil for an indemnity of three million *cruzados*, and an annual tribute of sugar for a decade or so. Apropos of this suggestion (which naturally encountered great opposition in Portugal) he wrote in August, 1648, that the Hollanders had taken more sugar in six months than the ten thousand chests which would have been paid to them in a decade according to his plan. It is arguable whether the Dutch would in fact have been con-tented with an average of a thousand chests a year, when there were so many more to be had for privateers' pickings. Privateering in the United Provinces was almost a national sport, as witness the popular Zeeland proverb, *Schijt in den Handel alseer Buyt te halen is*. But Vieira, ever fer-tile of ideas, had another and as it proved more practical suggestion.

This was the formation of a powerful chartered company, something on the lines of the Dutch West India Company which had proved so effective with ledger and sword—chiefly with the latter it must be confessed. Vieira's original plan (in 1641) was for two companies, one for India and one for Brazil, but the former never progressed beyond the paper stage. His idea was that the capital for these two chartered companies should be furnished by the New-Christian (or crypto-Jewish) financiers of Lisbon, and by the Portuguese Sephardic Jews who had fled to Northern Europe in order to avoid the rigors of the Iberian Inquisitions. In order to induce these oppressed classes and exiles to invest their capital in the projected Portuguese companies (and to leave the Dutch India Companies in which some of them were interested), it was essential to guarantee all investors from persecution by the Inquisition. It was on this point that the scheme first broke down, since that all-powerful tribunal utterly refused to countenance what it regarded as an infamous pact with Satan's emissaries.

Vieira nevertheless did not give up hope, and the steady deterioration of Portugal's international position, culminating in her exclusion from the Treaty of Westphalia, added force to his persuasive arguments. It was in the critical days of 1649 that he wrote his celebrated *Papel forte*, whose argument he resumed forty years later in the following succinct terms:

1. If Portugal and Spain together (from 1580 to 1640) could not prevail against Holland, how can Portugal alone make head against both Holland and Spain? 2. The Hollanders have eleven thousand topsail ships and a quarter of a million sailors: count the number of our ships and sailors, and see if we can resist the Dutch who are fighting us on all the seas of the four quarters of the globe. 3. The councilors of the king of Castile advise their monarch to prevent at all costs the conclusion of peace between Holland and Portugal; whilst his ambassadors are active to this end, regardless of expense. What can be more senseless than for the councilors of the king of Portugal to advise him to act as the Spanish councilors desire?

We have said that the progress of events gave added cogency to Vieira's arguments, so let us briefly review the former. The negotiations culminating in the Treaty of Westphalia had released for service elsewhere Dutch armed forces which had been tentatively earmarked for use against Spain. In August, 1647, the States General decided to help the West India Company with both men and ships on a generous scale, something for which the directors had previously agitated in vain. Twelve States' vessels, including the new flagship *Brederode*, pride of the Dutch Navy, were detached to reinforce the W.I.C.'s chartered shipping, the total fleet amounting to over thirty ships carrying about six thousand men. It is true that administrative red-tape, contractors' corruption, unseasonable weather, and the intrigues of the Portuguese ambassador at The Hague, Francisco de Sousa Coutinho, combined to delay the departure of the fleet until 26 December 1647; whilst it was subsequently storm-bound for weeks in the English Channel, the wretched troops dying like flies aboard the cold, wet, and ill-provided transports. Nevertheless the fleet finally reached Recife at the end of March, 1648, and its presence in Brazilian waters effectively removed the danger of any direct attack on Pernambuco.

A year before De With's belated arrival, Sigismund von Schoppe, a German veteran of many Brazilian campaigns, had landed on the island of Itaparica in the Bay of All Saints (February, 1647) with the idea of establishing there a "new Dunkirk," thus blockading the Portuguese colonial capital so closely that no shipping could go to or from Bahia, which was faced with the prospect of dying from inanition. News of this bold stroke reached Lisbon at the end of April, 1647, and the king sent forthwith at early dawn for the ubiquitous António Vieira, who had forecast just such a move some six months previously. Indeed, Schoppe was not carrying out a new plan, but one which he had openly advocated for many years before the *Heeren XIX*, or governing Board of the W.I.C., sanctioned this scheme in April, 1646.

On the flustered monarch's asking his Jesuit guide, philosopher, and friend, what was to be done now that Von Schoppe had carried out his pet project, Vieira made the obvious retort that a strong armada must be sent to raise the blockade of Bahia as soon as possible, and in any event before Schoppe could be reinforced from Holland. This, however, was easier said than done, since the royal treasury was empty, and neither the king nor his Council of State could think of any way to raise the cash necessary for the fitting out of an armada, which was estimated at 300,000 *cruzados*. This was Vieira's opportunity, and he retorted dramatically, "Fie on the ministers of the crown that they should tell the king of Portugal that there is no way of raising 300,000 *cruzados* with which to succour Brazil, which is the only valuable place that we have! Now I trust in God that with this patched cassock I shall be able to guarantee Your Majesty the whole of this sum to-day." Vieira then went to a Jewish friend of his from Bahia, Duarte de Silva, and suggested to him that he should advance the money in return for an impost on the sugar arriving from Brazil. De Silva replied that the business was too much for him alone, but that he would try to obtain a fellow-Israelite as co-guarantor. This he did, and Padre Vieira proudly took his two protégés to confirm their offer with the king that same morning.

It was thus with the aid of (*pace* the Holy Office) "tainted" Jewish money that the Armada Real do Mar Océano of about twenty sail left the Tagus on the 18th October, under the command of António Teles, created Conde de Vila Pouca de Aguiar and governor of Brazil for the occasion. Von Schoppe evacuated Itaparica and raised the blockade of Bahia on hearing the news of the armada's approach, so António Teles found the Bay of All Saints empty of hostile shipping when he cast anchor there on Christmas Eve, nine days after the Dutch had left. Eight months later, Salvador Correia de Sá e Benevides, in command of a squadron likewise largely prepared with the financial aid of Duarte de Silva and his co-religionists, recaptured Angola from the Dutch, thus restoring to Brazil her most profitable slave market. The Portuguese colonial empire had been saved from collapse by the money raised from his New-Christian friends by Padre António Vieira—a singular if patriotic combination of Jews and Jesuits.

The fleet of "Double-With," although too late to forestall António Teles at Bahia or Salvador Correia at Luanda, was nevertheless master of the Brazilian seas, and the danger to the homeward-bound sugar ships from Rio, Bahia, and Cape Saint Augustine was nearly as acute as ever. But the critical situation, and the efficacy of Jewish financial coöperation in preparing the Portuguese armada of 1647, had finally resolved King John IV's doubts. This monarch now strongly supported Vieira's project for the creation of a chartered Brazil Company, whose financial sinews were to be supplied by Portuguese Jews, crypto- and otherwise, both at home and abroad, in return for the exemption from confiscation of their capital (whether invested in the Brazil Company or elsewhere) by the Inquistion. At this point it is necessary to explain just what such a step involved, and why it was regarded with such aversion by the vast majority of Vieira's compatriots.

Jewish unpopularity was more due to religious bigotry than to anything else, for it seldom assumed dangerous proportions so long as the government or the clerical hierarchy did nothing to encourage it. Jews, or persons of real or alleged Jewish ancestry, were often employed by the Portuguese kings as tax-farmers, tax-collectors, monopolists, and so forth. As is the way with short-sighted human kind, the hatred aroused by the exactions of these crown agents was vented against them and their race rather than on the monarchs and ministers who originated or sanctioned such burdensome imposts. Jews were likewise prominent as surgeons and physicians, whilst the death-rate from the ministrations of medicos in the seventeenth century was alarmingly high. Popular prejudice ascribed to the malice aforethought of the Jew what was really due to the universal lack of sound medical and surgical knowledge. Despite the fact that a good deal of inter-marriage, and still more inter-breeding, took place between all classes of the population and those of Israelite descent, popular hatred of the latter increased rather than diminished. This unfortunate class was known by such opprobrious epithets as *christão-novo* (New Christian), *marrano* (swine), or by a more ambiguous but equally significant ellipsis, *gente de nação* (People of the Nation) mention of the hated Israel being deliberately omitted. It was widely believed that Jewish men menstruated like women, that they exuded a foul smell, and that they had the stump of a tail at the end of their vertebrae. Such fatuous fables were propagated by the more bigoted of the monks and clergy down to the nineteenth century at least.

Some modern defenders of the Holy Office of the Inquisition claim that it imposed at least a semblance of legality on the persecution of Jews, and at any rate avoided the recurrent pogroms and lynchings from which they had previously suffered. This may be so, but the proceedings of this tribunal bear more resemblance to those of such fine flowers of twentieth-century culture as the German Gestapo, the Japanese Kempeitai, and the Russian Ogpu, than to procedure in an average law-court. Suspects brought before it were not at first told on what charge they were arraigned, nor were they ever given the names or the opportunity to cross-examine those who had given evidence against them. This property and capital were impounded on their arrest, their families being literally as well as figuratively turned on to the street; and although they had the theoretical right to have their worldly wealth restored to them if ever they were honorably acquitted, either of these two contingencies seldom occurred. It can easily be imagined what facilities this tribunal provided for informers, blackmailers, and the settlement of old scores, and what a premium it put on the spread of envy, hatred, malice, and all uncharitableness. This will be readily apparent to anyone who takes the trouble to read through some of the original witnesses' depositions, many hundreds of which have been printed by the Portuguese scholar and archivist, António Baião.

As is often the way with organizations of this kind, the Inquisition arranged to have much of its dirty work done by others, partly to save its own "face," and partly to involve other bodies in its own nefarious activities. Obstinate sinners were handed over (after being duly tortured of course) or "relaxed" to the secular arm for disposal without shedding of blood—a Holy Office euphemism for burning a person alive. Similarly, although the confiscated wealth and property of all its prisoners ultimately came into its own coffers, it came by way of the crown fiscal in the first instance, though woe betide this official if any of the money stuck to his fingers. Ever since the institution of the Inquisition in Portugal in the middle of the sixteenth century, the New-Christians had made repeated efforts to have at least this confiscatory clause removed from the *Regimento* (Standing Orders) of the Holy Office; but although they had spared neither bribes, entreaties, nor promises to this end they had never achieved anything more than partial and fleeting relaxations. The inquisitors opposed this concession tooth and nail, for they stated categorically that they could not continue to function without the funds which they derived from this source. The crown was also loath to lose this particular income, since if it did so it would have to provide for the upkeep of the Inquisition out of its own revenues.

It will thus be realized that António Vieira stirred up bitter opposition when he formulated his proposal to attract Jewish capital to his projected Brazil Company, by specifically exempting investors therein from the penalty of confiscation of either goods or capital, even if convicted of the crimes of "Heresy, Apostasy, and Judaism." The inquisitors were already deeply suspicious of those New-Christians who had been formally "reconciled" with Holy Mother Church. The reverend gentlemen complained (no doubt correctly) that such reconciliations were mere shams, the victims still continuing to obey the Law of Moses in their hearts whilst outwardly conforming to Catholicism lest worse befall. One inquisitor advocated that not only should all such New-Christians be refused the Eucharist, but added that if the precepts of canonical law were enforced, any *christão-novo* who once relapsed should pay for it with his life, quoting Saint Augustine as saying *Lupus nadit, Lupus reddit.* This was perhaps an extreme view, but there was more general support for the stand of the inquisitor-general (Dom Francisco de Castro) and his council, who declared on the 25th June 1647, that the penalty of confiscation was the one most dreaded by crypto-Jews; for the formal stigma of Judaism meant little to them, whilst they could avoid death by an outward recantation. "And if with such a heavy penalty, Judaism has continued to flourish recently for our sins, what will happen when it sees itself free and immune therefrom?"

Vieira had, however, scored a great point in getting the vacillating King Dom John IV on his side; since if this monarch, at the Jesuit's prompting, really decided to waive the enforcement of the confiscatory clause, the Inquisition had no means of getting hold of the Jews' money, as it came ostensibly through the channel of the crown fiscal. The battle was now fairly joined, and this round went to Vieira and against the "Fortress of the Rocio" (Fortalesa do Rossio), as the great Jesuit termed the Inquisition after the name of the Lisbon square where its headquarters were situated. Devout Catholic as he was, Dom João did not venture to take so drastic a step merely on the promptings of Vieira, but he submitted the proposal to exempt Jewish and crypto-Jewish capitalists from the penalty of confiscation (*izenção do fisco*) to a large number of theologians and experts in canon law, as well as to the inquisitors. Needless to say, the latter were wholly hostile to the proposal, and claimed that the king had neither the right nor the power to enforce any such measure without the explicit written approbation of the pope. The Jesuit theologians of São Roque and Santo Antão, on the other hand, unanimously declared (in August, 1647) that such a measure was not only lawful but necessary, and that King John could enforce it with a clear conscience.

The king and Vieira now went ahead with their plans, but the formal incorporation of the Brazil Company was delayed for six months, partly because Duarte de Silva and others of the principal intended directors were busy with the preparation of António Teles' armada and Salvador Correia's squadron throughout the autumn, and partly because the theological wrangles with the Inquisition and its supporters still continued. The arrest of Duarte de Silva, one of the principal investors in the projected Brazil Company, by the Inquisition in 1648 also delayed things, it is to be presumed. By 6th February, 1649, all was ready, and on that day the king sent for the bishop-inquisitor-general and his council. On their arrival at the palace, he had the terms of the *alvará*, or decree formally embodying the Brazil Company, read over to them. These terms expressly included the *izenção do fisco*, whereupon the bishop and his colleagues respectfully but emphatically protested against them. The king in his turn equally politely, but still more emphatically, rejected their protest, telling them that the danger to Portugal and Brazil was so great that the foundation of this company (which other theologians had assured him was justified) was the only possible means of saving the situation. He added that they would be very unwise to make any outward demonstration of their opposition, which he would strongly resent. He then dismissed the fuming inquisitors.

The inquisitor-general subsequently suggested that the master should be referred to Rome for approval or rejection, but the king replied (on 29 March) that this was inadvisable at present, since the Papacy could hardly adjudicate fairly on the question, being hostile to the Portuguese government, but that he would do so in due course. Meanwhile, however, the Lisbon inquisitors had appealed on their own initiative to the pope, who promptly sent them a brief declaring King John's move null and void. The king was much annoyed when he heard this news, and sending for Dom Francisco de Castro and his colleagues once more, he read them the riot act in no uncertain terms. Portuguese kings have always been distinguished for their devotion and often for their bigotry; and seldom can a Lusitanian monarch have taken so strong a line with such puissant representatives of the church. He not only upbraided them for their disloyalty and warned them against attempting to enforce the papal brief, but reminded them that a few years previously the inquisitors had availed themselves of his support in refusing to recognize the validity of a papal brief obtained by the Jesuits against them in a bitter sectarian dispute with the Evora Inquisition.

But Bishop de Castro and his colleagues evidently knew their man. Secure in both papal and popular approval of their stand, they refused to yield, and in the end it was they who had the best of the struggle. Despite Vieira's persuasive eloquence and the subsequent development of events, the king gradually weakened under the strain of such intense disapproval in nearly all quarters. Two years later he reluctantly recognized the validity of the papal brief, albeit he did insist that money invested in the Brazil Company (as distinct from Jewish money invested in other enterprises) should remain immune from confiscation, save in very special circumstances and on certain conditions agreed with the company's representatives. Meanwhile Vieira could at least boast of having achieved something which had earned him more than a night's repose; for the Companhia Geral do Estado do Brasil which he created was the means of saving Portuguese America from the Dutch.

The statutes of the company as set forth in the printed *alvará* of 8 March 1649, make interesting reading when compared with those of its rival body, the Geoctroyeerde West-Indische Compagnie. We have not space to summarize more than a few leading points of the fifty-two articles in the original *instituição*. The preamble which is addressed to the king, clearly reflects Vieira's original conception. The company's area in Brazil is given as extending from Rio Grande to São Vicente inclusive, including Dutch-occupied territory. Investors of all classes and nationalities would be eligible to become shareholders in the company with a minimum subscription of twenty *cruzados*, for a term of twenty years beginning on Easter Day, 1649. Option of a ten-year extension on the same terms was stipulated. The company promised to fit out a fleet of thirty-six warships, each with a minimum of twenty to thirty guns, and to find crews for the same. This fleet was to be divided into two squadrons of eighteen warships. Each squadron would make an annual voyage to Brazil, and all other Portuguese vessels from Continental Portugal and the Atlantic Islands sailing thither would have to make the round voyage convoyed by one of these two squadrons. The subscription list for investors in the new company was to remain open to all and sundry for one calendar month in Lisbon, three for the remainder of Portugal, seven for Madeira and Azores, and for a year in Brazil, after which the lists would be closed. All subscribers would have to pay one-third of their investment in ready cash and the balance in two instalments of four months each.

The governing board was composed of nine directors (*deputados*), eight of them merchants, with a representative of the Lisbon municipality who was likewise to be taken from the mercantile community. All directors must have a minimum individual investment of one thousand *cruzados*, and could serve for three consecutive years. Eight were to be elected by a majority vote of the shareholders, the ninth being nominated by the judge and governing board of the Lisbon municipality. In addition, the Lisbon mercantile community (*i.e.*, the crypto-Jews) were to nominate another eight councilors who could be summoned to board meetings whenever necessary, when they would have the same voting powers as the remaining nine. All the company's officials were to be selected and appointed by the directors, and could be dismissed or removed at their pleasure. Appointments were triennial. The treasurer's accounts were to be audited by the board accountant and two directors. This meant that the shareholders had not even the semblance of control over the company's finances, and in this respect the Brazil Company differed from the Dutch Company. Board meetings were conducted at a large round table in order to avoid wrangles over place and precedence.

It was categorically stipulated that the governing board was to be completely independent of all the crown courts and tribunals, as also from interference by the Inquisition. The triennial governing board would only have to account to its successor for its doings, and of course to the king if necessary. In this respect it enjoyed much greater freedom of action than its counterpart in the W. I. C. (or would have done if the statutes had been properly enforced). Its legal affairs were to be handled by a *juiz conservador*, a peculiar official with far-reaching powers. He was empowered to deal summarily with minor cases without right of appeal. Lawsuits involving large sums of money were to be handled by him in a special court nominated by the king from officials selected by the directors

—a packed court, if ever there was one! A procurator-fiscal was appointed on similar terms.

Special facilities were accorded the company for securing shipbuilding supplies and labor, it being specifically exempted from interference by the crown officials who on the contrary were enjoined to help it, particularly arsenal and dockyard authorities. The company was allowed to build ships not only in continental Portugal (Lisbon, Oporto, Aveiro, Pederneira, Alcácer) but in Brazil (Bahia, Rio de Janeiro, São Vicente, and Maranhão) on the same terms as the crown. Facilities were also accorded for chartering English, Swedish, Hamburg, and other ships laden with ship-chandlers stores and artillery. Under royal license, foreign ships could also be chartered by the Brazil Company to sail in its sugar fleets. Similarly it could supplement the shortage of Portuguese soldiers and sailors by enlisting English, Scandinavians, or Germans to serve in its convoys.

It was recognized that sea-power was the key to the situation, and the company was therefore authorized to appoint its own admirals and sea-captains, subject to confirmation by the crown. Its armed forces were recognized as being on the same footing as the royal army and navy, whilst terms of service, recruitment, etc., were virtually identical and counted equally in respect to rewards and pensions. Furthermore, the governors of Brazil were expressly forbidden to commandeer any of the company's ships or men during their stay in the colony.

No vessel of any kind could leave Portugal, Madeira, or the Azores for Brazil, and *vice versa*, unless it sailed in one of the company's biannual convoys. Dispatch boats with urgent military or naval intelligence formed the only exception to this rule. The sailing of a convoy had to be announced two months previously, by posting up notices of the sailing date in all the principal ports. Originally, Lisbon was the only European terminal port, whilst those of Brazil (in 1649) were Cape St. Augustine (in lieu of Dutch-occupied Recife), Bahia, and Rio de Janeiro. Later this was altered, Oporto and Vianna getting their share, whilst Pernambuco was added to the list of Brazilian ports after its recapture from the Hollanders in 1654. The master of any vessel sailing to or from Brazil other than in the regular convoys had his license endorsed and his vessel confiscated. The Brazil Company was awarded a special flag, having the royal arms on one side and the picture of Our Lady of the Immaculate Conception on the other, with two inscriptions, *Sub tuum praesidium* and *Pro fide pro patria mori*—a somewhat ironical choice in view of the almost exclusively Jewish origin of the company.

The company's privileges included the monopoly of supplying Brazil with the four most essential imports (other than slaves) for the colony, *viz.*, wine, cereals, olive oil, and codfish, and these at rates fixed by itself. As regards the return cargoes of sugar, tobacco, cotton, and hides, the company was entitled to levy a tax on every chest, bag, or bale imported, in accordance with a sliding-scale laid down. It was accorded the complete monopoly of all Brazil wood exports from the four *capitanias* of Rio, Bahia, Ilheus, and Pernambuco, but paid an import tax at Lisbon on this commodity.

Capital once invested in the company could never be withdrawn, but shareholders could sell or transfer their shares to others, in whole or in part, at the prevailing market price. Only shareholders with an investment of over five thousand *cruzados* could vote in the triennial election for the eight directors. Capital invested in the company by both Portuguese and foreign nationals was specifically exempted from confiscation by the Inquisition or by any other tribunal. Even in the event of war between Portugal and the country of a foreign investor, the latter did not forfeit his investment or dividends; whilst all substantial foreign merchants resident in Portugal had to subscribe to the company according to their means, on pain of not being allowed to participate in the colonial trade anywhere. These statutes were confirmed in the most categorical and solemn manner by the king on the 10th March, three days after another *alvará* had been promulgated, formally exempting New-Christian investors from having their capital confiscated by the Inquisition "for the crimes of heresy, apostasy and Judaism." Padre António Vieira's triumph appeared to be complete, and the Portuguese Jews seemed on the threshold of emancipation from their long night of oppression; but the forces opposed to the company were only momentarily foiled and they soon returned to the attack.

Truth compels us to add that they were not the only forces of reaction. Along with the professional Jew-baiters of the Holy Office, and clerical obscurantists of every sort and kind from mitred bishops to begging friars, were to be heard the complaints of sailors, merchants, and skippers from ports like Vianna, Aveiro, and Vila do Conde, to say nothing of the Azores and Madeira. They clamored against the blow dealt to their coastal shipping by the company's insistence on well-armed vessels of large burden, and complained bitterly of the evils flowing from the company's monopoly of the four essentials of Brazilian colonial life, wine, olive oil, cereals, and codfish. Nor were their complaints entirely frivolous, for as the Marquês de Niza wrote from Paris in November, 1648 (when the formation of the company was still under discussion), "Monopolies of those articles which form the necessities of life always proved to be highly prejudicial to those monarchs who authorized them, for even though some benefit is derived by the royal exchequer therefrom, the harm suffered by the common people far outweighs that strictly limited advantage." This early apostle of free trade found many supporters in Portugal, and after a few years of acrimonious discussion the company's privileges were drastically reduced. But meanwhile it had achieved at least one of its avowed objects, the preservation of Catholic Brazil. *E senão veremos.*

When the armada of António Teles and the squadron of Salvador Correia left the Tagus in October-November, 1648, thanks to the funds supplied for this combined armament by Vieira's Jewish friends, the Jesuit wrote to one of his correspondents that "the port of Lisbon was left without a pinnace, the dockyard stores without an anchor or a cannon." If this was really so, it is all the more creditable to Portugal's resilience that a year later the Brazil fleet of sixty-six sail left the Tagus (4 November 1649) convoyed by eighteen galleons supplied by the new company, under the command of the Conde de Castelmelhor, with Pedro Jacques de Magalhães as admiral or second-in-command. This at a time, be it remembered, when none of the Armada Real of 1648 had returned from Brazil, and when the Hollanders were still picking up Portuguese prizes by the score in the Atlantic. Some of these ships were chartered foreign vessels, including at least four English, but the great majority were Portuguese. If anyone doubts that Portugal was still a maritime power of importance in the middle of the seventeenth century, these facts and figures should surely disabuse them.

The Hollanders at any rate were speedily disillusioned. Just when the West India Company and the Zeeland privateers were looking forward to lusher pasturage than ever amongst Portuguese shipping in the Atlantic, they found themselves confronted by well-armed vessels sailing in well-disciplined convoys, relatively immune from attack save by powerful squadrons. Whereas single caravels and pinnaces had proved easy game, the embattled fleets of the Brazil Company were a very different proposition. The Hollanders had watched with keen interest, not unmixed with apprehension, the struggle in Portugal which preceded the formation of the Brazil Company, and their reaction can be seen from the contemporary pamphlets printed in Amsterdam and The Hague. King John IV's *alvará* of 7 February, formally releasing Jewish capital invested in the Brazil Company from confiscation by the Inquisition, and the *alvarás* of 8/10 March incorporating the Brazil Company were translated and printed in Holland within a few weeks of their publication in Portugal.

The pamphleteers noted that at this stage Dutch opinion towards the Luso-Brazilian problem could be roughly divided into the following three viewpoints. Firstly, the proponents of an offensive *guerre à l'outrance*, with a view to the capture of Bahia and all Portuguese Brazil. This was the policy advocated by the directors of the W. I. C., and by the Provinces of Zeeland and Groningen; it was exemplified by the dispatch of the powerful expeditions under Banckert (1646), Witte de With (1647), and Haulthain (1650). In fact, Zeeland's adherence to the peace with Spain in 1648, was only secured because Holland and the other provinces promised to prosecute vigorously the war against the Portuguese in Brazil. Secondly, there were those who advocated standing on the defensive in Pernambuco, and relying on an intensified privateering war at sea to bring the Portuguese government to heel by entirely disrupting Lusitanian maritime trade. This was the policy actually in vogue in 1649, although its virtually sole advocates were those born privateers, the Zeelanders, with their motto of *schijt in den handel alseer buit te halen is.* Most of the remaining provinces were advocates of the third policy, which was to open peace negotiations with King John IV, on the basis of formal Portuguese recognition of Dutch Brazil within its boundaries of 1645, and an assured supply of slaves from Angola. Such were the viewpoints of the Dutch in Holland, but of more practical importance was the situation as seen through the eyes of the beleaguered Hollanders at Pernambuco, to which we will briefly turn our attention.

By a stroke of luck for the Portuguese, Admiral Witte de With's fleet (or most of it) had left Brazil for Holland between September and November, 1649, mainly on account of want of victuals and supplies, although clearly the admiral and the council of Recife were on bad terms. Hendrik Haecxs and his colleagues were thus seriously perturbed when they received news on the 16th February 1650, that a large Portuguese fleet was in the offing, estimated at fifty-seven sail in all. This fleet remained cruising between Olinda and Cape St. Augustine for a week, during which time the local Dutch squadron of six sail under Commander Caspar Goverts vainly tried to cut off and capture some of its components. A hot skirmish between the Dutch squadron and three chartered English ships, each of forty guns, "wearing red English flags at the stern and pennants from the foremast yards," took place on the 19th February off Recife Roads. No lasting damage was sustained by either side, although for three hours the contending ships appeared to be "wrapped in flames and smoke" to the anxious watchers at Pernambuco.

Next day an oxhead of Spanish wine was sent off to the Dutch squadron "to encourage the crews," but despite this "Dutch courage," Govert's squadron failed to take a straggler from the fleet, the frigate *Santa Luzia,* under Captain Bernardo Ramires de Esquivel, who beat off all the Hollanders' attacks on two successive days (February 21 and 22). This naval action was watched, not only by the Dutch at Recife, but by the blockading Luso-Brazilian forces under the Mestre do Campo Francisco Barreto de Meneses. So critical did the frigate's position appear against odds of six to one, that Barreto sent a message to Ramires, advising him to run his vessel ashore to avoid capture. Ramires replied with true Portuguese *pundonor* that whilst he might save his life ashore he preferred to preserve his honor at sea. In the end the Dutch drew off, sorely battered, and the three Portuguese army commanders (Francisco Barreto, João Vieira, and André Vidal) wrote to the victorious Ramires that they would rather have been his soldiers aboard ship on that occasion, than generals ashore. All that the Dutch squadron secured in the course of the week's fighting was one straggler from the fleet, a pinnace with sixty thousand guilders. This solitary prize formed a marked contrast to the scores of laden ships and caravels captured annually in previous years. The armada reached Bahia on the 6th March, 1650, almost exactly four months from the day it had sailed from the Tagus.

The terms of the Brazil Company's charter were violated in the return voyage of the first fleet of 1649–50. Instead of sailing via Bahia in convoy, the sugar fleet from Rio made the return voyage independently. The English admiral, Robert Blake, was blockading the mouth of the Tagus and intercepting all Portuguese shipping, in revenge for the protection afforded by King John IV to Prince Rupert's royalist privateers. Orders had been sent to Bahia, instructing the fleet not to sail until the coast of Portugal was clear; but Antão Temudo, commander of the Rio detachment of twenty-three sail did not call at Bahia en route. He was thus surprised by Blake off the Tagus on the 27th September, and although he escaped into Setúbal with the flagship, eight of her consorts were sunk or captured by the English. Meanwhile the Bahia squadron had either received the warning or were luckier, since bad weather forced its return to Bahia, whence it sailed for Lisbon for the second time on 24 September, 1650. The English admiral had previously stopped the outward-bound Brazil fleet on 21st May, 1650, and confiscated nine chartered English ships which he incorporated in his own squadron. The return voyage of the belated Brazil fleet of 1649–50, was apparently unmolested by either Dutch or English, since eighty merchant ships from Brazil convoyed by eighteen warships are recorded as entering the Tagus early in 1651. The Armada Real under António Teles which was returning from Bahia in company with the combined Brazil fleet was less lucky. A severe storm off the Azores caused the loss of four of the finest galleons (*São Pantaleão, Santa Margarida, São Pedro de Hamburgo,* and *Nossa Senhora do Conceição*) on the island of São Miguel during the first week of January 1651.

Despite these losses, the Portuguese still managed to find the wherewithal to equip a Brazil fleet of sixty sail which appeared off Recife on the 25th February, 1652. Haulthain's fleet of twelve "capital warships" had been in Brazilian waters since May, 1650, and formed the nucleus of a respectable squadron which was now dispatched to shadow the Portuguese armada, in order to cut off any stragglers therefrom, or to bring part of it to action if a favorable opportunity should occur. In this Haulthain failed, as the convoy kept such excellent order that although the Hollanders shadowed the armada for nearly two weeks, they were unable to pick up a single prize. An inconclusive naval action was fought off the Bay of St. Augustine, when one of the largest Portuguese galleons accidentally caught fire and blew up from the explosion of its own powder-magazine, "not a splinter of wood being recovered." Apart from this disaster the Brazil fleet suffered no loss, whilst the Dutch returned crestfallen to Recife Roads on the 8th March, empty-handed save for "lame excuses, unnecessary to relate here," as Hendrik Haecxs noted despondently in his diary.

The Dutch admiral had now been nearly two years in Brazilian waters. His ships' bottoms were foul, his supplies all but exhausted, some ships having rations for only one week left. Being unable to get further provisions from the equally empty company's stores ashore, he took "French leave" like his predecessor, Witte de With, and sailed for Holland in the middle of March, 1652. When the homeward-bound Brazil fleet of sixty-seven sail was sighted by two Dutch privateers S. E. of Recife on the 10th August that year, there was not another vessel of the W. I. C. left at Recife to send out to shadow this armada, and a fishing-boat, as the only craft available, was sent off instead. The loss of local sea-power by the Dutch coincided with the outbreak of the first Anglo-Dutch War of 1652–54, which in its turn rendered it difficult (if not impossible) for the Hollanders to send further reinforcements to Pernambuco for so long as this bitterly contested struggle lasted. The Portuguese were not slow to avail themselves of this opportunity. When the annual Brazil fleet appeared off Recife on the 20th December, 1653, the general, Pedro Jacques de Magalhães, and the admiral, Francisco de Brito Freire, easily allowed themselves to be persuaded into blockading the Dutch stronghold from the sea, whilst Barreto, Vieira, and Vidal pressed their attack from the land. With the command of the sea (which alone had encouraged the hard-pressed Hollanders to hold out for so long) now gone, Dutch hopes of relief sank to zero. The besiegers, on the other hand, at last saw their efforts crowned with success, and pressed home their attacks with such determination that the Dutch capitulated on honorable terms on 27 January, 1654. The *Ileada pernambucana* was over at long last; but it should not be forgotten that those who bore the brunt of the battles ashore from the Monte das Tabocas onwards, would never have been able to reap the reward of their labors but for the passing of local sea-power from Dutch to Portuguese hands.

This decisive stroke was only made possible through the formation and action of the Companhia Geral do Estado do Brasil, which whatever its political and economic shortcomings, had thoroughly justified its existence from the strategic point of view. The company was the brain-child of Padre António Vieira, and well might he write in 1689, to his critic the Conde de Ericeira, that it was *his* company which "brought always from Brazil the sinews wherewith to sustain the war against Castile, to maintain the kingdom, to recover Pernambuco, and still today helps with prompt and lavish means in times of greatest need."

Another Article of Interest

Boxer, C. R. "Salvador Correia de Sa e Benevides and the Reconquest of Angola in 1648." XXVIII (1948), 483–513.

The Portuguese slave depot of São Paulo de Luanda in Angola was captured by a Dutch expedition sailing from Recife in 1641. The capture brought immediate benefits to the Dutch, the Portuguese reaction being one of intensified anti-Dutch activity. Rebellions against the Dutch broke out in Maranhão in 1642 and in Pernambuco in 1645. Salvador Correia de Sa e Benevides led the Portuguese recapture of Angola in 1648. The recapture was attended by high casualties and the Portuguese attackers appeared to be losing when the Dutch surrendered. The struggle for Angola was primarily a struggle for the most lucrative slave market in West Africa, and the reconquest of 1648 saved the Portuguese colonial empire and Portugal herself.

20. The Guerra dos Emboabas, Civil War in Minas Gerais, 1708–1709

MANOEL S. CARDOZO

The relatively peaceful nature of the history of Brazil has often been emphasized, but this article informs the reader about a violent conflict in the mining district of Minas Gerais, an important interior region which has been the center of many controversies. Professor Cardozo of the Catholic University of America explains how the frenzied search for gold by the various competing groups in the mining camps led to grave disorders.

Although the rapid development of any frontier country has always been accompanied by tension and disorder, many such regions have been able to rise from a state of virtual anarchy to one of comparative social stability without recourse to armed conflict. In Minas Gerais, where the discovery of gold created a multitude of difficult problems, that transition was not effected in a peaceful manner. Over a period of several months, from 1708 to 1709, the principal mining region of the Brazilian interior was the scene of bloody skirmishes between opposing factions. The forces of government and religion eventually restored a semblance of order out of an almost absolute chaos, but the *Guerra dos Emboabas* between the natives of São Paulo on one hand, and "outsiders" from Baía, Rio, and Portugal on the other, left a festering sore which was not easily healed.

I

Only a little more than a decade before the outbreak of hostilities, the news of the discovery of gold in Minas Gerais by São Paulo *bandeirantes*

From Volume XXII (1942), pages 470–492.

had been exultantly welcomed. ". . . those Mines," wrote a former governor-general of Baía, "are said to be of such extent that gold will be mined there as long as the World exists. . . ." Earlier, in 1697, the governor of Rio could affirm that the Caeté mines alone "extend in such fashion along the foot of a mountain that miners are led to believe that the extraction of gold in that particular locality will be of great duration. . . ." Even the *Conselho Ultramarino* of Lisbon was willing to believe that the mines were the richest that had ever been discovered. Although fantastic rumors, embellished with each retelling, were accepted as truths, the fact remained that abundant deposits of the precious metal had at length been found, after so many years of futile search, in the "most expansive heart of that world Emporium," in that "resplendent diamond" of the finest quality which was Brazil.

At the beginning of the eighteenth century, the fondest hopes of Brazilians and Portuguese bid fair to be realized. Baltazar de Godói made some twenty arrobas of gold, partly from mining and partly from farming. Francisco do Amaral collected more than fifty arrobas from his multiple pursuits in Minas Gerais. Manuel Nunes Viana and Manuel de Borba Gato each made slightly less. Garcia Rodrigues Pais and João Lopes de Lima collected five arrobas from their stream; Domingos da Silva Moreira, from mining and trade, five arrobas; Amador Bueno da Veiga, eight arrobas. Tomaz Ferreira was reputed at one time to have more than forty arrobas. Dionísio da Costa found auriferous sand which is reported to have netted him a pound of gold in each panning.

Such reports of enormous wealth naturally drew thousands of people to the interior. Over the three principal highways from São Paulo, Rio, and Baía, a steady stream of adventurers and pioneers—Brazilians and Portuguese, Negroes and Indians, mulattoes and mestizos, priests and laymen—poured into Minas Gerais. In Rio, the great entrepôt of the mining fields, the exodus of the free colonists threatened to depopulate the city and the surrounding countryside. In São Paulo and Baía the same situation obtained; and even in Portugal the Province of Minho was so depleted of its man-power that it soon experienced a shortage of agricultural laborers. Certainly the history of Portuguese colonial expansion has witnessed no like displacement of people.

On the eve of the *Guerra dos Emboabas*, the Jesuit Antonil had philosophically observed that "there is nothing so good that may not give rise to many evils. . . ." During the first years of the gold rush, when the new Ophir harbored a heterogeneous population of some fifty thousand people, the lust for the "beautiful and precious metal" gave a wide scope for action to all that the "covetousness of man" could desire. The priest describes the shocking crimes that remained unpunished, the venality of the many fugitive or apostate clerics who, in defiance of their superiors, led scandalous lives. Brazil had never seen a more highly charged and corrupt society; nor one in which "haughtiness, lasciviousness, ambition, pride, and brazenness" reached such dangerous extremes. In the thirst for gold, life and property were violated. Much bad blood existed between *Paulistas*, who were the original settlers, and the later arrivals from Portugal and others parts of Brazil. "No prudent person," Antonil concludes, "will fail to realize that God permitted the discovery of so much gold in the mines to punish Brazil with it, just as He is punishing Europeans with iron at a time so plagued with wars."

II

Xavier da Veiga, author of a curious miscellany of information entitled *Ephemerides mineiras*, cites the oppression by the *Paulistas* and their unwillingness to share the control of Minas Gerais with the newcomers as the principal cause of the civil war of 1708–1709. This observation by no means contains the whole truth, but it focuses attention on one of the important grounds for discontent. The *Paulistas* had never looked with favor upon the influx of people from other parts of Brazil, principally from Rio and Baía, and from the mother-country. Why should strangers profit from the discoveries which the natives of São Paulo, at the cost of much sacrifice, had made? Quite symptomatically, the São Paulo *Câmara*, in 1700, had requested the home government to limit the awarding of land grants in Minas Gerais to *Paulistas*. The governor of Rio held this demand to be unreasonable. It was clear to him, as he wrote to the king on June 20 of the following year, that the other residents of Brazil were also "vassals of Your Majesty." In view of the governor's remarks, the petition was allowed to be forgotten; but the *Paulistas* did not resign themselves to the neglect of Lisbon.

They voiced their resentment against the intruders in Minas Gerais in opprobrious terms. People from Baía and northern Brazil were generally dubbed *Baïanos*. Natives of Portugal and the Atlantic islands were called *Emboabas*, an Indian word of obscure etymology applied to "foreigners" in general. Proverbially vindictive, *Paulistas* were not loath to attack the persons and property of the detested encroachers. They resented the droves of "outsiders" who, unlike themselves, shunned the risks of mining for the often more lucrative occupation of buying and selling. They complained bitterly of the monopoly of the sale of fresh meat which Francisco do Amaral Gurgel and Francisco de Meneses, a Trinitarian friar, enjoyed. Aptly did the Conde de Assumar, more than twenty years later, describe the true wealth of the mining fields as commerce. ". . . although some miners have made fortunes by extracting gold, the number of those who have ruined themselves in attempting to do so is infinite. . . ." In the Rio das Mortes district on the eve of the war, the rivalry between *Paulistas* and non-*Paulistas* reached a fever; in the Rio das Velhas area the situation was no better. With fuel in abundance for the fires of discontent, by the year 1708 Minas Gerais was on the verge of grave happenings. Only one hope for peace remained: the energetic intervention of the colonial government.

This, to be sure, would have involved an extreme effort, for Minas Gerais, ten years after the beginning of its gold rush, was still without effective political control. Though the area was theoretically subject to Rio de Janeiro, the inadequate number of crown officials, appointed at the turn of the century in the more important mining fields, was never able to cope with the needs of the population. The appointment of José Vaz Pinto in 1702 as superintendent of the mines, and the promulgation in the same year of an elaborate mining code might have proved the salvation of Minas Gerais; but Pinto's mission was a lamentable failure, and he returned to Rio in 1704.

Aware that the anarchy of Minas Gerais could not be long endured, on June 12 of the following year the queen regent of Portugal ordered the governor of Rio, Dom Fernando Martins Mascarenhas de Lencastre, to visit São Paulo for the purpose of restoring order in the gold fields. In a second letter dated two days later, the queen cautioned the governor to employ extreme tact in dealing with the situation. She instructed him to announce publicly that his departure for São Paulo was in nowise motivated by the desire to punish the guilty but rather to insure a better control of the mining areas and supervise the collection of the Fifths. He was authorized to avail himself of the assistance of the leading *Paulistas* and to promise them, in return for their coöperation, four patents of nobility and as many habits of the Order of Christ as he should think necessary.

Dom Fernando replied to the queen's letters on January 15, 1706. He was at that time preparing to carry out her instructions and had already selected the bishop of Rio to assume control of the government of the captaincy during his absence in the south. Nothing came, however, of these efforts. When the governor finally made up his mind to act, the *Guerra dos Emboabas* had already reached a crucial stage. It was then too late to prescribe a quick remedy for the evils of a frontier society.

III

The immediate cause of the armed strife between *Paulistas* and the other inhabitants of Minas Gerais was a personal misunderstanding between Jerônimo Pedroso de Barros, member of the most prominent *Paulista* family in the mining fields, and Manuel Nunes Viana. The latter's history may be briefly told.

Although the highway from Baía to Minas Gerais had been officially closed since 1701 to the passage of people and goods, excepting only herds of cattle for the sustenance of the settlers in the mining fields, the prohibition did not deter the residents of Baía either from entering Minas Gerais or from engaging in contraband trade. Among those interested in the forbidden business was Manuel Nunes Viana, a native of Viana do Castelo,

Portugal, owner of extensive properties on the Rio São Francisco in the Baía hinterland and head of a large concern which supplied Minas Gerais with many of its necessities. Because of his great wealth, his numerous crimes, and his intrepid character, as a contemporary wrote, Viana soon became the recognized leader of the contraband traders, and in the endless quarrels with the *Paulistas* also came to be looked upon to defend the interests of the non-*Paulistas* in general.

Under normal circumstances the differences between the two men might have been easily ironed out, but the moment was hardly one for conciliation. Viana subsequently reported that the misunderstanding had grown out of his refusal to countenance a dishonest act on the part of his opponent when both were in Caeté at the beginning of October, 1708. The incident led to high words, whereupon Viana challenged the *Paulista* to a duel. The challenge was accepted, but Barros, alleging "safer rather than honorable pretexts," avoided the encounter.

The discomfiture suffered by Jerônimo Pedroso de Barros was interpreted by his partisans as an affront to the *Paulistas*. With Jerônimo's brother Valentim as leader—Valentim, so it was said, had vowed to "kill the sons of Portugal"—a large party of relatives and friends, provided with more than six hundred blunderbusses, was organized. Word was passed about "that on a given Monday they should all meet in Caeté" for revenge.

The chief crown official in those parts at the time was Manuel de Borba Gato, an uncle of the two Barros. On October 12, 1708, acting apparently to favor his nephews, he posted a public notice on the church doors of Caeté banishing Viana from the district of the Rio das Velhas within twenty-four hours under the penalty of arrest and confiscation of his property. On the following day Viana wrote a formal letter of disavowal to Borba Gato, who was at his house in the Arraial do Rio das Velhas and not in Caeté. In his letter he categorically denied the accusations made and questioned Gato's authority to banish him. Protesting his own and his confederates' loyalty to the king, Viana accused Gato of favoring the *Paulistas* to the detriment of the other settlers of Minas Gerais, and of siding with Jerônimo Pedroso.

The refusal of Manuel Nunes Viana to leave Caeté greatly increased the danger of a serious upheaval, but Borba Gato remained undaunted. Taking the matter into his own hands, he posted a second public notice in which he prohibited the residents of the area from aiding or abetting the outlawed Viana on pain of arrest and confiscation of their property. The measure was obviously designed to intimidate all *Emboabas;* yet it only aroused their resentment.

The imminence of grave disorders and the possible realization of the numerical inferiority of his countrymen convinced Borba Gato of the opportuneness of a personal intervention. He therefore decided to leave his home in the Arraial do Rio das Mortes for Caeté. Disagreeable incidents had already taken place when he arrived. Two slaves belonging to Viana had been killed and other crimes committed. The situation was hardly the most propitious for conciliation. Nevertheless, Borba Gato, overcoming the difficulties which had earlier seemed insurmountable, brought Viana and Pedroso together.

The truce was of short duration. No sooner had Borba Gato, at the end of November, 1708, returned to his house in the Arraial do Rio das Mortes than armed conflict broke out between the opposing factions. According to the testimony of one of Viana's confederates, Borba Gato's second public notice prohibiting the residents of the area from assisting the *Emboabas* was so excessively interpreted that the homes of many innocent people were wantonly sacked and property valued in excess of five arrobas of gold was destroyed. Borba Gato, on the other hand, in his letter to the governor of Rio on November 29, 1708, wrote that shortly after his departure from Caeté the partisans of Viana forcibly obliged the neutral settlers to oppose the *Paulistas* by ordering many of them on pain of death to accompany the aggressors to Viana's camp. Be that as it may, it was rather the killing of a Portuguese in broad daylight in the streets of Caeté by the natural sons of José Pardo, a *Paulista*, that brought matters to a head. Incensed by this act, the *Emboabas* of the region, some two thousand strong, including reinforcements from Sabará, rose in revolt, repulsed their opponents, and killed Pardo.

During the disorders the apparently unfounded rumor was spread that the *Paulistas* were secretly disposing of their properties in order to be free to kill the ringleaders of the opposing faction and to make a hasty retreat. The disaffected elements in turn prepared to forestall these plans for revenge by executing a certain number of *Paulistas* and by driving all the others out of the Rio das Velhas country. Fortunately, better counsel was later taken. It was then decided that no *Paulista* or his slave would thenceforth be allowed on pain of death in an *Emboaba* camp at night, and that such a man could not be accompanied by more than two pages in the daytime. Other measures designed to restrict the liberty of the natives of São Paulo were also taken.

While the *Paulistas*, thus seriously rebuffed, were forced to evacuate the Rio das Velhas area, the *Emboabas* from Sabará, Arraial do Rio das Velhas, and Caeté, under the command of Manuel da Silva Rios, a Portuguese, Agostinho Monteiro, a Pernambucan, and Luiz do Couto, a native of Baía, aided and abetted by a number of apostate or renegade religious, including the Trinitarian, Frei Francisco de Meneses, met at the Caeté home of Manuel Nunes Viana during the early part of December, 1708, organized themselves into a militia corps, and chose Viana as their general. The *Paulistas*, in the meantime, retreating to the Ouro Prêto district, prepared a counter-attack. Disquieting news was periodically received by their victorious opponents. At Pascual da Silva the rumor was spread that Jerònimo Pedroso de Barros had considered the settlement "very appropriate . . . for a skirmish or a march. . . ." At Itatiaia the *Paulistas* had assertedly vowed to kill all "foreigners." Their preparations for revenge assumed alarming proportions. Four hundred men were reported at Itatiaia; another large detachment was reported in the Rio das Pedras area.

These military preparations aroused the *Emboabas* of Ouro Prêto, Antônio Dias, and Cachoeira do Campo, especially after it was rumored that the *Paulistas* were planning to seek revenge for their defeat in the Rio das Velhas area by destroying the three settlements, which were then without organized militia. Many of the inhabitants went about their business with considerable apprehension; others, as a means of insuring their safety, voluntarily cast their lot with the *Paulistas*. When, however, through the looting of certain letters, the truth of the latters' intentions was finally made known, the *Emboabas* of Ouro Prêto also decided to act promptly. On December 20, 1708, they rose in revolt against the natives of São Paulo. They then proceeded to elect Domingos da Silva Monteiro, a disaffected *Paulista*, as their military commander for the counter-attack which everyone supposed was imminent. Within a few hours fighting against the common enemy broke out in Antônio Dias and Cachoeira do Campo. The precipitous turn of events had taken the harassed *Paulistas* of Ouro Prêto completely by surprise. At two o'clock on the following morning, depressed by their defeat, they retaliated by setting fire to Ouro Prêto. Nine tradesmen's camps were burned, and a great quantity of property, including sixteen arrobas of powder, was destroyed.

Shortly thereafter Manuel Nunes Viana arrived in Cachoeira do Campo from the Rio das Velhas at the head of a numerous company. The spread of hostilities had by this time made apparent the need not only for coördinated military action but also for some sort of governmental control. A meeting of the most "respectable and experienced" residents was thereupon called. Viana was proclaimed governor-general of the entire mining area to rule until such time as the home government might send regularly constituted officials. He was given special powers over the Rio das Velhas territory, where he lived. For his secretary the new governor chose the Carmelite Simão de Santa Teresa, a native of Baía, and for his aide and military commander, with the rank of colonel of foot, Antônio Francisco da Silva, a Portuguese adventurer who had seen service in Nova Colônia do Sacramento. Bento do Amaral Coutinho, a native of Rio de Janeiro, was elected major-general of Ouro Prêto and environs in substitution of Domingos da Silva Monteiro, whose loyalty to the *Emboabas* was challenged. Mateus de Moura was named superintendent of the mines and given the specific duty of collecting the crown tax on gold. Captains were appointed, bodies of infantrymen were organized with their respective colonels of militia and of foot. A regiment was created in Ouro Prêto, Antônio Dias, Pedro Faria, and Ribeirão do Carmo, and another in Cachoeira do Campo. A close union of the Ouro Prêto and Rio das Velhas districts was agreed upon for mutual protection. The necessity of "bringing

the Rio das Mortes area into union" with themselves was likewise conceded, "not only because the 'outsiders' there have been forcibly deprived
of arms and liberty, according to information received privately, but also
because it would serve as an advance post and as a warning to those who
might wish to attack the settlers of Minas Gerais (as though they were
Frenchmen and at war with the Crown of Portugal) from São Paulo and
the towns below, as they are at present threatening to do." As a preventive
measure against possible violence, the insurgents further agreed to disarm
all *Paulistas* and their slaves. The position of the *Emboabas* being thus
assured, a mass was celebrated by Frei Francisco de Meneses at the church
in Cachoeira do Campo, first, as an act of thanksgiving for the victories
achieved and, second, to consecrate Viana in office. The new governor spent
a week in Cachoeira. At the end of December, 1708, he returned to Caeté,
leaving in the hands of substitutes the prosecution of the war in the still
unpacified areas of Minas Gerais.

The situation of the *Paulistas* in the Ouro Prêto area was daily becoming more critical. A number of them, accepting the assurance that they
would not be molested, voluntarily laid down their arms. Others, more
intransigent in their stand, were disarmed forcibly, while still others, rather
than subject themselves to the *Emboabas*, fled to the Rio das Mortes sector.
It was here that their compatriots were preparing a last stand. Under the
command of Valentim Pedroso de Barros and his brothers, and Fernando
Pais, the *Paulistas* had concentrated their forces in various woods, for the
most part along the Rio das Mortes where, unable to take the offensive,
they defied their enemies. They had, moreover, closed the road to Rio de
Janeiro, refusing to allow the passage of the caravans that supplied the
Minas market, and confiscated all arms, powder, and lead they could find.

In Ouro Prêto, meanwhile, plans were made to attack the *Paulistas* in
their last stronghold on the Rio das Mortes. By public proclamation, Bento
do Amaral Coutinho, in supreme control of the area since the departure
of Viana for Caeté, ordered all *Emboabas* attached or subordinated to
Paulistas to declare their allegiance to him within a stipulated three-day
period under penalty of being considered traitors and outlaws. Viana in
turn aroused the *Paulistas* by boasting that he and his followers were going
to "conquer them," burn their stocks of foodstuffs, prevent the passage
of caravans from the settled areas, occupy the woods, and strike at the
opportune moment "to obtain revenge for so many complaints. . . ."

Toward the end of January, 1709, one thousand armed men, commanded by Coutinho and supplied with eight small field guns, finally
launched the expected attack on the Arraial do Rio das Mortes. No difficulty was encountered. The settlement offered little or no resistance and
was quickly taken. Coutinho then hunted down the small guerrilla bands
roaming the countryside. He was unable to engage the *Paulistas* in formal
combat, but many of them were forced to retreat to São Paulo. Against a
body of *Paulistas* still at large in a copse some five leagues from the Rio

das Mortes settlement, Coutinho sent Captain Tomaz Ribeiro Corço at the head of a numerous escort, yet all attempts to dislodge them proved futile. Furious at the outcome of events, Coutinho marched against them in person. He surrounded the wood where the *Paulistas* were entrenched, but at first met with no greater success. In the meantime the enemy had climbed the trees and, camouflaged by the thickness of the foliage, opened fire, killing a Negro and wounding several soldiers. These tactics of the *Paulistas* made it difficult to attack them. After a siege of a night and a day, however, the beleaguered men begged for peace, offering to give up their arms for the customary honors of war. Coutinho accepted the terms but did not keep them. "... as soon as the *Paulistas* presented themselves to him and gave up their arms (oh ferocious cruelty, unworthy of human breasts!), he said that the *Emboabas* should kill those who had caused so many evils and deaths. ..." The butchery practiced on the helpless *Paulistas* was pitiless; before long the field was covered with the bodies of the dead. The name "Rio das Mortes" had not, indeed, been a misnomer.

The Rio das Mortes campaign was the decisive blow of the war. Repeatedly repulsed by their opponents, the *Paulistas* sought refuge in São Paulo. The three principal mining fields of Minas Gerais, Rio das Velhas, Ouro Prêto, and Rio das Mortes, were now in the hands of Manuel Nunes Viana, supported by a nondescript following estimated all the way from fifteen to thirty thousand men. "... you people there have your battles," a Rio correspondent wrote to a friend in Lisbon toward the end of January, 1709, "but we are beginning to have ours as well, though not against the French or Spanish. ..."

IV

The colonial authorities of Rio, who exercised political jurisdiction over the mining area, followed the course of events in Minas Gerais with great concern. Not only was the income of the royal exchequer threatened by the almost total suspension of the proceeds from the Fifths, but the commercial interests of the city, already handicapped by the infrequent arrival of trade fleets from Portugal and by the decline of the price of sugar, also began to suffer from the unsettled state of affairs in the interior. Business was practically at a standstill in the gold fields; and the caravans that regularly supplied the Minas Gerais market over the road from Rio were forced to turn back at the Rio das Mortes. Debts were left uncollected, for there was no way to force miners and other settlers to discharge their obligations. The extraction of gold in these troublous times was, moreover, almost completely abandoned; each man thought only of defending himself, his family, and his property.

Rio merchants and others with economic stakes in Minas Gerais were naturally affected; and it is little to be wondered at that a good many people in the coast city should have seen bankruptcy staring them in the face. The plight of the exchequer, as suggested above, was equally serious. The king would feel the unfortunate repercussions of the civil strife in Minas Gerais, an anonymous correspondent wrote to Portugal from Rio on February 10, 1709, "because he will receive neither Fifths nor coin, and, in fact, there are none. To tell you the truth, brother, everyone will suffer the bad consequences, and I especially, for God so willed it that in this crisis I should have my money in Minas Gerais. . . ." Debtors, he added, were unable to pay their accounts "since not even a dram of gold is mined; nor is there any business; and I wish to tell you frankly that, when these difficulties are solved, it will take much more than two years for the mines to get back to normal. In the meantime, may God have pity on the many people who have their wherewithal in those parts!"

Faced with a problem of unprecedented proportions, Dom Fernando Martins Mascarenhas de Lencastre, governor of Rio, felt that only his presence in Minas Gerais would quell the disturbance. He planned the trip to the interior with no very open or conciliatory mind. In his letter to the king of February 14, 1709, he described Manuel Nunes Viana as a "bandit" whose seditious activities had created the difficulties. The *Paulistas*, Dom Fernando wrote, should be restored to power, not only because they had discovered the mines, but also because they alone were capable of exploiting them and increasing their production. Without the *Paulistas*, he felt, the mines would soon come to an end, for the other settlers were unable or unwilling to make new discoveries. Since the governor considered the natives of São Paulo "more useful" to the best interests of the exchequer, he was determined to expel from Minas Gerais all settlers who had entered through the Baía hinterland. He would, as a consequence, establish a more rigorous control over the Baía road and suggested that troops from the Baía garrison should be ordered to Fanado, the most strategic point on the long highway from the Brazilian capital to the gold fields.

The receipt of Bento do Amaral Coutinho's letter of January 16, 1709, only served to arouse Dom Fernando's antagonism further. He refused to admit the claims and aspirations of the *Emboabas*. Writing a second time to the king on February 16 of the same year, the governor attacked the legality of the new regime set up by Manuel Nunes Viana and the moral character of its principal leaders. He considered Viana a usurper who had dared to repulse the *Paulistas* and establish laws of his own with the ostensible purpose of restoring liberty. Mateus de Moura, a resident of Rio and Viana's appointee as superintendent of the mines, was the alleged assassin of his own sister. Such people, Dom Fernando said, made up the chief supporters of the rebels. Even Bento do Amaral Coutinho, a bitter critic of the *Paulistas*, was known to have killed a son of Pedro Gago da Câmara and to have given vent to his cruel fury by inflicting more than sixty wounds on the victim.

Accompanied by four companies of dragoons, with their officers, and by *Desembargador* Antônio Luiz Peleja, who had recently arrived from São Paulo, Dom Fernando Martins Mascarenhas de Lencastre left Rio at the end of February or very beginning of March, 1709. Before his departure he informed the São Paulo *Câmara* and other municipal bodies of that captaincy of his intention to visit the mining fields to "pacify doubts" and confidently invited the *Paulistas* to return once more to Minas Gerais. He fully expected to be able to rely on their support. The governor, however, was actually less hopeful of the success of his mission than he was willing to admit openly, for he wrote to the king on February 16, 1709: "The fact that Manuel Nunes Viana has not informed me of these breaches of authority and of these appointments [*i.e.*, officials appointed by the insurgent governor] leads me to fear that he may refuse me his obedience and that, seeing me en route with considerably less force than his, he may prevent me from advancing. . . ."

The news of the governor's decision was received by the victorious settlers of Minas Gerais with consternation. Many foolishly believed that Dom Fernando was bringing an ample supply of chains and other iron instruments to punish them. Fearing his reprisals, the insurgents agreed to refuse him their obedience and prevent him from entering the mining fields.

Upon hearing of the arrival of Dom Fernando in Minas Gerais, Viana, at the head of a numerous following, left Ouro Prêto for Congonhas do Campo, a few leagues away, where the governor then was. When they reached the latter's camp, the insurgents defiantly shouted: "Long live our general Manuel Nunes Viana! Death to Dom Fernando if he should not wish to return to Rio!" A meeting between the two men was nevertheless arranged and the rebel governor conferred with his superior for a little more than an hour. Viana seems to have assured Dom Fernando that the "disturbance was against his wishes and that the people had brought him . . . very much by force; that the reason why they resisted was the widespread fear that he [the governor of Rio] was going to punish them; but that if he [Dom Fernando] wished to continue his journey, he [Viana] personally would not prevent him." In view of such non-committal assurances, the governor thought it wise to retrace his steps rather than risk the doubtful outcome of an adventure which had already filled him with fear. He left the mines as he had found them, in the hands of the rebels.

The first reports of the difficulties in Minas Gerais had, in the meantime, reached Lisbon, where they provoked justifiable alarm. On August 12, 1709, the *Conselho Ultramarino* unanimously agreed that the situation, as described in Dom Fernando's letters of February 14 and 16 of the same year, merited "a very prompt and efficacious remedy. . . ." As one councilman expressed it, any delay in applying the prescribed "remedy" might provoke an even greater conflagration in Minas Gerais which might conceivably spread to the other southern captaincies, thereby jeopardizing the "inestimable treasure" of the mines and endangering Brazil as a whole.

Yet the *Conselho* was unwilling to believe, as Dom Fernando believed, that the entire responsibility for the civil war in Minas Gerais lay with Manuel Nunes Viana and his partisans.

Since Antônio de Albuquerque Coelho de Carvalho, Dom Fernando's successor in office, had already arrived in Rio from Portugal when the *Conselho Ultramarino* was called upon to solve the difficulties in Brazil, the crown was advised to order the new governor to Minas Gerais and to authorize him to proclaim a general amnesty. Only the two ringleaders, Manuel Nunes Viana and Bento do Amaral Coutinho, were to be excluded from sharing in it, for their past activities were deemed to justify the full penalties of the law. The *Conselho* felt that Carvalho should be permitted to resort to force if necessary. He should be authorized to take as many soldiers from the Rio garrison as he should see fit. Additional soldiers, over and above those who could be taken from Rio without weakening unduly its military defenses, should be supplied by the governor-general of Baía.

On August 19, 1709, the recommendations of the *Conselho* were approved by the crown; three days later a royal letter embodying the proposals was despatched to Carvalho. These plans, however, proved to be unnecessary, for the governor had earlier resolved on independent action. Leaving Gregório de Castro de Morais in charge of Rio, Antônio de Albuquerque Coelho de Carvalho, escorted by two captains, two aides, and ten soldiers, set out for Minas Gerais in July, 1709.

The situation in the mining fields, meanwhile, had become increasingly favorable for conciliation. Uneasy over their position, fearful of the reprisals of the mother-country, the *Emboabas* were now anxious to sue for peace. They impatiently awaited the day when they might safely return to their homes and occupations, for the principal objective of the uprising, with the overthrow of the *Paulistas*, had already been achieved. Accordingly, when word was received of the governor's arrival in Rio, they despatched Frei Miguel Ribeira, formerly Carvalho's secretary during the latter's term of office as governor of Maranhão, to invite the new executive to Minas Gerais and assure him of their obedience "to all the precepts of the King and orders of his governors."

The arrival of the friar in Rio on the eve of the governor's departure for the interior greatly raised the latter's spirits. The unexpected development augured well for his plans; and he made haste to confer with the rebel leaders. The success of his mission was probably more complete than he had hoped. At Caeté, the scene of the first serious uprising of the war, received by the inhabitants "with the greatest demonstrations of love and obedience," Carvalho met Viana for the first time. They never saw each other again. As dramatically as he had risen to power, the *Emboaba* governor, whose praises more than one chronicler and historian have since sung, voluntarily retired to his properties in the Baía hinterland. The way was thus left clear for the pacification of the mining fields.

From Caeté, Carvalho visited the other settlements of Minas Gerais, in each of which he was received with equal cordiality. He approved the several posts created by Viana and, in the majority of cases, confirmed the appointment of those who were serving the same offices. He also created a number of new posts for the administration of the area. Then, after a measure of order had been restored, he left for São Paulo in the attempt to dissuade the *Paulistas* from a proposed invasion of Minas Gerais.

The atmosphere in São Paulo, as the governor undoubtedly knew, was far from ideal. Still smarting from the defeat suffered at the hands of the *Emboabas*, the *Paulistas* had resolved to avenge their discomfiture, possibly incited, as Rocha Pita suggests, by their womenfolk. The disgruntled *Paulistas* thereupon collected an expeditionary force of twelve hundred men and, under the command of Amador Bueno da Veiga, left for the mining fields.

It was this makeshift body that Antônio de Albuquerque Coelho de Carvalho, on his way to São Paulo, met at Guaratinguetá, in October, 1709. The governor attempted at once to dissuade the invaders from the undertaking, but without avail. Giving up his plans, therefore, to visit São Paulo, Carvalho hastily left for Paratí, and thence for Rio, from where he warned the settlers of Minas Gerais of the impending danger. The warning was timely. A large body of *Emboabas*, quickly mustered for defense, fortified themselves at Ponta do Môrro, in the Rio das Mortes area, and obliged the *Paulistas* to halt. The latter now entrenched themselves on a hill overlooking the settlement. For more than a week thereafter shots were exchanged by the contending factions but without advantage to either side. When, however, the news was received that numerous persons from other districts of Minas Gerais were marching on the Rio das Mortes to join the defenders, the *Paulistas* resolved to abandon the struggle and retreat to São Paulo. Early one morning, as unheralded as at their arrival, they gave up their positions, shrouding their movements in such complete silence that they departed unsuspected by their opponents.

V

With the failure of the invasion, the war in Minas Gerais finally came to an end. The bitter rivalry between *Paulistas* and *Emboabas* gradually subsided; peace brought the promise of effective political control exercised through regularly appointed officials. Yet the termination of hostilities did not result in a permanent calm. Martinho de Melo e Castro remarked in 1788 that "of all the peoples who comprise the several captaincies of Brazil, none were more difficult to subject and reduce to the obedience and submission which vassals owe to their sovereign than those of Minas Gerais." The Portuguese minister of state, upon whose shoulders rested many of the responsibilities of colonial government, thus registered the long series of disturbances which the captaincy, ever since its beginning, had caused the mother-country; but he might have added by way of explanation that no area in Brazil had gone through a more tumultuous evolution. Some eighty-five years before, at the turn of the century, Antonil was convinced that gold was not an unmixed blessing. In Minas Gerais, unfortunately, the *Guerra dos Emboabas* was not to be the only proof of that assertion.

Other Articles of Interest

Cardozo, Manoel S. "The Collection of the Fifths in Brazil, 1695–1709." XX (1940), 359–379.
With the opening of Minas Gerais, the crown losses in the fifths became more significant, and measures of control were attempted. Four smelting plants were established to estimate the fifths before shipment to Portugal for coinage, yet contraband gold continued to flow to Portugal. In 1702 a mint was established in Rio, but much bullion escaped coinage. Both church and administrative officials defrauded the crown, and Portugal was still attempting to find a solution when revolution broke out in Minas Gerais.

————. "The Last Adventure of Fernão Dias Pais (1674–1681)." XXVI (1946), 467–479.
Fernão Dias Pais, a bandeirante, is perhaps more respected and popular in Brazil than any other colonial figure. Born in São Paulo in 1608 of white descent, he was one of the wealthiest residents of the captaincy. His final adventure, undertaken when he was sixty-six years old, was an expedition to discover emeralds and silver in the interior of Brazil. While the expedition cost him his life in 1681 and failed to discover precious stones or metals, it did direct the attention of the *Paulistas* to the Minas Gerais territory.

---

21. The Rise of the Brazilian Aristocracy

ALAN K. MANCHESTER

Brazilian history received little attention during the early years of the *HAHR*, despite the efforts of such scholars as Lawrence F. Hill and Percy A. Martin. Professor Manchester of Duke University was one of the few who cultivated this field, and he demonstrated his mastery both of the modern period through his standard work *British Preëminence in Brazil* and of the colonial years in the present article. The rise of the landed gentry in Brazil, with their distinctly New World orientation which in-

From Volume XI (1931), pages 145–168.

creasingly led to friction with peninsular Portuguese, may be compared with the concurrent development of creole interests in the Spanish American colonies.

On February 15, 1823, only five months after Dão Pedro had proclaimed the independence of Brazil from Portugal, George Canning, in an official dispatch, offered to recognize the new government if the young emperor would abolish the slave trade immediately and unconditionally. In view of the peculiarly close relations which had existed between England and Portugal for centuries, recognition by Great Britain would mean instant success for the Brazilian revolution; yet Dão Pedro was unable to pay the price demanded by Canning, since, as José Bonifacio regretfully reported to the Brazilian chargé, any measure which precipitously abolished the slave traffic would endanger the very existence of the government itself. The interests engaged in the trade, powerful as they were, might possibly be faced successfully; but there was no hope of a victorious conflict with the owners of the great plantations. The government did not share the opinion held by the agricultural people of Brazil, Bonifacio continued, but that class was the powerful element of the country and, enticing as the bait was, Dão Pedro could not purchase independence at the price demanded by England.

The landed gentry, who were able to limit the action of the emperor so effectively, formed a distinct social and political element which identified itself with Brazil in preference to Portugal. Colonial-born, and bred in a society that looked back on achievements in which the mother country had little or no share, this class during the three centuries preceding independence had originated a native aristocracy antagonistic to the element which was Portuguese by origin or tradition. In the creation and development of this aristocracy certain factors had operated which were common to all sections of the colony while others were peculiar to certain geographical divisions; yet both the general and the sectional factors had served to foster hatred between the two classes of colonials. The antagonism which divided the revolutionist forces under Dão Pedro into constitutionalist and absolutist originated in this traditional cleavage between the native Brazilian aristocracy and the element in the colony which was Portuguese by birth or tradition. The constitutionalist, or patriot, was the inheritor of the traditions of the Brazilian aristocrat, whereas the absolutist was the descendant of the Portuguese group. The rise of this native aristocracy, therefore, was a decisive factor in the Brazilian struggle for independence.

The cleavage between the *masombo* and the Portuguese began early in colonial days with the caste distinction which existed between the noble and the peon of the first conquests. Later this class distinction was modified to include among the native aristocracy the descendants of the ignoble followers of the conquerors, of early settlers regardless of social position of such ancestors, and of the *masombo* who had attained to some colonial governmental position and had perpetuated in his family the right to hold office. The last of these stipulations furnished a door by which later immigrants could enter the Brazilian aristocratic class.

Except for the public functionaries, nearly all of whom were sent from Portugal, the emigrant to Brazil before 1700 was a stable colonist. After the disillusion of the first decades and before the gold and diamond rush of the eighteenth century, the Portuguese who emigrated to Brazil were inspired not by hopes of plunder but by the desire to acquire better living conditions in the virgin colony and to establish stable fortunes. Consequently, the Portuguese who settled in the colony during this period abandoned to a certain extent their rights in Portugal, identified themselves with Brazil, and strove to climb to the social status of the native nobility. The first great emigration, which occurred after 1580 when the subjection of Portugal by Philip II caused Portuguese families of the best type to flock to the colony, brought so many free settlers to the country that from a total population of 57,000 in 1584 the colony grew to 150,000, perhaps even to 200,000, in 1640. The colonists who dominated after 1600 were of a type that was capable of creating wealth, of taking possession of the land, and of defending the colony without the assistance of the mother country. Thus by the beginning of the seventeenth century there had been created a distinct and powerful group in the colony which identified itself with Brazil in preference to Portugal.

The economic foundation of the colony, during this formative period and prior to the discovery of gold and diamonds, was land. In the north, principally in Bahia and Pernambuco, sugar was the staple; tobacco and cotton were also grown from Espirito Santo northward; cereals and fruits were the source of wealth in Rio de Janeiro and São Vicente, although sugar was grown along the coast in Rio; and cattle furnished the means of existence in the extreme south, in São Paulo, in Espirito Santo, and in the backcountry of Bahia, Pernambuco, and Parahyba. Deprived of any dream of fortune from gold, silver, or precious stones, the colonists fell back on agriculture, ranching, and fishing; the possession of land thus became the paramount desire of the Brazilian.

The colonist secured possession of a plot of land by obtaining grants by *sesmaria*. During the régime of the *capitanias* the lord proprietor *(donatario)* was empowered to divide at will all lands of his *senhoria* among applicants, irrespective of the social status of the person applying, provided only he were a Christian. At first the captain-mór as well as the captain could grant such petitions in the name of the *donatario*, but later the right was restricted exclusively to the governors of the various provinces. The lands were granted to the applicant to be owned by him and his heirs in perpetuity, the owner henceforth to pay the tithe of the produce of the soil due the crown. The king retained the right to found villas and cities on land granted if the future should reveal the advisability of such action while wood proper for naval construction was reserved for the crown. The holder of the grant, who received only a provisional title at the beginning, was obligated to cultivate the land granted, to fix roads to ports, quarries, or bridges, and to mark off his land, within three years after receiving his grant. At the end of that period, he obtained a permanent title to his *sesmaria* if he had complied with the conditions specified. After 1695, however, holders of *sesmarias* paid a quitrent *(foro)* proportionate to the extent of land in their possession—in Rio, from one to two milreis per league and in Pernambuco, six and four milreis according as the *sesmaria* was near to or distant from Recife. It was forbidden to grant *sesmarias* to religious orders or to ecclesiastical personages; but if grants should come into the possession of the church by donation from the original grantee or his descendants, tithes had to be paid by the church to the crown on such property.

Sesmarias were granted to the applicant for such services as the conquest of new land, the defense of settlements at the time of Indian raids, aid in expelling French, Dutch, or other foreign intruders, or simply as a reward for developing effectually land already in his possession. New land was granted in many cases in response to the plea of the applicant that his family had grown so large that additional room was necessary. At first little restraint was exercised in conceding grants to whomever should petition and every colonist was richly endowed with land. Many of the small owners were unable to develop their grants as required by the terms of the *sesmaria* and thus lost their permanent title whereas the richer few who were able to acquire slaves enlarged their holdings by increasing the size and number of their *sesmarias*. At the same time, these more powerful *senhores* seized lands of Indians which lay in the district occupied by their grants and by various methods despoiled the smaller farmer of his possessions.

Thus although *sesmarias* were conceded to all who might petition, the land gradually became consolidated in the hands of owners who were able to obtain and develop large tracts. Consequently, there grew up a class of big proprietors, around whom was grouped a large number of descendants who worked for the lord somewhat after the manner of the feudal vassal. The small farmer resisted the encroachments of the large proprietor; but backed by the *camaras* (town councils), the big owners gradually forced the submission of the small, independent agriculturist. Those who were able, remained as renters on the big estates; those who were unable to maintain even the independence of a renter, placed themselves under the protection of the large proprietor, paying him service in return for food, clothing, and shelter. It was in this condition, a condition amounting to peonage, that the great majority of the rural population—*mestiços*, Indians, and Portuguese—of Brazil remained throughout colonial times.

Thus during the seventeenth century there developed in the colony a distinct social class which was dependent on land for its position. The large landowner established his family socially as well as financially while he arrogated to himself absolute power over slaves, dependents, renters, share-croppers, mechanics, overseers, members of his own family, in fact, over all who existed on his possessions. An aristocracy native to the colony resulted.

The basis of class distinction in the north was land adapted to the cultivation of sugar, for the *senhor de engenho* carried in Brazil the distinction which titles granted in Portugal. The sugar plantation, or *engenho*, was virtually a small kingdom ruled over by the *senhor*. Slaves of the hoe and sickle, mulattoes and Negroes assigned to house work or the mill, boatmen, carters, cattlemen, shepherds, fishermen, woodcutters, carpenters, nurses, overseers, the numerous mechanics of the mill, and a priest who served as chaplain of the plantation, all looked to the *senhor* as their master. On the larger plantations there were 150 to 200 slaves in addition to the renters under obligation by contract to send their cane to the mill of the *senhor* who received half to four-fifths of the sugar so milled. Sometimes the *senhor* sold land outright to small farmers on condition that the cane be sent to the *senhor's* mill while money was often loaned to owners of free farms on condition that the borrower send his cane to the lender's mill with one-half the sugar resulting going to the *senhor*. By 1700 there were, besides those under construction, 146 *engenhos* in Bahia, 246 in Pernambuco, and 136 in Rio de Janeiro.

As early as 1584, more than one hundred colonists in Pernambuco received annual incomes of over five thousand *cruzados* while some gained over ten thousand yearly. A Jesuit *visitador* who traveled from Bahia to São Paulo between 1583 and 1590 discovered riches comparable to those of Lisbon. The college at Bahia had three thousand *cruzados* annual income besides the produce from land in its possession. Sixty persons resided in the college, "enjoying an excellent living" where "there never lacked a cup of wine from Portugal". One *senhor* near Bahia reaped eight thousand *cruzados* profit yearly and possessed a private chapel, exquisite in its marvellous carving, cornices, and ornaments. In Pernambuco the *senhores* assumed the style of a titled count of Portugal with "beds of crimson damask fringed with gold and rich coverlets from India". Some of them were worth forty to eighty thousand *cruzados;* their women and children dressed in velvet, damask, and silk; and each *senhor* owned three or four blooded horses. In Pernambuco, mourned the reverend father, there was "more vanity than in Lisbon".

In the north, therefore, the native aristocracy resulted from the position which wealth, derived from sugar, bestowed on the *senhor de engenho*. In the south, social distinctions originated from other sources, for while the *Bahiano* or *Pernambucano* was resting on his bed of crimson damask fringed with gold under rich coverlets from India, the *Paulista* slept in hammocks, ate with tin spoons on bare planks, and dressed in the simplest of clothes. In contrast to the eight thousand *cruzados* annual income of the

Bahia *senhor,* the total value of the possessions of the most prosperous inhabitants of São Vicente between 1578 and 1603 did not pass five hundred *milreis* (1,250 *cruzados*). The total valuations given in the inventories of this period range from one hundred to five hundred *milreis,* the latter seldom being reached. Slaves, cattle, pigs, horses, grain, some few farm implements such as sickles and hoes, town houses and buildings on the farm, household articles of the most meagre kind, and land form the principal items listed. The inventory of one Matheus de Siqueira of the villa of São Paulo, captaincy of São Vicente, is typical of the more well-to-do *Paulista* of the late seventeenth century. His estate included a town residence and a farm. In town he had: two buildings (posts driven in the ground with tamped mud packed hard for walls, and thatched roofs) valued at 64$000; a box with lock and key, seven chairs, two cupboards, sword and scabbard, sunhat, one coat, one pair of pants and one suit (all used), and five silver spoons and one silver platter. On the farm he owned three hundred *braços* of land with one league and a half of backwoods *(sertão),* valued at 50$000; four slaves (80$000); two copper kettles and one copper utensil (28$500); three swords (10$200); 128 *varas* of cotton cloth (10$240); fifteen hoes, seven sickles, seven mattocks, some tin articles, used carpets, and a few other items; money to the value of 16$000; and thirty *arrobas* of cotton (9$000). Sixty-three Indians are listed by name as belonging to the estate with no valuation given.

The poverty of the São Paulo region was proverbial; even the Jesuits almost despaired of any material prosperity. Fernão Cardim, who was so enthusiastic over the wealth of the north, reported a land healthy in climate but poor and sparsely settled. This condition resulted from the failure to find a profitable agricultural product and from the fact that the mountains rose abruptly from the sea, leaving no rich coastland belt. But this universal poverty became the driving force which initiated one of the greatest movements in Brazilian history and created an aristocracy peculiar to the region of São Paulo. Thrust on over the mountains by the necessity of finding richer land, the colonist of São Vicente discovered the interior plateau which sloped westward toward the Paraná-Paraguay basin. Since no commercial connection with Portugal kept the faces of the colonist turned eastward, the *Paulista* buried himself in the interior, independent of the mother country. Land was obtained easily by *sesmarias* with settlements centered in the eastern side of the plateau near the base of the mountains, but slaves from Africa or the Amazon valley seldom reached a market so far south of the prosperous sugar region. Impelled, therefore, by the lust for a richer land, by a desire to drive the Spaniard back, and by the necessity of obtaining Indian slaves, the *Paulistas* began the famous expeditions to the interior called *bandeiras.*

The effort of Portugal to penetrate the interior ceased after the opening of the coast from the mouth of the Amazon to Iguapé, south of Santos. Further expansion was due to the initiative of the Brazilians themselves, who explored the region that lay almost exclusively beyond the line of demarcation. Between 1526 and 1700, unsupported, with men and material resources drawn from the sparsely settled, poverty-stricken captaincy of São Vicente, these *Paulistas* expanded to the Andes on the west, to the Plata on the south, and to the Amazon on the north. Since this exploit, which more than tripled the territory of the colony, was exclusively Brazilian, the colonist thereafter cherished a vital tradition in which Portugal had no share. Moreover, in contrast to the northern colonist, no economic tie bound the *Paulista* to the mother country; self-sufficient on his plantation, he asserted his independence of royal authority and exercised an absolute power over the persons on his possession equal to that of the *senhor de engenho*. The rudely dressed *bandeirante* and his descendants belonged to a native aristocracy no less than did the silken-clad *senhor* of the north.

The creation of this land aristocracy native to the colony was aided by the rural character of Brazilian colonization. In contrast to the Spanish in South America, the Portuguese settled in the country. That the original Portuguese *conquistadores* of the sixteenth century did not wish to colonize in towns, is evidenced by the fact that they petitioned for *sesmarias* which lay beyond the limits of the villas marked out by the governors despite the fact that it was expressly permitted to secure grants within towns. As late as 1767, Governor Cunha reported to Lisbon that the nobility of the country was scattered throughout the captaincy, living on plantations, remote from town and from each other. Rio did not have a person capable of serving as a member of the town council, he complained, since it was inhabited only by mechanics, fishermen, sailors, mulattoes, blacks, and some few business men. Governor Luiz Antonio de Souza reported that the villa of São Paulo was a desolate place in which to live, since despite all his efforts to entice the plantation owner to occupy his town house, the *Paulista* persisted in burying himself in the jungles, coming to town only during certain festive or solemn occasions.

It is evident, therefore, that the economic basis of the colonial aristocracy was land; but the legal basis lay in the right to vote in the elections of the *camaras* of the towns. The colony of course was governed by functionaries who were sent from Portugal, but local administration was left to the colonist, who exercised his right by means of *camaras*. In general there were three members, one judge and two *vereadors*, who appointed the city officials, voted and enforced fiscal measures, imposed taxes, policed the city and settlements, and attended to hygienic conditions, water supply, construction of streets, and such measures of local interest. It was due to the efforts of the *camaras* that the citizens of Maranhão, Bahia, Rio de Janeiro, and São Paulo were granted privileges conceded to the city of Oporto.

The *camaras* maintained their power during the greater part of the colonial period. With or without royal sanction, the *senado da camara* set the pay of Indians and of free laborers in general and established the price of articles made in the mechanical shops of the colony, of meat, wheat, salt, rum, cotton thread and cloth, medicinal drugs, and even of the manufactures of Portugal. It likewise regulated the value of money; issued provisions for agriculture, navigation, and commerce; imposed and refused tributes; deliberated over *bandeiras*, missions, peace and war with the Indians, and the creation of settlements and frontier posts; imprisoned public functionaries and private individuals; made political alliances with other *camaras;* and called to its presence and nominated or even suspended royal governors and captains. Many of these powers were conferred by law on the governors and captains but the repeated orders from Lisbon to restrict the jurisdiction of the *camaras* purely to local affairs were fruitless except in the capitals where the governors resided. It was only in Bahia, and later in Rio, that the governor or viceroy maintained complete dominance over the town council; elsewhere the *senado* attained political functions so extensive that any action of the governors was impeded or rendered impossible without the consent of that body.

The members of the *camara* were elected from a list of *homens bons* which was revised annually. Only persons of untarnished blood *(pessôas limpas e de geração verdadeira)* were included in the list; the exercise of any mechanical trade or the selling of merchandise over the counter sufficed to debar a name from the list; Jewish or Negro blood (Indian blood was clean) was considered impure; while laborers, slaves, and the degraded were excluded. The people (by which is meant the *homens bons*) were convoked at the order of the *camara;* these elected the five or six electors who in turn selected the judge and the *vereadores.* The judge and the *vereadores* then appointed the officials who should serve for the next three years, writing a set for each year on separate lists and sealing them in the shape of a sphere (called *pelouro*). At the beginning of the year the *ouvidor* (royal judge in charge of the administration of justice in the captaincy) attended a meeting of the *camara;* the box containing the three lists was opened and the *pelouros* placed in a hat; a boy selected one; and the officials indicated thereon were read out and inducted into office at once. The other lists were replaced, the box locked with three keys, and the same ceremony was repeated the second and third year with a new election thereafter. Both the judges and *vereadores* who composed the *camara* and the officials appointed by them were chosen from the lists of *homens bons.* The presence of the name on the list entitled the person named, therefore, to vote, hold office, and take his place among the native nobility.

The power of this Brazilian aristocracy was increased by the system of universal military service employed in the colony. In addition to the regular standing army maintained by Portugal, there were the militia and the *ordenanças*, the commands of which in great part were given to Brazilians. Those of the *homens bons* who were not occupied in municipal offices sought military commands to guarantee their positions.

In opposition to the colonial aristocracy of the land there developed a social group consisting of the new arrivals from Portugal. Concentrating on commerce, a phase of colonial life despised by the Brazilian aristocrat, these newcomers made business their chief concern. As Viceroy Lavradio reported in 1779, the Europeans who came to Brazil were so successful in achieving their purpose that the entire commercial life of the colony was in the hands of the Portuguese element. The majority of this class never lost sight of the idea of returning to the mother country; and many, after acquiring wealth, left the colony. Others, shifting the center of their interests and climbing into the native aristocracy by marriage and the acquisition of land, merged with the Brazilian party. Yet this element in the population of the colony remained socially one step above the lowest class, ranking below the rural proprietors and the *senhores de engenho*. These Portuguese were never admitted as a class into the aristocracy of the colony.

Thus before 1700, certain permanent characteristics of the social life of Brazil were definitely established. By that date there had arisen a distinct and powerful element in the colony which identified itself with Brazil in preference to Portugal. Aided by the rural character of the population and by the system of militia employed in Brazil, this class of colonists had created an aristocracy which was based economically on land and legally on the right to vote in the elections for the *camaras*. Jealous of its position, this colonial aristocracy forced new arrivals into commercial and mechanical pursuits with the result that there developed a Portuguese class which cherished antipathy for the Brazilian aristocrat. It was this traditional antagonism which emerged as a decisive factor in the events which occurred after 1821.

In April of that year, when the fat, irresolute king, at the insistence of the *côrtes*, was forced to return with his court to Lisbon Dão Pedro, eldest son of the king of Portugal, was appointed prince regent of Brazil; yet almost coincident with the departure of Dão João from Rio de Janeiro the *côrtes* began to manifest its purpose of limiting the powers of Dão Pedro and of restricting the liberties of the co-kingdom. In consequence of an order issued in April, which detached all provincial governments from Rio and made them subject directly to Portugal, petty provincial and municipal *juntas* sprang up throughout the colony, each corresponding with Lisbon and refusing to pay revenue to Rio. Thus, though nominally regent of all Brazil, Pedro really became merely governor of Rio and the southern provinces. The bank, looted by the king and despoiled by the directors, failed in July, and the treasury of the prince was empty. In September, the dissolution of the co-kingdom was completed when the *côrtes* by decree (September 29, 1821) abolished the chancery court, the treasury, the *junta* of commerce, and the various tribunals and establishments set up during the residence of Dão João in Rio; at the same time Dão Pedro was peremptorily ordered home. Two days later another decree appointed governors-at-arms for each of the provinces of the colony. It was clear that the *côrtes* intended to reëstablish the colonial status of Brazil which had been abolished when the colony was raised to the rank of co-kingdom in 1815.

The issue divided the inhabitants of Brazil into two camps: one approving the action of the *côrtes* and favoring the return to the colonial status, the other insisting on the equality of the two kingdoms under one ruler. To the first belonged those Portuguese who had immigrated during the thirteen-year residence of the court at Rio or who still looked to the mother country as the center of their interests although they had resided in Brazil before 1808. These Portuguese constituted that part of the commercial class which hoped to reëstablish its ancient privileges and monopolies. Every foreigner was an interloper in their eyes and the treaty of commerce of 1810 with England was the special object of their detestation. They formed the element which, with the soldiers and functionaries who looked to Lisbon for their positions, remained loyal and forced a civil war during the struggle for independence.

To the other camp belonged the Brazilian aristocracy and those Portuguese who, by marriage or interest, had become rooted in the colony by social and financial ties and had severed connections with the home land. The Brazilian element of this class found it impossible to relinquish the gains which had been obtained since the *carta regia* of 1808 had taken the first step toward releasing the colony from its subjection to the mother country, while the Portuguese element was faced with ruin when the *côrtes* threatened to restore the exclusive, monopolistic system of colonial commerce. Both parties of this camp looked to Dão Pedro to lead their resistance to the decrees of the *côrtes* and, if necessary, to save them by proclaiming the independence of Brazil from Portugal. Both elements, uniting to bring every influence to bear which might lead the young prince to disobey the orders despatched from Lisbon, coöperated in inducing Dão Pedro to defy the *côrtes* and raise the cry of "Independence or Death".

During the early part of the revolt, the two groups continued to coöperate in supporting Dão Pedro in his struggle against the loyalists and the feeble efforts made by Lisbon to subjugate the colony. Yet as the loyalists were expelled or silenced and the forces of the mother country were driven home or seduced to the revolutionist cause, a distinct cleavage began to appear between the two parties which supported the prince. The element of Portuguese origin favored an absolute monarchy under Dão Pedro, with a government entirely independent of the Lisbon court but with the crowns united under one family. To these absolutists belonged the Portuguese office-holders who had been thrown out in 1821 by the suppression of the Brazilian courts and governmental departments, a large number of the wealthier families, that part of the Portuguese commercial class which was profiting by the direct trade carried on under the open-door régime, and some native Brazilians who, while they admitted the advantages of constitutional government, yet denied the policy of applying it to the ignorant population of the new empire. The Brazilian party, on the other hand, favored a constitutional monarchy totally independent of Lisbon, while a large element in the group leaned toward republican ideas. To the constitutionalists, or patriots, belonged the plantation owners, the descendants of the conquerors and early settlers, and the backcountry dwellers, in short, the native aristocracy springing from the land. The constitutionalist of Dão Pedro's time, therefore, was the inheritor of the traditions of the Brazilian aristocrat, whereas the absolutist was the descendant of the Portuguese element in the colony.

The final success or failure of the struggle for independence in Brazil depended on the support which both the absolutists and the constitutionalists gave Dão Pedro; yet the two elements were too hostile to coöperate except under the threat of immediate failure in their struggle for independence. Consequently, as success became assured, the divergence between the two parties grew so acute that the conflict between constitutionalist and absolutist superseded independence as the paramount political issue in Brazil. The independence of the colony was recognized by Portugal in 1825; but it was not until six years later that the constitutionalists by expelling the absolutist Dão Pedro succeeded in freeing Brazil from the Portuguese. Thereafter the destiny of the empire lay in the hands of the native aristocracy: Brazil at last was controlled by the Brazilians.

---

22. Feudal and Capitalistic Elements in the Portuguese Settlement of Brazil

ALEXANDER MARCHANT

The early history of Portugal in the New World has been little investigated by scholars in the United States. This study by Professor Marchant of Vanderbilt University skillfully states the opposing views of those who emphasize the feudal or the capitalistic elements in the donatário period of Brazilian history (1534-1549). The author then adds his own conclusions and with a firm grasp of European, especially Portuguese, history and of sixteenth-century Brazil gives a provocative account of that controversial subject, the nature of Portuguese rule in early Brazil.

From Volume XXII (1942), pages 493-512.

In the decade of the 1530's, Dom João III of Portugal undertook the colonization of Brazil. He gave large grants of lands and powers to certain of his subjects as *donatários*, or proprietary landlords and, in return, required them to defend and settle the land, at their own cost. Such of the grantees as survived the first difficult years of colonization divided some of their lands among the settlers whom they had brought with them and began to grow colonial crops for export to Portugal.

Though few students of Brazilian history question the order of events in the founding of colonies in Brazil, they do differ as to the interpretation to be placed on those events. One group interprets the settlement in feudal terms and gives the name of the Brazilian Middle Ages to the fifteen years between the coming of the *donatários* in 1534 and the institution of a general royal government in 1549. Another group finds almost nothing feudal about the settling of Brazil, rejects any terminology that echoes the mediaeval, and considers that the settlement may be interpreted only as capitalistic. Indeed, the order of events appears to give support to both opinions.

Because the word "feudalism," like "capitalism," may mean all things to all men, it is well to state that the definition used here is the one now most commonly accepted by mediaevalists in the United States. Feudalism, as it flourished principally in France during the eleventh and twelfth centuries, was a political arrangement between members of a military upper class of knights in which military services were given by vassals in return for hereditary grants of powers and of land (the fief). It did not include the dwellers on the manors of the knights nor, later, the townsmen, for, while they supplied the economic base for the feudal class, their occupations remained economic and not political. Occasionally feudalism is defined broadly as a class system in which those who held land also held political power, accompanied by many rights over the property of inferiors, and were warriors by profession.

The fullest and more recent exposition of the settlement of Brazil as a feudal matter appeared in 1924, in the monumental collaborative *História da Colonização Portuguesa do Brasil*. The occasion was the centenary of the independence of Portugal from Brazil, once a neglected step-child, but later the foundation and stay of Portugal's overseas empire. The general editor, Carlos Malheiro Dias, not only discussed the question in prefatory remarks but also in a separate chapter entitled "O Regímen feudal das donatárias anteriormente à instituïção do govêrno geral (1534–1549)."

His premise was simply that the small resources of Portugal and the preëmption of many of them by the attempt to dominate India made necessary some scheme for settling Brazil that would not cost much in men or money. The system of *donatários* that was applied to Brazil, for all that it was impermanent and failed in defending the land, was the only one compatible with the need for defense and the financial limitations of the crown. To colonize and defend his captaincy, the *donatário* was given great rights and powers in his *carta de doação*. At the same time, carefully stated obligations to the king were laid on him in his *foral* which closely limited his freedom of action. The fact that he was going to set up colonies in a wild and distant new world did not free him of restraint by the crown, for the captaincy, says Malheiro Dias, was not given him to exploit as a plantation, but to govern as a province.

If in sketching the rights and duties of the *donatário* Malheiro Dias did not state explicitly what he means by "feudal," he soon suggests the color with which he invests the term. The *cartas de doação* and the *forais* were drawn up in Portugal by men who had inherited the experience and traditions of more than a century of governing an empire. The privileges in the instruments were to stimulate the zeal of the *donatário* and to make his dangerous outpost attractive to his pride and to his ambition to command. Brazil, in short, was founded by nobles and gentry who went there to burnish the splendor of their arms and blazons and to restore fortunes dissipated at court. Their settlements were agricultural and without towns, aristocratic in direction and free from the influence of the mercenary interests of townsmen. The class of the *donatários* and their privileges rooted in Brazil a nobility of blood and assured it a species of emancipation that avoided the stigma of colonial servitude. This opinion Malheiro Dias rested on the celebrated introduction by Oliveira Viana to the Brazilian census of 1920. When Oliveira Viana added that "all the long colonial period is one of the splendor of great landholdings," Malheiro Dias agreed that "the first cycle of Brazilian colonization is an undertaking of the nobility, with each captaincy adorned with its heraldic blazon."

From this much of Malheiro Dias's work, it may be gathered that his concept of feudalism is much broader and also much vaguer than the one defined at the beginning of this paper. It meant the giving of lands by the king in return for their defense by the *donatário;* an agricultural society, dominated by men of noble and gentle blood and with warrior spirit.

The critics of the feudal interpretation do not hear the din of chivalric war in the settlement of Brazil. Professor Simonsen, from whose recent *História econômica* much of recent interpretation seems to flow, does not find reasonable the emphasis that national historians have placed on the feudal aspect of the system of *donatários*. Indeed, he attacks the school represented by Malheiro Dias as much for a misunderstanding of European mediaeval history as for a misunderstanding of Brazilian colonial history.

He commences with the poverty of Portugal and with the need for an economical method of colonizing Brazil. But from this point on he diverges from Malheiro Dias. The basis of mediaeval society, he says, referring to Schmoller, was fixed social classes. The serf was not able to change his social and economic class and become an artisan, and the artisan could not become a gentleman. Such a society of fixed classes no longer existed in Portugal at the time of the settling of Brazil. Everyone was going to the New World to make money, to better himself, and to rise in the social scale. Further, the king himself was no longer simply a feudal overlord. With his navigation policies, his commercial monopolies, his manipulation of the royal currency, and his manoeuvres with the Venetian spice trade, he was "um autêntico capitalista." His vassals (to whom Professor Simonsen refers in quotation marks) were not behindhand, and were no more than exploiters on a grand scale. The privileges given them were not concessions to their pride and ambition to command (as Malheiro Dias said), but rather, assurances of profit-making to induce them to accept grants in Brazil. Likewise, the magnitude of the powers given the *donatários* did not indicate feudalism, for powers of equal extent are given even today to admirals of fleets, to generals of armies, and to governors in times of emergency. That the powers and titles were hereditary meant only that they were concessions for an unlimited period. What Professor Simonsen does find in the granting of powers and titles that is feudal is some of the formal terms used in the documents themselves, but this he discounts, for some of this language remains in use today.

While making use of the contradictions in Malheiro Dias's work in challenging the feudal interpretation, Professor Simonsen does not go far into the question of what interpretation should be put on the settlement of Brazil. Because his book covers the economic history of the entire colonial period, the few years of the *donatários* must be despatched quickly. He finds, consequently, that capitalism was indicated by the love of gain, with the king as the leading capitalist in Portugal and the *donatários* as his imitators in Brazil. When the king gave the settlers concessions, such as exemptions on their exports, he used characteristically capitalistic processes that have their counterparts today. Professor Simonsen does not say what these processes were, and, offering no instances or examples, he leaves their recognition to the general acquaintance of the reader with economic history.

Even the recent large-scale history of colonial Brazil at present taking shape in the hands of Dr. J. F. de Almeida Prado does not carry the discussion beyond this inconclusive stage. Dr. Almeida Prado accepts Professor Simonsen's opinion that the grants made by the king were not feudal, that only in the *forais* did any element remain that might be called feudal, and that the grants should be placed against the patterns of capitalism that were in full development in the Renaissance. Later he characterizes simply as capitalists some of the noble and powerful men who were considering building sugar mills in Pernambuco. But, unhappily, he does not consider that the demands of his volumes permit him to dwell on the subject and, consequently, he does not specify the patterns of capitalism that were followed.

The most thorough continuation of the criticism begun by Professor Simonsen has been, curiously enough, not along economic but along political lines. In less than a dozen pages of antitheses, Dr. Raúl de Andrada de Silva takes a body of prevailing notions accepted by historians about the donatarial period and casts them against the model of French feudalism of the twelfth century. Beginning with the poverty of Portugal and the need of a cheap means of controlling Brazil, he considers the giving of Brazil to *donatários* in return for their defending it a juridical act analogous in some respects to the giving of a fief by a suzerain in return for its defense by a vassal. Further, the giving of lands in *sesmarias* (measured pieces subject to certain stipulations) by the *donatários* to the settlers and their giving lesser portions in turn to other settlers suggests an analogy with the subinfeudation of feudal France. Likewise reminiscent of France is the giving of such lands for life and, above all, in return for personal services, especially in time of war.

Dr. Andrada de Silva's closer examination of the captaincies does not satisfy him that the chain of analogies continues. In Portugal itself at the time of the settlement of Brazil the king had overcome the desires of his vassals for equality and for decentralized government and had become king over all, not *primus inter pares*. In Brazil, in the captaincies, the powers of the *donatários* were likewise limited. Into each captaincy the king sent royal officials to collect royal taxes and administer the royal justice side by side with the taxes and justice of the *donatário*. Even in dispensing his own justice, no *donatário* could follow his own desires, for he was bound as a subject of the king to judge according to the *Ordenações manuelinas*, the code of Dom Manuel, and not according to local *costumeiros*.

While Dr. Andrada de Silva does not give the term "feudal" all the vague meaning with which Malheiro Dias had invested it, he does include the economic in his discussion. He does not find the captaincies feudal in this use of the term, for, while self-supporting, they were intended for trading and were not the self-sufficient household economy of the mediaeval manor. Like Malheiro Dias, he considers feudalism also as a sort of class division, but in this respect he finds only the most attenuated analogies between the social classes of the middle ages and the division of the captaincies into nobles, Christian peons, and Indians. The captaincies had no bourgeoisie in the sense in which such a body existed in France, its church was not a part of a feudal system, and in it slavery took the place of serfdom.

In conclusion, Dr. Andrada de Silva finds analogies principally in the juridical aspect and in the hereditary character of the grants. Even the giving of grants for life does not seem to him proof of feudalism, for he recalls Professor Simonsen's opinion that they were only concessions for an unlimited period.

Before examining the *cartas de doação* and the *forais* themselves in order to obtain an independent basis of judgment, it is well to have in mind the various meanings that have been given the term "feudalism." An economic meaning, aside from its general inaccuracy, is entirely inapplicable, for it implies comparison of the self-sufficient household economy of mediaeval France with the plantation and trading economy of Brazil. Two other meanings are more acceptable. The one preferred here is that of a purely political arrangement between the members of a military upper class. The other is that of a class system in which the landholders hold political power. The test of the political meaning is the performance of military service by the landholder in return for his land. The test of the other is harder because the meaning is broader and vaguer, but may be found in the rights, motives, and activities of the upper class, in this case the Brazilian landholders.

The *carta de doação* given to Duarte Coelho, *donatário* of Pernambuco, which is typical, first described the boundaries of the lands and declared the grant to be hereditary. It gave the *donatário* jurisdiction in all civil cases involving less than one hundred thousand *reais* and gave him the exercise of the death penalty in criminal cases involving slaves, heathen, Christian peons, and free men. Persons higher in the social scale were privileged, but he had the power to banish them or to fine them not more than one hundred *cruzados*. Regardless of social condition, he could impose the death penalty in cases of heresy, treason, sodomy, and the making of false money. He was also given the right to found towns and appoint officers; to issue licenses for mills, saltworks, and other enterprises; to levy taxes and tithes; and to hold certain monopolies. He was given as his own property within his whole grant a tract ten leagues wide, which was tax-free and inalienable.

The *foral* gave in detail the obligations of the *donatário* to the king, such as the king's fifth *(quinto)* on all metals, and the obligations of the settlers to the *donatário*, such as the tenth *(dízima)* and twentieth *(redízima)* on certain articles. It gave the *donatário* the right to give land in *sesmarias* on two conditions: that the *sesmeiro*, or recipient, be a Christian and that he pay a tithe to the Order of Christ. In conclusion it required all "the dwellers and inhabitants and people" of the captaincy to serve with the *donatário* in time of war if necessary.

Tested against the definition of feudalism as a political system of members of a military class in which land was given in return for military services, the provisions of the *cartas de doação* and especially of the *forais* do not appear feudal. The duty that they laid on the *donatário* was that of colonizing the land, not necessarily that of military service. In this essential matter of giving land in return for military service, the conditions are clearer in the relation of the *donatário* to his settlers. It will be noted that in the *foral* land was given in relation to the religion and the tithe-paying of the *sesmeiro*. Military service was put at the end of the document and was something that could be claimed by the *donatário* in time of war from all the inhabitants of the captaincy, regardless of land tenure.

Tested against the broader definition of feudalism as a class system in which the landholders had political rights or were warriors by profession, it may be seen that the provisions of the *cartas de doação* and *forais* likewise do not appear feudal. In short, whatever residue of the feudal may have remained in the terminology of the *cartas* and *forais*, the parties to the instruments were not all of the upper military class nor were they agreeing to a feudal instrument. It is therefore perhaps superfluous to point out that the king himself described his action at the head of the *carta* as an *intervivos* donation, a concept of the Roman law far removed from the conditions of landholding of feudal France.

II

If the above discussion has suggested reasons for rejecting feudalism as a proper description of the founding of Brazil, it has not at the same time suggested an alternative description. Professor Simonsen, Dr. Almeida Prado, and Dr. Andrada de Silva all accept capitalism as the alternative, as if none other could exist once feudalism had been rejected. But if capitalism is accepted, what is needed next is a differentiation of the kind of capitalism practicd by the *donatários* from the many other kinds that were being practiced then or have been practiced since.

In order to suggest a contrast with "feudalism," "capitalism" may be said to mean the investment of sums of money, with profit as a motive, to make more money. So broad a definition does not specify the various types of capitalistic enterprise that the kings of Portugal and the merchants of their nation had developed in commercial exploitation of the Atlantic and Indian oceans since the time of Prince Henry the Navigator.

So far, this discussion has concerned principally the instruments governing the settlement of Brazil. Now it will examine the economic aspects of how the *donatários* actually went about the business of colonization. But first it should take into account the fact that, by the time of the founding of Brazil, three types of capitalistic enterprise had become usual, each one fitted to particular circumstances of trade that the Portuguese had found in pushing along the African coast and to India.

While that expansion of Portugal overseas has well been called a crusade, it was a crusade in which commercial advantage was not forgotten. Readers of Azurara's chronicle will recall how prominently commerce appeared as one of the motives that led Prince Henry to invade the lands of the infidel. The prince, indeed, was among the first to develop the overseas trading company that early became a characteristic of Portuguese commerce when dealing with regions where trade was already active. Before the middle of the fifteenth century he was a shareholder in the Lagos company and took one fifth of the profits. In 1441 he founded a great company, with a capital of seven hundred and ten thousand *reais brancos* and with income guaranteed by profits from the slave-trade, for the discovery and development of trade with islands not owned by Spain. All capitalists of the realm were invited to participate and many did, including a large number of Jews. The companies gave Portugal a share of the trade in gold, ivory, slaves, and other wares that had long been controlled by Mohammedan traders along the African coast. Factories were planted at trading ports and goods, collected by factors, were taken to Portugal in the ships of the companies.

A second form of doing business grew up in the second half of the fifteenth century, when the king took over as a royal monopoly the trade built up by the private companies. Henceforth, royal factors were added to the private ones, the ships sailed under royal control, and all trade was by royal license. With few changes, but with an increase in the number and armament of the warships that escorted the trading vessels, this was the method of commerce applied to India after 1500.

In dealing with regions where trade did not exist, such as the unpopulated islands of the Atlantic, the prince applied yet another way of doing business that combined commerce with colonization. The islands were given in whole or in part to *donatários*, who colonized them at their own cost. They received certain taxes and monopolies that gave them revenue and control over their settlers and proceeded to grow sugar and other crops. Once settlements had become established and productive, traders in Portugal formed companies to deal with the islands on the terms used in the factories in Africa.

This third method, when applied to Brazil, was intended to settle people for the double work of defending the land and making it productive. The king divided Brazil between the Atlantic and the vaguely defined Tordesillas Line into twelve captaincies and gave each to a *donatário* under the provisions of *cartas de doação* and *forais*. Because Brazil was too obscure and India still too attractive, the high-born and wealthy did not take the grants. The first *donatários* were only of the *pequena nobreza* and the middle class, some trained in war in India, some in the fleets, and some in government offices. Some among them were landowners in Portugal, others had their government salaries, and some of the soldiers had acquired fortunes in India.

Even so, the *donatários* did not have large resources with which to undertake at their own cost the settlement of Brazil. Duarte Coelho, the *donatário* of Pernambuco, appears to have put his entire Indian fortune into the venture. Three other *donatários* had to sell their properties in Portugal to pay for their expeditions. A fourth, Pedro de Góis, the *donatário* of Paraíba do Sul, associated himself with Martim Ferreira, a capitalist with several thousand *cruzados* ready for investment. Góis took charge of the ships and the settlers and went to Brazil, while Ferreira remained in Lisbon and watched the investment from there. Góis does not seem to have put any money into the partnership, but to have contributed his experience and willingness to go to Brazil. In short, because these men had drawn so heavily on their capital, they might be expected to attempt to make their captaincies profitable as soon as possible.

Sugar appears to have been the crop to which all these men looked as the means of recouping their expenditures. The Portuguese had earlier carried sugar to Maderia from the Levant and Sicily and, as the climate of Brazil seemed comparable to that of Madeira, it appeared likely that the *donatários* could successfully grow sugar in Brazil. Certainly the way in which towns and plantations were laid out in Brazil suggests how completely the *donatários* were devoted to the scheme of growing sugar. On landing, the *donatários* and their settlers set up a few houses and a fortification. Then, with the aid of the natives, they laid out plantations around the town. As soon as they could, they began to build *engenhos*, mills for grinding the cane and preparing the sugar.

Examination of some of the captaincies will cast light on how their business was conducted, even though not all the captaincies were successful. Of the dozen provided for, four were never settled, and four succumbed after settlement to the attack of hostile natives. The survivors—São Vicente, Pernambuco, Pôrto Seguro, and Ilhéus—lasted well beyond the institution of the royal government in 1549.

Pedro de Góis, as has been seen, went to his captaincy of Paraíba do Sul in Brazil and left his partner Ferreira in Portugal. By 1545, less than ten years after receiving their grant from the king, Góis had already laid out canefields and had finished one sugar-mill run by water-power. He borrowed men from the neighboring captaincy of Espírito Santo who were familiar with sugar and with their aid was clearing more fields. At the same time, he was busy building two more mills to be run by horse-power. One was to be solely for the use and the profit of himself and Ferreira, but the other was to be used, for a fee, by the settlers. He had enough labor for the work, for he had Indian slaves working at the mills while free Indians were helping him clear and plant more fields. Altogether, the prospect was bright, for he expected to make two thousand arrobas of sugar that year "... e dahi pera diante mais." At the same time, he requested his partner to send sixty Guinea slaves and twenty salaried men. Shortly afterwards he returned to Portugal to collect more resources. Unhappily, Indian attacks in his absence had destroyed much of his settlement and continued hostilities finally drove him and his settlers away to Espírito Santo.

Vasco Fernandes Coutinho, the *donatário* of Espírito Santo, whose captaincy was also destroyed by Indians, was even more active in the sugar business. By 1545 he had five water-mills built, of which two were already in operation. He expected two more to be working by January of 1546. Besides these, he had two horse-power mills built of which one was already working. In 1546 he expected to produce one thousand arrobas of sugar. Those who knew considered his sugar to be as good as the best from Madeira. Indeed, so active and promising did Espírito Santo appear that the king's factor residing there recommended that the king build a royal factory or some place for loading sugar in order to facilitate the levying of customs. Shortly afterwards, like Góis, the *donatário* returned to Portugal to collect more resources to put into his captaincy, this time to aid him in finding gold and silver as well as expanding his sugar plantations. He returned to find his settlement all but entirely swept away by Indian attacks from which it did not recover for over fifty years.

The captaincy of São Vicente was the first captaincy to be established. Though Martim Afonso de Sousa, the *donatário*, spent only a year or so in

Brazil before going on to India, he kept watch on his lands from afar. It was in his captaincy that sugar was first planted, and he early ordered the building of mills to grind the cane. Other *donatários* sent to him for cane for their own fields. Shortly afterwards, many families of Italian sugar-growers who had been working in Madeira left the island for the new sugar-fields of São Vicente. By 1545 he had six mills with more than three thousand slaves working in them and on the surrounding plantations. To protect his lands and settlers, he was able to hire mercenary soldiers, but it is not clear whether they were paid from the profits of his exports of sugar, or whether he paid them from the booty that he was winning in India. His captaincy remained at peace with the natives and he gave orders that wealthy merchants might go and build themselves sugar mills and great plantations. In 1568, for instance, Gaspar Schetz of Grobbendonck, a Flanders merchant and capitalist, had rich sugar lands and a mill in the captaincy and sent out factors to supervise the works. Such plantations and mills still existed in the 1580's.

While much the same story, *mutatis mutandis*, may be told about the other captaincies, the case of Pernambuco shows most clearly how a *donatário* intended to make his fortune from his captaincy. Duarte Coelho, as has been seen, made a large fortune in India. His expedition was perhaps one of the largest and, accordingly, one of the most expensive. By 1542, when he had planted a great quantity of cane and almost finished his first mill, he was still feeling the financial strain.

The situation that Coelho faced in Pernambuco was not simple. Pernambuco had always been a favorite place for collecting brazilwood and that trade was still being vigorously pursued by companies operating under royal license. At the same time, because the land and the climate were good for sugar, more and more people were starting to build mills. To this economic activity in itself Coelho did not object, for one of the things he desired was the settlement and profitable exploitation of his captaincy. What he did object to in the case of the brazilwood traders was that, as they operated under royal license, they were not under fiscal or judicial control. He protested against the rapacity with which they had cut wood, for by 1546 the nearest substantial forests were now twenty leagues from his town. As Coelho saw it, this was a waste of his captaincy, and one from which he derived no compensation in taxes. Many of the new sugar planters he considered a detriment to his captaincy, for they came to make a profit and not to help defend the land. Contractors and armateurs were dealing with his settlers for their crops, and the settlers in turn were expanding their holdings to produce more. In need of room, they were taking lands from the Indians, and, in need of labor, they were attacking and enslaving other natives. In time, they provoked retaliatory native wars for which they were unprepared. To prevent the Indians from coming too close to his main settlement, Coelho was forced to defend these persons whether he wished to or not. Though at this time Coelho was still complaining to the king of being poor and spent, he was able to hire mercenary troops to help fight off the hostile natives.

From about 1550 on, he began to balance his books. For a few years before, he had been making arrangements with persons in Portugal to go to Brazil and build sugar-mills and, presumably, to defend them. Of the obligations to him of these persons and other settlers he kept careful record, in order to calculate his taxes. Some of the wealthiest *(poderosos)* of the new settlers built mills, and others less wealthy laid out more plantations of sugar, cotton, and foods. Even so, when in 1550 he told the king that the captaincy went on well and had five mills built and at work, he complained that he himself had yet to make a profit, so great had been his expenses.

While Duarte Coelho himself probably did not enjoy much of the profit that eventually came from his defense of his lands, his son became one of the wealthiest men in all Brazil. About 1580, the son was receiving nineteen thousand *cruzados* a year from the tenth on sugar-mills alone, in addition to the profit from sugar grown on his own land. Indeed, in Pernambuco the operation of an agricultural colony for profit had its greatest success. Many men, said a wise observer, return wealthy to Portugal who went to Pernambuco very poor. Fifty mills and wide sugar-fields provided the sugar which forty and fifty ships a year came to carry away. More than a hundred men had incomes of between one thousand and five thousand *cruzados* a year, and there were even some with eight, ten, or twelve thousand *cruzados* a year.

III

Whatever may have been the emotional temper of the *donatários* and their interest in deeds of arms against the Indians, they were not members of a feudal society and they did not found feudal landholdings in Brazil. The *donatário* did not hold his lands from the king simply in return for feudal services and neither did the *sesmeiro* owe such services for the lands he held from the *donatário*. Likewise, the holding of land in Brazil did not necessarily bestow on anyone except the *donatário* political powers and rights over the property of his inferiors.

On the other hand, the *donatários* were clearly capitalistic in the sense of investing money for profit. They were planter capitalists and not primarily traders, and their investment was in land and slaves. Only after the *donatários* had begun plantation economy in Brazil did merchants, organized in trading companies and investing not in land and slaves but in buying, selling, and transporting sugar, bring to Brazil another and more obviously recognized type of capitalism.

Appendices

Recent Articles on Historiography

Arnade, Charles W. "The Historiography of Colonial and Modern Bolivia." XLII (1962), 333-384.

Barager, Joseph R. "The Historiography of the Río de la Plata Area Since 1830." XXXIX (1959), 588-642.

Bishko, Charles Julian. "The Iberian Background of Latin American History: Recent Progress and Continuing Problems." XXXVI (1956), 50-80.

Corbitt, Duvon C. "Cuban Revisionist Interpretations of Cuba's Struggle for Independence." XLIII (1963), 395-404.

Griffin, Charles C. "Francisco Encina and Revisionism in Chilean History." XXXVII (1957), 1-28.

Griffith, William J. "The Historiography of Central America since 1830." XL (1960), 548-569.

Hoffmann, Fritz L. "Perón and After." XXXVI (1956), 510-528; XXXIX (1959), 212-233.

Humphreys, R. A. "The Historiography of Spanish American Revolutions." XXXVI (1956), 81-93.

Lavretskii, I. R. "A Survey of the Hispanic American Historical Review, 1956-1958." XL (1960), 340-360.

Oswald, J. Gregory. "A Soviet Criticism of the Hispanic American Historical Review." XL (1960), 337-339.

Potash, Robert A. "The Historiography of Mexico Since 1821." XL (1960), 383-424.

Ross, Stanley Robert. "Bibliography of Sources for Contemporary Mexican History." XXXIX (1959), 234-238.

Stein, Stanley J. "The Historiography of Brazil, 1808-1889." XL (1960), 234-278.

———. "The Tasks Ahead for Latin American Historians." XLI (1961), 424-433.

Smith, Robert Freeman. "Twentieth-Century Cuban Historiography." XLIV (1964), 44-73.

Szászdi, Adam. "The Historiography of the Republic of Ecuador." XLIV (1964), 503-550.

Walne, Peter. "Guide to Sources for the History of Latin America, British Volume." XLIV (1964), 375-276.

Dana G. Munro	Princeton University
J. Fred Rippy	Durham, North Carolina
France V. Scholes	University of New Mexico
Lesley B. Simpson	University of California, Berkeley
Arthur P. Whitaker	University of Pennsylvania

Readings in Latin American History

Lewis Hanke

Columbia University

Volume I: To 1810
Volume II: Since 1810

Volume II

Introductory Note
Part One: Revolutionary Period
Part Two: General
Part Three: Mexico and Central America
Part Four: Spanish South America
Part Five: Brazil

A List of Recent Articles on Historiography
A List of Editors
of the Hispanic American Historical Review